Warren County, Ohio and Beyond

Dallas R. Bogan

HERITAGE BOOKS
2011

HERITAGE BOOKS
AN IMPRINT OF HERITAGE BOOKS, INC.

Books, CDs, and more—Worldwide

For our listing of thousands of titles see our website
at
www.HeritageBooks.com

Published 2011 by
HERITAGE BOOKS, INC.
Publishing Division
100 Railroad Ave. #104
Westminster, Maryland 21157

Copyright © 1997 Dallas R. Bogan

All rights reserved. No part of this book may be reproduced or transmitted in any form or by any means, electronic or mechanical, including photocopying, recording or by any information storage and retrieval system without written permission from the author, except for the inclusion of brief quotations in a review.

International Standard Book Numbers
Paperbound: 978-0-7884-0678-2
Clothbound: 978-0-7884-8605-0

Dedicated to the Residents of
Warren County, Ohio,
Past and Present.

CONTENTS

Chapter I

WARREN COUNTY

HISTORIAN RECOUNTS 18TH CENTURY WARREN COUNTY EVENTS FOR READERS........................PAGE 1

UNDERGROUND RAILROAD MOVED EFFICIENTLY, SILENTLY THROUGH COUNTY............................PAGE 6

AMERICA'S COWBOY HAT HAD BEGINNINGS IN WAYNESVILLE.....................................PAGE 10

A SHORT HISTORY OF OLD DEERFIELD TOWNSHIP ....PAGE 13

CHRISTIAN NULL HOMESTEAD IS A SPRINGBORO LANDMARK.......................................PAGE 15

LEBANON ONCE BATTLED MORROW IN BID FOR WARREN COUNTY SEAT...............................PAGE 19

EARLY COUNTY SETTLEMENTS AND THE SWAMPS..PAGE 22

CORN CANNING WAS ONCE A TOP COUNTY INDUSTRY ....PAGE 24

THE SPIRIT MILLER THAT INHABITED THE OLD WELCH MILL......................................PAGE 26

MARCH MARKS 80TH ANNIVERSARY OF WARREN COUNTY UNDER WATER..............................PAGE 29

HARVEYSBURG SUFFERED DEVASTATING FIRE IN 1939 ....PAGE 33

HISTORIAN CLEANS OUT HIS FILES WITH VARIOUS TIDBITS ON COUNTY.........................PAGE 35

MORE BITS AND PIECES OF WARREN COUNTY HISTORY ....PAGE 41

PIONEER VILLAGE HOLDS OLD TIME FOOD AND MUSIC FESTIVAL.................................PAGE 43

HISTORIAN TAKES A LOOK AT THE LOCAL NEWS OF 1909......................................PAGE 47

A GLIMPSE AT WARREN COUNTY SCHOOL NEWS IN 1930
....PAGE 50

HISTORIC SCHOOL BEGAN IN HARVEYSBURG.....PAGE 54

BOXWELL LAW GAVE FARM YOUTHS CHANCE TO CONTINUE EDUCATION................................PAGE 56

SOME OF WARREN COUNTY'S HORSE RACING LEGENDS
....PAGE 58

WARREN COUNTY LONG KNOWN FOR WONDERFUL TROTTERS
....PAGE 61

WARREN COUNTY TOOK BUTLER LAND, AND GAVE BACK TO CLINTON COUNTY..........................PAGE 65

SETTLERS COULDN'T HAVE "SETTLED IN" WITHOUT LOCAL INNS..............................PAGE 70

Chapter II

TOWNS AND VILLAGES

WARREN COUNTY TOWNS AND THEIR NAME CHANGES
....PAGE 77

REMEMBERING THE 'FORGOTTEN' LOCAL TOWN OF COZADDALE....................................PAGE 82

RECALLING THE HISTORY OF THE LITTLE VILLAGE OF OREGONIA................................PAGE 86

FIRE TOOK ONE OF COUNTY'S LANDMARKS IN 1909
....PAGE 90

HARVEYSBURG - "TOWN BY THE LAKE" ORIGINATED WITH COL. BUFORD.................................PAGE 93

HISTORIC LYTLE OFF THE BEATEN PATH......PAGE 102

HISTORIC LITTLE MOUNT HOLLY NESTLED IN WAYNE TOWNSHIP....................................PAGE 107

CARLISLE WAS PART OF WARREN COUNTY'S 'WESTWARD EXPANSION'..................................PAGE 113

UTICA ONCE A THRIVING HAMLET............PAGE 118

HISTORY OF KINGS MILLS DATES BACK TO 1799
....PAGE 120

FROM PALMYRA TO KIRKWOOD - THE EARLY PROGRESS OF MASON......................................PAGE 125

SPRINGMAN'S HISTORY OF MASON VALUABLE RESOURCE
....PAGE 130

THE TINY COUNTY VILLAGE OF FOSTER IS RECALLED
....PAGE 135

SOUTH LEBANON IS THE OLDEST TOWN IN WARREN COUNTY......................................PAGE 140

Chapter III

TRANSPORTATION

LOCAL SETTLERS DEMANDED ROADS THROUGHOUT WARREN COUNTY......................................PAGE 145

EARLY CANAL SYSTEM PLANS BEGAN IN LITTLE MIAMI VALLEY......................................PAGE 149

DO YOU REMEMBER THE D. L. & C. RAILROAD?
....PAGE 152

TRACTION LINE ONCE LINKED ALL CORNERS OF WARREN COUNTY..PAGE 157

FLATBOATS BROUGHT EARLY SETTLERS DOWN RIVER TO OHIO VALLEY.....................................PAGE 162

THE CINCINNATI, WILMINGTON AND ZANESVILLE RAILROAD..PAGE 166

HISTORIAN DETAILS EARLY CANAL CONSTRUCTION
....PAGE 170

Chapter IV

AMERICAN CIVIL WAR

CIVIL WAR: THE FIRST DAYS IN THE COUNTY
....PAGE 176

A HISTORY OF THE THIRTY-FIFTH OHIO VOLUNTEER INFANTRY..PAGE 180

WARREN COUNTIAN McLEAN LED CIVIL WAR OHIO BRIGADE..PAGE 185

OHIO'S SQUIRREL HUNTERS DEFENDED CINCINNATI
....PAGE 188

LOCAL CIVIL WAR VET REMEMBERED..........PAGE 190

GENERAL R.C. SCHENCK EARLY MILITARY HERO
....PAGE 194

Chapter V

BIOGRAPHICAL SKETCHES

EATON FIRST COUNTY RESIDENT............. PAGE 198

REV. JAMES SMITH HAS MANY DESCENDANTS IN THE COUNTY..................................PAGE 202

ABOLITIONIST BUTTERWORTH HELPED SHAPE WARREN COUNTY..................................PAGE 207

JEREMIAH MORROW SHOULD BE CALLED THE FATHER OF OHIO....................................PAGE 209

JOHN MORROW INSTRUMENTAL IN WARREN COUNTY ....PAGE 213

WILLIAM HARMON LEGACY LIVES THROUGHOUT LEBANON AND BEYOND.............................PAGE 216

HISTORICAL FIGURE EVANS HAD ROOTS IN WAYNESVILLE AREA....................................PAGE 220

HON. JOHN McLEAN FOUNDED THE WESTERN STAR ....PAGE 224

GENERAL WILLIAM CORTENUS SCHENCK WAS FRANKLIN FOUNDER.................................PAGE 229

HISTORIAN FINDS GUSTIN A FAMILIAR WARREN COUNTY NAME....................................PAGE 233

MELVA BEATRICE WILSON..................PAGE 235

LT. CHARLES L. EARNHART: LEBANON'S WAR ACE ....PAGE 237

SERGEANT RALPH P. SNOOK DIED IN WORLD WAR I ....PAGE 239

GLENDOWER WAS HOME TO J. MILTON WILLIAMS ....PAGE 242

HISTORIAN TELLS STORY OF WAYNESVILLE RESIDENT ALLEN BROWN............................PAGE 245

UNION TOWNSHIP'S WILSON FAMILY KNOWN ACROSS U.S. ....PAGE 249

MOSES MILLER EARLY LEBANON RESIDENT OF NOTE
..................................PAGE 252

DEY VENTURED TO LEBANON FROM JERSEY, MET JACKSON, CLAY..................................PAGE 254

WILLIAM H. CLEMENT: ONE OF MORROW'S FOUNDERS
..................................PAGE 256

LEBANON RESIDENT LINCOLN BEACHY WAS AVIATION PIONEER..................................PAGE 259

CEPHAS HOLLOWAY A PROMINENT SHAKER LEADER
..................................PAGE 261

JAMES E. MURDOCH WAS CELEBRATED ACTOR AND PUBLIC READER..................................PAGE 263

CINCINNATI'S CROSLEY FAMILY HAD CLOSE TIES TO WARREN COUNTY..................................PAGE 266

HOLLINGSWORTH AND HAMILTON EARLY WARREN COUNTIANS
Rhoda Whitacre Hollingsworth............PAGE 271
Captain William H. Hamilton.............PAGE 273

GENERAL O. MITCHEL WAS A TRUE RAIDER....PAGE 275

CHAPTER VI

NATIVE AMERICANS

WARREN COUNTY ONCE HOME TO TWO OTHER "ANCIENT FORTS"..................................PAGE 279

CARLISLE FORT EXISTED ABOUT 2,000 YEARS AGO
..................................PAGE 281

THE MOUNDS OF OBSERVATION IN SOUTHWEST OHIO
..................................PAGE 284

OHIO MOUND BUILDERS NOT AS ADVANCED AS HISTORIANS THOUGHT................................PAGE 287

BOW AND ARROW GREATEST LABOR-SAVING INVENTION FOR FLINT-USERS...........................PAGE 290

HISTORIC OLDTOWN HOSTED TECUMSEH, DANIEL BOONE ....PAGE 295

WARREN COUNTY HAD ITS OWN SERPENT MOUND ....PAGE 297

Chapter VII

RELIGIOUS DENOMINATIONS

THE FIRST BAPTISTS IN OHIO AND WARREN COUNTY ....PAGE 302

JONATHAN TICHENOR: A PRESBYTERIAN PIONEER ....PAGE 307

MAINEVILLE CHURCH CELEBRATES INTERESTING HISTORY ON 150TH BIRTHDAY......................PAGE 310

SHAKERS MADE THEIR IMPACT ON WARREN COUNTY ALMOST 200 YEARS AGO....................PAGE 313

SHAKERS FACED SETBACKS WHILE IN COUNTY..PAGE 316

THE PASSING THROUGH OF THE PILGRIMS.....PAGE 319

Chapter VIII

LEBANON, OHIO

TAKING A PEEK AT LEBANON IN THE 19TH CENTURY ....PAGE 323

LEBANON ALMOST HAD ITS OWN "REDSKINS"...PAGE 327

LEBANON'S FIRST GRIST MILL ON TURTLE CREEK ....PAGE 330

BARRING OUT THE SCHOOLMASTER WAS A FAVORITE PRANK OF PUPILS..........................PAGE 332

THE BUILDING OF THE FIRST SCHOOLHOUSE IN TURTLE-CREEK TOWNSHIP..........................PAGE 335

LEBANON'S OPERA HOUSE WAS A CULTURAL LANDMARK ....PAGE 340

MARY HAVEN HOME HAS LONG HISTORY OF CARING FOR WARREN COUNTY CHILDREN IN NEED..........PAGE 345

THE OBSTACLES FACED AS LEBANON TRIED TO LURE A RAILROAD................................PAGE 348

THE FIRST BANKS OF OHIO AND THE CITY OF LEBANON ....PAGE 351

LEBANON MARKET HOUSES OF YEARS AGO......PAGE 355

WOMEN OF DISTINCTION AMONGST MULTITUDE..PAGE 359

'STORM OF CENTURY' ROCKED LEBANON AREA MORE THAN 100 YEARS AGO............................PAGE 363

Chapter IX

MISCELLANEOUS ARTICLES

ABRAHAM LINCOLN VISITS SOUTHWESTERN OHIO ....PAGE 366

LITTLE MIAMI WAS ONCE OHIO'S MOST IMPORTANT MILL STREAM..................................PAGE 372

PRINTING PRESSES CAME EARLY TO OHIO FRONTIER ....PAGE 374

ELECTRIC MULE COULD PROPEL A CANAL BOAT SYSTEM
....PAGE 378

TREATY OF GREENVILLE EXPANDED THE EARLY UNITED
STATES....................................PAGE 382

SOUTHWESTERN OHIO TOBACCO GROWERS SAW SOME TOUGH
TIMES.....................................PAGE 384

AUTOMOBILES OF YESTERYEAR STILL INTRIGUE
....PAGE 387

HARRY E. PENCE: LOCAL AUTOMOTIVE PIONEER
....PAGE 389

HISTORIAN DISCUSSES SEVERAL HISTORY TIDBITS
War Roads.................................PAGE 392
General George Rogers Clark...............PAGE 394
General Josiah Harmar.....................PAGE 396

BULLSKIN TRACE EXISTED THROUGH WARREN COUNTY
....PAGE 398

Preface

From the beginning, the residents of Warren County, Ohio, have contributed not only to the County, but to the nation as a whole. As one reads the contents of this book it will be fairly obvious just what has been given and the rewards received.

I am much indebted to the personnel of **The Western Star**, and its sister newspaper, **The Sunday Western Star**, located in Lebanon, Ohio, for allowing me to write for this fine organization. It has the distinction of being the oldest continuous weekly newspaper in Ohio, beginning in 1807.

History always had a place in these excellent publications.

Possibly the first to write on a somewhat regular basis concerning Warren County history in the **Star** was Anthony H. Dunlevy, his series beginning in the middle of the Nineteenth Century.

The next gentleman of note to write a series concerning history was Josiah Morrow, grandson of Jeremiah Morrow, the sixth Governor of Ohio. He wrote weekly from 1907 to 1928, a total of over 21 years.

Another excellent historian and writer was Marion Snyder, his articles appearing from the middle 1950's and extending to the early 1990's.

There have been many others who have contributed to this vast subject of history in the **Star**, too many to mention here.

Mr. Snyder passed away and I was asked to take his place. I felt very humble in this endeavor, because I was all too familiar with the writings of the preceding historians.

My column began in **The Sunday Western Star** in January 1993. This book consists of a selection of articles I wrote for this newspaper.

I have many to thank for my duration with the Brown Publishing Company, but I am especially grateful to the two top-notch editors I worked for, namely, Thomas Barr and Inga Kimple.

Most of all, I have to thank the many readers who have an interest in Warren County and its history. In these articles I have done much research and spent many hours trying to put my subject in perspective.

I have always tried to vary my subject matter, hoping to reach everyone at some time or another.

Because of the length of some of these articles, many were published in parts and printed in weekly segments. I have therefore combined these segments and made them into one story.

An acknowledgement of the many public facilities used in my research should be made.

Most of the material for this book was taken from the archives section of the Warren County Historical Society Museum, and the Warren County Genealogical Society, both located in Lebanon, Ohio.

I would also like to recognize the Mary L. Cook Public Library in Waynesville, Ohio; the Greene County Public Library in Xenia, Ohio; the Salem Township Public Library in Morrow, Ohio; the Mason Public Library in Mason, Ohio; the Cincinnati Public Library and the Cincinnati Historical Society; the Montgomery County Public Library in Dayton, Ohio; the Franklin Public Library in Franklin, Ohio; and the Middletown Public Library in Middletown, Ohio.

Without the support of my wife, Opal, this book would not have been written. Also, the support of our children, Edward, Karen, Kevin and Elizabeth has been so important.

Thank you.

Dallas R. Bogan

Chapter I

WARREN COUNTY

HISTORIAN RECOUNTS 18TH CENTURY WARREN COUNTY EVENTS FOR READERS

The earliest land owners between the Miamis (this land was originally called the Miami Country) were owners but not residents. John Cleves Symmes began sales to the pioneers in 1787, but because of the constant Indian raids, possession was next to impossible.

Wayne's victory over the Indians on the 20th of August, 1794 (Battle of Fallen Timbers), slowed down the frequent Indian commotion and disturbances. Still, occasional uprisings, horse thievery and frequent engagements with the whites led to no type of permanent agreement.

The treaty of peace, or the Treaty of Greenville (concluded August 3, 1795), virtually put an end to the Indian/white man engagements.

Before the peace settlement and shortly thereafter, protection from the Indian attacks was needed. A site was selected and entire neighborhoods would join in and erect what was called a blockhouse.

Small cabins were built which would surround the blockhouse; log pickets were built as fence lines for protection. This type settlement was called a station.

About a month after the peace agreement, on September 21, 1795, two groups of surveyors left Cincinnati to explore the Mad River area near Dayton, one under the command of Daniel C. Cooper, and the other under the surveillance of John Dunlap.

William Beedle was assigned to Dunlap's party. Beedle's purpose was to begin a new settlement. In his possession was a wagon, tools and provisions.

The party followed Harmar's Trace to Turtlecreek where Beedle, with his brother Francis, left to begin his community.

(The actual location of Beedle's Station stood west of present S.R. 741, north of the Hamilton Road, or County Road 13, east of Station Creek, and about one and three-quarters mile south of S.R. 63. A marker stands at the east side of the O.D.O.T. location, Division 8 building, noting the settlement.)

Beedle's Station was, according to most local historians, the first permanent settlement in Warren County. In Beer's Warren County History, the Hamilton Township section states that William Mounts and five other families settled in the County October, 1795.

The land was purchased from Robert Todd by William Mounts and Martin Varner. No blockhouse was erected, but several cabins were built in a circle surrounding a spring.

It was called Mounts' Station. (There is a stone monument in honor of this occasion located just south of the Little Miami River and across from the gravel pit on lower Stubbs-Mills Road.)

The names of the early families in this group were: William Mounts, wife and six children; Thomas Forsha, wife and children; Thomas Leonard, wife and six children; and Thomas Watson and family.

(Spelling of the Beedle family name is varied in different forms such as: Beedle, Bedle, Bedell and Beadle. However, in William's will and his deed from Jonathan Dayton, it is spelled Beedle. This spelling is a general acceptance in Warren County.)

In Littell's Early Settlers of the Passaic Valley of New Jersey, the following is written:

"William Bedell sold out his lands in October, 1792, to his brother-in-law, Nathaniel Littell, and with his sons-in-law and son, and their families, removed to a section of land that he purchased for $250 of Daniel Thompson, between the Miami rivers in Warren county, Ohio, where they all settled."

Beer's 1882 History states:

"William Bedle probably purchased from Daniel Thompson a land warrant issued by Symmes, as his deed for Section 28, Town. 4, Range 3, was executed by Jonathan Dayton and dated November 30, 1795."

Beedle's blockhouse was a dwelling built of round logs. Various ways were used in the construction of a blockhouse. The stockades were built with posts or logs solidly set in the ground and sometimes sharpened at the top, and arranged so as to enclose a region.

The stronger blockhouses were generally built conforming to each angle, and the lines between them filled with stockades or with cabins, one connecting the other, thus completing an enclosure.

The heavier built fortifications were constructed of heavy hewn timbers, and were sometimes of two or even three stories.

The smaller stations were built to accommodate fewer families and had a single blockhouse with cabins close by, and sometimes were without pickets.

The secluded blockhouses between the Miamis were typically crude buildings made with nothing but the common ax. The materials consisted of straight round logs, notched at the ends and hewed on the upper and lower edges to lie close together.

One identifiable characteristic of the blockhouse was that the upper part of the structure, above the height of a man's shoulder, was extended outward for about a foot or two over the lower part. This reasoning was that rifles could be thrust into the openings and defense of the blockhouse/station could be stabilized.

Judge Jacob Burnet describes life in the stations. He writes:

"Each party erected a strong block-house, near to which their cabins were put up, and the whole was inclosed by strong log pickets. This being done, they commenced clearing their lands and preparing for planting their crops. During the day, while they were at work, one person was placed as a sentinel to warn them of approaching danger.

"At sunset, they retired to the block-house and their cabins, taking everything of value within the pickets. In this manner they proceeded from day to day and week to week, til their improvements were sufficiently extensive to support their families. During this time, they depended for subsistence on wild game, obtained at some hazard, more than on the scanty supplies they were able to procure from the settlements on the river.

"In a short time, these stations gave protection and food to a large number of destitute families. After they were established, the Indians became less annoying to the settlements on the Ohio, as part of their time was employed in watching the stations.

"The former, however, did not escape, but endured their share of the fruits of savage hostility. In fact, no place or situation was exempt from danger. The safety of the pioneer depended on his means of defense, and on perpetual vigilance.

"The Indians viewed those stations with great jealousy, as they had the appearance of permanent military establishments, intended to retain possession of their country. In that view they were correct: and it was unfortunate for the settlers that the Indians wanted either the skill or the means of demolishing them."

Most of the early emigrants of the Miami Valley were Presbyterians. The Turtlecreek Presbyterian Church, built about 1798, was located a mile north of Beedle's Station. This was one of the first churches in Warren County, its members being mostly from New Jersey. (Isaac Miller and Francis Beedle were among those persons credited with starting the church.)

The church grew by leaps and bounds and became a strong congregational influence. Richard McNemar, its pastor, became involved in the great Kentucky revival and led nearly all the members out of the Presbyterian denomination, changing the church to New Light.

The Shakers, not long after the split in the church, accepted McNemar and many of the congregation into the Shaker faith. William Beedle, an elder in the church, followed McNemar into the New Light religion, but not into the Shaker denomination.

Completely renouncing the new Shaker sect, no part of Beedle's land was given to the Shakers, but his son, James, and his sons-in-law, Jonathan Davis and Elijah Davis, were declared in the Shaker records to be among the earliest converts.

One of the demands given by the mob of 1810 against the Shakers was that William Beedle be allowed to see his grandchild, a son of Elijah Davis. The reply was that the child was in the hands of his parents and the Shaker leaders had no control over the situation.

William Beedle's will, probated February 14, 1814, rewarded the family members who rejected Shakerism, while it left a very small inheritance to those who favored it.

He left title to his land, over 800 acres, to two daughters and two grandsons. His wife, Esther, would have the use of one-third of his estate and the occupancy of the best room in his house so long as she remained his widow.

His son, James received $10 in cash, and his daughters, Susannah Davis and Lydia Davis each $5.00 in cash, these children being Shaker converts.

His daughter, Phebe Mulford, was given a total of 186 acres.

Mary Holle, another daughter, received 180 acres.

William Beedle's grandson, John Davis, inherited a total of 200 acres.

Another grandson, John Beedle, was awarded about 250 acres.

UNDERGROUND RAILROAD MOVED EFFICIENTLY, SILENTLY THROUGH COUNTY

When this writer was a kid, he thought the Underground Railroad was a place where trains ran underground. As we all know, this was not the case.

The railroad had passengers, stations, conductors and routes in which it followed. It was a system in which the Negro slaves were transported through the free states to Canada.

The terms of the Ordinance of 1787 stated that slavery was forbidden in the Old Northwest Territory. This territory eventually became Ohio, Indiana, Illinois, Michigan, Wisconsin and Minnesota, the portion lying east of the Mississippi River.

Not all the slaves moved north; many stayed in the areas in which they were harbored. The County of Warren was amongst other counties which were a refuge for the Negro families.

The first two Negroes in Warren County of which there is written record were fugitives.

Francis Baily in 1796, described a Negro his party encountered on their way up the Little Miami to Waynesville. Hideously painted, a Negro appeared in the woods coming from the North and told the party of Englishmen that he was escaping from an Indian village; and "him we looked upon with the eyes of pity and of occupation, and did give him where with to continue his journey to Columbia."

The next Negro of record was a run-away slave from Kentucky. He was found very ill by William Smalley in Washington Township.

Several pioneer families in this County brought Negro servants with them. Many other pioneers came here at a sacrifice of money and long established homes in the South to get away from the conditions that were growing worse year by year.

Professor Wilbur Seibert, author of the book, "The Mysteries of Ohio's Underground," estimates there were about five thousand Ohioans which participated in the Underground Railroad, and that more than one-hundred thousand slaves found refuge in Canada.

Southern soldiers returning from the War of 1812 from the Canadian territory spoke of the life and freedom of the Northwest Territory. Overhearing this, the slaves created an avenue in which to escape. ("Managers" was the term given to the abolitionists who mostly planned the escapes.)

The names of those who signed on as "conductors" from Warren County regarding the Underground Railroad were: Abram and David Allen, Jacob Bateman, Henry T. Butterworth, Job Carr, R.G. Corwin, Joseph Evans, and Angelina Farr.

Thomas Hopkins, Isaac and Job Mullin, Valentine and Jane Nicholson, Edward, John and Samuel Potts, Achilles Pugh, Jonas D. Thomas, Fred and Jesse Wilson, and Jonathan Wright.

Jonathan Wright, a Quaker from Springboro, was in favor of "minding his own business" and not interfering with any matter which was accepted under the law, even though he felt it was wrong.

Wright was a saddle maker from Maryland and had Negro servants. He did not believe in interfering in the business of slave owners. If the law held slavery valid, he did not believe in aiding the escape of slaves as did many other Warren Countians.

Wright had a Negro named Frederick who hid his run-away brethren about the farm when they needed hiding.

He was anxiously waiting for Wright to turn away from the farm one night, for he had hidden a colored man there. Wright lingered and said: "Frederick, thee surely knows where the food is kept. Go out and get some." He did not let on that he knew Frederick was waiting for him to go so that he could get food for a run-away slave.

In Springboro in the 1850's, the Negroes organized and supported their own school.

Job Mullins, a Quaker from Springboro stated in his eighty-ninth year that he thought the most active days in the "Underground Railway" through Warren County was between 1816-1830.

With the passage of the Fugitive Slave Law of

1850, and the slave owners open passage into the slave free states, the bitterness of the two cultures became apparent.

Springboro, Waynesville and Harveysburg's Quaker communities were daring in their efforts in helping the escaping Negroes.

The road to Springboro (St. Rt. 741), was an artery in which the fugitives were transported. Marble Hall, at Otterbein Village, was rumored to be a stop-over for the railroad; also, the Green Tree Inn and the Red Lion Tavern, since torn down, were suspicioned to have been stops.

The early pioneers of Lebanon had little money. The early wealth of the County was brought by the Quakers from the slave States.

The Quaker settlements seemed to settle the more remote areas where they could set up their own places of worship. Waynesville, Springboro and Harveysburg were suitable for the trend of the time.

Jesse Wilson, a Lebanon Negro (now deceased), noted that his parents and grandparents worked for the Thomas Corwin family, and related stories of run-away slaves being hidden in the Phineas Ross house attic in pre-Civil War days.

Jesse told of his life in Lebanon. He said his grandparents came from Kentucky with their owner, Daniel Bedinger. He stated:

"Father was sold several times, and I recall his telling of the slave market, and of how the slave-trader would go along the road displaying his wares - Negroes in chains, to planters who would draw rein, stop, question the trader as to a likely buy in Negroes.

"The Thomas Corwin house was an underground station before the Civil War, so I've heard my mother tell. A hiding place was made for them up in the attic.

"My brother graduated from the old Normal School; he went nights to make his recitations. Professor Holbrook was nice - encouraged colored folk all he could. Our old Colored Public School was over back of French's Creamer. A cyclone blew our school in once and it was rebuilt. There just wasn't any system to our colored school; we had large classes and didn't get to recite every day. A bright colored child could go over to the white school; there we would get as much study and recitation in a day, as in a year at colored school."

In a letter from R.G. Corwin of Lebanon, written in September 1895, he recalls in his childhood seeing fugitives at Ichabod Corwin's (his father) house. R.G. seems to have continued his father's efforts in this work up into the 1850's.

The home of Francis Dunlevy has been known traditionally over time as an Underground Station.

Butterworth Station, near Foster, was the most southerly stop in Warren County, the station being operated by Henry Thomas Butterworth. Slaves were sheltered at the station in long sand filled bins in the sweet potato sheds. (Mr. Butterworth married Nancy, the sister of Thomas Wales and Jane Wales Nicholson of Harveysburg, who were also station operators.)

The route from Foster led to Oakland in Clinton County, with a branch leading from Mason to Springboro, via Lebanon. (There was possibly a direct line from Cincinnati to Springboro, with a branch off to Dayton from Springboro, also a branch line from Mason to Xenia.)

Achilles Pugh, a Quaker from Waynesville, was active for many years in Cincinnati in the abolition cause.

Waynesville's location was high atop the hill overlooking the Little Miami River. This strategic point was one of much benefit; the attic turrets affording a panoramic view of the area.

Local residents tell of a tunnel system from the river to the hideaways. The Miami House, built in 1826, which stood where the former Sonny's Drive-in was located, on the corner of Main and North, was said to have had concealed hideaways. This house was constructed to include a secret stairway and compartment reached by a trap door that opened to the secret compartment.

The basement included an entrance to a tunnel that ran from an opening on the Little Miami

River to the house. The tunnel extended across the street and down the west side of Main, and at some point up the hill, to the Haines residence.

In 1939, the W.P.A. installed a sewer system and initially destroyed the tunnel.

Mrs. Howard Stanley (now deceased), former resident of the Miami House, said in an interview in 1976, that part of a tunnel was visible in the basement when she lived there. She told of finding a hidden room about eight by ten feet from a secret stairway leading down about 12 to 15 steps from the attic. There, she said, she saw old hats, boots, straw and remains of ham bones.

The twenty-two room home of Noah Haines, which sits high on Third Street, is said to have a tunnel system that ran from a well at the rear and exited out the front portion of the home.

Other Waynesville area residences which possibly harbored the slaves were: the Evans Home at Main and Chapman; the "Diamond Hill" home of pioneer Abijah O'Neall on the Clarksvillle Road; and the Halfway House built in 1812 by John Satterthwaite at Third and Franklin.

There are possibly thousands of stories that traveled with the Underground Railroad. The individuals that had the foresight to record some of these happenings has allowed us to visit for a short time the past and preserve it for the future.

AMERICA'S COWBOY HAT HAD BEGINNINGS IN WAYNESVILLE

Waynesville has been involved in many historic occasions, but one such milestone seems to stick out more than any other.

America's favorite western hat, the Stetson hat, had its beginnings in this small town. Worn by such famous cowboys as John Wayne, Tom Mix, Gene Autry, Will Rogers, and the Lone Ranger, this "Boss of the Plains" found world wide attention.

John Batterson Stetson was born on May 5, 1830, in Orange, New Jersey. He was the son of Stephen Stetson, who was a hatter and a wise businessman. Stephen retired at the age of 50 with a bank account of $50,000.

Young John learned the hatter's trade from his father. Through bad investments, his father's funds were lost and John never received any financial gains.

John's health seemed to erode due to his diagnosis of tuberculosis. A prescription to move West where the air was dry and warm was the prognosis issued by his doctor.

His first stop was at Waynesville where he set up residence in his sister Louise Stetson Larrick's dwelling on South Main Street.

It was at this time that John made a decision to move to the area of St. Joseph, Missouri, where eventually he found work in a brickyard.

Through hard work and perseverance, John was promoted to manager which eventually led him to buy a piece of the business.

Two years later, the Missouri River overflowed and a half-million un-baked bricks were washed away, wiping Stetson out.

He tried enlisting in the Civil War, but because of his health he was rejected.

Later, with his health improved somewhat, he joined an array of prospectors who were hiking more than 700 miles to the "Pikes Peak or Bust" gold rush.

Somewhere in the area of Denver, Stetson started experimenting with possibly the hat that "Won the West."

His first experiment was: "he made a bow, using a leather thong and a tree bench. With it, he agitated clumps of shaved fur and kept them floating in the air. Slowly, he blew mouthfuls of water on the fur, which then matted and fell."

The thin fur sheets were then boiled and the procedure was repeated. With this process Stetson formed a hat with a high crown and broad rim to protect him from the rain.

Stetson's first wide-brimmed hats were made

fun of, but when a drifter came into camp and handed over a $5 bill for the first "Stetson," the world famous hat was on its way.

With John's health totally restored, and his bad luck of prospecting behind him, he sometime later returned to Waynesville to again reside with his sister, Louise.

It was at this time he conjured up the idea of starting a one-manned hat factory. His sites were set on Philadelphia. His sister loaned him $60 for his upcoming venture and in 1865 he was on his way.

The Philadelphians weren't exactly overwhelmed with the design of the cowboy hats. With a market that was practically non-existant in the eastern city, Stetson turned his attention to the southwestern portion of the United States.

"The Boss of the Plains" hat caught on with the cattle industry's personnel. Borrowing to the total extent of his credit, he made enough hats to supply the top clothing and hat stores in the Southwest. The rest is history.

The original three styles and prices were: rabbit, $5; beaver and rabbit combined, $10; and pure beaver, $30.

In 1970, the business almost folded. Two decades of falling sales in the hat industry had put the company into a great financial bind.

A small family-owned business firm, the Stevens Hat Company, located in St. Joseph, Missouri, acquired the ailing Stetson Company; machinery, label and all. (It was in this city that John B. Stetson on his way west, had earlier located and made his first fortune.)

Hat sales immediately took off after this acquired move. There are now virtually more than 100 other styles of Stetson hats ranging at different prices.

Among other dignitaries wearing the Stetson cowboy hat were: Harry Truman, Dwight Eisenhower, Lyndon Johnson; and among the television stars were Dennis Weaver, James Coburn and Burt Reynolds, to name a few.

General Custer wore one into his last battle, the Battle of Little Big Horn in 1876.

The Stetson House is still in existence on South Main Street in Waynesville. It is presently used as an antique store.

John B. Stetson died in 1906. At this time there were 3,500 workers producing 2 million cowboy hats a year. The "Hat that won the West" is a tribute to a never ending desire to fulfill a dream.

A SHORT HISTORY OF OLD DEERFIELD TOWNSHIP

Those of you who have a knowledge of the statistics of the State of Ohio know that it consists of 88 counties. The first county, Washington, was organized in 1788 and the last, Noble, was conceived in 1851.

A Constitutional requirement of Ohio states that no county shall contain less than 400 square miles, and that no county shall be reduced below that amount.

Ohio itself was never formed as a territory, only as a portion of a territory of the United States.

Governor Arthur St. Clair was appointed Governor of the vast Northwest Territory and established the first counties to his choosing.

Josiah Morrow has written about the different counties and townships before Ohio was formed. I shall now draw from his writings.

As was mentioned before, a county in Ohio forms 400 square miles or more, but Hamilton County in the Northwest Territory contained an estimated 5,000 square miles.

A report of Jacob Burnet, treasurer of Hamilton County, lists all monies paid into the county treasury by the different townships in the year 1799, the total amount being $3,633.49.

A list of these fourteen townships are: Columbia, Cincinnati, South Bend, Miami, Anderson, Springfield, Colerain, Fairfield, Deerfield, Dayton, Franklin, Washington, Ohio and St. Clair.

As you will notice many of these township names are the same as those towns or settlements which are now so-named.

William Mounts, the tax collector in Deerfield Township, had made the settlement called Mount's Station on the east side of the Little Miami, about three miles below the mouth of Todd's Fork in 1795.

Obed Denham, the tax collector of Washington Township (not to be confused with present Washington Township in Warren County), was a Baptist preacher who came from Kentucky and founded the town in Clermont County now called Bethel.

We shall now concentrate on old Deerfield Township. This large township comprised nearly all of the present county of Warren, except the current township of Franklin, the western portion of sections in Clearcreek, and ten sections of the fourth range in the northwest part of Turtlecreek. This area totaled about 30,000 acres in the neighborhood of Franklin.

Deerfield Township was much larger than the present County of Warren. It encompassed a strip three miles wide now in Montgomery and Greene, and extended eastward to the site of Wilmington, comprising about one-half of Clinton County. It also extended into Hamilton County along the southern boundary of present Deerfield Township.

This large township was organized by the commissioners of Hamilton County in 1797. It was given the name Deerfield, in honor of the first settlement which was made in 1795.

Elections of township officers were to be held at the house of David Sutton, then the most prominent pioneer in Deerfield.

By 1797 there were many settlements in progress in Deerfield Township, some being Beedle's Station, Mount's Station, Waynesville, Turtlecreek and Todd's Fork.

The old township was fairly new in 1799, but was beginning to become a force amongst some of the other townships. Among the tax receipts of this year Deerfield ranked fourth in Hamilton County.

On June 10, 1797, the commissioners of Hamilton County chose Benjamin Stites, Jr., assessor, and Isaac Lindley, constable and tax collector of Deerfield Township. The tax return for that year for the entire township was $111.15. Stites' fees were $5.20 and Lindley's, $2.30.

In 1798, Peter Drake was assessor and Joshua Drake, constable and tax collector. The fees of the assessor were $11.21; of the tax collector and constable, $4.13 each.

In 1799 Michael H. Johnson was assessor; his fees were $8.22; William Mounts was tax collector.

Timothy Boothby was "lister" of the township in this year, and made an inventory of the white male inhabitants twenty-one years of age and over. His fees amounted to $21.

Several attempts were made to make Deerfield Township a county. An act was passed for this purpose by the Territorial Legislature which met at Cincinnati in 1799, but Governor St. Clair vetoed the bill and it failed to become a law.

CHRISTIAN NULL HOMESTEAD IS A SPRINGBORO LANDMARK

A grand celebration was held Sunday, August 18, 1996, at the old Christian Null homestead, located high atop a picturesque hill in a portion of the Heatherwoode golf course, just south of Springboro, Ohio.

The Springboro Historical Society, a fairly young organization, accepted the challenge of restoring this two and one-half story log house to its original condition.

Many objections were raised regarding the project. However, with the vision and perseverance of the local Society, plans were made, executed, and today stands a monument to the past which everyone can be proud of.

In February 1995, two members of the Society, Charlie Logan and Gil Morris, introduced a plan to the Historical Commission, of which they are members, to completely renovate the decaying Null dwelling. In turn, the Commission presented their plans to the Springboro City Council, and approval was given.

City Manager, Ed Doczy, paved a way for the project, developing both a viable and financial plan.

Before the project got underway, an estimate of $200,000 was given to the Society for restoration of the building. However, Charlie and Gil accepted the monetary challenge and the job was done for less than $25,000.

Actual renovation began in March, 1995. Volunteer work crews from the Springboro Historical Society, the Historical Commission, and Springboro City Council worked Saturdays throughout the on-going process.

Charlie and Gil worked every Tuesday and Friday, weather permitting. They were joined in late March, 1996 by Paul Travisano, who had moved to the area from Chicago. And a tip of the hat to Charlie's daughter, Jane Perkins, for her part in the project. In all, more than 60 volunteers helped in the renovation.

One of the first jobs, and most assuredly the most difficult, was to place the dwelling back on its foundation, which was a mere four inches off. One reason given for this misalignment was the large earthquake of 1811.

Charlie and Gil hooked the old building up with cables and ingenious contraptions. Constant pulls were given. Finally, with one extra large groan, it slipped perfectly back into place.

The inside has been completely redone, except for a few minor adjustments. Five sections of logs were replaced on the east side. Most of the foundation was rebuilt, and the ground floor in the main room was restored. In this room is a giant fireplace that a person can stand upright in.

All the windows and doors were replaced.

In late 1995, Chris Payne, a Springboro High School sophomore, organized a group of scouts and their parents to do the chinking.

A porch was built onto the west side and both exterior wings were reboarded.

Gil and Charlie also used juvenile offenders assigned by Lebanon courts as workers.

The Christian Null Story

Our story begins in Virginia over 200 years ago. A somber group of men made their way to the home of the Henry Null family. They led a riderless horse and carried a saddle, sword and sidearms. Tragedy had struck. Their son Jacob was a casualty of the Revolution.

Especially affected by this bleak circumstance was 12 year old Christian Null. With the death of his brother, Jacob, Christian decided to carry the Null family name forward, and so at this tender age, he enlisted into the Revolutionary War.

At age 20, Christian had matured and achieved skills in the ways of the wilderness more-so than men twice his age. His father, having observed his skills and restlessness, gave him $500 and a mission. His assignment was to migrate westward to the grand frontier and purchase better farm land for the family.

His travels took him overland to the Monongahela River. Here he offered himself for work in order to secure passage on a flatboat heading down the Ohio River. He was refused by the men, but the ladies of the craft thought otherwise, speculating that he might be of some help.

In just three days Christian was selected as helmsman.

As they floated down the long winding river, a life threatening event occurred, the horses had kicked loose a board beneath the water level. Water quickly poured into the craft. The men stood frozen while the women screamed uncontrollably.

Christian jumped into the river, grabbed the loose board and forcibly pushed it back onto its pegs. All was not well yet, as the travelers bailed endlessly. Eventually, they reached their ultimate destination at Limestone (Maysville), Ky.

Christian worked, saved his money, and not until the Indian Peace Treaty in August 1795 could he fully explore the Ohio country.

Many trips were made north of the Ohio until

at last he found his homesite high atop a hill above Clear Creek.

Word was sent back home to Virginia for his brother Charles to join him in building a cabin on his newly purchased land.

A beehive of activity was now being performed in this new location. Large walnut and oak trees were being felled and carried to the pinnacle. A sizable two and one-half story home, constructed of square-hewn logs, was now being crafted.

Stone fireplaces, laid with rock from the valley of Clear Creek, were fashioned into each floor. One of these marvels consisted of a built-in oven.

The second floor and attic accesses consisted of a narrow stairway which turned 180 degrees in just six feet.

It was in the year 1798 that the Null log home was built. It is the oldest on-site exposed log building in Warren County.

After completion, Christian returned to Virginia for the rest of the family. By 1802, the Null family had settled into their new log home.

Christian Null was born in Harrisonborough, Rockingham Co., Va, in 1770. He married Kathryn Bone of Oldtown, Allegheny Co., Md. They raised all twelve children in their Clear Creek home.

After Christian's death, in 1832, Kathryn and the children moved westward. He is buried in the United Brethren cemetery on land that belonged to the Null family descendants until 1953.

The Taylor family assumed ownership of the Null residence in 1832. During their tenure two cribbed wings and a full-sized cellar were added. Some years later the cellar was used as a refuge for fugitives of the Underground Railroad.

The Celebration

Music for the celebration was supplied by the superb Centerville Community Band. An estimated 250 persons attended the ceremonious event. Fifty-seven Null family members were on hand, one from as far away as Salina, Kansas, and another from Mobile, Alabama.

Opening ceremonies were presented by Don Ross, Historical Society President. Speakers at the occasion were: Tom Sproat, site expert; Bob Wilson, Historical Society Vice-president and Historical Commission Chairman; Ray Wellbrook, Springboro Mayor; Ed Doczy, Springboro City Manager; and Bob Schaefer, Springboro Deputy Mayor. Renovation recollections were given by Charlie Logan and Gil Morris. All are Historical Society members.

Ribbon cutting ceremonies were executed by Society members along with Marlin Heist, former owner, and Emma Jane Null, family descendant. The second part of this ceremony was performed by Null family members.

Future Plans

Future plans for the building include group tours and will serve as a casual historical museum. Also, an annual Christmas event is in the plans. The city's Historical Commission and the City Council will periodically schedule events.

Already, Nancy Morris, local genealogist and Society trustee, has annual summer plans for traditional craftsmen and history experts. She is presently teaching the youngsters the art of spinning.

As the writer gazed at the delightful landscape from high atop this hill, my question was answered as to why a home in this setting. Surrounded by golf fairways and greens, and by stately homes, the old Christian Null log home stands as a symbol of the past with a link to the present.

(The writer greatly appreciates the assistance of Don Ross, Springboro area historian, for supplying material for this article.)

LEBANON ONCE BATTLED MORROW IN BID FOR WARREN COUNTY SEAT

Warren County was once a part of the huge County of Hamilton. Deerfield, being a large township of Hamilton County, comprised all of the present county of Warren except 44 sections about Franklin. This area also included a portion of Clinton County.

In 1799 residents of Deerfield Township asked the Territorial Legislature for a division of the County of Hamilton and asked that Deerfield be made the seat of justice of the new county.

On April 22, 1801, a meeting of the leading citizens of the township of Deerfield was held at the town of Deerfield (South Lebanon) which embraced the idea of a new county.

A meeting was held with the territorial Governor, Arthur St. Clair, for the sole purpose of making Deerfield the county seat. The committee was comprised of the leading citizens of the township. They were: Rev. William Wood, Robert Benham, Jeremiah Morrow, Nathan Kelley, Ignatius Brown, Ephriam Kibbey and John T. Hall.

After the formation of the County, March 24, 1803, by the first State Legislature of Ohio, Deerfield was contested for the new position of county seat by Lebanon, Waynesville and Franklin.

Deerfield, with its earlier establishment as a town, and Lebanon with a more centralized location, and with its designation as the temporary place of holding courts, encountered a struggle for two years for this prestigious vacancy.

The final decision was concreted by a special act of the Legislature February 11, 1805. At the time of the passage of this act, the County was represented in the House of Representatives by Matthias Corwin and Peter Burr, and in the Senate by William C. Schenck and John Bigger.

The House of Representatives was nearly equally divided on the passage of this act, and a motion to reject the bill was lost by the casting vote of the Speaker. Lebanon had won by a very narrow margin. Deerfield's last hope of becoming a county seat had been lost.

Morrow's Bid for the County Seat

In March 1879, the County Commissioners submitted the proposal of building a new courthouse, with the approval of the electors. The Commissioners issued a public notice to this account, and within one week Morrow held a public meeting in which a proposal was discussed toward the building of a new courthouse in Morrow.

Morrow's argument was that a new tax should not be established for the purpose of building a new courthouse; that those concerned should furnish the money and eliminate tax monies.

A written form read: "The friends of Morrow tender to the people of Warren County, the proposition to furnish the grounds and build the new courthouse by private donations free to the taxpayers, and we fully recognize the right of any and all other towns in Warren County to make similar propositions, leaving it to the people to say where their convenience and best interests require to its location."

At the April election, the electors defeated the tax. The tax proposal was again voted on in the October election of 1879, and again was rejected.

After the second defeat, the citizens of Morrow circulated a petition authorizing a vote on the question of the removal of the seat of justice at Lebanon. The petition stated the advantages of the county seat being located in Morrow, one of which comprised the juncture of two railroads.

A statement was issued saying: "Lebanon being off the railroad can afford neither markets nor manufacturing facilities and has failed to develop the ordinary advantages of a county town."

The citizens of Lebanon at first took the Morrow proposal in stride, however, after several months, the issue became a bitter struggle.

With Lebanon's tax hopes proven nil for the building of a new courthouse, the community requested the County Commissioners repair the existing building.

The argument for the citizenry of Lebanon stated in effect that Lebanon was on February 11, 1805, commissioned by the General Assembly of Ohio to be permanently established as the County seat.

The Morrow petition and the Lebanon rejection were presented to the Legislature. Months of this quarreling had virtually brought the entire County into the battle.

Signatures of the Morrow petition numbered 2,148; those who rejected the petition, 3,750.

With the vote in, the Morrow petition was brought before the Senate. This committee, upon hearing arguments from both perspectives, on February 12, 1880, agreed unanimously against the bill. The contest for the removal of Lebanon as a county seat was over.

EARLY COUNTY SETTLEMENTS AND THE SWAMPS

Early swamps in the County of Warren and surrounding areas were probably as much a hindrance for settlement as the great forests. These stagnations lay in places where we would least expect them.

The early settlers of Cincinnati found swamp land extended through the entire range of the town.

Jacob Burnet, a young lawyer, went to Cincinnati to practice law in 1796, eight years after the town had been settled. He found that during the summer amd fall months, the people were given to attacks of ague and recurrent fever.

A few years later, Daniel Drake went to the young town to study medicine and found in one spot a low belt of wet ground. It had been beaver ponds and were still annually filled with water.

He says in another tract in front of Fort Washington (Cincinnati) was still another pond in which ducks and other water fowl were regularly shot.

Lebanon, in its early days, would seem to have been well drained by the two branches of Turtlecreek. Dr. Daniel Drake's visit to the town, shortly after it was founded, thought its site was free from ponds, marshes and other social forms of disease.

In contrast, A.H. Dunlevy says that there were three parcels of wet and marshy ground on the original plat. He believed the circumstances contaminated the water of the wells in the oldest part of the town.

Swamps, bogs and marshes were common in the entire country when it was new. The Miami Valley, a well drained area, was not without its swampy places. Most every farm had some sort of drainage problem.

It would seem that the swamp lands would be low and close to the running water sources. But, according to the early topographphers, the wettest and most marshy land was found on the highlands separating the main water courses, while the driest land lay along the boundary of the streams.

Ohio geologists have expressed similar facts stating that: "The highest lands in the State and the summits from which the streams flow in different directions are not so well drained as those on the lower lands and on the slopes."

The divide between the valleys of two rivers is usually not a dry ridge but often level and wet ground.

The pioneers, in traveling westward from Lebanon through Warren County, found a sizable piece of swampy ground belonging to the Shakers. Part of the drainage of this swamp found its way to the Little Miami, and part to the Great Miami.

Wet miry land, bogs and swamps in the early settlement of the country were typical of watersheds that had any large span of surface.

The summit receives only rain water while the lower regions are often deluged with the drainage of the land lying above it. This accumulation of water thus tends to wash away obstacles and to cut channels which completely drain any ponds or swamps which have at one time been formed.

The higher swamps and pond water supply were responsible for the even stage of water throughout the seasons. The many springs that have been found on the lower levels also take their fresh water from this supply.

Before the clearing of the forests, many little flour and saw mills stood on the tiny streams which supplied waterpower for running them much of the year.

The machinery of these mills was simple and low-cost and the dams were effortlessly built of logs and brush. The farmers would work the mills during the rainy season and farm during the dry seasons.

Washington Township was long delayed in its development and settlement because of the swamp lands. Squire Samuel Harris, says in his history of the township that the highest lands in the township lie very near its center.

On this portion of land was a marsh called Sweet Gum Swamp. These waters moved northward by a slow stream into Flat Fork which empties into Caesar's Creek.

Flat Fork swamp lands were not developed until 1840 when John Hadley, John Wilkerson and the Harrisses opened farms upon it, which resulted in land favorably with any other in the township.

The largest body of flat and wet lands in the County was located amongst the original forests of Harlan Township.

This condition caused the township to have a sparse population during its first years of organization, delaying the first roads through it.

The first road law set up by the County Commissioners was in 1809, six years after the organization of the County. An answer to the settlement of the township laid in the clearing of the forests.

A drainage system was set up and the township land proved to be amongst the most worthy in the County.

CORN CANNING WAS ONCE A TOP COUNTY INDUSTRY

In the late 1800's and well up into the middle of this century, corn canning was one of the top industries in Warren County.

The writer well remembers the canning factory at Spring Valley, where he worked in the fall of '49. I lived in New Burlington at the time and would hitch a ride to and from the factory.

My starting wage was seventy-five cents an hour, later raised to ninety cents. My first job was stacking the cans in the crates.

Later I was assigned the chore of bringing the crates in from the outside. I'm sure many of the readers can relate to their own experiences.

Without going into the history of the corn canneries, the writer will try to focus on the actual operation itself. South Lebanon had a bustling corn canning business which was owned at different times by several different businessmen. In this article, we will focus on its methods.

Corn canning was a production type operation where every employee was assigned a particular job. The workers were very proud of their assignment, and the results proved this decidedly.

Mr. P.B. Dunham was superintendent of the South Lebanon Packing Company in 1884, its fourth full year of operation. About one hundred persons, young and old, male and female, were employed.

The factory was admired by all because of its system of order and perfect arrangement. Working conditions and safety were upper-most in the relationship between management and the workers.

This year, 1844, saw about one hundred and sixty acres harvested, the amount being about half the acreage because of the adverse weather conditions.

Beginning the operation, the corn was pulled from the stalk unhusked, and conveyed to the factory, and thrown on the upper floor.

After being husked by one set of hands, it was cut from the cob by another, conveyed to a chute by a third, and through this carried into a box below, where the canning machinery was brought into operation.

The machinery was operated by steam power, and moved in a trip-hammer fashion.

It consisted of an iron box, with a projecting tube about one and a half inches in diameter, which filled a can at every decline. A can per second was the goal.

When filled, they were quickly conveyed to the weighing table, where every can was increased or reduced to a certain weight, about two pounds. The operation was performed by two ladies, who were very quick and capable.

Cooking the corn was the next operation. It was then sealed with perforated tips, and placed in amounts of about four hundred each in an iron rack, and thence swung into a vat of boiling water.

After this first process, the cans, after cooking about fifteen or twenty minutes, were taken out.

The perforated tips were soldered perfectly air-tight, and the cans placed in a second boiler, where a second and final boiling process (perhaps an hour), completed the cooking.

The next process finds the canned goods being conveyed to the packing rooms, where the work of packing, labeling, etc., was completed.

The packing room at the time contained about 200,000 cans, which were being speedily shipped to Cincinnati, Chicago and points beyond.

Operating efficiently allowed shipments to be sent on time. No goods were shipped unsold. The corn was shipped with the label "Royal" imprinted on it.

The company, that season, shipped about 9,000 cases of two dozen cans each.

THE SPIRIT MILLER THAT INHABITED THE OLD WELCH MILL

Certain events happen which sometimes seem to be supernatural at times. Word is passed along concerning this event and eventually the story is stretched out of proportion. Such is the case of the old "Welch mill" which was located for years at the foot of the hill at Harveysburg. Our subject this week will focus on the "Spirit Miller of the Old Welch Mill."

A short history of the land layout and mill should at this time be appropriate.

Before the lake project, an exquisite little valley lay directly to the west beneath the Harveysburg hill. Geologists seem to think that before the last ice age, this area was once the bed of a lake, but the changes which took place at the close of the ice period closed up the original outlet. This caused the accumulated waters to open up a new channel, through which Caesar's Creek now flows.

The old Welch gristmill was built in 1839 by Amos and Samuel G. Welch, and Thomas M. Wales. It was the last one in operation in Massie Township.

It was forty feet square and three stories high, and worked three runs of stones.

It was last owned respectively by Isaiah Fallis, John and Thomas Fallis, George Wikle, William Harlan, William Starry, George Ross, Alfred Edwards and T.E. Lawrence.

The old mill at one time was the highlight of a large and successful trade. It was the centerpiece of the market and the gathering spot for nearby and distant citizens.

Up above the mill, near the western side, there were overflowing springs which had caused large marshes to exist.

The owners drained the bog and caused a discharge of waters into Caesar's Creek near the southern rim.

This small stream was known as Prairie Branch, and the entire valley was known to early pioneers as Little Prairie.

Our story now continues with a taste of ghostly fright. It seems that an old miller by the name of Hans Van Ripper was well remembered in the middle 1800's by many Harveysburg citizens.

Hans was normally a gentleman and respected by all who knew him, except when he allowed the Devil's own concoction, "good old-fashioned whiskey," to draw out an inner fire in him. This episode allowed the demon to take the place of the man, and become a fiendish fury.

The "legend" states that on one hot, steamy summer night a violent thunderstorm was raging with all the ferocity the heavens could yield. The might of the Devil seemed to lash out and at times flick its fire toward the earth in a vengeful manner.

Hans, in a drunken frenzy, appeared to display a disposition that complimented the unmerciful display of the heavens.

He cursed the storm, the lightning, the wind, and, as the events grew even more turbulent, his madness increased in intensity.

His employer, who was horrified not only at the storm but at his wild companion, started to leave the premises when Hans burst into a fresh barrage of profanities, and called on the Devil himself to come and help run the mill.

A graphic sheet of flame, a crash of thunder, a wild piercing scream, and a momentary vision was caught of a dark form sailing through the air, and the curses of Hans were heard dying away into the retreating storm.

The eventful night of Hans and his disappearance caused much commotion amongst the multitude.

Ill-fortune now hung over the mill as if being guided by some unknown force. Twice it was ravaged by fire and twice it was rebuilt. The dams had been swept away and the race was dry.

The vast wheel which turned the machinery was clogged with mud and hung idly rotting on its shaft. The windows were gone; the doors hung ruined on their hinges; and the moss grew on the roof in an aimless manner.

The old mill beckoned for the days of the past.

But the ever reaching hand of Hans Van Ripper dominated the events to his choosing.

It was said that not even the birds nor rodents would choose the mill as their resting place.

The eerie walks of the ghostly cast their shadowy form and strange shapes through the open windows, while the pale moonlight projected its remnant through the cracks of the rickety old building.

It was then the hound would stop in full chase, throw up his head, and break away into the most gruesome howls.

The horse of the overdue rider stops, with every limb trembling, with inflated nostrils, its eyes flashing and ears quivering, while neither blows nor persuasion will spur him to proceed.

On the fiercest nights, when the storm is in all its fury, it was said that lights shone from every window of the old mill.

Ghostly teamsters and their teams would again be seen driving into the mill-yard. Horses were again heard neighing in the mill-shed.

Sounds of water splashing over the great water-wheel were again distinctive. The distant sound of the groaning mill and its machinery once again rang out a in a spooky fashion.

Sounds of grain falling from the elevator buckets, the dull rumble of the millstones as they turn on their spindles, the hopper boy once again seen making his rounds, all of which seemed to be fashioned by the unknown.

On nights of immense storms and the awesome powers of the heavens are inflicted on the Earth, the old storytellers shake their heads, and tell the frightened child that Hans Van Ripper and the Devil are attending the mill.

MARCH MARKS 80TH ANNIVERSARY OF WARREN COUNTY UNDER WATER

The month of March marks the eightieth anniversary of the Flood of 1913. The Miami Valley was deluged with rain unprecedented in modern history, leaving the County of Warren with the greatest natural disaster in recent times.

The hardest hit was the city of Dayton. With Dayton completely swamped with water, because of the broken levees, the call for help rang out.

Lebanon, a city hardly recognized by name,

came to its rescue. The city of Dayton depended on Lebanon for telephone, telegraph and mail service.

The Dayton, Lebanon, and Cincinnati Railroad was the only railroad service to reach Dayton from Lebanon.

The Cincinnati, Lebanon, and Northern Railroad was the only exit from Cincinnati to Lebanon, thus allowing a connection from Dayton to Cincinnati through Lebanon. The railroad was used by the National Guard to aid and assist the flood victims.

Lebanon was set up as the mail center. Working twenty-four hours a day with no time for rest, the mail personnel painstakingly performed a duty that merited many credits.

It was said that Lebanon probably sent out as much as 10,000 loaves of bread. Much of this was baked by the women of the vicinity.

The Waynesville postmaster sent a mail wagon to Lebanon each day which consisted of mail from Waynesville, Lytle, Harveysburg and Corwin of this county; Spring Valley, and Bellbrook of Greene County; and Centerville of Montgomery County.

The towns of Morrow, South Lebanon, Foster and Oregonia each sent mail to Lebanon daily and Franklin was supplied at Lebanon for three days.

South Lebanon was assessed to be the hardest hit of the towns of the County. There were just a few homes on the foothills on the north side of the town that escaped the ravages of the Little Miami.

Some of the houses were carried into the swift current and parts of them were found between South Lebanon and Cincinnati. Many of the one story houses were completely covered with water, the occupants being rescued by boat.

One family, the Silas Hill family, consisting of an aged mother and an invalid brother, was forced to the attic. With the waters approaching rapidly, Mr. Hill took a rail of a bed and knocked a hole through the tin roof of the house, through which he pulled his mother and brother.

Thinking he placed them in safety upon the extreme top of the roof, was an oversight.

Being engulfed by the waters again, he secured a ladder which was swimming nearby. With this he made a bridge to the top of a tree which grew in front of the house. And over it they crawled and there, in the branches, they remained for seven hours before they were rescued.

Morrow was placed second among the County's casualties. The property on Railroad Street was completely wiped out. This being the principal business street, a total collapse of the town was evident.

Property in East Morrow was also a distressful situation. The water in the post office stood at about seven feet. The first sight of "laundered money" was seen by many of the residents at the local bank.

Senator John Holden had just arrived from Columbus to find as pretty a little cottage as any could wish, practically ruined, for the water had stood in it to the depth of five feet.

An old log house, which stood near the bridge at Morrow, is said to be responsible for the destruction of several bridges down the river. It was so well constructed that the mighty current of the Little Miami designated it to become a battering ram.

The greatest financial loss of the County was at Kings Mills. George C. King, who was in Chicago when the flood struck, estimated the loss to the King Powder Co. and the Peters Cartridge Co. at $150,000.

Talk of rebuilding was finally concluded when it was decided that their financial loss would be too great if they relocated.

The only major damage was done to the two companies, since the village of Kings Mills set high atop a hill.

The town of Foster's east side was completely wiped off the map, the double bridge being completely washed away.

Next to the east came the two story store building of Ben Rohling in which he carried a $12,000 inventory stock. It was said that the store remained intact until it struck the bridge at Loveland, about four miles down the river. There it went to pieces with a crash.

Opposite Rohling's store was a three story brick building belonging to Frank Maag. After the water struck it, not a brick was to be found.

East of Rohling's was a three story white brick hotel. The east end was knocked out by a floating barn and the two lower stories were heavily damaged.

The Pennsylvania station was a complete wreck. The telegraph operator conducted his business from a little table in a corner of the women's waiting room, having deserted the other parts of the building.

To the east of the railroad stood the Lutheran Church. It had filled with water which ran through the broken windows until the pressure took out the entire west wall. The organ and pews were completely swept away.

Seven deaths were reported at Franklin. Great losses were sustained by the Franklin Coated Paper mill, American Writing Paper mill, Franklin Wheel Works, and Brown-Carson-Schieble Manufacturing Co.

The west side, or the Mackinaw district, suffered most; practically all the houses were under water. Eleven houses were swept away by the ravaging current of the Great Miami.

The Miami Valley Chautauqua suffered heavily. All the buildings were swept away, except the auditorium.

At Oregonia, the store of John Sherwood suffered great damage, along with the residences along the railway. The immediate damage was cared for and assistance from Lebanon was not needed.

At Fort Ancient the bridge was swept away by the rushing current of the Little Miami. There was some water damage to the property paralleling the river. The water rose to a height of three and one-half feet higher than ever before.

A total of six bridges were washed away in the County. Their locations were at Fort Ancient,

Mill Grove, Stubbstown, Kings Mills, Fosters and Loveland.

Estimates at the time were in the range of $150,000 for the roads and bridges and $150,000 for the approaches to the bridges and pilings; a total of $300,000.

Roads in the flood areas were ruined. At Fosters the water had washed holes in the road up to four feet deep.

One day after the flood a railroad car came from Cincinnati to Lebanon. It was guarded by ten blue coats with Winchesters.

The merchandise contained $300,000 in cash consigned from the First National Bank of Cincinnati to John H. Patterson at Dayton. Patterson confided that the residents of Dayton need not wait on the State of Ohio for their needs, but the money shall be distributed to the needy and Ohio could recompense him.

HARVEYSBURG SUFFERED DEVASTATING FIRE IN 1939

"It was the nearest I've been to eternity." These were the words spoken by Charles Thompson concerning the worst fire in Harveysburg's history.

On January 27, 1939, at 1 A.M., a devastating fire swept downtown Harveysburg and destroyed three businesses and a portion of a residence and garage. The blame was placed on an overheated stove in the pool room of Charles Thompson.

According to Mayor Carroll Smart and Marshall Carl Pottorf, the Lebanon fire department, with Fire Chief Dunham, Ralph Palmer and Jack Wills in attendance, made heroic efforts to extinguish the fire during the five hour battle.

The Wilmington fire department was also called upon and worked courageously. Harveysburg Fire Chief Adam Campbell and his volunteers, numbering about 175, worked until weary.

The wind blew briskly from a northerly direction causing the flames to move rapidly and spread to the residence of Thompson, where his wife and son-in-law were sleeping.

McDonald's barber shop, the Harveysburg post office, the drug store, and the rear of the Carroll Smart garage were engulfed in flames.

High tension wires in the center of the village melted causing total darkness until about 4 a.m.

This event proved hazardous to the firefighters trying to contain the fire.

"Bob," Charles Thompson's dog, was the only fatality of the blaze. Thompson's loss, besides the building, was about $200 in silver and about the same amount in bills.

The silver was found in a melted state and returned to Thompson by one of the firefighters.

Thompson retired to his room above the pool room about 9:30 p.m. The downstairs business was left in the care of Howard Debord.

According to Debord, he closed up about midnight. Thompson stated that about an hour later he was terrified by the smell of smoke.

Choking and coughing, he staggered downstairs and into the restaurant where he saw the flames advancing up the wall behind the stove. Thompson fought his way to the door and fell into the street.

Louis Snell had just returned from work in Dayton and spotted the commotion. He immediately rushed to the town hall and sounded the fire alarm.

Members of the local volunteer fire department instantly reacted to try to control the fire before it spread to the other buildings.

Mayor Smart, seeing the fire was out of control, called upon the Lebanon, Wilmington, Dayton and Waynesville fire departments for their aid.

The local post office was in jeopardy causing the Postmaster, Charles Madden and his assistant, R.E. Hurst and others, to rescue the mail. It was transferred to the Jeffries restaurant across the street.

All the Government property was saved except the lock boxes.

The water in the four fire cisterns and five deep wells was almost depleted, but to no avail, the flames still spread in a frightful manner. Flying embers from the fire landed on the roofs of the Smart garage and Doster's feed store causing damage.

After five grueling hours, the fire was quenched. The trucks of Frank McCarren of Harveysburg, and A.C. Roblitzer, Waynesville, busied themselves hauling water from Waynesville to fill the depleted wells in case of another fire eruption.

The temperature held at or about 18 degrees causing much of the water to freeze.

The next day, and for some days afterward, curious on-lookers from many different neighborhoods frequented the site of the fire.

School was dismissed by H.C. Milligan, superintendent of the Harveysburg schools, because of the loss of water, and also because many of the students were tired in body from fighting the fire.

The garage was owned by William McCarren and operated by Carroll Smart; it was covered by insurance.

Sabin McDonald was the owner and operator of the local barber shop and was not covered by insurance, although he was in the insurance business.

The pool room was owned by Thompson and was covered by insurance, but not the contents.

Thompson's residence, owned by J.W. Snell, was nearly an entire loss and was covered by insurance.

The post office building was owned by Anna Madden, wife of Postmaster Charles Madden, and covered by insurance.

HISTORIAN CLEANS OUT HIS FILES WITH VARIOUS TIDBITS ON COUNTY

The following is information which contains loose ends that the writer has laid back, and do not include enough material for a complete article. Many are quotes from newspaper articles and the like. The first four features were taken from **The Warren County Record** in 1902.

"The old well-sweep has almost vanished. How familiar was the square board box that rose from the well-curb and the long pole that spanned above, the well always open to the air, and the dank, narrow bucket, that was attached by a chain to the aerial pole, and was placed on a ledge, all dripping with cool, good water. The contention will always be made, at least until the present generation dies away, that we have never had such water as it was."

"The toll-gate came years after the early settlement, but it has passed away, and that so long ago that many well-grown people may never have seen one. When a little white house, standing close to the road, hitched by a rope to a half-leaning pole, and giving one the impression that the house was linked to a post on the other side of the road, appeared to your vision, you had to pay, or the toll-bar came down to stop your progress. Now there is not a toll-bar spanning any road in Warren County."

"Along the roadway we had milestones. They are practically all gone. The milestone had a shape, width, and a bright surface not unlike many gravestones. It had the number of miles to some place, and the number of miles from some place, carved in the stone. It served a good purpose in its day, but the need of it passed, and the stone gave place to something else, and its life went out with the rapid march we have been making."

"An enterprise of great importance in the early history of Lebanon and Warren County was the building of the Miami Canal from Dayton to Cincinnati. On the completion of the canal, and on the day that the first boat was to pass through from Dayton to Cincinnati, there was a great celebration at Franklin. A large delegation went over to Franklin from Lebanon. Some went in carriages, but the majority went on horseback, that was the customary way of traveling in those days. Being only fourteen years of age, I was rather young to be a delegate, but I went with the others, all the same, and, riding my own horse, felt about as big as Thomas Corwin, or anybody else.

"The boat left Dayton that morning, and was due at Franklin early in the day, but, as yet, there was but little water in the canal, which caused the boat frequently to drag on the ground, making progress slowly. Finally, when the horn blew, and the boat came in sight, [about 1828] there was a great rush for the canal, and very soon both banks and the bridges at street crossings were crowded with people, and, as the boat passed under the first bridge, there was a great shout. The people were very enthusiastic.

"The arrival at the present day of an ocean war vessel would not cause as much excitement as that little canal boat did that day. The name, painted in large letters (Alpha of Dayton), was very appropriate. Very soon after this there was a daily line of passenger boats from Dayton to Cincinnati. These were called packet boats, for passengers, making about five miles an hour. This was rapid transit in those days. At about this time the daily line of four-horse stages from Cincinnati to Sandusky was established. this was progress." (The last article was written by William Ferguson II, an early resident of Lebanon.)

Last Tribe of Ohio Indians
Pass Through Lebanon

The Wyandottes, who had earlier been known as the Hurons, came from north of Lake Erie and settled on the south shore of that lake, mainly about Sandusky Bay and westward to the Maumee. They gradually spread out until they occupied most of northern Ohio. **The Western Star** inserted an article in the paper which concerned the last of the Indians. It said:

"On Monday, the 17th of July, 1843, an Indian tribe - the Wyandottes - passed through Lebanon. This was the last tribe left in Ohio, and they were removing to their far distant home west of the Mississippi River.

"They were removing at their own charge, in wagons and on horseback, and made quite an imposing appearance. There were, in all, about one hundred and fifty wagons and carriages, eighty of which they had hired for the occasion, and the remainder belonged to themselves. From Cincinnati they go by steamboat to a point not far from their destination. They number, in all, between seven and eight hundred, but a part of their people have gone across by land with the stock, and a few yet remain behind to close up their business.

"The tribe is comparatively wealthy. Besides the large sum received in hand, their annual annuity will amount, we understand, to about twenty-two dollars a head, men, women and children. In addition to this they have allotted to them west of the Mississippi perhaps four times as much land as they owned in Ohio, and their stock, in horses, cattle, etc., is very considerable.

"The Wyandottes are far advanced in civilization, and have many men among them of wealth and education. They appeared to be well prepared for the toils and fatigues of the journey, and, withal, happy and contented in view of their change of condition and prospects.

"Still, one could not but feel melancholy at witnessing the exodus from our borders of the last of a powerful race, which, in times gone by, held undisputed possession of this broad land. But their council fires have gone out; their wigwams are deserted. No more their shrill whoop resounds through the interminable forest, starting the game from its lair to meet the fatal ball of the hunter.

"They have passed away! Peace, civilization and science have taken their place, transforming the trackless wilderness into cultivated fields, and rewarding the laborer for his toil. They are gone! May the Good Spirit guide and protect them!"

Some Interesting County Names

In Washington Township there was a settlement of people and a school house that was known by the name of "Leather Ear." The founding or reasoning for the name is not at the present time known to this writer.

East of Lebanon, on the road to old Mather's Mill was a place known as "Buzzard's Glory." It was a small area located west of the Little Miami River. Perhaps the area got its name from a resting point of the huge fowl.

The name "Dog Street" should ring a bell to many residents south of Lebanon. The lands that skirt Muddy Creek have long been called this name. "Mary Ellen" and "Blue Shinn" were many years ago common names for locations along the Little Miami River. "Hoptown" is a familiar nick-name for Hopkinsville.

Businesses of Waynesville in 1853

The following businesses were listed in the Waynesville Miami Visitor dated December 14, 1853.

There were two saddle and harness making establishments in Waynesville, one who was Chandler & Ebright, Main St, between North and Miami.

The harness prices ranged from $10 to $25 for single, and from $20 to $75 for double seats; their saddles varied in price from $5 up to $25.

The other establishment was possibly owned by G.W. Satterthwaite, the business being conducted by Mr. John Borden. It was situated on the corner of Main & Miami Streets.

There were possibly two or three grocery stores in town, the number not being absolute.

Four blacksmith shops were listed, the names being: T.B. McComas, on Miami Street; Levi Hartsock, upper end of Main Street; Mr. Crispen, at the foundry; and D. Eberly on the Public Square. Mr. I.V Fairholm occasionally did a little business at his shop east side of Main Street in the back.

There were no wagon making establishments in town.

Carpenters were too numerous to count. A.E.

Merritt and H.W. Printz had shops and helpers, the latter number not given.

Seven or eight doctors was the count given, but no names were supplied.

One drug store was listed, the former owner being Asa Trahern. It had been purchased by H.W. & E.R. Printz.

The chain pump business was run by George M. Zell.

There were two hotels in Waynesville and one in Corwin, viz. the Hammell House, on Main Street, operated by E.P. Yoemans; The Morrow House, located on the corner of Main and North Street, owned by R. Morrow; and the Woodruff House, in Corwin, owned by Mrs. Woodruff. There was one livery stable in town, William Rogers, proprietor.

There were two saw mills and two flour mills, one of each at the upper end of town, Wright & Baily, Proprietors, and the other two at the lower end, A.H. & J.P. McKay, proprietors.

The town had one cooper shop, that of L. Umphry, North Street. In Corwin, A. Cadwallader had a shop.

Early Settlers and their Residency in the County

New Jersey was represented in the County by several diplomatic officials, namely, John Cleves Symmes who was Chief Justice of New Jersey, and the originator of the Symmes Purchase.

An associate of Symmes in his purchase was Jonathan Dayton (for whom Dayton was named), a Revolutionary War officer.

Another associate, also a resident of New Jersey, was Dr. Elias Boudinot, also as Revolutionary patriot. Dr. Boudinot was a President of the Federal Congress and afterward first President of the American Bible Society. It was certainly possible for so many of the early settlers of New Jersey to settle in Warren County.

The Quakers came from Pennsylvania, Virginia and the Carolinas, settling largely in the northern and eastern parts of the County; Waynesville soon became a prominent place among the Friends. Opponents of slavery came from the slave states to live in the first free State organized in the Northwest Territory.

MORE BITS AND PIECES OF WARREN COUNTY HISTORY

Other Times

The many means of living or survival accompanied the pioneers. With no means of manufacture or simply to say "every thing was done by hand" was a true statement. The next four segments will explain somewhat the methods of living within their means.

It should be noted that a "spider" was the handiest and most commonly used of all pioneer cooking utensils. It was just like a skillet, except that it had a very long handle. It also had legs attached to it and could be set right over the fire. There was also an iron rim on the cover, so that hot coals could be piled under the spider and on the top of the lid. No flame was allowed to blaze around it. Deep iron kettles which the pioneers brought with them were highly treasured, because for many years iron was not available west of the Alleghenies. The griddle was much like the spider, but had no legs or cover.

Soapmaking was a process in which the pioneers settled into in the spring of the year. Now enough soap was made to last through the year. Wood ashes saved during the winter were put into a barrel. Water was poured through the ashes and allowed to trickle out through a hole in the bottom. This brown liquid or "lye" was then boiled in a large kettle with fats and grease saved from the year's cooking and butchering. The mixture was cooked slowly until it thickened to form a soft, jellylike, yellow soap.

Candlemaking was a much needed skill since the pioneers depended upon this means of light for their night hours. The wicks were made of rolled cotton, silky down from milkweeds, or tow string, slipped over a candle rod and dipped in melted tallow. The tallow clung to the wick and hardened. The dipping continued until the candles had become thick enough. Later, tin molds were used and as many as six, eight, or more candles could be made at once. The melted tallow was poured into the molds and then allowed to cool around the homemade wicks.

Homemade clothes were worn by most of the pioneers. Deerskins and pelts of fur-bearing animals often were used. Later, when the settlers began to raise sheep, the wool was sheared, washed, combed, carded, and spun into yarn. A dye was made from berries, leaves, and bark. The yarn was dyed before it was woven into cloth on a loom. Learning to spin and weave was part of every girl's education.

Proposed Trolley Route

The Western Star, on July 16, 1908, published news of a new trolley system. The article contained information concerning a new trolley road which was to pass through southern Warren County.

There were two routes spoken of: one route was from Cincinnati to Milford, through Goshen to Pleasant Plain and Butlerville, and thence to Wilmington and Washington C.H., with an extension to Xenia. The terminus would be at Columbus.

The second route would pass from Cincinnati to Montgomery, through Maineville and Butlerville and probably Morrow and thence to Wilmington and Columbus.

The approach to this project was that the road would be in air line; "the cars would be propelled by compressed air."

Upon investigation of this new type of locomotion it was said (after the purchase of the new cars) the maintenance on these particular carriers would be minimal.

A meeting at Goshen, with the chief promoter, met with approval. A statement was made that as soon as the right-of-way was cleared the project would be underway.

Apparently the project never got beyond the talking stage. There is no evidence of this line being routed except on paper.

Six 'Little Red' Schools are Sold

Five one-room schools in the Lebanon school district and one at Hopkinsville were sold at auction Saturday, August 17, 1940. Auctioneer Virgil Russell was in charge of the sale of five at the courthouse; the other sold in the afternoon at Hopkinsville, with Karl M. Brown being in charge.

The Merrittstown School, the location being north of Lebanon on U.S. 42, was sold to Mrs. Charles Irwin for $1,515.

The Greenwood School, east of Lebanon, was purchased by Ray Lucas for $420.

John Goddard was the high bidder on the Independent School at a figure of $565.

The Hart School, west of town, was sold to S.S. Baals for $775, and Albert Arthur bought the Pleasant Hill School for $550.

The Hopkinsville School was sold to Mrs. Geneva Snider, of Hopkinsville, for $1,160.

PIONEER VILLAGE HOLDS OLD TIME FOOD AND MUSIC FESTIVAL

"And a fine time was had by all!" This was the general feeling the writer experienced when he visited Pioneer Village Sunday, June 25. The 60 acre site was the nucleus of fine entertainment for the entire family.

The theme was entitled "Ole'Tyme Music & Food Festival." And indeed one came away with the feeling that the clock had been turned back to another time and another place.

Entertainment included many locals displaying their talents, as well as groups from distant localities.

Have you ever heard Willie Dunn, Lebanon's local C.P.A representative, play the banjo? Or have you ever listened to Carlisle's Curt Noe and his "talking" harmonica?

Another special treat was "Squawkbox," and their guest, Hillary Gregg, from Dayton.

Three dulcimer groups were highlighted; the Mountain Dulcimer Society of Dayton, the Cincinnati Dulcimer Society, and the Mountain Dulcimer Troupe from Middletown.

Many other musical groups, along with several bluegrass bands were present, all displaying the heritage the village depicts.

Superb gospel groups exhibited their talents in the old Friends Church.

Since the program included the word "food," let us examine the menu for the three day event. Foods were served by ladies wearing their 1800's attire which made the menu that much more appealing.

Scrapple, corn fritter, cabbage chowder, pumpkin soup, hominy & sausage, red flannel hash, turnip stew, homemade bread with butter, bean hole beans, sorghum popcorn balls, along with many fine desserts were served.

Have you ever seen "cloggers" perform? Or are you interested in "square dancing?" The G. & M. Cloggers, the Down Home Cloggers, the Country Cousins, and the Honey Bee Squares, all entertained in the old time dancing tradition.

As one would frequently say, just follow the crowd and there would be a story-teller in the center.

Such was the case! The village was graced with the presence of Cherokee Chief Gray Eagle, of the Over the Hill Tribe of Louisville, Kentucky, and his spouse, Red Bird.

Many tales were shared by the Chief concerning the American Indians, along with a question and answer session.

The location of this story-telling venture was at the Samuel Heighway cabin, the writer's favorite site.

Don Richards says the log structure was built around 1793-95, and is considered the oldest existing structure of its kind in Ohio. It was moved to the site from about a mile below Waynesville.

The general layout of the building was built in such a way that paralleled the Indian wigwam. It has open ends at the top of the side walls and a fireplace in the center. This setup allowed a perfect draft for the smoke to exit through the top of the dwelling.

Pioneer Village is uniquely located on Pioneer Village Drive, just off Oregonia Road, between Harveysburg and Oregonia.

It has not always been the village it is today. Miriam Lukens says the village had its start in the spring of 1973.

The first festival was held in September of the same year. Only one cabin was in existence during this event, the Levi and Elizabeth Cleaver Lukens cabin, built in 1807.

The Lukens family migrated to the area and purchased 1,000 acres along the banks of Caesar's Creek, which included the present site of Pioneer Village. (The Lukens log house represents architectural dwellings typical of the hard-working Quaker settlers in the Warren County area.)

When Pioneer Village was in the planning stages, the council was advised that a venture of this sort would last but about five years.

However, some twenty-two years later, it has grown into a well landscaped tract of land that comprises nineteen reconstructed log buildings, and many out buildings which appropriately fit in with the times.

The village originally started out as 12 1/2 acres until about 1976, when the council asked the Corp of Engineers for additional land. It was ultimately granted fifty additional acres.

Mrs. Lukens says that she and Bill Lukens went on the road searching for someone with a horse and wagon to supply transportation for the visitors through the village site. They eventually found one in Centerville, and this method of travel was solved for several years.

She also said a cow was obtained for the village and the visiting children were shown the art of "milking."

All the log buildings were disassembled at

their original site and reassembled at the village site, all except the Friends Church.

Cozy fireplaces are neatly fitted inside the log cabins, portraying a time of yesteryear. Also included within are furnishings of the same period.

Warren County is indeed fortunate to have within its boundaries a fine facility such as Pioneer Village. The main function of the association is to "bring history alive in the community."

Needless to say, like many other organizations, "volunteers" are the backbone of the village.

They are too numerous to be mentioned in this column, but they know who they are. (I am told that additional volunteers are always welcome.)

The village is open year round. The actual construction personnel consists of retired volunteers dedicated to their work, as evidence points out. They are on the grounds every Friday, year round, weather permitting.

If one were to inquire into a specific cabin, or to the actual building of the cabins, these gentlemen would gladly share the knowledge they have acquired.

The only income for this fine organization is the festivals they have, and monies collected from the membership dues. No public funds are used.

Sharon Kingan, one of the dedicated trustees, says their motto is: "To forget one's ancestors is to be a brook without a source, a tree without a root."

According to the village events schedule, the next occasion is entitled "Caesar's Creek Rendezvous."

It will portray personnel dressed as trappers, hunters and the American Indian. There will be over 100 tents set up and all their wares will be on display. This event is scheduled on July 15 and 16, 1995.

HISTORIAN TAKES A LOOK AT THE
LOCAL NEWS OF 1909

What's in a newspaper? While we scour the local headlines and world news sources, possibly the most "human interest" stories are buried deep in the classified ads or in a miscellany section of the paper. This week we shall review the small news happenings of 1909 as published in **The Western Star**, primarily reported in Lebanon.

On New Year's Day an owl made a noise like a fire alarm, and saved the home of Mrs. Elizabeth Kell in Lebanon from destruction by fire.

Soot had gathered in a closed grate and was smoldering when accidentally the owl toppled in.

An investigation was held as to the cause of the noise, the consequences being that a disastrous fire was averted.

One week later Joe Herron smashed all records of eating when he devoured in one meal 17 egg sandwiches, a large crock of oyster soup and drank sixteen cream pitchers of water without stopping.

A short time later, with the "hungries" still gnawing at him, he devoured ten dishes of ice cream with the average of 51 seconds per dish.

The same week Ike Lerner, a junk dealer, mistook a gasoline can for a coal oil container and an explosion followed which blew every stitch of clothing from his body. Shrieking with pain he dashed home by a route through back yards.

A short time later a large fox terrier belonging to Frank Maple, formerly of the Genntown area, wandered all the way back from Nebraska where he had been taken by his master removing to that State.

Late in February an earthquake of large magnitude was felt in the Lebanon area. An artesian well which had been bubbling forth crystal water for half a century suddenly ceased to produce.

In contrast, a spring located on the Albert Brant farm, near Lebanon, which had been dry for twenty years, again began to flow more freely than ever.

On March 10, Will Fraser was peeling a banana when a large tarantula fell onto his plate.

After a desperate confrontation the spider-like being was killed.

The following week the French Brothers Dairy Company reported a valuable cow on their Valley farm was missing.

It was found dead and an autopsy was held. It was found that the cow had eaten nails and wire and that these objects had worked through the animal's system, penetrating the heart.

The month of March brought forth a beautiful Sunday in which the residents of Lebanon were treated to the rare sight of a man riding an old-fashioned cushioned tired "High Water Bicycle."

It was the property of Raymond Decker and was purchased for $1 from R. Wilds Gilchrist, who paid $150 for the machine when new, not so many years before.

The middle of April finds O.A. Hutchinson telling of his alarm clock cat at his home.

Should the family members oversleep the feline lightly trips lightly across the keys of the family piano and the alarm is given.

On May 10, John Mann, a traveling salesman appears in Lebanon on a regular trip and it is found that he has a broken back, but that the vertebrae had been spliced by tiny gold wires and the man was enjoying the best of wealth, excuse me, health.

With the close of the public schools, Miss Roberta Hart made a record of attending school for a period of ten years and never being tardy.

On July 1st, lights similar to those of the aurora borealis, reflecting from the northern skies, attracted much attention in Lebanon.

An investigation followed which showed the illumination to come from a search light on the Algonquin Hotel in Dayton.

The middle of July found that a hen belonging to Thomas Keever, of East Main Street, completed the remarkable feat of laying 107 eggs in 107 days.

One week later the town clock took a tantrum and struck thirteen times instead of one o'clock following the noon hour.

At two o'clock the clock failed to strike at all, but an hour later the correct stroke was given.

Early in August fish were found living in a deep well on the property of Mary Ruch, having thrived there over a year from the time they were washed there by a flood in Turtlecreek.

Late in the same month **The Western Star** staged a contest and invited all the farmers in Warren County to bring in their stalks of corn.

The largest stalk measured 17 feet and 7 3/4 inches with the first ear 11 feet from the ground.

Following this occasion James Colbert presented a stalk growing in the public school yard which had ten perfectly developed ears of corn.

September was marked with freaks of nature. Cherry blossoms burst forth on a tree in the yard of John A. Thompson.

A leech of eight inches in length was caught by Miss Josie Williams north of Lebanon and presented to Lebanon University.

Nine fully developed papaws in a cluster were found by Miss Gurtrude Grown in a woods near Lebanon.

A volunteer hill of potatoes developed until at the digging 22 fully developed potatoes issued forth.

On October 10, a large python snake owned by Charles Hauser, of Franklin, was sold to a traveling show. It had been a pet for nine years living in the house with the family.

The following week found Dudley E. Foss, residing near Maineville, walked eight miles to dine with his daughter in Morrow. He was 92 years of age.

A few days later a horse belonging to Harry Mosteller, a resident of Mason, dropped dead in its harness so frightened did it become at the passing of an automobile.

October found that a valuable horse belonging to Samuel C. Kersey killed itself by jumping astride the manger, thus breaking the ribs which pierced the heart.

Warren County was graced in October with the distinguished presence of Mrs. Elizabeth Martin of Paris, Ky. She was originally Elizabeth Bird and in turn married men by the name of Martin, Crow, Robin, Buzzard and Martin again.

Toward the end of November a horse belonging to Eli Downey, frightened on Main Street and ran away striking an electric light pole and knocking out the lights in the Main Street church during the evening preaching service.

The beginning of December was like a second spring with violets blooming and buds bursting as in the spring time.

The same week found a large white eagle had been shot at Cedar Bluffs, on Caesar's Creek, by hunters from Dayton. The wing measured six feet from tip to tip.

Within the next few days, Mrs. Al Keever, living near Lebanon, while dressing a hen, found three fully developed eggs with hard shells.

A GLIMPSE AT WARREN COUNTY SCHOOL NEWS IN 1930

Inserted into **The Western Star** April 24, 1930, was news from several local schools. The writer at this time will try to bring back the happenings of yesteryear.

Ridge School

An "Easter Egg Hunt" was given on the preceding Friday afternoon which proved to be a very exciting affair. A gold and silver egg was furnished for each division by the teacher. Virgil Jackson found the gold and Louise Drake the silver in the upper section, while in the lower Berneda Morgan the gold and Donald Armour the silver. After the hunt the children were treated in the school. The first graders were given baskets filled with chicken and eggs and the upper grades chocolate bunnies.

Jimmie Cochran and Emmor Bailey, Jr., visited the school on the previous Friday, so that they might get their diphtheria test.

Miss Dorothy Corwin and her niece, Pollyana Ayers, visited the school the previous Friday.

Only one pupil failed to secure a "blue bird" seal the past week.

South Lebanon School

An honor roll list for the fifth semester was handed out which included: second grade; Elsie McIntosh, Kenneth Allen, Richard Doughman, Junior Smith, Phyllis Galbreath, Louise Hammiel. Third grade; William Collier, Willie Adams, Elsie Herald, Verna Gabbard. Fourth grade; Glen Smith. Fifth grade; Edra Rowland, Estel Allen, Albert Frye.

An orchestra was organized and played for the first time on the preceding Wednesday afternoon with Miss Helen Stevens as the director. The instruments included nine violins, three cornets, one clarinet, and piano.

Miss Delma Wells of Columbus was a visitor to room V on Monday, visiting Miss Velma Gose.

The South Lebanon grade baseball team played the Maineville team on the preceding Friday at Maineville; the latter being the victors by the score of 8 to 6.

Hart School

The "Reds" were losers to the "Blues" in the Health Contest. In consequence, the "Blues" were treated to an Easter party. Those on the Red team were: Arabella Rainey, Ruth Brown, Farrie Slusher, Ellen Miller, June Rainey, Edwin Miller, Darrell Thompson, Homer Slusher, and Lawrence Edginton. Edwin Miller was in charge of the entertainment and planned many interesting games, one in which was carrying hard boiled eggs on a tablespoon to a basket. Della Slusher was the winner.

Arabella Rainey was in charge of the eats and with help from the other girls, home made candy, sandwiches and popcorn was served. Each child was left a candy bunny by the Easter bunny.

The school board had their regular meeting at the school Friday past. New equipment was checked, which consisted of new buff adjustable blinds, as well as paper towels and holder, dictionary shelf, stereographs, reading glass, and thermometer.

Merrittstown School

Marjorie McClure went home with Miss Foster to stay all night Saturday in order to go to church at 6:30 a.m.

Eileen Earnhart burned a large blister in the palm of her right hand the previous Saturday.

The honor roll included: Eileen Surface, Mary Surface, Maurice McClure, Leslie Rothman, Billy Clark, and Opal Downing.

The previous week found all the students spending one afternoon in the woods picking flowers and playing games.

Helpers for the week were Virginia Surface and Marjorie McClure.

The preceding Friday found the students having an egg hunt in the school yard. After the hunt each student had a basket of Easter candy.

The perfect attendance roll for the two previous weeks were: Maurice McClure, Leslie Rothman, Arthur Phillips, Victor Earnhart, Robert McKeever, Leslie Earnhart, Harold Sears, Betty Clark, Eileen Earnhart, Ada Kendricks, Eileen Surface, and Marjorie McCluure.

Morrow School

The following students were on the honor roll for the fifth and sixth weeks test. They were: Alberta Parker, 85.5; Ruth Emma Stack, 97; and Romona Hizar, 96.

Winners of the third and fourth grade geography test were the third graders.

Those receiving 100 in spelling the previous week were: Miriam Achterman, Patricia Bennington, Eda Brown, Jane Easley, Ruth Hofer, Clyde Lee Conner, and Erle Miranda.

Morrow high school won their third straight baseball game by defeating Waynesville the preceding Friday by the score of 16-2. B. Thompson had a perfect batting showing and Milton Marlatt had three hits in four at bats.

Loretta Whitacre left the Bethesda Hospital the previous Saturday, and she was expected to be back in school in a few weeks.

Western Row School

Benny Downing was introduced to the students of the third grade as a new pupil, which set the enrollment for the school at 42.

Those who received 100 in spelling for the week were: Lydia Dumford, Evelyn Bates, Harry Dumford, Albert Barnes and Harold Dumford.

The county nurse made a visit to the school and found the children to be in good health.

A visit from the music teacher found all the students excelling with good grades.

Mamie Whitsel was absent from school on account of sickness.

Lick School

A visit from the County nurse found the students to be in good health.

A practice of the first graders was that when they received good grades in spelling, they wrote it in their spelling books which they have made.

Emma May Bercaw visited the school in hopes she would be a student the following year.

Some of the girls brought violets for the teacher and arranged them on her desk.

An interest in baseball has caused several automobiles to stop and watch the students play.

Foster School

Plans for the Closing Day Program were in place for May 17, at 1:30. A basket dinner was the usual feature of the forenoon.

The following list of students who had not been absent or tardy during the whole school term were: Vivian Rhodes, Mary E. Begley, Mildred Rhodes, Rema Gose, Ruth Mastio, Dortha Haney, Elmo Testerman and Eugene Maag.

The snake season was once again started. The pupils captured one the preceding Wednesday.

The honor roll for the past six weeks was: eighth grade, Rema Gose; seventh grade, Elmo

Testerman; sixth grade, Richard Juterbock; fifth grade, Mildred Rhodes and Edith Gose; fourth grade, Rachel Brenner; third grade, Adolph Leder; second grade, Walter Perry; first grade, Glen Reynolds.

The teachers desk was adorned with wild flowers which the children had brought.

HISTORIC SCHOOL BEGAN IN HARVEYSBURG

The village of Harveysburg had the first free Black School built in the Northwest Territory. It was built in 1831 by Dr. Jesse Harvey, with his wife Elizabeth Burgess Harvey as its first teacher.

A planter from Richmond County, North Carolina, Stephen Wall, sent agents north to locate an area or town in which his slaves could be educated. He was recommended to Dr. Jesse Harvey, and with the subject addressed, Dr. Harvey promised to open a Black school the following fall. Financing of the school was by the Grove Monthly Meeting of Friends, of which the Harvey's were members.

In the fall just before the opening of the school, Mr. Wall brought a number of bright young mulattos to Harveysburg. The children, numbering eight, were of three mothers and one father, their master.

Along with Mr. Wall's children were other children, numbering twenty-five, which were also to be educated in Dr. Harvey's school.

Mrs. Harvey was a housewife, and mother of three children. She taught in the Academy of Sciences for two years; Isaac Woodward taught the school until his death and again, Mrs. Harvey was the teacher.

Mr. Wall, in his last will and testament, filed in 1846, set free the following slaves; "Little John and Alfred, children of Rody, also $1000 from my estate. Also to John and Alfred all the land I now own in the State, $5000 to Dr. Harvey to be laid out in land, $200 to Moses Burgers."

Harveysburg Quakers were highly criticized for an institution comprising of an all Black school. However, opinions changed when positive sentimentality toward the oppressed people and opposition to the slave owners seemed overwhelming.

With the new trend in tact, the Harveys were highly criticized for not having integrated schools. Dr. Harvey was the first to integrate by building a seminary in 1837 which included classes for black students as well as white.

The school closed in 1845 and from it came the building for the Zion Baptist Church.

Stories of Underground Railroad tunnels in Harveysburg extending to the high banks of Caesar's Creek, have been constantly told. The one time Harvey homes and the former Masonic Hall on Maple Avenue are said to have been underground stations.

Sealed up places in the basement of the former Sabin home is on the list. The last resident in the Wales home was Dewey Simpson, who told he had found a secret entrance to an attic over the kitchen.

The Black school, customarily known as the East End School, operated from 1831 to 1906 as a one room school house, until it was merged with the other Harveysburg schools.

The Harveysburg Historical Society, which was formed in 1977, has spent considerable time and money on the restoration of the building. Lucy McCarren said Wilberforce University showed considerable interest in the building as an extension of its Black history center, but money was the deterrent.

The Historical Society members bought the building in 1977 from Daisy Nash for $10,000. The monies raised by the society through different events were to be matched by various private and public grants.

The Bullskin Trace was the main north and south thoroughfare for Indian travel. It was also one of the main tracks for the Underground Railroad. Following this trace from North Carolina to Harveysburg was perhaps the main reason that Mr. Wall contacted Mr. Harvey concerning his interest in a school.

BOXWELL LAW GAVE FARM YOUTHS CHANCE TO CONTINUE EDUCATION

With the attention the schools seem to be getting on the ninth grade proficiency tests, the writer searched through his files and found some material concerning another type of test, which in accordance should be of some interest to Warren Countians. It was a testing procedure called the "Boxwell Law."

Alexander Boxwell was born in Frederick County, Virginia, and became a resident of Ohio in 1857, settling with his parents at Springboro, Warren County.

At the age of 20 years, he entered Ohio Wesleyan and subsequently took up the teaching trade which he practiced for sixteen years. While in this endeavor he studied law and in 1881 was admitted to the Ohio Bar.

He served for a time as Justice of the Peace and later was elected to the Ohio Legislature for a period of ten years, at one time becoming Speaker of the House.

School attendance was made mandatory through a law which was incorporated in 1877. The law, being lax in enforcement, was practically forgotten.

Consequently, in 1889, a new statute was written which incorporated the use of truant officers and set age standards between the age of eight and fourteen. If the student was between the age of fourteen and sixteen, and had a job, he or she could be excused.

Being a teacher and a member of the Warren County Teachers Association, and with his influence as a Legislator, Alexander Boxwell pursued a way in which to incorporate a fair practice of allowing the country schools students to be admitted to high school without the added expenses.

A council of teachers appeared before the

Committee of Schools and presented arguments for a bill proposed by Mr. Boxwell, which in turn provided "that the boy or girl in the country schools shall have an equal opportunity with the pupils in the town or city schools."

The Boxwell Law gave an opportunity to the aspiring young adult, whose roots were on the farm and not in the city, to proceed with his or her education.

The new law, which was passed in 1892, stated in certain terms "that township boards of education are obligated to pay the successful applicants' tuition at the city school of their choice, but the students must provide for their own transportation or living accommodations."

Under the new law, an examination was given that tested the scholastic skills of the rural students. It set up a sort of qualification standard in which the student could participate through a testing procedure.

Subjects in which testing was given were: orthography (spelling and language study), reading, writing, arithmetic, English grammar and composition, United States history including civil government, and physiology.

Two examinations were to be given a year. Passage of these tests made the student eligible for admission to any high school in the County in which the pupil lives, or some neighboring County.

Successful applicants, where each student presented an oration, or read an essay, were arranged to meet at regular township commencements. The law also read that a County commencement of all graduates under this act should also be held.

The Boxwell Law had clearly done more for the country schools of Ohio than any other law passed previous.

The way of the "one room schoolhouse" was struggling in its composition of too little education and no future for advancement. The new Law was an opening for the bright young students who wished to excel and make a place in society.

In the remaining space of this article, I will

give some examples of the tests required. See how you do on them.

U.S. History.
1. Name the two oldest settlements by the English in the territory of the U.S.
2. Give the date of the beginning and close of the French and Indian War.
3. In what year was the Stamp Act passed?
4. When and where did Washington first take command of the American army?
5. When and where did the first Continental Congress convene.
6. Give the date of the assembling of the American army.
7. Name in their order the presidents of the United States.
8. Name two battles of the War of 1812.
9. What territory was gained by the Mexican War?
10. When and where did General Lee surrender the Confederate Army?

SOME OF WARREN COUNTY'S HORSE RACING LEGENDS

Sleepy Tom

A race horse by the name of "Sleepy Tom" was owned by Steve Phillips of Waynesville. He was a totally blind horse who has become a legend in Warren County.

Sleepy Tom started as a delivery horse carrier for **The Cincinnati Enquirer** between Dayton and Xenia.

Newspapers of the times were delivered from Cincinnati to Dayton by train. Horses and wagons were then engaged in transporting the papers to other towns.

Rivalry between **The Sunday Enquirer** and **The Gazette** (later **The Commercial Gazette** and then **The Commercial Tribune**) was intense.

A hefty circulation battle always broke out between the two papers, until **The Enquirer** bought the blind pacer from a Xenia livery stable.

A crowd always gathered at Beatty's Tavern in Xenia to await the arrival of Sleepy Tom. The reverence of the Sabbath was set aside as much betting was wagered.

The sanctity of the church-goer was by-passed for the mere speculation of the newspaper delivery contest. Sleepy Tom always won.

This fine racer was foaled in the Old Tavern Stables in Bellbrook, Greene County, in 1866. He came from fine stock, being sired by Tom Rolph.

Isaac Dingler, his early owner, was impressed with Sleepy Tom's abilities to race, and some training was given him, but the horse being blind put a halt to any interests in racing him.

He was repeatedly traded and with his loss of sight, he was withdrawn from his modest racing debut.

Phillips interests in the training of pacers and trotters had just begun when he bought Sleepy Tom for $40.00 and a quart of whiskey. He was then put through regular rigorous training.

He was first put to the test under Phillips in the traditional "Jimtown" (Jamestown, in Greene County) fair meet and showed promise. He won the race and proceeded to win all his races in neighboring events and fair entries.

Tom won two spectacular races at the Greene County fairgrounds and attracted the attention of Frank T. Stark, a railroad man and a race horse buff. An agreement between Stark and Phillips was struck and greater things were in store for Tom.

At Chicago, on July 24 and 25, 1879, when Tom was 13 years old, the most famous racing celebrities ever gathered watched him race.

He won the third, fourth and fifth mile heats in 2:16 1/2, 2:16 and 2:12 1/4 respectively. He defeated the world famous Mattie Hunter. He crushed the great Rowdy Boy, and handily won from Lucy.

It was said of Sleepy Tom by those who followed him, that he was the greatest and most graceful natural pacer that ever lived.

Though moody and unhappy in his stall, he was at home when strapped between sulky shafts. His longing for the sweet smell of the track in his nostrils was forever unchanging.

Phillips ultimately sold Tom for $10,000. Age increasingly began to take over and he was again sold and traded, drifting to different parts of the country. The life of a legend ended in a stable fire in a western town.

Nightingale

Another Warren County horse that made headlines was a horse named "Nightingale." She was owned mutually by stockholders and officers of the First National Bank of Franklin. She won every race in which she was entered in the years of 1892 and '93. She won more than $90,000 in her career.

When her racing schedule included the raceway at the Franklin Fairgrounds (formerly situated on the extreme west end of Franklin, in the vicinity of Hollywood), the railroad companies were compelled to run special trains to oblige her fans. Her admirers included large crowds along with a band welcoming her home.

Her housing included a barn built especially for her with lace curtains at the stable windows. Her appearance of beauty with a sleek brown coat was an attraction of great elegance.

Her driver, John Picket, took her to Lexington, Ky., in 1895, where she lost to a horse called Hamilton Nightingale.

Franklin residents, allegedly, along with Franklin Bank personnel, bet large sums of money on this race.

Coincidental or not, the bank failed at this very time, and Nightingale became known as "the horse that broke the bank." Court litigation showed that the losses were not directly related to the famous race.

In contrast, the bank examiner said that "he knew exactly why the bank closed and without further explanation Nightingale was held responsible."

Nightingale was included in attached assets

and was lost forever to her Franklin owners. Her fancy stable burned to the ground and was never rebuilt.

WARREN COUNTY LONG KNOWN FOR WONDERFUL TROTTERS

Shanghai Mary

In the early days of Red Lion there seemed to come a great deal of history concerning Warren County. One of these events concerns a great racing horse known as "Shanghai Mary."

In the early part of the nineteenth century there lived in the Red Lion area a man named Goldsmith Coffeen and his family, who had removed from the State of Vermont. He was widely known as a horse breeder and manufacturer of liniments, which he claimed were suitable for man or beast.

Coffeen and his partner, John Irons, owned a magnificent dark chestnut sorrell horse with white legs named Iron's Cadmus. He was the sire of Pocahantas who later became the ancestor of many great performers, including the Axworthy family.

Our subject, Shanghai Mary, was sired by Iron's Cadmus. She was one of the most intriguing horses among the old time affiliated brood mares.

Iron's Cadmus was trained as a pacer and an effort to make him trot jumbled the poor horse up so badly that his gait totally disappeared.

He was sired by Beach's Cadmus from a pacing mare that his breeder, Goldsmith Coffeen, had received in trade from a horse-trader.

Iron's Cadmus passed through many hands and was finally sold for $2,000 and shipped to St. Louis.

On the trip west by boat, the horse caught cold and died a few days after his arrival. He was eighteen years of age. It is estimated that 80 percent of all harness horses in the United States came from Iron's Cadmus.

Shanghai Mary made her public debut in 1869

when John H. Wallace called the attention of Charles Bachman to a doubt of Shanghai Mary's daughter, Green Mountain Maid. A slip of paper concerning the sale of the mare at a price of $450, said in certain terms that the mare was out of Shanghai Mary by the celebrated running horse, Lexington.

Bachman's secretary, Mr. Shipman, was sent to western New York and Ohio to establish the authenticity of the mare's birth. Shipman returned with a report which showed that Shanghai Mary was foaled in 1847, which made her older than Lexington.

While still searching for some history on Mary, Shipman learned that the Wilcox Brothers of Livingston Center, N.Y., while purchasing sheep from some farmers in eastern Ohio, met a young man on the road near Canton. He was riding a three year old chestnut filly with four white feet, a blaze on her face, and a stubby white tail which had been eaten off by calves.

The boy said he had ridden her about five-hundred miles and had intended to trade her for a blind mare that the Wilcox Brothers had taken in trade for some sheep. A trade was made and the boy simply rode away and disappeared.

Wilcox Brothers broke the white-faced mare to harness; she exhibited great speed and was started in a number of races in New York, none of which were ever reported as the Angelica mare.

Eventually the Angelica mare became known as Shanghai Mary. Using the latter name she was passed to Samuel Conklin of Middletown, N.Y. He bred her to Harry Clay in 1861 and got the filly afterwards known as Green Mountain Maid.

She was of a small nature, wild and was never broken to harness; even age could not tame her. (Green Mountain Maid died on June 6, 1888, having been the ancestor of many racing horse legends.)

An investigation was made by Hershel I. Fischer, former editor of **The Western Star**, into the disappearance and reappearance of Shanghai Mary. He found that a son of Goldsmith Coffeen,

Thaddeus, had become outraged at his father over wrongful conduct toward him as a jockey, and that one day in the fall of 1850 he disappeared from home.

It was common report that Thaddeus had taken the filly in exchange for his jockey services.

It was thought in the fall of 1850 that the appearance of a filly near Canton, named Shanghai Mary, and a description of Coffeen's filly named Shanghai, were the same horses. The actual testimony of Thaddeus would settle the controversy, but he was not to be found.

The fleeing of Thaddeus Coffeen across the State of Ohio with the great filly Shanghai Mary (and her soon to become famous career) to the New York traders, and his disappearance, has earmarked Warren County to become "The Mother of the Trotters."

Pocahontas

In 1844, John C. Dine purchased a bay mare who was a graceful trotter and was much more adaptable to racing than ordinary farm horses.

Knowing practically nothing about horse breeding and raising, the Dines were encouraged by the ultimate speed of the mare to visit the home of Iron's Cadmus with hopes to get a fast runner.

In the spring of 1846, Dine and his neighbor, Abe McKinney, each took their mares to the Cadmus stallion. Upon arrival both mares were in season. The stallion had already served six mares that day and a coin was tossed to see which of the two mares would be served first.

McKinney won the toss and his mare became number seven for the day. The Dine mare dropped a large, strong filly which was later to be known as Pocahontas.

With the death of John Dine in 1848, an auction was held and the two year old filly was bought by Dine's son, William, for a price of $30.

At the age of three, she was broken to ride, but her withers were so low that a device called a crupper had to be used to keep the saddle from slipping forward. Consequently, her tail stock became sore and her saddle soon became useless.

Dine worked the horse with much ease. One day she was handed over to a young lad who worked her so hard that she was badly restricted in both legs. She was presumed to be of no use to the family, so she was sold to a neighbor for $51.

The winter of 1850 found her doing common farm work. She was then traded to Abraham Pierce for another three year old.

Pocahontas afterward passed through the hands of several owners.

In 1852, Pierce bought her back for use in a four horse team for hauling logs, and the following year she was sold to William Potter for $135. She was now located a few miles from where she was foaled.

Potter noticed the unusual amount of energy the mare had and took her to the farm of L.D. Woodmansee who owned a half-mile track. Her first race paced in the saddle was 2:58. She was then sold to the owner of the track for $180.

Being shipped to Cincinnati to be raced on that track, she won her first race in a time of 2:40. It was at this race that she acquired her name "Pocahontas."

Cincinnati residents gathered to watch with great interest the race between their fast pacer Ben Higon and Pocahontas. Their conclusion was that a greenhorn from the country was easy prey for their well-known pacer. Pocahontas won in 2:34.

Dunham and Hooper bought half interest in the pacer for $1,000. The mare was then shipped to New Orleans where she won three races.

In the meantime, Pocahontas had been turned out to pasture where a young colt had got to her. Before starting in the last race, she was found to be in foal. The owners had to enlarge by six inches in width the sulky axle; she won her race in that condition.

On April 21, 1854, she foaled a colt that was later named Tom Rolf. This was but two months and nine days after she had won her last race with a time of 2:20. The colt was placed with a mare that had lost her offspring, and Pocahontas immediately went back into training.

She won many races before her end. A story goes that in her later years a boy on a runner challenged her to a race one morning at Cincinnati. The two were even at the half way point, then the mare turned on speed and left the runner behind. Her time was said to have been 2:08 1/2, running the last half in 57 1/2 seconds.

Moquette

Lebanon had another horse that held the world's record in 1896 of 2:10. His name was Moquette. Frank and Isaac Drake, who owned a livery stable where the old Goodwill store was located, was the owner. He was a horse of immense reputation with his picture and story featured in many newspapers and magazines.

(His speed was almost unapproachable with a time nearing 2:04, before being beaten at Fleetwood Park, N.Y.)

He was raced in Chicago and raised much enthusiasm with Warren Countians who had bet on a first place finish. His second place finish in the Windy City caused the Drakes to sell him.

His portrait, which hung over the door at the livery stable on Main Street, was said to have been painted by Marcus Mote, the noted Warren County painter.

WARREN COUNTY TOOK BUTLER LAND, AND GAVE BACK TO CLINTON COUNTY

Warren County was established by an act of the first General Assembly of the State of Ohio, passed March 24, 1803. Out of the large territory of Hamilton County, as it then existed, Warren, Butler and Montgomery Counties were formed by one act, and by the same act the County of Greene was formed out of Hamilton and Ross.

Warren County contains nearly exactly 400

square miles. Originally this county contained no territory west of the Great Miami.

After Clinton was formed (1810) it was found to contain less than 400 square miles (both Ohio Constitutions provided that no new county was to contain less than 400 square miles).

In 1815, the Legislature took 11 square miles, being a strip along the eastern boundary (Eaton Township), from Warren and added it to Clinton, and at the same time detached from Butler a small tract west of the Great Miami and attached it to Warren.

This gave to both Clinton and Warren the area of 400 square miles that was constitutionally called for.

Virginia, in 1784, gave up her rights of the western territory to the General Government. This opened up the lands for future purchases.

John Cleves Symmes, an ex-member of Congress and Chief Justice of the State of New Jersey, applied for purchase rights of the lands between the two Miami Rivers.

This tract originally called for a total of 2,000,000 acres, but when his contract was made to Congress this amount was reduced to 1,000,000 acres. It was then found that there were only approximately 600,000 acres from the head of the Miami Rivers to the mouth.

The monetary exchange was only for about half of that acreage, consequently Symmes received a deed for only 311,682 acres.

The northern boundary of Symmes Purchase runs along an east/west line, passing from a point on the Little Miami, a short distance from Oregonia (Freeport/Oregon), to the Great Miami River, about three miles below downtown Middletown (it closely follows Todhunter Road in Butler County).

This line parallels an east/west course aligned with Emmons Road for a short distance, and also the line follows closely the Monroe Road line in Lebanon.

Thus, the line north of this was later called Congress Lands and sold for $2.00 per acre and the line below this was bought by Symmes for 66

2/3 cents per acre. This acquisition was called the Symmes or Miami Purchase.

The price to be paid for this tract was payable in certificates of debt due from the United States.

How the price came to be fixed at 66 2/3 cents per acre is explained by the fact that the Government estimated the value of the lands at one dollar per acre, but as they were to be sold in very large tracts, one-third of the price was to be deducted for poor land and land covered by water.

The Symmes Purchase contained more good land than any other tract of the same scope in the State.

In the prospectus of the terms of the sale and settlement of his purchase, issued at Trenton N.J., November 25, 1787, Symmes announced that after May 1, 1788, the price of land would be $1.00 an acre, and, after November 1, 1788, still higher.

Symmes exceeded his patent authority by selling lands that he had no deeds to. His unauthorized sales extended past the line which was surveyed one-mile north of Lebanon. Waynesville, Franklin, Middletown and Dayton were included in this area.

The first deed for land in Warren County recorded at Cincinnati was from John Cleves Symmes to Moses Kitchel of Morris County, N.J., for an entire section (640 acres) in Deerfield Township, near Kings Mills.

It was dated April 10, 1795, and the consideration for the 640 acres was $425 "in certificates of debt due from the United States." This was exactly the price Symmes had paid the Government, two-thirds of a dollar per acre, payable in certificates of greatly depreciated value.

The first land entry recorded in the Military Lands in Warren County was an entry recorded in the name of Clement Read. Read had his choice of all the lands in the County east of the Little Miami.

This land chosen extends along the river about

a mile and a half above Corwin. In describing the land, its estimated distance below Old Chillicothe (Old Town) in Greene County is given. Also, reference is made to the road cut by General George Rogers Clark in his expedition against the Indians in 1780, and also to an old sugar camp of the Indians on the land entered.

There were 122 surveys made in Warren County, many of which were made as late as 1831 or 1832. The surveys listed in this county are as such: Nathaniel Massie, 57; Gen. Wm. Lytle, 38; James Galloway, Jr., 6; John O'Bannon, 3; Duncan McArthur, 1; and the remaining 17 were made by various surveyors at a later date.

The first permanent settlements in Warren County were made by William Beedle at Beedle's Station, five miles west of Lebanon, in September 1795, and by William Mounts at Mounts Station along the Little Miami River near Stubb's Mills Road.

Mr. Beedle did not get his deed until November 13, 1795. The money consideration is not given, but it is believed he purchased one section (640 acres) upon which he settled for $250.

Major Benjamin Stites, the founder of Columbia, now a part of Cincinnati, owned some 10,000 acres in scattered sections, chiefly in the eastern halves of Union and Turtlecreek Townships.

Samuel Manning was one of the earliest settlers on lands east of Lebanon, coming here about 1796. He purchased of Benjamin Stites the half-section (320 acres) on which is now the northeast part of Lebanon, paying $320 for the half-section, or $1.00 per acre.

Mathias Corwin, father of Governor Thomas Corwin, and John Osborn purchased the half-section east of Manning's, each paying Stites the same price. Corwin paid $100 for the northeast quarter and Osborn $100 for the southeast quarter. This was a little less than two-thirds of a dollar per acre.

A little later Captain John Tharp purchased the half-section of which is the southeast quarter of Lebanon, which includes Harmon Park and the County Home farm, paying $1,000 for the 320 acres, or a little over $3.00 per acre.

Jeremiah Morrow received deeds from Symmes at three different dates, the price advancing with the time: in 1800, for 210 acres at $1.50 per acre; in 1803, 212 acres at $3 per acre; in 1805, for 90 acres at $4 per acre.

On February 3, 1796, Samuel Heighway, Reverend John Smith and Dr. Evan Banes contracted for the purchase of 30,000 acres on the Little Miami about the site of Waynesville.

The contract was made with Judge Symmes and the purchase price was $1.25 per acre, but only one thousand dollars was to be paid in money, the remainder in certificates of indebtedness due the United States, so that the price of the whole tract the speculators expected to pay did not exceed 25 cents per acre.

Heighway and the other two purchasers were equal partners and each was to reserve for himself 3,000 acres for his own use, as Heighway agreed to advance the first 2,000 pounds of the purchase money as soon as Congress should demand the payment, he was to have the first choice in selecting his 3,000 acres.

The settlement of Waynesville did not begin until March 1797, more than a year after the contract for the purchase was signed. At this time Heighway asked $2.00 an acre for land outside the town and $6.00 for a town lot, the purchaser agreeing to build a house in a certain time.

As Judge Symmes failed to obtain from the Government a patent for the lands north of the Monroe Road line in Lebanon, as described earlier, his contract for their sale was voided.

The first owners of land about Waynesville obtained deeds not from Symmes, but from the United States Government and the price paid was probably in no case less than $2.00 per acre.

The towns of Franklin, Dayton and Waynesville were all laid out on lands which Symmes had contracted to sell but for which he was never able to give deeds.

Heighway and his associates were involved in

law suits concerning their lands which continued for several years and their speculation it seems was not a profitable one.

Some later Wayne Township land prices were: In 1803, Nathaniel Massie deeded to Ezekiel Cleaver 135 acres for $404.75; John Overton to Abijah O'Neall, 621 acres in Griffin's survey for $1,255; in 1805.

Benjamin Anderson to Abijah O'Neall, 1,000 acres on Caesar's Creek, for $2,000; in 1807, Thomas Posey to Jonathon Wright, 298 1/2 acres in Survey 1056, for $297; in 1807, Abijah O'Neall to Robert Millhouse, 210 acres on Caesar's Creek, for $72.10.

The first settlement on Todd's Fork above its mouth was made by William Smalley in 1797. He had been a hunter and guide for surveying parties and had traversed the whole region. He selected for himself a fine tract in Warren County near the Clinton County line.

In 1801, he received a deed from General Lytle for 600 acres of excellent land, the purchase price being only $200. In 1806, he sold to his brother, Benjamin, 100 acres of this tract for $300.

Ten years later after the organization of the County, or about 1813, several hundred acres of good land in the neighborhood of Hopkinsville, and not far from the state road, were purchased at $1 per acre, while land of the same quality on the same road, west of the river, would bring six dollars an acre.

As was stated earlier, all the lands west of the Little Miami and north of Symmes Purchase were called Congress Lands and were sold to purchasers at public land offices. The uniform price fixed by Congress for all public lands, without regard to quality, was $2 per acre. Not until 1821 was the price of Government lands lowered to $1.25 per acre.

SETTLERS COULDN'T HAVE "SETTLED IN" WITHOUT LOCAL INNS

The early inns, or taverns, were the first big businesses in Warren County. Without these occasional stops for rest and relaxation, not only for the passengers, but for the horses, the early stagecoaches could not have survived.

Bartering was a way of life for the early settlers. The inn was frequently a bartering center. The first migrants in the new territory used beads, tobacco, codfish, ginseng, bone, blankets, peltry, and numerous other articles, including knives and gunpowder, for trading purposes.

The early inns knew the statesman, scholars, doctors and lawyers, outlaws, evangelists; circuit-riders, priests, salesmen, tourists and the curious travelers.

The requirements for obtaining a tavern license in Ohio were, "the applicant must be of good moral character; the tavern must be necessary at the place designated; the applicant must furnish suitable accommodations; and the applicant must be a suitable person to keep tavern."

The cost of a tavern license for one year ranged from three dollars to ten dollars depending upon the situation, size and local conditions.

A worthy woman could, in Ohio, obtain a license to run an inn, but in New England the law required that should an inn-keeper die, his widow must provide a fit man that is Godly to manage the business.

The early inns provided temporary housing which included a bed, a meal and provisions for his horse.

In 1798, before the actual clearing had been made for the roads, the tavern-keeper paid $1.00 per bushel for corn; $1.50 per bushel for wheat; $4.00 per 100 pounds of flour; 65 cents per bushel for potatoes; and 75 cents per bushel for oats.

From 1800 to 1810, unrefined sugar cost 35 cents per pound; chocolate, 3 shillings 6 pence per pound; tobacco 4 cents per yard.

In 1801, board in a backwoods tavern was $1.00 per week, and a fraction of a week at the rate of $1.50.

Indian corn, turnips, pumpkins, cranberries, wild game, domestic fowl, and copper distilled whiskey cost next to nothing. Apples cost $3.00 per bushel - but the keeper got along without them.

Two quarters of venison sold for 25 cents, butter 10 cents or less per pound. Fish was found in abundance in the streams, but the Indians were the only ones to feast on this delicacy. Few pioneers enjoyed this luxury of the water.

Advertising signs of the early inns were identified with pictures since many early settlers could not read. Some of the inns were also the first post offices in the County.

Franklin's Charles Lang kept a tavern on the corner of Center (Main) and Fifth Streets. Nathaniel Coleman kept the Mansion House in 1837. Washington Coleman opened a hotel in his three story residence on Center Street between Fourth and Fifth Street.

Aaron Reeder opened the first hostelry in Franklin prior to 1814.

The Bull's Head Tavern in Franklin was operated by Joseph Hurst, later, after his death, managed by his wife.

A hotel was later operated by Mrs. Hurst, William Harrison, and Samuel Ross on the corner of Fifth and Front Streets.

The Exchange Hotel was founded by Francis McGalliard in 1836 on the corner of Sixth and Canal Streets. He was also the owner of a hotel on the corner of Sixth and Center Streets.

In Springboro, Jeremiah Stansel operated a hostelry under the name of Washington Hall. The building built prior to 1837 is located at 40 South Main Street. It was renamed the Morton House in 1852 after it was purchased by Joseph and Rhoda Morton.

Featured in the hotel was a second story ballroom which was used for social events.

In later years it was purchased by Mr. and Mrs. Samuel Masters and became known as the Masters Hotel.

Another location in Springboro was on the corner of Franklin and Main Street. This large brick residence was used as a stagecoach stop.

The Mason Hotel was the main stop at Mason. An advertisement in **The Western Star**, dated Feb. 4, 1842, states:

"The undersigned offers for sale, for cash or in exchange for land, or property in Lebanon, the tavern stand in Mason known as the 'Mason Hotel.'

"It is a spacious building conveniently situated and well calculated for a public house. The stables and out-houses are convenient and substantial. Attached to the premises is a lot on one acre of ground. The payments will be made easy."

Peter W. Wikoff operated a hotel in Mason. Some believe that he operated his hotel in his home. This residence was located at 318 Reading Road. It has been told that it was used as an exchange for horsemen.

After changing horses at this location, the farmers would proceed on to Cincinnati. This was also a stop for the mail riders and stagecoaches. The hotel had an attic room which housed the Negro workers.

Morrow's old Charles Hotel (built prior to 1859) was located directly across the street from the Pennsylvania Railroad station (formerly Little Miami Railroad) on Main Street. This was a main passenger stop for the railroad.

The building at 130 Main Street was once the Sawyer House. The 20 room hotel is now an apartment house. It was the former residence of John Scheurer, a German shoemaker. Scheurer operated a shoe shop at the residence; the shoes were made in the upstairs area.

The Morrow House had the distinction of being the second house built in Morrow, it being constructed in 1844.

The Miami House was erected one-half block east of the railroad depot; the Imperial House was located on the present site of the Morrow Lumber Company.

Roachester had the "Sign of the Lion and

Eagle" hotel. It was operated in 1826 by Elijah Thomas.

Rossburg had a tavern and store about 1824 operated by Lewis Sever.

Ralph Markham purchased from William Crosson a lot in which Markham built a two-story brick hotel, which later became known as the Pleasant Plain Hotel.

Pleasant Plain (formerly New Columbia) was on the Cincinnati and Marietta Railroad and was a station stop. There was reported to have been five taverns or inns in this village at one time.

Butlerville once had a tavern. The Butlerville Hotel is located on what was a busy stagecoach route. The building is still in existence, but is slowly giving away to time.

Dennis Dalton says the bricks were fired at the community's old brickyard. He also says cattle drivers driving their large herds east along Sugar Run Creek were frequent guests at the old hostelry in addition to stagecoach travelers.

James Corey is possibly the first to build an inn in Wayne Township. This log tavern was built in Waynesville on Wabash Square in 1800. The Hammell House Stand was the name remembered by the many area travelers.

The inn was purchased by James Jennings prior to 1806. He later built a frame building.

John Worrell acquired the tavern in 1817, which included several lots, for $600.

Other known owners were; Samuel Beck, Robert Way, Richard Cunningham; Keene, Barnhart and Durand; N. McLean, Enoch Hammel, and W.O. Gustin.

Gustin remodeled the inn in which he added electric along with hot and cold running water.

An inn was kept by David Holloway on Third Street in Waynesville in 1805.

Samuel Martin operated a large two-story tavern on the northern edge of Main Street in 1808.

The Halfway House was built in 1812 by John Satterthwaite. It was the stage stop for the

Opposition Stage Line. It is located on the corner of Third and Franklin Streets in Waynesville.

The Miami House was built in 1826 by Joshua Ward. It was located on the northeast corner of Main and North Streets. Some of the proprietors were; Israel Woodruff, Joshua Ward, 1828; Brice Durran, 1830; and S.M. Linton.

The Panhandle Hotel at Corwin consisted of a saloon and a grocery store. The hotel later became the Arnold Hotel. This hotel was destroyed by fire after a chicken brooder attached to the back of the building caught fire.

Harveysburg's hotel was named the Central Hotel. It was used by the many businessmen and travelers of the time.

It was purchased by Mr. and Mrs. Frank Wilson in 1894. Under their guidance it became one of the premier hotels in this part of the State.

The Black Horse Inn at Mount Holly was located near present U.S. 42 on Main Street. This small town was on the main stagecoach route between Cincinnati and places beyond. The inn was a four room two story brick structure. Another name for the inn was the Black Bear Inn.

Another stagecoach stop in the Mount Holly area is the location of the Smith family home situated on the corner of Mount Holly Road and the Old Stage Road.

Ichabod Corwin established the first tavern in Lebanon. This business was built in 1796 on the east side of Broadway between Mulberry and Silver Street.

The house was purchased in 1800 by Ephriam Hathaway. It then became known as "The House of Ephriam Hathaway." It was named, in 1803, "The Tavern of the Black Horse." It served as the first courthouse in present Warren County.

Jonas Seaman applied for and received a license "to keep a house of Public Entertainment." This site was later to become the location of the Golden Lamb, Ohio's oldest hotel.

Ichabod Corwin also built a two story brick inn known as The Green Tree, located on the corner of Rt. 741 and Greentree Road. This establishment was operated in 1818 by Samuel Baird; later by John Baird.

William Ferguson established the Indian Chief Hotel in Lebanon in 1805. The inn was located near the present site of the Lebanon fire department.

The Indian Queen Hotel is located on U.S. 42 north of Lebanon.

The Henry Clay House was on the site of the present Public Library.

The Warren Hotel was located on the corner of Warren and High Streets. It was operated by S. Calvin.

The Mansion House was located on Main Street two doors east of the Indian Chief. It was operated by John Worrell in 1852.

The Exchange Hotel was operated by David Egbert in 1843. It was located on the corner of Mulberry and Mechanic.

The Bull's Head Inn was located on the northeast corner of Mulberry and Mechanic.

The Crossed Keys Tavern, located in Washington Township, was built by Benjamin Rue in 1802. It has the distinction of being the oldest rock structure in Warren County. Rue later became manager of the Golden Lamb.

The Fort Ancient Hotel was located at the railroad crossing at Ft. Ancient State Park. Its history is practically unknown.

Daniel Foster founded an inn at Foster's Crossing as early as 1809.

The Liberty House at Foster's Crossing was operated by M. Obergefel.

Ridgeville also had a tavern as early as 1825, which was operated by William Patton.

David Sutton operated a tavern in South Lebanon which was the seat for local government.

Chapter II

TOWNS AND VILLAGES

WARREN COUNTY TOWNS AND THEIR NAME CHANGES

Warren County, I'm sure like many other counties in Ohio, had an array of name changes in the numerous communities, some being nicknames and others being official changes.

Reasoning for this variation is quite possibly due to the post office name changes. Since the post offices were official government offices, there was no possible way to delay a change if the higher-ups requested it.

Early railroads had quite a bit to do with the naming or changing the name of an already established settlement. One such example was Carlisle.

Some towns had a spelling change. For instance, Harveysburg was originally spelled Harveysburgh; Springboro was spelled Springborough; and Dallasburg was spelled Dallasburgh.

The original post office at South Lebanon (established in 1828) was named Deerfieldville, with the name change to South Lebanon coming in July 1871.

The post office at Dodds was created as Dunlevy.

The earliest post office at Mason/Palmyra was named Kirkwood. The initial name for the post office at Maineville was spelled Mainville, without the "e."

South Lebanon, in Union Township, was first named Deerfield. It was established in 1795 by John S. Gano, Benjamin Stites, Sr., and Benjamin Stites, Jr. The town was laid out into 144 lots,

29 of them were given to the first settlers for building houses or cabins. This was the first authorized town in Warren County.

Dodds, which is situated in Clear Creek Township, was changed from Utica when a post office was established in 1881. It was a station on the Dayton, Lebanon & Cincinnati Railroad (DL&C). It also had a canning factory, school and church.

Fort Ancient Heights was the former name of Fort Ancient, it being located in Washington Township. The founding proprietor was W. H. Carney. A post office was established on the Little Miami Railroad May 28, 1846, with Thomas C. Nelson as the first postmaster.

Carlisle is located in Franklin Township. Its original name was the "Jersey Settlement." In 1852, when the Cincinnati, Hamilton and Dayton Railroad made its entrance, the name was changed to Carlisle Station. On November 29, 1882, the name was permanently converted to Carlisle.

Foster is located in Deerfield Township. This was a station on the Little Miami Railroad and the Montgomery Pike, which is also the crossing of the Little Miami River by the pike.

It was named after the Foster family. Henry Foster built a mill and a hotel on the east side of the river, and his son James H. Foster was the leading merchant of the town. The name of the post office was changed three times, first Foster's Crossings, next Fosters, and lastly, Foster.

Franklin is one of the oldest communities in the County. It was established in 1796 by William C. Schenck and Daniel C. Cooper. In 1800, William C. Schenck bought out Cooper's interest and became sole proprietor. Franklin, in the early days of its existence, had a nickname of "Schencktown."

Fredericksburg is situated in Salem Township. It lies on the north bank of the Little Miami River opposite the mouth of Todd's Fork. It was settled in 1818 by Nathaniel Harrell (it is now a part of Morrow). A later name was Bridgeport.

Oregonia is located in Washington Township along the Little Miami River. It first took the name Freeport in 1820, but when it was found that a town of the same name existed in Ohio, the name was changed, in 1845, to Oregon, thus becoming the name of the post office.

However, refusing a name change, the railroad company used the name Freeport and the post office used the name Oregon. A compromise was made in the fall of 1882 through the efforts of Frank Sherwood and Dr. George W. Henderson, and the name Oregonia was adopted by both parties.

The site of Kings Mills was originally called Gainsborough. It was established in 1815 by Ralph W. Hunt who laid out 140 lots. The pioneer town was probably named after Gen. Edmund P. Gaines, who had distinguished himself in the defense of Fort Erie. It is located in Deerfield Township.

Genntown is located in Turtle Creek Township. It was named for Colonel Jethro Genn, who located a short distance northeast of Lebanon. It was originally called Leelan with a post office being established January 28, 1888.

Hageman, a station on the old Cincinnati, Lebanon & Northern Railroad (C.L.& N.), is situated in Union Township. A post office called Camp Hageman was established in 1879, named after Henry Hageman, father of Rev. R.S. Hageman. It was also called Hageman Station.

Wellman, located just south of Harveysburg on Oregonia Road, is a part of Massie Township. Its original name was Henpeck. A post office of this name was established on May 28, 1890, with the name of Wellman being established May 17, 1894. It was a settlement of a dozen lots.

The first settlement on which the city of Lebanon sits was originally called Turtle Creek. It was founded in September 1802, by Ichabod Corwin, Silas Hurin, Ephriam Hathaway and Samuel Manning. It was divided into 100 lots. A nickname for the city is the City of Cedars.

Level was a railroad station and post office located in Harlan Township. It was appropriately named from the topography of the region. It was first called Windsor. The location is about three miles east of Butlerville on the M. & C.

R. R.

Lytle was originally named Raysville. It also had a nickname of Minktown. It was platted in 1856, the location being in Wayne Township. It was laid out by M. Mills and other proprietors.

Lytle was a station on the Dayton, Lebanon, & Cincinnati Railroad (D.L.& C.). Tradition has it when the post office was established, a number of names were submitted to the Postal Department at Washington and all were rejected. The name Lytle, caught by a glance on the label of a shoe box, was then submitted and accepted.

Maineville was established about 1815. Its property is in Hamilton Township. Silas Dudley and Seth G. Tufts laid out the town into 69 lots. It was named long before it was platted. It was named after the State from which many of the early residents had emigrated. It was originally called Yankeetown.

Millsborough, located in Salem township, was founded in 1804. It was located on the Little Miami River near the intersection of Stubbs Mills and Mason-Morrow Roads. It was later called Stubbstown from the Stubbs Mills located there.

Morristown was founded in 1816, it being a part of Turtlecreek Township. It was later called Green Tree from a tavern of that name; its location was north of Union Village. Joseph Kenan and John Wickersham were the original proprietors laying out 32 lots, it being vacated in 1853.

Mount Holly's original name was Shattersburg. This name was used prior to 1819. There is no information as to why this name was used. An official settlement was made in 1833 in Wayne Township. Jacob Pearson was the original proprietor laying out 25 lots. It was named for Mount Holly, New Jersey.

Pleasant Plain's initial name was New Columbia, known later by some as Plumsock. It was founded in Harlan Township in 1852. Samuel Craig was the original proprietor with an establishment of 32 lots.

Mason's pioneering name was Palmyra, being

authorized in 1815. Major William Mason was the proprietor with an assemblage of 16 lots. The name was changed from Palmyra to Mason by the Legislature in 1835.

Roachester's first name was Salem with the first settlement being made in 1816. Mahlon Roach and James Roach were the first proprietors with an establishment of 40 lots.

The Senior Powder Mills were located in Washington Township in the Mill Grove/Hammell vicinity. The mills made gunpowder during the First World War. This area was called Blue Shinn.

Socialville, in Deerfield Township, was made a post office in 1878. The place, for a time, had been called Mormontown from the conversion of some of its residents to the faith of the Latter Day Saints.

Shakertown was settled in 1805 in Turtlecreek Township, it being so named because of the Shaker settlement. The name was later changed to Union Village in 1810. It is now known as Otterbein Village.

Red Lion's original name was Westfield. Absalom Crane, in 1817, was the founding proprietor with an outlay of 36 lots. This village was named from the sign on an early log cabin with a red lion standing on his hind legs and his fore paws elevated. The first post office was established in 1834 and was named Red Lion.

Some of the names mentioned in this article, along with others, are now ghost towns, towns with no existing identity. A mention of a few of these are: Black Hawk, Edwardsville, Osceola, and West Woodville, Harlan Twp.; Comargo and Dallasburg, Hamilton Twp.; Fort Ancient and Hammel, Washington Twp; Morristown, Turtlecreek Twp.; Henpeck and Hickoryville, Massie Twp.

The early atlases of Warren County show the precise locations of the preceding towns. The atlases are available at the public libraries, societies, etc...with the dates of the early maps being 1856...1875...1891...and 1903. These maps not only show the towns, but the nearest land owners and the acreage owned.

REMEMBERING THE 'FORGOTTEN' LOCAL TOWN OF COZADDALE

Cozaddale is a forgotten little town located in the extreme southeastern portion of Hamilton Township. It is intersected by the Cozaddale-Murdock and the Roachester-Cozaddale Roads.

This little farm town was founded in 1871 by John Jackson Cozad. Perhaps the evolution of the Cincinnati and Marietta Railroad (formerly the Hillsborough and Cincinnati line, now the Baltimore and Ohio Railroad) played a large part in the founding of the town.

The area of Cozaddale was originally named Spence's Station. The 1903 Atlas says that the acquisition of this name originated with John W. Spence, who for many years after the completion of the railroad, was assigned the duty of general storekeeper, postmaster, and railroad agent and held these positions for at least thirty years.

It is with doubt that Spence's Station had a post office. This writer has a complete collection of all the names and dates of all the early post offices and postmasters in the County and I cannot find any reference to Spence's Station.

Cozad owned 323 acres to the North and West above his village. He purchased the land, from which his town developed, from Daniel Snell. He had nearly 200 lots in his plat, with a division of eight streets.

John Cozad formed a building association which had general backing from the people. However, opposition was met with his project, but, after two years it appeared that Cozad would win out.

After several cottages and one large three-story building had been erected, trouble began and the association folded, which practically ended the progress of the small town of Cozaddale. Cozad apparently left the area sometime in 1873.

The French Brothers Creamery was established in 1890 at great expense. The creamery was equipped with a machine for manufacturing ice. The daily capacity of this mechanism was four tons.

The Odd Fellows lodge was organized in Cozaddale September 2, 1873. The identification of the lodge was Cozaddale Lodge No. 557, I.O.O.F.

Cozaddale's post office was originally located in Dallasburgh. On June 2, 1871, John J. Cozad was named the first postmaster of Cozaddale.

Other postmasters were: William Renshaw, 23 June 1874; Austin P. Simonton, 15 Dec 1885; Charles N. Tigar, 6 Aug 1887; William Renshaw, 18 June 1889; Nicholas Sanning, 12 Aug 1892; Charles N Tigar, 6 Dec 1893; William Masters, 17 Nov 1897; Edson C. Gaskill, 13 Dec 1902; Frank C. Fryburger, 21 Aug 1913; and Theodore A. Tigar, 13 June 1917.

John Jackson Cozad was born on his father's farm near Allensville, Ohio, in 1830. Apparently dissatisfied with his home life, Cozad ran away at the age of 12. His next home was on the riverboats running up and down the Ohio and Mississippi. His occupation was dealing faro, a card game.

He later turned up in South America, and still later in the California gold fields.

He married Theresa Gatewood of Malden, Virginia, in 1858. Two sons were born to this union, namely, John A. and Robert Henry Cozad. At about this time he was engaged in promoting business in his home State which eventually led to the founding of Cozaddale, Ohio.

Cozad, in his early 40's and still on the lookout for "better things," ventured to the new State of Nebraska. Looking for a new town-site led him to the north bank of the Platte River, which was bisected by the Union Pacific Railroad.

He bought 40,000 acres of prairie from the railroad and then ventured to round up settlers. In 1873, some 30 settlers arrived, mostly from Ohio, and the town of Cozad, Nebraska, was born.

John J. Cozad became a hay tycoon in his new State. In due time, Cozad, as a farmer, had constant quarrels with the cattlemen. These frequent encounters forced him into exile.

Cozad, feeling despondent over his farmer

status, had an argument with a man named Pearson. Pearson pulled a knife and Cozad consequently pulled a gun and killed Pearson.

The fugitive, Cozad, immediately got out of town. His wife sold all his holdings, and with her two sons, she discreetly slipped away.

John Jackson Cozad and his family completely disappeared. For about 75 years nothing was heard of the Cozad family.

Two years after the incident at Cozad a gentleman by the name of Richard Henry Lee appeared as a property owner on the boardwalk at Atlantic City, N.J. Lee was a very tight-lipped man, as were his companions and sometimes business associates.

His constituents included a struggling young artist by the name of Robert Henri, identified as a nephew, and Frank Southern, who was identified as a brother-in-law.

John Jackson Cozad and his two sons, Robert Henry and John A. had been located.

Lee/Cozad lived a quiet life among the residents of Atlantic City. With his two sons he ran Lee's Pier, which encompassed an amusement center of gambling, drinking and exhibits, including a bicycle railway out into the ocean.

The city fathers of Atlantic City decided to widen the boardwalk. A right-of-way was sought across Lee's property and he refused, and consequently constructed a barrier across his section of the walk.

The city still tried to cross his property. Lee apparently drew some of the Cozad fire from within and began to tote a pair of six-shooters.

Council members apparently saw the happenings that were almost evident and decided to widen the boardwalk around "Lee's Fort." Lee quickly started buying all the surrounding property.

The case was taken to the New Jersey Legislature and a bill constituting a beach front park took almost four years to pass, which gave them power to condemn property.

Lee had lost. By 1900 he had disappeared. The boardwalk can well remember "Lee's Fort."

Lee/Cozad died in New York City in 1906 of

pneumonia. He was buried in Pleasantville, N.J. His remains were later removed and interred in Providence, R.I.

John A. Cozad, alias Dr. Frank Southern, became a distinguished Philadelphia physician. He served as a member of the City Council of Atlantic City for three years.

Robert Henry Cozad, alias Robert Henri, went on to become one of America's best known artist. His finest canvas was one in which he painted his father's portrait.

Robert Henri was born in Cincinnati on June 25, 1865. He was educated in Cincinnati at Chickering Institute, it being one of the largest private schools in the country.

His first aspiration was to be a writer. However, his creative talent as a boy showed a great deal of artistic quality, an art career being his final decision.

In 1886, he entered the Pennsylvania Academy of the Fine Arts in Philadelphia.

Henri abandoned Philadelphia in 1888 and traveled to Paris hoping to find a niche. After two years, finding himself dissatisfied with the quality of teaching and his own individual progress, he decided to return to the United States.

In his youth the master occupied himself with painting landscapes, waterfronts, city streets and industrial subjects. Later his projects turned to portraits.

He involved himself in painting common people such as Negro and Dutch children, Spanish gypsies, Irish peasants, and the brightly clad American Indians and Mexicans.

He always emphasized that "the beauty of a work of art lay in its execution rather than in the subject." He also contended that "a picture of a tramp painted in a vigorous and original style was more beautiful than a hackneyed portrait of a society belle."

Although he won many medals and prizes for his work, he emphasized that prizes were generally awarded to the wrong artists, and that competition amongst artist was ridiculous.

Robert Henri began teaching in Philadelphia in 1891, traveled to Paris and taught in the late nineties, and for about three decades taught at art schools in New York. He taught and inspired many of the great artists in America.

Henri was the author of "The Art Spirit," a book that encouraged his generation and continues to be used by aspiring young artists. His influence among the youth tended to teach independence, originality and individuality in each specific circumstance.

Robert Henry Cozad, alias Robert Henri, died in New York City on July 12, 1929. Shortly before his death, a canvass of his constituents, artists, dealers, collectors and museum officials, named Henri as one of the three most important living artists in the United States.

When researching this family the writer was fascinated with the whole aspect of the adventures which surrounded such a prestigious relationship. This is just another positive notch in the relationship of Warren County and its people.

RECALLING THE HISTORY OF THE LITTLE VILLAGE OF OREGONIA

As we tour this beautiful county of ours, we should not forget to visit the quaint little town of Oregonia. As one drives to the little village from any direction, a more picturesque view cannot be found.

The town is bounded on the west by the Little Miami River and a row of steep hills, and on the east by a sheer cliff-like bluff.

To this writer, the total scene would seem to be an artist's paradise.

Oregonia was settled by Nebo Gaunt in the year 1802 or 1803. According to Beer's History, he built a mill in 1802 that passed to the ownership of Judge Ignatius Brown and David Brown, and was known as Gaunt's and Brown's Mill til probably about 1820.

In connection with this mill David Brown built

a paint mill for the manufacture of Spanish brown and its compatible shades, the materials being obtained from a point above the mill.

Samuel Harris wrote in his history of Washington Township, that Gaunt was "an ingenious man, and could work as a millwright, carpenter, wagonmaker, blacksmith, etc.

He afterward built a two-story frame house and made nearly all the nails in its construction. It also seems that Gaunt set up the first blacksmith shop in the township.

According to information the writer has found in the Warren County Museum, the Gaunt family was among the Quaker families migrating from Wateree and Bush River, South Carolina. The names of Nebo, Zebulin and Zimri Gaunt are mentioned, and they could have been sons of Samuel Gaunt.

A copy of a document dated October 23, 1776, was witnessed by a "Nebo and Zimri Gaunt." It was a description of a Quaker meeting that said: "In this vintage might be seen the person of Samuel Gaunt, dressed with all the precision of a Quaker, but neat as a pin."

Oregonia first took the name Freeport in 1820, but when it was found that a town of the same name existed in Ohio, the name was changed, in 1845, to Oregon, thus becoming the name of the post office.

However, refusing a name change, the railroad company used the name Freeport and the post office used the name Oregon.

A compromise was made in the fall of 1882 through the efforts of Frank Sherwood and Dr. George W. Henderson, and the name Oregonia was adopted by both parties.

The first post office in Oregonia was established February 5, 1846, with William H. Hamilton as its first postmaster. Other postmasters up to December 8, 1882, when the name was officially changed to Oregonia were: Jonathan Sherwood, Daniel Robertson, John M. Dougal, Martin T. Ely and Francis Sherwood.

Oregonia seems to be a sleepy little community now, but at one time it was an enterprising little village. Beers History of 1882 states that "there are at present in the village one flouring mill, one saw-mill, two general stores [Sherwood's and Mason's], two blacksmith shops, a wagonmaking shop, express and post offices, United Brethren Church [now the United Methodist Church, sometimes called the Unity Chapel] and a public school; Thomas C. Kersey and George W. Henderson, physicians, and twenty families."

Harris writes that: "David Kinsey built a carding mill in 1816, and about the same time a cotton factory was built by a company, the latter being burned in 1818. How long the carding mill was operated after the burning of the cotton mill is not known.

"James Van Horn had a blacksmith and auger factory and Elijah or Elisha Vance had a pottery business about 1820.

"Mark Armitage, a farmer, had an auger factory near by. A large frame was erected in 1844 for Charles Nixon to be used as a paper mill, but not being used for that purpose, the machinery was operated from some time for a barrel factory."

The settlement at Mather's Mill on the Little Miami, below Oregonia, was situated near the present Lebanon & Wilmington/Corwin Road. The date of this settlement was earlier than 1807, David Van Schoyck and Lewis Rees being there at that time.

Rees built the mill in 1807; it was later sold to Richard Mather, who settled there the same year.

George Zentmire settled at this time some distance below the mill and built the dam for Mather. He was a Virginian of German descent, spoke the German language fluently and was a Revolutionary War soldier. His cabin was by a spring below the mill.

In addition to the mill, Richard Mather set up a store and smith shop. He brought with him Jacob and Richard Ashmead as millers. Others coming the same season were: Jacob Horn, blacksmith; Jacob Longstreth, storekeeper; Samuel Couden; Irishman John Frazee and others.

John Bradbury, a native of England, came to Oregonia in 1873 and established a blacksmith and wagon shop which he operated for 15 years. On January 1, 1888, he sold half interest to Thomas R. Spencer, and at that time the firm name was changed to Bradbury and Spencer. It was this year that the first bridge was sold.

Steam power along with iron working machinery was later incorporated into the firm. Charles A. Spencer was taken into the company in 1895, and on May 28, 1896, the name was changed to the Oregonia Bridge Company.

Capital stock for the newly formed corporation was set at $50,000 and the firm incorporated with John Bradbury as president; Charles A. Spencer, vice-president; and Thomas R. Spencer, treasurer and general manager.

Because of the growth and expansion of the firm, it was moved to Lebanon in 1903.

Hazel Spencer Phillips wrote a short history on Oregonia. In it was enclosed a personal segment associated with her experiences in the little town. She writes:

"My father [Charles A. Spencer] worked hard every night to build the cupboards in the house, the out-house and the wood shed, and to saw out the pickets for the fence across the front to keep us in the yard. While thus engaged, a big iron crane swung around while unloading iron from a railroad car and the hood cut his lip badly. Auntie Fan came through the gate from her house every single day to dress the cut.

"I remember Uncle John Bradbury, and Auntie, who made lovely laces on a pillow, and Uncle John piling all of the Spencers into a hammock in the front yard at Uncle Tom's and swinging and singing until dark, all his English songs and an American favorite, 'While We Were Marching Through Georgia' - a good swinging song.

"At regular intervals the steam boiler at the shop had to be scraped and cleaned. My little Dad was elected to do this. As soon as the boiler was cool enough, we would all troop across the tracks and stand by with lighted lanterns until he emerged safely again.

"The first telephone was installed in the shop and we all listened and talked over the miracle.

"Then each noon and night, when the steam whistle blew, all the little Spencers trooped up the path to the steps of Sherwood's store, never beyond the steps, to wait for our fathers.

"Sherwoods will forever be associated in my mind, not for the mail from the post office or the sweets from their store, but for the long beans and the heavily scented blooms of the catalpa trees which we gathered while we waited there.

"I remember a fish so big they could hardly squeeze it into a big washtub. I remember a large white crane, spread out on Mother's black silk petticoat for a picture made by Mabel Sherwood.

"I remember the wonderful music by the Oregonia band, wafted over the evening air as they practiced somewhere nearby.

"I remember the echoes from a cannon made by my Dad, fired from the hill back of town in a salute to a black-draped funeral train, probably McKinley's.

"I remember Dr. Kersey, calling us to the fence, with hands filled with tiny, tiny bottles for our dolls; Uncle Tom's milk cow on the hill; the old concord coach, minus the running gears; in the barn yard where we played traveling; the peddlers with packs on their backs; tramps begging food at our doors; and always in the silence of a small rural village, the sound of the horses's hoofs on the wooden floor of the bridge."

FIRE TOOK ONE OF COUNTY'S LANDMARKS IN 1909

One of Warren County's landmarks was erased by fire the night of December 23, 1909. The old Oregonia Merchant Mill had long been the pride of the community.

On a cold, dark, sleepy Thursday night in December, the little village of Oregonia was awakened by the sounds of roaring flames. Cries of "the old mill's on fire" were shouted by nearly all the residents.

Flames were already leaping at the darkness of the skies when a rescue by the citizens was attempted. Smoke completely covered the valley and eventually filtered away into the night.

There was no organized fire department in the small village and a bucket brigade was formed. Efforts were made to extinguish the flames, but to no avail.

Seeing clearly that the mill could not be saved, and fear of the fire spreading, screaming women and weeping children ran from their homes in a desperate panic taking all the possessions they could carry.

Men were sprinting here and there, shouting orders and readying their efforts to deter the flames from their homes.

For miles around, the fire could be seen. The eerie red smoke filled scene saturated the skies of the extremely cold night with a cast of spooky fright. One by one the walls fell, a puff of smoke and cloud as their witness.

The heat from the fire was so intense that it was deemed necessary to throw water upon the clothing of the men fighting the fire to keep them from burning to death.

The nearest building was 75 feet away and it received a good scorching, as did Cody's store and other houses.

As dawn filtered through, a mere skeleton of a once thriving business, a landmark, was evidenced. Fire and its disastrous efforts once again triumphed.

The cause of the fire remains to this day unexplained. The flames were first seen in the southeast corner of the third floor. The main chimney was located at the northeast corner, the belief that possibly an overheated flue was the culprit.

Another theory was that perhaps it was started by the sparks from a passing train, or by internal combustion. One source says it was started by a firecracker.

The mill was named Spencer & Monroe and was owned by John K. Spencer and Charles Monroe. It had just been recently sold to W.E. Schwartz of Clarksville, Texas.

The new landlord was to have taken over on New Year's Day. With the transfer of the property, the insurance ran out and had not been renewed.

An estimate of the loss to the property and the contents was placed at $12,000. The value of the building was fixed at $7,000. The contents were still owned by Spencer and Monroe which were partially covered by insurance. The estimated loss was $4300 with $2000 insurance coverage.

A couple of names mentioned as joining the ranks of the brave were Will Craddock and Bert Hollingsworth. The housewives made a grand effort by supplying coffee and the essentials to the firefighters.

The Morrow fire department was called upon for assistance. The men were loaded on a Pennsylvania special ready for departure when a call came that nothing could be done.

Spencer spoke to **The Western Star** about the tragedy. He said:

"The old mill was the pride of my life, as it was to almost every resident of Oregonia. We were cleaning up our business and the afternoon before the fire I took a walk through the entire mill to see if there was anything yet to be done before we turned it over to the new management.

"I was happy when I saw how our foreman John Myers had left things in as neat condition as it was possible. But there were pangs of regret that I was about to turn my back upon the old mill probably forever. Little did I think that in a few hours it would be a mass of charred ruins.

"When first told of the fire I hurried to the mill and opening the doors, dashed for the third floor to turn on the pumps that would start our own fire fighting apparatus. I saw at once that it was impossible to do this and no sooner had I run out of the door than the floors fell in and I saw the building was doomed."

The first mill on this site was built in 1802 by Nebo Gaunt. On Christmas night, 1852, fire totally consumed Gaunt's Mill. Two years later, Isaac Stubbs and Jonathan Sherwood brought the machinery of the famous Whitehill Mill (located below Lebanon on the Warren County Canal) to Oregonia and set up a top quality flouring mill.

In 1885, Albert Stubbs bought the mill and operated it until the spring of 1903. It was then purchased by Spencer and Monroe.

HARVEYSBURG - "TOWN BY THE LAKE" ORIGINATED WITH COL. BUFORD

Harveysburg has in recent times been known as the "town by the lake." However, each village has its own history.

It is neatly situated about 100 feet above the original course of Caesar's Creek. Its land lies in the Virginia Military District of land distribution. The original owner under this jurisdiction was Colonel Abraham Buford, deed recorded August 6, 1787.

The second proprietor was Rhoden Ham who located on it in March, 1815. William Harvey was the next owner and proceeded to lay out Harveysburg in 1828. Harvey divided the town into forty-seven lots along the state road, now known as S.R. 73.

Harveysburg, like many other small communities, was a Quaker settlement. One of the beliefs of the Society of Friends was nonviolence in any form. This encompassed the slavery issue.

This small town has on its east side (approximately one-half mile) an old Indian trail called the Bullskin Trace. This trace, or trail, was at one time one of the main routes the Negro slaves used for their escape from Southern oppression. The principle objective of the slaves was to traverse the Northern States and exit into Canada. This trace served the purpose.

The Bullskin Trace was an extension of the many trails which wound through the South. It started its Ohio course at the Ohio River, near the town of Rural on S.R. 133 (Rural was washed away in the 1913 flood), east of Cincinnati and wound its way through the State to Detroit, Michigan.

Mrs. Walter McCarren notes that many of the slaves came up from Cincinnati through Lebanon on present U.S. 42 and proceeded east on Middletown Road, which, before the lake project, was complete to Harveysburg.

I have before me a paper written by an early resident of the vicinity of Harveysburg, Jane F. Wales Nicholson. She was born in 1806 and died in 1906. She was the daughter of Mr. and Mrs. Isaac Wales. I will humbly endeavor to rewrite portions of her story. She writes:

"I can recall many features for our new home which I greatly enjoyed as a child. My father worked on the land all day, sometimes in the evening would be busy in the blacksmith shop. I being small could just reach the great bellows. It was interesting to watch the iron grow red, and then see the sparks fly as it was struck on the anvil. My father made hinges and all the iron work needed for the new brick dwelling, which he soon prepared to build, except nails--these he bought at Cincinnati, and made the purchase by carrying down a load of bacon, which sold at two cents per pound. It took five days to make the journey then from Harveysburg to Cincinnati, two to go and two to return, leaving one for business there.

"There was plenty of game in the woods. It was not unusual to see a flock of thirty or more wild turkeys fly up from the ground and alight on the tall trees. They were fond of the beach-nuts that covered the ground.

"Squirrels were abundant, and very destructive traps were set on every few panels of fence around the corn field, and it was the duty of the morning to go around and gather up the dead squirrels and re-set the traps.

"One quiet Sabbath when our parents had gone to Waynesville meeting and we were alone, we were startled to see eight deer walking one after the other, in Indian file down the bank of the creek, and drink from the salt lick near where the bridge now stands.

"There was abundance of native fruit - excellent wild plums, crab apples and wild gooseberries, which made excellent pies when green, cut when ripe the beards hardened to thorns, and made it difficult to eat. There were wild raspberries, and black berries sprang up wherever the ground was cleared.

"The first opening on the new farm was appropriated for an orchard. There were no nurseries near and it was difficult to get fruit trees. One neighbor brought his trees all the way from Kentucky, on horse-back - besides peaches and currants. We could get but sixteen apple trees, two of these died and the remaining fourteen were cherished with greatest care.

"Three acres first cleared were sowed in rye the first fall, which ripens early, and would be off in time to sow wheat the next fall. When ripe, my father's hand cut it all with the sickle, in the absence of a wind-mill my mother helped him winnow it with a sheet. Their first little harvest lay piled up on the bare floor, when the officers came and took it all for a muster fine. The Friends ignored all obligations to train for war, and one neighbor south of us on the Miami, had, at great pains, collected a flock of forty Merino sheep, the first in that section of the country, and the officer took them every one to pay his muster fine.

"Improvements of all kinds came slowly but surely - compared with the present comforts, the first settlers endured many privations. There were no washboards; the soiled clothes had to be rubbed with the hands or pounded in a barrel. The houses had very little except necessary furniture, of which the loom, the wheel, the cards and reel, the break and hackle were an essential part. Every new farm had its flax field. The fabrics for clothing and bedding were made in the home; and the two Miami's, which have since turned so many mills for manufactories, then flowed free from duty along their wooden banks. The improvements and inventions have been greater in the last 70 years than ever before. In the next 70 they may be still greater.

"The recreations and amusements were determined by the necessities and industries of the time. For young people, apple cuttings; for men, huskings and log-rollings, while matrons would quilt and pick wool.

"Travel often interrupted by swollen streams over which there were at first, no bridges; heavy rains and melting snow would so increase the little runs along the hills that fed Caesar's Creek, that it was often impassable at the ford.

"Many and frequent were the water-bound travelers waiting for its fall. I recall one incident that caused great anxiety: The Friends who had discarded form in worship retained some rigid ones in regards to dress; one of the desirable symbols was the Quaker bonnet, its crown of stiff folds of intricate pleats, was what few bonnet makers attempted. Those who could sent to Philadelphia for their bonnets; in a large assembly, as a Yearly Meeting we could always tell the Philadelphia bonnet although they were also made at Richmond and at Waynesville.

"There was to be a wedding at Friends' meeting in Wilmington. The bride and her attendants came to Waynesville for their bonnets, and sent for them a day or two before the ceremony. The messenger did his errand, and came by on his way back on horse-back, well loaded with hand-boxes, and finding Caesar's Creek roaring too loud between the banks, he could not cross.

"He stopped with us. Next morning the creek was rising; he waited all day - no fall. Next morning was the day of the wedding. The creek still too high to ford, what was to be done? Would the wedding take place without the bonnets? A council was held, S.G. Welch, an obliging young man, volunteered to see them safely over the angry stream in time for meeting. He did so by going down the stream a few miles to a shallow ford, and got them there in season. Long afterward, he had the happiness to see his nephew married to a daughter of the bride."

First School in the Neighborhood

"We did not have books and papers in such numbers as are seen on the tables today; but such as we had were chaste and good. I have now the copy of Stearne's Reflection that my mother used to read, and several volumes of Addison's Spectator that her father loved.

"There was a great desire among the people to educate their children. Some other neighborhoods had schools, but they were far from us, and thick woods intervening. Father and a few others met to select a place on his farm for the school house. The intended patrons all volunteered their work. They brought their axes and cut the trees and cleared a place for the house. They felled a large oak tree to make clap-boards for the roof and puncheons for the floor. Next day they brought horses and log chains to drag up the logs - a froe to rive the boards and dress the puncheons.

"The chimney was built of sticks filled with mud, some stone slabs for the back wall, no jams - the fire-place occupied the entire end of the room. Stones instead of andirons held up the burning logs. Three or four logs from, four to six feet long with scaly bark between, made the cabin shine with light, and feel warm and comfortable. Boards were nailed over the openings of logs inside plastered with mud on the outside to keep out the cold. A board door with openings for light completed the first house of education between the Miami River and Caesar's Creek. But how were the children to find their way there? It was all dense wood excepts a field now and then cleared and planted in corn and pumpkins. The fathers took the course, and blazed the trees, and made a path through the under-brush. And over this narrow road through the woods, young feet traveled, many and many a day. We were afraid of the wild hogs. They were ugly looking creatures - red in color, with sharp noses and tusks. In winter they lived on acorns and beech-mass, under the dry leaves in summer they lived on the mussels which abounded in the creeks.

"On our way to school, we had our little trees picked out to climb, in case we should meet a bear, as we were told they could not climb small trees. Our first teacher was Judith Welch. It was feared that a young woman could not manage boys, but she gave a good satisfaction for several months. A large tree felled before the door, served for a table. To this we carried our blankets and ate our mid-day meal.

"When the nooning was over the teacher came to the door and called 'books, books!' Bells were scarce in those days - we could hardly get one for the cow, and had none to spare for the school.

"The next teacher was Robert Way, a Pennsylvanian, but had taught in Athens, Ohio. He brought the three readers: the Introduction, English reader and Murray's Sequel; also a grammar by John Comley, a Quaker preacher. I still have those old books.

"Some one passed the school house one day and found that all was still and orderly; they mistook the quiet for idleness, and reported no learning there, because the pupils did not 'say out of their books.' They called a meeting to investigate and the teacher had to explain his method. He was a member of our family a part of time--was a diligent student and studied late at night, wishing exercise before retiring, that he might sleep well, he would walk briskly, up and down the yard from the gate to the house. Passersby who did not understand this gymnastic exercise, reported him. The neighbors watched him and became alarmed, fearing reason was dethroned; this also had to be explained. He had many prejudices to contend with. One of his older pupils, F.K., had a turning lathe. Mr. Way got him to turn a sphere of wood upon which he traced the countries, the zones, and meridians - thus making a globe to study geography from.

"The young man's mother was distressed, she thought it blasphemous for man to imitate the works of God. She was, however, a strong character in the community, a German by birth--had united with Friends in the South where she walked seven miles to their meeting, often carrying a child in her arms, but such was her early training that she could not divest her mind of superstition. Robert Way remained a popular and useful teacher through a long life. He afterwards taught my children and later, had a school for boys in Springfield, Ohio.

"The next teacher was Isaac Thornburg, a native of North Carolina and a graduate of one of her institutions. He was learned in Greek, Latin and Hebrew, which few of his pupils needed. I remember, Owen Evans, Cornelius Clark and Webster Welch studied the languages. We had but few school months in the year, for the children, both large and small assisted their parents at home.

"A school in the O'Neal neighborhood was superior to ours in numbers. By boarding at our grandfather's and walking two miles we were able to attend this.

"The first teacher I remember there was Morris Place, a Friend from Richmond, Ind. He was succeeded by Thos. O'Brien, also a Friend and just from Ireland. He was a cousin to William Horton, who was also from Erin, a fine scholar and successful teacher.

"Thos. O'Brien had the hot temper and old country severity in governing children, which did not agree with the liberty loving natures under our institution. Aside from this, he was pleasant, kind, a very capable teacher; but his threats, 'I'll flog you if you don't do thus and so,' rang continually through the room, and he too often put in into practice. Both my nature and training revolted at this, for there never was a switch in my father's house.

"One day, in the forenoon, he announced that he would whip M.E. before night. I did not relish my dinner and trembled all day for fear the threat would be executed. I don't remember the offense, a light one, but he was to be made an example before the school.

"This little boy, not over twelve, took off his linsey coat and bore the stripes bravely. I felt like going to the boy and comforting him. I could not study any more that day. I found an excuse to remain at home next day for fear of a repetition of this sad practice. If teachers and parents would practice kindness and forbearance, they would lay a much better foundation for knowledge and goodness, than if they used threats and punishment.

"Outside of school he was a refined, genial man, very intelligent and good company. He was a frequent guest of my parents, and afterwards often sat at my own table as long as he lived. I have met many of his pupils in Indiana, and we have tried to excuse his severity, and use of the rod as a remnant of the arbitrary rule of his own country. Let us hope there is a reformation there as well as here in the treatment of tender children, whose unfolding minds look to us for help and strength.

"Owing to the enterprise of Dr. Jesse Harvey, Harveysburg was favored with a high school and boarding house to accommodate pupils from a distance and those too remote to attend as day pupils. Excellent teachers were employed, David S. Burson, who graduated at Friends College, Haverford, Penn., and William Horton, before mentioned. Dr. Harvey was fond of the natural sciences, and had besides a botanical garden, a good museum, and from time to time specimens of wild animals.

"Early in the twenties my father hired a colored laborer to help him clear the land, which was a very difficult thing to do. He gave one man the use of twelve acres for five years if he would deaden the timber and cut down all the trees that were one foot in diameter and under.

"This black man, known as Sam Green, came from South Carolina with Wm. Henley. He had 'bought his sef,' to use his own expression, vis., had hired his time of his master - worked for wages elsewhere - and kept the overplus, and after it had accumulated to the price of his manhood, paid this to his master, and by this means made a present of himself to himself. He was honest and industrious and assisted in clearing many a field of stumps and roots that others might turn the soil with an uninterrupted plow-share.

"But as old age crept on, the horrors of his early life in slavery, stood so vividly before him, that he became deranged. He would hide around in fields and woods, thinking that the slave-hunters were seeking him to take him back to slavery. He carried with him a long stick into which he had driven nails to defend himself.

"Once he stayed out so long that he was almost starved. My sympathy with him was great, he confided all his fears to me and asked me to conceal him. I took him up in the garret where I hoped he would rest; but he stole out and went again to the woods. Shortly after he was found sitting up by a tree, dead. This was a very sorrowful case. My interest in him prepared me for further work which I afterwards had to do for the poor unfortunate Negro in his efforts for freedom.

"About this time there were many slaves fleeing from their masters and from blood-hounds on their track. On their way to Canada they required shelter, food, clothing and transportation. In this capacity I worked for twenty years - until all were free by the Emancipation Proclamation. Hundreds that passed through, stopped at my house - ate at my table - I heard their tales of hardship; their desire for freedom, and the danger and sacrifice they were making to obtain it. Many had left near and dear relatives behind; some mothers left babes in the cradle.

"Nearly every one had a story of tragedy of pathos that will fade with the memory that now holds them. In the record of one year the number that came was eighty-six, but in other years I know we had many more.

"We were but one short night's ride from Cincinnati, and to our home came the slave, Lewis, whose case is notable, because the first tried under the Fugitive Slave Law of 1850. The trial was in Cincinnati, and lasted many days.

John Jollif aided by Rutherford B. Hayes tried all the technicalities of the law to secure his freedom, but in vain. He sat in the court room between his master and the state marshal who had him in custody.

"While the sentence was being read that remanded him to slavery, Lewis slipped his chair back quietly, arose, and before the judge had finished reading, stepped into a group of colored people conveniently near, one handed him a hat, another pointed to the door.

"The court room was crowded but a way opened to let him pass. In a moment he was in the street and gone, before the multitude in the court house could realize what had happened. He made his way out of town and hid for a few hours in a colored grave yard.

"At night the sexton brought him to a friend's house in the city. In the disguise of a woman they took him to the basement of a Presbyterian Church, where he remained concealed for several weeks in one of the committee rooms, his meals being carried to him.

"One morning he came out dressed as a nurse with a veil over his face and a child in his arms, took a seat in a carriage with the pastor and his wife, Dr. and Mrs. Boynton, and before sunset they were at our fireside.

"A little daughter, was rather astonished to see an awkward molatto woman go upstairs, and come down a brisk slender young man.

"The foiled master claimed one thousand dollars from the marshal for the loss of his slave: but by compromise he received but eight hundred.

It is known that the marshal, disguised as a Quaker, visited, under various pretenses, our and other neighborhoods of Friends in hopes of finding Lewis and saving his money."

HISTORIC LYTLE OFF THE BEATEN PATH

There is a quaint little town named Lytle that lies just off the beaten path of modern civilization. No interstate, no U.S. highways, just a few country roads pass through this historic town.

It lies in the northwestern section of Wayne Township just on the border of Wayne and Clearcreek Townships. The roads that pass through are: Lytle Road, Lytle Five-Points Road, Lytle Ferry Road and Township Line Road.

Much of the information in this column was taken from an article written by Mr. Walter Kenrick.

Lytle's first name was Raysville, named after Alexander Ray, who came to the area with his wife, Debra, and six daughters about 1807.

Ray purchased, from the founders of Waynesville, Banes and Heighway, a complete section of land consisting of 640 acres. He sold some lots, but was unable to give a clear deed because the original owner of the land, John Cleves Symmes, could not give a clear title.

Passage of the Enabling Act by the Government allowed the purchasers a clear title, but not without paying an extra two dollars per acre.

By 1810, many changes were made to the town. The population was made up mostly of people from Bucks County, Pennsylvania.

Expansion of the village was commenced in the form of tradesmen setting up their own businesses.

Wagon makers, blacksmiths, shoe makers, tailors, hat makers, coopers, grain makers, auger makers, and plow manufacturers made up the bulk of the enterprises.

At this time more than forty covered wagons reached the County from Pennsylvania. The main road through Lytle was then called the Pinckney Road. This road was started prior to 1804, being possibly an old Indian trail. Part was called Raysville and part was called Pinckney Road. It is now Lytle-Ferry Road.

The first nursery was established by Silas Wharton. He acquired twenty-two and one-half acres for $91 in the northeast quarter of the section.

Edward L. Kenrick established a store in 1827.

Sales recorded for March 12, 1827, were:

Thomas Wharton, 42 pounds of iron at seven cents per pound, $2.94 and a mole board for $1.75; John Belsford, two pieces of glass, eight cents; Elizabeth Jackson, credited with 11 dozen eggs at two cents per dozen and seven and a half pounds of butter at five cents per pound. Coffee sold at 22 cents per pound, tea at $1.25, molasses at forty cents a gallon.

The Wharton brothers were blacksmiths and wagon makers, Thomas Goodell was the tailor and Biddle Hay made Quaker hats.

Cornelius Morford built a saw mill and was operated afterwards by William and Richard Duke, and after them by Frank H. Duke.

The forest of the area at that time was thick with walnut trees and the mill supplied the means for the building of many of the houses.

Raysville was platted in 1856, with twenty-two lots, by Mahlon Mills and his brother, Owen. The Mills brothers owned eleven of these lots and for a number of years ran a pork packing business. They butchered as many as 100 heads of hogs a day and also acquired dressed hogs from the neighboring farmers.

Their manufacturing facilities were set up to make lard, barrel it and pork, which was sold in Cincinnati.

A story goes that a farmer brought in a four horse wagon load of dressed hogs, but because of the cold weather the hogs were frozen solid. The meat was covered and allowed to stay in the wagon. Six weeks later it thawed enough to be processed.

The Mills brothers establishment kept two cooper shops busy making barrels for their packed goods. One of the cooper shops was located in town and the other was near the intersection of S.R. 73 and Township Line Road. These shops were also known for making whiskey barrels.

As we all know a cooper is a barrel maker or one who repairs barrels. The sides of a wooden barrel (strips of wood) are called staves.

The staves are wider in the middle than at the

ends which makes the wooden barrel bulge in the middle. The reason for this bulge is strength.

The barrel is then bound together by metal or wooden hoops. The heads, or top and bottom of the barrel, are formed by flat wooden circles that fit into grooves near the ends of the staves.

In the neighborhood of Lytle white oak trees were plentiful. These trees were selected by the coopers as prime wood.

The Dayton, Lebanon and Cincinnati Railroad came to Raysville about 1883. An official name was then needed for the village because of this event, and the addition of a post office. Mr. Walter B. Kenrick suggested the name Lytle which was taken from a shoe box from the Lytle Shoe Company of Cincinnati.

The first post office was opened June 5, 1882. The first postmaster was John A. Kelsey. Other postmasters and dates were: Elmer E. Keever, July 15, 1895; Samuel L. Williamson, February 5, 1896; and Charles E. Johns, December 16, 1897.

The postal service was discontinued November 30, 1918, which was then moved to Waynesville.

A new store was built in 1867 opposite the Methodist Church. The name of the original owner or builder is unknown. However, in later years it was bought and operated by Isaac Sellers and his son-in-law, J.A. Kelsey.

The general store of Sellers and Kelsey was moved, in 1885, to the area of the railroad where they operated it for a number of years.

The business was sold in 1894 to Elmer Keever, who later sold it to C.E. Jones, who in turn sold it to Elbert Wallace of Red Lion.

In the early days, as repair was being made on a stone bridge, a family of minks was uncovered in the bridge. The town was then referred to for many years as Minktown rather than Raysville.

The first religious meetings were held in the homes of individuals until 1824, when Charles Hall sold to the trustees of the Raysville Methodist organization land in the area of the Pinckney and the future Franklin Road.

A log structure was used for over 20 years for

the first church. This was replaced in 1847 by a frame building. In 1860, a large frame church was built which was destroyed by fire some 12 years later. The present church was completed in 1873.

Some years later, in 1915, a complete remodeling was done. An addition of an entrance hall, two small rooms in the west end of the building, and a belfry was added.

A basement, an assembly room, a modern kitchen, and rest rooms were added in the year 1952.

A log cabin also served as the first school for Lytle students. This was located at the southwest corner of Section 16. Another school was located one and a half miles northeast of Raysville towards Ferry.

The Raysville students had a walk of about two miles to attend school. The roads at this time were atrocious. After a period of time, and many squabbles over this long walk, a new school building was constructed just east of town in 1876.

In 1895, an operation was initiated which would organize a special jurisdiction to include District No. 4, 12, and 3 in Wayne Township and 10 and 11 in Clearcreek. When accomplished a successful school district was in utilization for about 20 years.

Due to an increased teaching staff, which was required by the State, and a small tax duplicate, they were forced to close the school and return to the township method, and some years afterward were relocated into the Wayne Township precinct at Waynesville.

The railroad's appearance changed the town somewhat. Morris Silvers bought an acre of land from Jacob Lamb and built a grain elevator.

Purchasing five more acres from Lamb, Silvers added a lumber yard. After three years, Silvers made an assignment to a lawyer named Dechant, who sold the assets of the business at auction and the property to Mrs. Morris Silvers.

Mrs. Silvers sold the property on August 31, 1883, to John Simonton and his son, Lon, of Lebanon. Lon later inherited the business and conducted a successful firm for 37 years. He afterward sold the enterprise to Everett Early on June 23, 1923.

Early expanded his establishment by enlarging both the buildings and business. He became one of the main shippers on the Cincinnati, Lebanon & Northern and Dayton Lebanon & Cincinnati Railroad lines.

Harvest time saw the business receiving as much as 100,000 bushels of wheat for shipment.

Early incorporated the business in 1937, the corporation name being Early Elevator, Inc.

Under this name he branched out into several other lines, which included liquid nitrogen. He later sold, in 1952, to Carl Pitstick.

Edwin Sweny and Josiah Hough constructed a tile mill in which they manufactured and sold many rods of tile. The mill was later sold to Frank Hamilton, then to Sidney Coon, and later to J.M. Stacy, who sometime later concluded the making of tile.

Everett Early bought the land, on which he had a coal and feed business for five years, from the Stacey heirs.

Dr. Dyche opened an office in the early 1880's for his medical practice. Attending the locals for several years he later sold his business to Dr. James W. Ward, who at that time was a newly trained medical student.

Dr. Dyche attended the community for about 25 years in a sufficient fashion and in 1911 he retired to his farm near Harveysburg, where he died in 1944, leaving his widow, Dora Nelson Ward, who died two years later.

HISTORIC LITTLE MOUNT HOLLY NESTLED IN WAYNE TOWNSHIP

There is a little town that lies in Wayne Township in the northern half of the County known as Mount Holly. It is located just off U.S. 42 near the Greene County line. Like other small towns it has its own history.

Mount Holly was laid out in 1833 by Jacob

Pearson; the town consisted of 25 lots. The original name of the town was "Shattersburg."

Earlier history finds the Buckles family purchasing land and settling in the locale in 1797.

They had originally lived at Columbia in 1790, a town along the Ohio River, now a part of Cincinnati. There were five girls and four boys, their names being; Robert, William, John, James, Mrs. Henry Simmons, Mrs. Culbert Watson, Mrs. Edward Dyer and Mrs. John Heaton. One of the girls never married.

A small stream named Bear Branch ran through the Heaton farm. The highlight of this name was the fact that Heaton once, while hunting, shot a bear from a tree near the stream, the bear falling into the stream. Thinking it dead, he hustled to the area and started to stick it with his knife. The bear suddenly sprang up and lunged at Heaton, thus giving him a fight before the bear was finally killed.

The vicinity of Spring Valley, just north of Mount Holly, had the only tillable land within the locality of the early settlers. Their cabins were some distance away and it was a chore to keep the Indians, bears, squirrels, etc., from destroying their crops.

The Buckles family had no means of trading except a small log cabin which had been built and used as a store in the village of Waynesville.

The first house built at Mount Holly was a log house. It was the congregating place for the women with their washings.

This house was built by John Everhart, who was a brick maker and mason. He moved to Waynesville from Cincinnati in 1806.

Having walked the entire distance, he related his passing of a band of Wyandott Indians encamped at Cold Springs below Waynesville. The Indians, because of ceding their lands some years ago to the Government, were apparently searching for new hunting grounds. It was not unusual in that period of time to see large bands of roving Indians.

Mrs. Ellen Marlatt, when a mere youngster, remembered seeing a band of four hundred pass through Mount Holly. The old chief and squaws stopped at a tavern in the settlement and ate their dinners.

William Rye remembered seeing the same band camped below Waynesville and states that the old Chief was very sick and died before reaching Cincinnati.

John Everhart, after leaving Waynesville in 1808 or '09, built a cabin on the Edward Hartsock farm. He resided there until the building of the house mentioned at Mt. Holly.

Jackson Allen, from Virginia, built the first mill dam and saw mill in 1814. While building the dam Allen caught the ague and spoke of leaving the area and returning to Virginia. His friends tried to convince him to stay, revealing to him a cold water cure.

Catching him at the mill one day with a chill coming on, they gave him a rigorous ducking. Without reason he got well and gave up all cause to return to Virginia.

John Satterthwaite bought a mill site in 1819 from Robert Huston, upon which he built his grist mill where the more recent Marlatt mill stood.

The masons and millwrights for this mill came from Mt. Holly, N.J. The burrs for it were brought by pack horses over the mountains; they were brought in sections and were put together and banded here.

The farmers had formerly gone to Waynesville to have their grinding done, but now they could do it locally.

A Mr. Heaton was the first Miller, thence being succeeded by Alexander Hayslip.

A contest was entered into by Satterthwaite and Hayslip as to who could raise the largest hog. Each contestant picked a pig from a stock known as the "English." After a period of time two enormous hogs evolved.

Satterthawaite's hog was claimed the winner, weighing in at its death at 1400 pounds. It was shown throughout the United States and then shipped to England.

A man named Elliott took over the mill after Mr. Hayslip. Stephen Cook then bought the property and held it until 1843.

Riley Brinker was one of the millers and was employed by the different owners in later years. The mill then passed from Mr. Cook to John Kinney, and then to Mr. Pence.

A time period from 1845 to 1868 registered a large business at the mill. The business was so good that some of the old-timers said that traffic was backed up for almost a mile waiting their turn. In the meantime a distillery had been added.

Samuel Ellis built a one story house in 1823 for the purpose of a blacksmith shop. Other early blacksmiths succeeding him were; Everhart, Clingan, Weller, Caldwell, Hartsock and Doron.

John Morford built a pottery about the year 1825, its operation being very successful for a number of years.

About this same time John Githens constructed a wagon shop.

Near the site of the Marlatt mill, a mill called the Fanning Mill Manufactory was built in 1830 by a Mr. Patter, with Levi Frazer being in his employ.

Jacob Pearson was the first storekeeper in Mt. Holly. His store stood on old main street. Other early store and grocery keepers have been Watson and Taylor, Grant, Hill, Fox, Holcomb, Craft, Frazier and Carey.

The Pence house was a tavern between 1840 and 1850. Noah Jones also had a tavern in 1823 known as the "Black Bear." The identity of this tavern was portrayed by a large black bear painted on a white board.

The old stage roads had run west of town until the pike was built in 1839. Subsequently, with the new road being built, Mt. Holly was allowed the advantages of the stage coaches and team traffic through the village. Tavern keeping was then launched into a great enterprise.

The post office was moved from Transylvania (near Spring Valley) to Mt. Holly in 1843. The early postmasters were: Samuel Hill, 8 March, 1843; Peter DeHaven, 7 March, 1844; Aaron Mintle, 26 June, 1845; Josiah Craft, 29 July, 1845; George Sims, 4 September, 1861. The post office was discontinued 20 April, 1863.

The coopering business was established in the early history of the town. Among the first coopers were John Everhart and sons, Nathan and Emanuel; and George Sims and J.W. Marlatt.

John Everhart was alleged to have invented the endless chain, since used in different kinds of horse power. His claim was made in 1834; its purpose was to be used in the cooper business, but before the patent could be confirmed, it was stolen from him.

Aden Haines had a successful saddle and harness business which was later carried on by Foster Ward and William Cornell.

David Wilson lived on a farm south of Mt. Holly and worked the cobbler business for the neighborhood. George Mayer, a Methodist minister also worked at the trade.

Jacob Pearson, the founder of the town, was the Methodist preacher in the town and vicinity. Jacob's wife, Rebecca, is buried in the old cemetery on the former farm of Jesse Hartsock. At one time there was an old church on the grounds called Bethel.

Mrs. Ellen Marlatt attended this church in her childhood. She remembered being in the church at the time the first train ran on the Little Miami Railroad; the minister at that time was Joseph Hill.

The preacher and the entire assembly rushed to the scene and stood and watched the train in bewilderment. Some thoughts ran rampant even to the point of this being a wild animal. All agreed that it ran fast enough to cause a wind to blow.

The first school in the town was held in about 1830; the location was in the building of John Githens. It was taught by George Sims who at that time was a cooper, a tavern keeper and was an avid huckster.

John Sims and his wife were among the other

early settlers; he built his home in 1829.

Other early settlers who helped establish Mt. Holly were: Hoover, Clevenger, Smith, Cornell, Hartsock, Archer, Jones, Vetter and Gretsinger.

Possibly the most prestigious person to visit the little village of Mt. Holly was Coates Kinney, the world renowned poet.

He was born November 24, 1826, at Kinney's Corners, near Penn Yan, Yates County, New York. He was the second son of Giles and Mira Cornell Kinney.

The Kinney family moved, in 1840, to Springboro, Ohio. In 1842, the family moved to a house on the road from Waynesville to Ridgeville. Young Coates attended Ridgeville School, the school apparently triggering in him an uncanny desire for learning.

At this time he was learning, with no inner satisfaction, the trade of coopering. Perry Staley, being his instructor, saw in this young boy an attitude for learning. Staley started bringing books for the young lad to read, rather than seeing him working at the boring trade of coopering.

He later started work in the saw mill at Mt. Holly. His mind seemingly wandered while in the employment at the mill. It was this wavering that caused him to lose this job.

Kinney obtained an education and eventually taught school at Mt. Holly.

"Rain of the Roof," one of the best known poems at the time, was reportedly written at Mt. Holly by Coates Kinney.

Kinney says: "I slept one night next the roof in the little farm cottage which our folks lived in....In the evening there came up a gentle rain, which patted on the shingle roof two or three feet above my head....Here I lay and conceived the lyric and then went to sleep. It haunted me next day, which was bright and green and glorious; and on a walk from Spring Valley to Mt. Holly I composed most of the poem. It was the easiest production I ever wrote."

CARLISLE WAS PART OF WARREN COUNTY'S 'WESTWARD EXPANSION'

Deep in the northwest corner of Warren County lies a quaint little village named Carlisle. It is one of the oldest settlements in the County, with the earliest inhabitants settling shortly after 1800.

Harriet Foley, editor of "Carlisle, The Jersey Settlement in Ohio," has graciously allowed this writer to draw much material from her book.

The area of Carlisle was not always in Warren County. The State of Ohio was formed on the first Tuesday of March, 1803 (date debatable), and Warren County was established March 24, 1803.

Clinton County was formed in 1810. It was found not to have enough territory to establish the 400 square miles that both Ohio Constitutions called for. At this time Warren had just over 400 square miles.

Clinton County expanded westerly which caused Warren County to expand in a westerly direction. In 1815, the County of Warren extended to the west side of the Great Miami, thus consuming a portion of Butler County.

The early residents of the Carlisle area migrated from New Jersey. Like many other pioneers they moved with their families over the Alleghenies on pack-horses, or down the Ohio River on flatboats.

Land sites were chosen, cleared and homes were crudely built. It is said that a family could clear and burn an acre of ground in about three weeks. The new home consisted of a huge fireplace along with home-made furniture.

The first land owners were thought to be the Barkalow brothers. In about 1804 it is thought they bought land from the mouth of Twin Creek to the Great Miami River dam and thence as far west as Carlisle.

At the same time Arthur VanDerveer, of Freehold, New Jersey, bought land above them. Other early land owners were: Hendrick Lane, Daniel DuBois, Dr. Benjamin DuBois, the Schencks,

Denises, Conovers, Van Tuyls, and the Francises.

Some other land owners from the twenties to the fifties were: Dickey Francis, Kinny Anderson, the Chamberlains brothers, Wykoffs, Conovers, Emleys, and Bairds, to name a few.

The "Jersey Settlement," as it was known far and wide, had a definite foothold on civilization.

Transportation at this time was simply by horseback. The roads were atrocious, merely wagon tracks. The farmer rode his horse to the mill with his corn and wheat; his wife rode to market and visited distant friends; and the preacher, lawyer and doctor all making their rounds on horseback.

Some years later toll-roads were established and one of the old tollgates was located on the southwest corner of State Route 123 and Central Avenue.

In the early days of the settlement, Dr. Benjamin DuBois was the only physician on the west side of the river, having settled here in 1804. He was a doctor of wide renown.

The first church in the Jersey Settlement was established on August 14, 1813, at the house of William Barkalow, which was called the New Jersey Presbyterian Church. The first meetings took place at different residences and barns.

A Mr. Monfort was ordained and installed as the first pastor June 14, 1814. The membership was 22 and the salary for the pastor was $150 in half-yearly payments.

The first church was built in 1815 just back of the present building, with a land donation of two acres given by Daniel DuBois.

As time went on markets were established and prices more or less conformed to the times. Wheat was 12 cents a bushel, butter from 3 to 5 cents per pound, and eggs 2 to 3 cents per dozen.

Foreign imports were high with the price of coffee set at 50 cents per pound, tea 80 cents, and gingham 50 cents per yard.

The first grist mill in the area of Carlisle was the old Van Derveer mill which sat on the east side of the Great Miami River, just north of Pennyroyal Road on Old Rt. 25 below the dam site.

It did a great business, but it came to a halt in the 1860's and went into the hands of a receiver. The machinery was moved to Franklin and the old building was left to decay, leaving no identifiable trace.

The Van Tuyl grist mill was located on the Van Tuyl Road (now Martz Paulin Road, established in 1817) which stood on Twin Creek near the intersection of Martz Paulin and Dian Drive.

Miss Dora Fleming, late resident of Carlisle, was calling with a friend on an old gentleman in Lebanon. It was mentioned that she lived in Carlisle. He said: "That Jersey settlement! The smartest women on earth live over there. Get up and do a big washing and go visiting for dinner on Monday. The men will treat you like a king, give you a big dinner and then cheat you out of your eyes in a horse trade."

The Cincinnati, Hamilton and Dayton Railroad (C H & D) revived the Jersey Settlement which allowed the vicinity to expand. The railroad ran over a three mile course through Carlisle Station.

The first excursion train traveled over the road from Cincinnati to Hamilton September 13, 1851; trains began running regularly between Cincinnati and Dayton on September 22, 1851.

Carlisle Station was the only railroad in the proximity of Franklin and Germantown, this being the only passenger and freight shipping depot in the entire vicinity.

Everybody was out to see the first train pass through. A Mrs. Winters tells how she, a mere child, ran with schoolmates to see the cars, and then fled in terror in the opposite direction as the awful monster went rolling by.

Mr. George Carlisle, vice-president of the C H & D, purchased about 150 acres from Benjamin DuBois, and Benjamin and George Conover, which he platted into 30 lots.

He offered the villagers a triangle of land to build a "Literary Society" meeting house if they would call the community "Carlisle." The building is still standing and is the old section of Carlisle's town hall.

With the coming of the railroad, a freight depot, warehouses, a post office located in a general store, stockyards, livery stable, and a boarding house were established.

The freight depot was located along the C H & D tracks behind the Gross Lumber Company. For years the station was just a railroad car.

Eventually a fine passenger station was built. Mr. Patrick Sweeney was freight agent for many years. Mr. Mulford Tapscott was the first ticket agent, and a Mr. Chase took care of the station which was also a boarding house.

The "Mackinaw Railroad" was brought to Carlisle Station in 1887. The train station was moved to the northeast junction of the Cincinnati Northern and the Cincinnati, Hamilton and Dayton, which was located on Park Drive.

The "Literary Society," previously mentioned, was formed March 20, 1856. There were five trustees elected who were: Henry Eby, William Hendrickson, Jacob DuBois, Norman DuBois, and Andrew Baird with J.C. Fleming as clerk. On March 22, a meeting was held at Mr. Eby's storeroom and a resolution was made to build a good hall.

A dedication for the new building was held on May 17. There was singing by a choir, a building report given, and an address by a Reverend Hall and Reverend Weaver was delivered.

Aside from the donation of the land by Mr. Carlisle, the total cost of the building was a little over $1200. A subscription of $400 was presented which left a debt of over $800. The final payment was made in March of 1860.

Some of the early enterprises of Carlisle were: a Mr. Yehring had a dry goods store; Mr. Tunis DuBois for several years had a dry goods store; and a Mr. Eby owned a grocery store.

After his death Mr. Stevenson bought the grocery, and about 1858, sold out to Mr. Alfred and Lew Craig. A new building was built by the latter and was later owned by Charles Mount.

A livery stable was located at the northwest corner of Park Drive and Hillcrest. The business thrived as people came to park their wagons and carriages in order to catch the train to places far and wide.

Next to the town hall was a blacksmith shop and a saloon establishment. Mr. Dye had a harness shop where Breeding's home is located.

With the advent of the railroad, and Carlisle established as a large shipping station, an elevator was built and first run by a Mr. Green. He later sold his business to John Hankinson.

The latter lost his sight and later sold it to Owen Gross and William Basore. Mr. Gross bought out Mr. Basore and when he retired, his son James took over, and after his retirement, the establishment reverted to his son James, Jr.

The first post office was named Carlisle Station. A chronology of the early post office and postmasters is as follows: "Carlisle Station," Jacob M. Tapscott, December 3, 1852; Henry Eby, February 18, 1854; Tunis V. Dubois, September 30, 1858; Alfred S. Craig, May 31, 1865. Alfred S. Craig, June 15, 1869. Changed to "Carlisle," November 29, 1882. Alfred S. Craig, November 29, 1882; Albert W. Barr, June 2, 1893; Charles Mount, April 21, 1897; Ethel VanDerveer, August 1940 to May 26, 1961.

The Carlisle post office became a branch of Franklin post office May 26, 1961. At this time there was not enough revenue to set up delivery service independently. The residents were spread out too far to frequent the post office.

The different addresses at this time were: Rt 1, Germantown; Mounted Route Miamisburg; and Mounted Route Franklin. With the move and a promise from Franklin, Carlisle was allowed to keep their name and address.

Mrs. Ethel VanDerveer (now deceased) stated that the school was a two-story brick with the first six grades in the two rooms down and the seventh and eighth grades grouped with the high school upstairs. Some students had two years, some three and some had four years of high school.

When the new building was built across the road, the old building and ground were sold to Mrs. Howard Monger. She had the old building torn down and houses were built with part of the salvaged material.

UTICA ONCE A THRIVING HAMLET

It seems the small hamlets in Warren County go unrecognized as to their history and location. Utica is one of these remote areas.

Utica lies on the corner of Old Route 122 and Utica Road in the extreme south-eastern portion of Cleacreek Township. It is easily passed by, it being identified as just another bend in the road.

While researching Utica, I found it had its own definite character and history.

It was easily recognized in the latter half of the 1800's, it being another of the County's bustling communities. An early writer of the town said: "Few compare with Utica in point of socialbeness, friendly greetings, hospitality and neighborly friendship."

As near as the writer can estimate, the time period of the following description is between 1850 and 1890. Utica had one store, one blacksmith shop, one pork house, one saw-mill, one cabinet shop, one harness shop, one school, one saloon and one good writing school.

Jehu Mulford owned the store, sold out and bought land below Lebanon. The store was purchased by Benjamin A. Stokes who kept it for some years.

He then moved to Ridgeville, became a banker (not at Ridgeville), and accumulated a great sum of money. The store was later run by Samuel Carey who was described as a "kind and accommodating man."

Lewis Kling, along with his son, owned and operated the local blacksmith shop, the name of the establishment being, of course, "Kling & Son." Excellent and timely service was their mark with the community and surrounding areas.

The porkhouse was co-owned by Benjamin A. Stokes, Jake Davis and William Wright.

Alexander Lewis owned and operated the cabinet shop. He was was said to have been the best cabinet maker in the State at the time. He was also employed at one time in Cincinnati.

Michael Matthews conducted the shoe shop business.

There is no name attached to whom the harness shop trade was carried on by.

Andy Patton was the school teacher. He later studied medicine under the tutelage of Dr. Moses Keever.

Abe Brandenburg was the saloon owner. He was said to have died in the poor-house.

John Murly owned and ran the local saw-mill. His reputation was staked on doing every kind of work on short notice and at reasonable terms.

The schoolhouse was made of logs with a fire-place on one end with a row of glass, probably the size of the window which would be ten or twelve inches by fifteen feet. It was called the Buttermilk Schoolhouse.

At a later time, another schoolhouse was built which was said to have had an upper story that was used as a Grange Hall. The hall was probably used more by the owls and night birds than by the members of the Grange. The school was kept by B.A. Hathaway.

A meeting house was built by the United Brethren Church. It was organized by H. Toby.

The membership soared at first, but soon dwindled. At a later time the church became very successful with its attendance once again viable.

The 1875 Warren County Atlas has a diagram of Utica (page 78) which shows the location of the residents, church, store and the school. Town lot owners were: S. Kirby, D. Graham, L. Grove, W. Davis, H. Brandenburg, R. Ivins, L. Kling, J.W. Phillips, L. Rogers, W. Pence, E. Marsh, J. Merritt, and G.A. Poisett.

Benjamin A. Stokes was mentioned as an early businessman in Utica. He was also the founder of "Dunlevy," January 17, 1850, at which location the writer cannot find. Dunlevy is in my files as a post office which was later changed to Dodds, August 29, 1881. Benjamin A. Stokes was its first postmaster, June 17, 1850.

The writer hopes he has shed some light on one of the small villages that has since become just a crossroad on a map.

HISTORY OF KINGS MILLS DATES BACK TO 1799

Kings Mills is a small town which lies in Deerfield Township and goes almost unnoticed except by its residents. The town has a rather long and unique history which dates back to 1799, when William Wood built a grist mill on the bank of the Little Miami River. We shall now at this time review the history of this fine town as seen by one of its late residents, Constance Witt.

Elva Adams (since deceased), former director of the Warren County Historical Society, planned a project to go out into the communities of Warren County and set up interviews with different individuals to preserve the histories of these communities.

A committee consisting of Miriam Lukens, Chairman, Constance Witt and Alma Kintzel was chosen to develop the undertaking. An enormous work was done and these works are preserved in the Warren County Museum.

Constance Witt grew up in Kings Mills. After spending her adult life teaching in Cincinnati, she retired in Kings Mills.

Her father, George Edwin Witt, was a multi-talented man. In 1903, he worked in Cincinnati on Eighth Street in a buggy and carriage shop, receiving 11 cents an hour.

Among his many skills was that of a painter, cornet and slide trombone player. He sought employment through the Kings Powder Company, and as Providence would have it, Percy Bolmer, who was the cornet player in the band, passed away, which left an opening for Witt in the band. He was hired as musician and also as a painter for the company.

Mr. Witt moved to Kings Mills in 1903. He had previously married Christine Weis of Maineville. Both were to spend the rest of their lives in Kings Mills or Maple Park, a subdivision of the town. Christine Witt died in 1929 at the age of 48, and Mr. Witt died in 1975 at the age of 96.

Witt's paint shop was located down the hill from the Cliff Hotel along the river road. Its location was in a cool shady spot where "long stemmed violets grew in the spring."

The Cliff Hotel was located at the top of the hill on the corner. It was a two story building with sixteen rooms, eight on the first floor and eight on the second. The dining room and kitchen were in the basement.

The Manse was a building on College Street, located between Church and Miami Streets. It was a rather long building similar to a row of condominiums, except that it was all painted the same color.

The church was the gathering place for all the community. Revered Spindler was the minister; Mr. John Wilson was the Sunday School Superintendent; and his daughter Margaret was a teacher.

Mr. Witt was the choir director and also joined in the singing. Mrs. Witt was Constances' Sunday School teacher, and when Constance moved to another class, she took her teacher with her.

Witt, among his other professions, was also local librarian. The post office was located in the lower part of the library at that time. Ida Cline and Margaret Wilson were post mistresses.

The library had an auditorium upstairs with a stage and a balcony. The entertainment included class plays, the Lyceum Course, minstrel shows, and, of course, picture shows.

Popcorn, as now, was always sold to the patrons. The rattling of the paper bags was quite noticeable until this delicacy was all gone.

The shows had no voice sounds; the words appeared below the picture. Occasionally someone could be heard reading the lines out loud to a possible non-reader.

Constance related one event to Mrs. Lukens. She said:

"Occasionally the show must have been 'scary' because one evening I rushed across the street to our home afterwards, hurried through the dark living room and ran into the glass in the bookcase. From that time on, we could get the books out of the bookcase without opening the door."

Kings Mills had a bandstand which was located behind the library.

The brass band practiced in the building or on the roof (which had a railing) in the summer evenings. One special occasion at Music Hall in Cincinnati found the band marching down the aisle playing "The Stars and Stripes Forever." The spirit of the band instilled a spark into the other bands and all joined in playing the gallant marching tune. The occasion was a memorable one.

The school housed all grades from first through high school. Constance graduated in 1925, there being only six in the class. With this small number, they could all jump into a classmate's Ford and drive to their class outing.

The barber shop was located in one room of the house on the corner of King Avenue and Miami Street. A room addition was later added below for the barber facilities. It was later moved to the old traction depot.

Popcorn and hot roasted peanuts were served across the street. Mr. Trimble prepared this delicacy and charged five cents a bag.

Other points of interest was the Kings Powder Company office, located down the hill. Farther down were the buildings for charcoal and sulfur, as well as a little building on the right of the steps which housed paint.

The keg shop and mills were along the race and river road. The Peters Cartridge Company buildings were just across the river. The magazines where powder was stored was located on Magazine Hill.

Recess at school meant play-time. One of the

favorite games of the children was a rugged game of "prisoner's base." Choosing sides was very important. Helen and Mahlon Wood were generally chosen first because they could run the fastest.

Some more of the memories of Constance was that a circus was staged in her back yard. Her brother, Byron, had a goat and wagon.

Mr. Witt built Constance and her sister, Geneva, a doll house. He built a teeter-tooter, and also what they called a trapeze. Skating was allowed on the new sidewalks, but never on Sunday.

When the Witt family moved to Maple Park, the kids had a bicycle to ride to school, although the one mile trip was made most of the time on foot.

A hiking club was formed in high school by Miss West and Mrs. Harbaugh. Anyone hiking one-hundred miles during the school year received a felt emblem.

The Fourth of July was celebrated in those days much the same as today. Firecrackers, flower pots, sparklers, and "snakes in the grass" were much in accord for the grand celebration. Witt lighted and held the Roman candles. Care was taken in lighting the various fireworks and no injuries were reported.

Halloween, Valentines's Day, and Christmas were all exciting times for the children. Christmas time found the family gathering around the piano, all joining in the singing. The family had their own orchestra. Geneva played the violin; Byron played the drums; Witt played the cornet or slide trombone; and Constance played the piano. Mother was the audience.

Winter evenings, when the snow and ice were just right, found the children gathering around Mr. Harry Misel, a neighbor, who owned a bobsled. The gates at the bottom of the hill would be opened, and the length of King Avenue would be just enough space to gather up enough speed to conquer the hill.

Around the Cliff Hotel they would travel and down through the opening. Constance was the youngest and therefore got to ride in front of

Harry, who would steer the sled.

A family of any size in those days would have to economize.

Witt resoled the shoes; a large garden was utilized in addition to picking strawberries, raspberries, blackberries, and robbing the fruit trees. Canning was a necessary chore for Mrs. Witt. Byron joined in and gathered hickory nuts and walnuts.

Apples were bought by the barrel; chickens were raised; the hunting season brought many delicacies; Mrs. Witt baked pies, cakes and bread. Butchering was a necessity when the weather cooled. The cured hams were hung in the cellar and lard was made. Ice was cut from the river and stored in sawdust for the summer months.

The iceman knew the quantity consumed by the family and brought it in a large block for the icebox. Pieces would be left in the wagon to melt, and, with consent from the iceman, the assembled children would consume the small scraps.

Traveling merchants were rather thickly populated in those days. A meat wagon came from Brewster's butcher shop in Mason. Mrs. Witt would choose and order the family's choice of meats which were delivered to the door.

The dogs, which possibly knew the timetable of the meat wagon, gathered and all the trimmings were thrown to them. Mr. Nunner, a store owner in Hopkinsville, drove a covered wagon filled with groceries to Kings Mills.

Among other traveling merchants was a man who came around and fixed umbrellas; one sharpened scissors; another carried a huge pack of clothes for sale strapped to his back. Also included was a woman who sold men's hose, and a roving photographer who captured the early family in a retrospective pose.

The traction car was available to go to Cincinnati or Lebanon. During World War I, the baggage car of the traction line was used to transport laundry to Cincinnati and back. Witt collected the laundry, mostly from the hotel.

A system was set up which included the making out of a slip for each bundle. The work was done in the Witt's kitchen on King Avenue by he, Mrs. Witt and Aunt Rose Ford. The laundry was transported by traction car and returned washed, ironed and neatly wrapped.

Constance would often take a train to Foster. She had to walk down the hill to the station, board the train, make the trip, and was met in Foster by her grandfather with his horse and buggy for the ride to Maineville.

Electricity, being unavailable in this day and time, meant excessive labor. Promptly on Monday mornings Mr. and Mrs. Witt got up at four o'clock and heated the boiler of water on the coal stove. A bar of Tag soap had been previously cut up in the water the night before. Mr. Witt routinely turned the machine and emptied the water before going to work.

Clothing irons were heated on the stove. The Witts had a large iron that burned charcoal.

The icebox was used constantly, but food was sometimes covered and set on the cellar floor to keep cool. Hand sweepers were used; rugs were put outside on a line and beaten with a carpet beater.

When someone passed away, the casket was placed in the home before the church service and a wreath was put on the front of the house.

Another type sign was a quarantine sign. If it was placed on the front door of a home, this meant that a contagious disease such as scarlet fever was present, and visitors were requested not to linger.

Such is the story of a dedicated historian, Constance Witt, who found time to compose the history of a family and a town.

FROM PALMYRA TO KIRKWOOD - THE EARLY PROGRESS OF MASON

This writer has quite a selection of material regarding the city of Mason. However, with the kind permission of Rose Marie Springman, I will attempt to draw from her very informative book, "Around Mason, Ohio: A Story."

William Mason, the founder of Mason, Ohio, was a soldier in the Revolutionary War. He was only sixteen at the time of enlistment and served his time as a private in the war for independence.

In 1789, General Josiah Harmar, who was a Revolutionary War General, gathered up an army to defeat the native Indians which were assembled to the North in what is now Greene County.

In 1790, with an army of 300 regulars and over 1100 volunteers, they left Fort Washington (now Cincinnati) for an encounter which ended up as a total defeat for General Harmar's army. William Mason was one of these soldiers.

Apparently the Mason family landed at Columbia (now a part of Cincinnati), and William Mason's brother, John, a Baptist preacher, stayed in this frontier town.

William's brothers, Samuel and James, removed to Palmyra, Tennessee. There is a possibility that William traveled to this locality for a visit.

Mason purchased 80 acres along the Little Miami River in Columbia Township from John Cleves Symmes on December 18, 1798.

William Mason's first marriage was to Mary McClelland of Cincinnati. He at this time was 38 years old. Their first birth was a daughter, Maria, just a year later. Their second child, Samuel, was born in 1801.

Some of the first settlers in Deerfield Township were greeted with massive forests which consisted of trees of many different varieties such as: giant elms, oaks, walnuts, maples, ash, hickory and cherry. The denseness of the trees and foliage was so considerable that only the Indian trails could be used for transportation.

Another deterrent for the early pioneers in Deerfield Township was the abundant amount of wild life. Such creatures as poisonous snakes, bear, deer, wolves, wildcats, and other small animals were at first a hindrance, but soon became a source for food.

After the peace treaty with the Indians (the

Treaty of Greenville) in 1795, settlers began to trickle in. Some of the men and their families that entered Deerfield Township in 1796 were: Joseph Coddington, Moses Kitchel, Jeremiah Morrow, Thomas Espy and John Parkhill.

The next few years saw John Meeks, Robert Witham, John Bigham, Stephen Bowyer; Benjamin Ross, Peter Tetrick, Joseph Scofield, Judge Jacob D. Lowe; the Clark brothers, John, Elisha and Brazillia; amd Benjamin Dodds, along with many others.

Shortly after peace with the Indians, schools of log structure were being erected. The early innovators were definitely interested in education.

These structures were furnished with slanted boards nailed to the walls for desks; the benches consisted of split logs, and a stone fireplace was essential for the colder days.

The schools were generally on a four month per year schedule. The classes consisted of spelling, reading, the Bible, and limited arithmetic.

The early Baptists of the township found solace worshiping in each others home. In 1804, they were recognized and admitted into the Miami Baptist Association. There is the possibility that William Mason's brother, the Rev. John Mason, was accountable for the congregation.

Sometime later, a church not yet built, allowed the members to hold their services in a log schoolhouse along Muddy Creek near the Butler County line.

A church was built later just west of this location along with the establishment of a cemetery. The first names recorded at the church were: John Seward, T.T. Brown and Robert Witham.

In 1808, just seven years before the founding of Mason, the Presbyterian denomination was founded and were gathering in each other's homes for worship. At this time they called themselves the Unity Congregation of the Presbyterian Church.

On December 3, 1812, Noah Cory and David Williamson, the first elders of the church, acquired a lot for $10 from Susan and George

Howard. An adequate church was built.

Families of the first church were: George, Mary, Peter and Hannah Williamson; John and Hannah VanDyke; Judge Jacob D. Lowe; Peter and Catherine Wikoff; John and Jane Lynn; John and Mary Monfort; and Noah and Hannah Cory.

In 1813, Jacob D. Lowe gave to the Unity Congregation a lot just west of the location of their church to be used as a cemetery. This cemetery was used until the early 1870's.

William Mason married again May 11, 1811, to Sarah Murphy, age 21. William and Sarah had four children, Elizabeth, William, Jr., Cynthia and Sarah.

The War of 1812 found twenty-six men from Deerfield Township involved in routing the British. Mason, at this time, aged 52, hired a substitute named Solsberry to go in his place. Mason furnished Solsberry with the essentials and supported the man's wife and family for the duration of his term.

Jacob Derrick Lowe platted a town of sixteen lots on his father's land (Section 31) in 1814. Each of the lots were proportioned five rods by 18 rods 3 feet deep. Two intersecting streets called Harmony and Mechanic were named. The town was named Unity.

In 1815, William Mason platted a town on the property he owned. He duplicated the sixteen lots that Jacob Derrick Lowe did the year before on his plat. Mason decided to change a part of the road from Cincinnati to Xenia. He met with no opposition.

The main road ran southwest to the northeast through Mason's real estate, however, he wanted it to run straightaway east and west.

Mrs. Springman says:

"Starting at the section line on the east side of his property and just north of Muddy Creek, he struck a line due west for a distance that would accommodate two blocks and then angled southwest to meet the original road again. Each of the two blocks was divided into 3 one-half acre lots on each side of the new road.

"Dividing the blocks was a road called Bedle

Station Road, possibly a trail from the North laid out years before to connect this original settlement in Warren County with the main road to Cincinnati.

"On the north side of Mason's new street the lots were only one deep but on the south side four saleable lots behind those on Main Street were planned along a narrow stream of water running from a natural spring to Muddy Creek."

Palmyra, Tennessee, was mentioned in this article previously. Mason possibly named his new town, Palmyra, from the town in Tennessee.

Mason sold only one of his lots by 1816 and none again until 1821. His first sale was lot number 6 to James McCowen for $25. However, Mrs. Springman makes mention of several names being registered on the assorted lots. She says that perhaps the lots were being rented or possibly leased to the assignees.

The Union Methodist Society was organized in 1820. The meetings were held in a log house about two miles east of Palmyra. The name Union was possibly favored because many of the congregation farmed in nearby Union Township.

Members of this assemblage included the following families: Frederick Cline, Brazillia Clark, Michael Bowman, Levi Bowyer, Stephen Bowyer, Elisha Clark, Joel Hanly and John Clap.

A community called Stringtown, located northeast of Palmyra, was situated along the primary road between Cincinnati and Xenia on present U.S. 42.

Just north of the new town a school called the "Old Stone Schoolhouse" was built; it was later used as a recreation center.

A wool and carding mill was built by Richard Sibbett just south of the school, but the venture turned sour and the mill was converted into a hatchery. Stringtown's advancement turned nil.

On April 26, 1823, William Mason sold Lot number 11 to Thomas Fugate for $100, the location being on the northwest corner of Main Street and Section Road. A hotel was built on this corner and for about a hundred years it prospered under many owners.

Down through the years William Mason sold his lots to many families who came to be well-known residents in the County. Among these names were: George Bolander, William Lytle, Jr., Abram Parmeter, Mason Seward (Mason's nephew), William N. Kirkwood, John Kean and Archibald Hosbrook, to name a few.

On May 31, 1828, William Kirkwood bought lot number 12 and this might possibly have been the location of the first post office in Palmyra.

William Mason apparently moved from his farm to a house south of town previous to 1830. The house was located on Road Street and faced east toward Muddy Creek.

A well was situated on the property in which the water was brought up by means of a well sweep. Mason's granddaughter, Flora Tetrick, wrote in her journal: "Grandfather was drawing water and fell in the well head foremost, struck his head and drowned. Ma had his hat for years, a silk plush colonial style, and the cut in the hat was about four or five inches. He drowned in February [1830]."

Palmyra had an official name change on April 25, 1835, to Mason. Apparently a mistake had been made on the part of the federal post office. They had listed the post office in the town on their records as Kirkwood, possibly because the postmaster was named William Kirkwood.

Palmyra was the name suggested by the post office department. However, there was another town by the name of Palmyra in Ohio, and consideration was given to VanBuren as the new name.

Mason was the new name accepted for the pioneer town in honor of its founder. An official consent by the personnel in Washington, D.C. concreted the decision.

SPRINGMAN'S HISTORY OF MASON VALUABLE RESOURCE

Rose Marie Springman is undoubtedly the foremost historian of modern times in the vicinity of Mason. Her book, Around Mason, Ohio: A Story, is possibly one of the most complete accounts of a town history this writer has read.

She also chronicled an abstract concerning the town's history during the 1965 sesquicentennial celebration of the village's founding.

The writer first inserted an article (August 29, 1993) which outlined Mason as one of the first settlements in Warren County. I intentionally stopped during the year 1835. It is during this time period that we shall continue. With Mrs. Springman's kind permission, I shall now draw from these works.

Mason was incorporated in January, 1839, and it was officially accepted by the residents in March, 1840.

An election was immediately held and Mason Seward was elected as the first Mayor. Other elected officials were: Recorder, Joseph Paulding; Treasurer, Peter Voorhis; Marshall, William Walker; Trustees, Ezra Dawson, Abram Durrell, Stephen Murphy and Ephriam Meighan. All held their offices for a period of ten years, until the next scheduled election.

One point of interest that intrigued me was the fact that Deerfield Township had amongst its citizens official Overseers of the Poor. These gentlemen were appointed to oversee the welfare of the population and those ill-adapted to earning a living.

This type person was actually sold on a yearly basis to the lowest bidder. The Overseers could also force undesirables and oppressive persons to leave the township.

Mason was conveniently situated on the road from Cincinnati to Columbus. A newspaper clipping of 1897 details the "early" wagon trains that passed through the village. The article described in effect:

"The principle freight from New York to Cincinnati was hauled in wagons of four, six, or eight horses and these large trains sometimes filled every hotel and stable in the village. Saloons were then unknown; every little house kept root beer, gingerale and sometimes small beer, but the liquid refreshments were always found in the 'tavern.'

"The crack of the whip and the encouraging work of the driver was hailed by the citizens with interest, as it meant meals for man and beast, and in many cases, liberal portions of the overenjoyment."

The early settlers of Mason, primarily because of the personnel, and most assuredly because of the caustic road conditions, were to become self-sufficient.

Sawmills, gristmills and every other type enterprise were founded and operated by the locals.

A gristmill was in operation by the 1850's, its wheels being powered by Muddy Creek.

A sawmill was operated by Sight Mahan.

Raising his own broom corn, Billy Thompkins made and supplied brooms for the town. He was also the village gardener, and was said to have amused the villagers with his "English" brogue.

Mr. Scofield built and sold chairs from his own shop.

Peter Walsh owned and operated the "wagon-maker" shop.

The village shoe-makers were Ellis Kitchel and "Old Man" Hutchinson.

Squire VanDyke was the owner/operator of a jewelry shop and a gun shop. He was said to have been an expert in both professions.

A blacksmith shop was run by "Ole Josie" Bursk. He had the reputation of keeping five fires going at one time during working hours.

Snack time substances were provided by John Thompkins in the form of ginger cakes and cider. Eliza Backus and a Mrs. Farmer were confectioners, no doubt with a knack for this vocation.

The general store had its place in every community. William Leitch, William White, Benton Holdcomb, J.G. Murphy and William S. Dodds owned such enterprises in Mason.

A writer who signed himself "The Old Gray Head," wrote during the period of the nineties that: "The present stores are palaces in comparison to the dark, low ceilinged, 7 X 9 business rooms of old where the dry goods man sold sugar, calico, old rye, pine tar, turpentine and nails, in fact, everything from a needle to a threshing machine."

Of course every community had its own slaughter house. Peter Wikoff and James Bowyer operated the one in Mason. It was said that they sometimes carried as much as $20,000 in their pockets at one time for their business transactions.

Distilleries were scattered about in the County, four or five being in the vicinity of Mason. Corn and rye liquor were considered a commonplace drink. Good rye whiskey was advertised by the early marketer at forty cents a gallon.

Mason was well known for their two potter shops, folks coming from near and far to the village for their pottery. These establishments were owned by William Jared and Silas Ballard.

Jared was claimed to have killed a Negro man and promptly exited the village. Residents claimed the ghost of the murdered man was occasionally seen about town.

Mason played an important roll in the Civil War (1861-1865). Deerfield Township sent a total of 212 men into the military ranks. Most served in Company A, 69th Regiment, Ohio Volunteer Infantry. The names of the volunteers in this Regiment, and other personnel, are listed in Beers History, pages 644 and 645.

Skipping to the 1870's, we find the population of Mason to be about 400. The town government was at this time paid on a yearly wage basis, the salaries being: the Mayor, $9.80; the Marshal, $15.00; the Street Commissioner, $21.00; and Council Members, $9.00.

In 1874, the first jail was built at a cost of $143.00. Also the same year, the council purchased its own printing press, complete with supplies, at a cost of $28.60

Expenditures for the town government in 1875 were $372.59. The mayor received a raise of 20 cents which elevated his annual salary to $10.00.

Rent for a meeting room for the council was

approved at a figure of $5.00 per year.

The first jury trial in Mason was held in 1876.

A dozen street lights were installed on Main Street in the summer of 1877, the total cost being $118.34. The lamp lighter was salaried at $4.00 per month for his daily chore.

Also in this year, the first enclosure was built in which to keep stray hogs, cattle, horses and mules.

Mason, like many other towns in the County, had atrocious roads. Main Street was often referred to by the citizens as the "Mason Jars."

A town law required all the men in town to donate two days' work per year on the streets. This was practiced well into the Twentieth Century.

A railroad was next in line for the village. The Cincinnati & Northern Railway Company completed a three-foot gauge railroad from Cincinnati thru Mason, and on to Lebanon in May, 1881. Mason residents were jubilant concerning this new form of transportation through their town.

This railroad was later, in 1894, widened to a standard gauge (4 ft. 8 1/2 in.), and was renamed the Cincinnati, Lebanon and Northern.

The budget for the year 1882 included a general fund of $200.00, a street fund of $100.00, and a police fund of $50.00.

An engineer had been hired the previous year for a fee of $137.00 to set grades and plat the streets.

Frank Bone, County Engineer, in 1882, was employed to provide curb line markers.

An ordinance was passed by council, in 1883, to forbid the playing of baseball and marbles in the corporation. A fine of $2.00 was imposed, along with a 24 hour jail sentence to violators.

The red brick building on the corner of Main and West Streets was built in 1887 by George Tetrick. It housed a clothing store and the Mason Bank on the first floor, the second floor being the location of the Mason Opera House.

A place of elegance and amusement were provided for the townspeople in the "Gay Nineties," as well as visitors to the Opera House. A seating capacity of over 300 was housed in this exquisite building.

High school commencement programs, musical recitals, dances and the Mason Dramatic Club, all used the Opera House as a gathering place for their particular activity.

Town activities were all centered around this fine establishment, until the school auditorium was constructed on East Street in 1937.

A team of horses and wagon moved ever so slowly in delivering the first bank vault into the town of Mason in 1888. The event actually caused a sensation amongst the townspeople as they viewed the careful unloading of this equipment and its installation.

In 1921, the First National Bank and The Mason Bank merged, the subsequent name being the First Mason Bank.

There is much more to write about this quaint little city, but we shall stop at this time, and perhaps at another time, finish the rest of the story.

THE TINY COUNTY VILLAGE OF FOSTER IS RECALLED

Foster lies in Hamilton and Deerfield Townships, with the Little Miami River bisecting it. Roads that lead to it are the Old Three C Highway, the Fosters-Maineville Road, the Socialville-Fosters and the Davis roads.

The once booming town was named after the Foster family. James H. Foster came to the area in 1841 or 1842 and built a mill and hotel on the east side of the river. The hotel was named the "22 Mile Stand," it being located 22 miles from Cincinnati.

James was considered the leading merchant of the town until his retirement in 1865.

A most unique event happened in the village of Foster on February 13, 1861. The presidential train of Abraham Lincoln passed through the town on its way to Columbus from Cincinnati, traveling on the historic Little Miami Railroad.

An early history of Foster, written in 1868, and inserted into **The Western Star**, points out that the turnpike and railroad crossings were located on the east side of the Little Miami.

The article also states that forty-seven houses were grouped together at corners on both sides of the river. Twenty-seven of this total consisted of business houses and shops.

There were three dry goods and grocery stores, a merchant tailoring house, two boot and shoe establishments, a first class boarding house, a grain depot, a flouring mill, a saw mill, a distillery, a railroad depot, a cooper shop, a blacksmith shop, five beer saloons, and a toll gate house. A quote is made that "of these saloons we have just five too many."

There were two express offices, a post office, a telegraph office and a railroad ticket office.

Mention is made by the writer of the article that there were no schoolhouses or churches, but there were two day schools kept, and a Sabbath school.

The day schools were allocated for the smaller children, and for those who were unlikely to walk one-and-a-half or two miles to the larger district school.

One was a German school and the other American; each was taught by ladies of the village. The writer indicates that a visit had been made to the latter and it was well conducted.

The Sabbath facility was a union school. Although small, the officers and teachers were determined to keep it up.

Foster's population, in 1868, was aggregated at 180. One-hundred and five were German, fifty were American, and twenty-five were Irish.

The German residents were an industrious and business type group. Most owned real estate and acquired a comfortable home with a few acres of ground.

A gristmill was located on the river and cut off about an acre of ground, which formed an island that incorporated three residential homes and a saw mill. The timbers of the covered bridge were framed on this island.

As we now continue our own story with respect to Foster, we find a Mr. M. Obergefell, a German immigrant, arriving from Cincinnati in 1865. He was a merchant tailor by trade and made clothes for the Civil War soldiers while a resident of the Queen City.

He was the builder and proprietor of the "Liberty House," and lived next door. It was said that he could serve up a "square meal" and a "suit of clothes" in equal fashion.

Earl Maag, a former resident, said there were stone cattle pens underneath the hillside building of the Liberty House.

Maag's grandfather purchased the dance hall from Obergefell and renamed it Maag's Hall. The establishment continued in use for dancing until about 1930. Maag said dancing was mainly quadrilles and that German type bands and fiddlers performed.

According to the 1903 Warren County Atlas, Brazilla Clark is credited with building the first mill in Foster in 1806.

Possibly the most significant resident of this quaint town was Governor Jeremiah Morrow. His gristmill was one of the foremost mills in the territory. (More on this mill in another article.)

Augustus Hoppe was a miller for Jeremiah Morrow. He later purchased the Foster Mill from Seth Greely in 1886.

The milling enterprise was a fruitful family business until January 1944, when a mill accident took the life of Edward Augustus Hoppe, son of the original proprietor.

The mill produced cake flour from soft winter wheat and supplied Lebanon and Cincinnati bakeries until its shutdown. It was said to have used a fine silk cloth to sift the flour so that in the end it was truly "as fine as silk." It also produced and distributed pancake four and cornmeal.

The "Pride of Miami" was the mill's top brand. It also did custom grinding for families who brought in their wheat, corn, rye, barley and other grains used primarily for hog feed, as Warren County was one of the major suppliers of processed pork in early times. (The foundation of the old mill and much of the mill race is still in existence at this writing.)

Hoppe's Island was a get-away paradise in the 1920's and '30's. Families from near and far frequented the island paradise for entertainment as well as for relaxation purposes.

The island is a physical protrusion into the Little Miami, it originally being formed by the mill race of Hoppe's mill. However, a portion of the mill race is gone and the formation of an island is no longer visible.

Provisions of the entertainment circle included swimming, canoeing, picnicking, dancing, or perhaps just the place for a family gathering.

Mrs. Bernice Hallam, daughter of Edward Augustus Hoppe, recalled that on Sundays it was impossible for visitors to reserve a picnic table unless at the premises as early as 5 a.m.

Before the horseless carriage, many people drove their horse and buggies to the park.

The famed band leader, Ace Brigode, owned and managed the park for a while, but afterward discontinued it.

After the death of Mr. Hoppe, in 1944, the island went into private ownership. It never again enjoyed the success it had between WW I and WW II.

Glenn and Vivian Irwin purchased the 30 by 50 structure which was, as was previously described, the historical Liberty Hall. The dwelling is located on the 13 1/2 acres which was formerly the mill site and that of Hoppe's Island, now called Glenn Island. (The State purchased the grounds several years ago and transformed it into a public park.)

Travelers, in stagecoach days, crossed the river when traveling the old Montgomery, Hopkinsville and Wilmington Pike, now known as the Old 3 C Highway. They could not have envisioned that the progress of Foster would be put on the back burner because of the huge viaduct that would span the Little Miami many years later.

The viaduct was started in October 1936, and completed October 1, 1938. For the readers who are interested in statistics, the bridge, at a cost of a half a million dollars, took over 90,000 man-hours to complete. Approximately 9000 cubic yards of concrete and 1,200,000 pounds of reinforcing steel were used in the structure.

Six spans, varying in length from 155 to 175 feet, support the viaduct. The deepest concrete pier is securely anchored, its foundation being 27 feet below the water level.

The mile and a quarter project, which includes its approaches, was unique due to the fact that it spanned three forms of transportation; water, rail and motor.

At the center pier, the roadway stands slightly over 75 feet above the Little Miami River.

The post office name in Foster was changed three times, first Foster's Crossings, next Fosters, and lastly, Foster.

"Foster's Crossings" first postmaster was Joseph T. Matthews, his tenure beginning October 27, 1859.

Later postmasters and dates were: William S. Foster, 17 Nov 1863; Daniel K. Gordon, 13 Oct 1865; George W. Thompson, 7 Mar 1866; Albert A. Cooling, 18 Nov 1867; William W. Burroughs, 6 Jan 1874; and, lastly, George B. Fouche, 28 Aug 1883.

"Fosters" was the next selected name and was begun January 7, 1884, with George B. Fouche still retaining the position of postmaster. He was followed by Peter B. Hall, 2 Feb 1887; and again, George B. Fouche, 10 May 1889.

The new name, "Foster," took effect June 7, 1893, with Jacob Englert as postmaster. He was followed by Ernst Hoppe, 29 May 1897; Louise Hoppe, 18 Oct 1910; and John Maag, 8 July 1915.

A long standing tribute to the past was the home of the "Blue Danube Tavern." Long before the turn of the century, it was a fashionable three-story hotel and restaurant.

Earl Maag said his aunt, Theresa Englert, operated the building as a summer resort from 1892 to 1907.

During the flood of 1913, a big log reportedly washed downstream and knocked out one end of the building. The old wooden bridge was also washed away in the flood.

It retained the Blue Danube Tavern name from 1934 until the tavern was purchased in 1975 and completely remodeled. The building, which sits next to the new bridge structure (the George Terwilleger Bridge), is now known as "The Train Stop Inn."

The tavern, prior to its renovation, was known as "a jumping off spot for trouble." One former deputy sheriff said:

"As I remember it, Foster was a thriving little town, full of all kinds of fights and shootings. We never had many calls to the Blue Danube, but when we did, it was a good one."

The last few years saw a gradual decline in the one time prosperous village. As the older citizens moved on it left a vacancy that could not be filled as in olden days.

SOUTH LEBANON IS THE OLDEST TOWN IN WARREN COUNTY

South Lebanon has the distinction of being the oldest town in Warren County.

Originally named Deerfield, the town was, in all probability, laid out in the autumn of 1795, although no date of the survey is available.

One of the first men to explore the lands on the Little Miami was Major Benjamin Stites of Essex County, N.J.

In 1786 or 1787, he descended the Ohio River with a flat boat load of flour and other articles to Limestone (Maysville), Ky.

While in Limestone a band of Indians stole some horses and other merchandise from Stites.

Consequently, arrangements were made to assemble a party of frontiersmen to pursue the culprits to their camp. They followed the trail down the Ohio and up the Little Miami to a point a few miles north of Xenia.

His stolen property was not retrieved, but on

the return trip down the valley of the Little Miami, Stites and his party carefully observed the beauty and fertility of the countryside.

Sometime later, he met Judge John Cleves Symmes of New Jersey, and sparked an interest in the judge concerning a possible speculation of purchasing all the lands between the two Miamis.

(Symmes did purchase all the lands from the Ohio River to an east/west point paralleling the Monroe Road in Lebanon, between the Miamis.)

The name Stites did not turn up as one of the parties in the purchase of the lands, however, he became the owner of 10,000 acres near the mouth of the Little Miami. On this land he founded the first town between the Miamis, Columbia.

He also purchased about 10,000 acres in Warren County, and became the owner of all the land on which the eastern part of Lebanon now stands. This purchase also included lands in which Deerfield (South Lebanon) was laid out.

Major Stites thought that a town situated on the large tract he purchased could be an asset and would add value to all the lands in his acquisition.

Major Benjamin Stites, Benjamin Stites, Jr., and John Stites Gano laid out the town of Deerfield on a top-notch portion of land on the north side of the river. Its location was thirty miles above the Ohio, and was the first town laid out on the Little Miami above Columbia.

The new village was platted with 144 lots of one-half acre each; a total of 100 acres must have been used. Four of the lots were donated to the public, and there was little doubt that these lots would possibly be used at a future time for county buildings, should the town become the county seat.

A custom generally used in the Northwest Territory was that the proprietor of a new town would offer a lot as a gift to any settler who would make a clearing and build a cabin upon it. Deerfield, as well as Columbia and Cincinnati, followed this plan.

The town plat was not recorded until April 23,

1802, and a total of twenty-nine lots were given to the first settlers.

"The Centinel of the Northwest Territory," a Cincinnati newspaper published from 1793 to 1796, says in its concern regarding the establishing of Deerfield:

"That the number of lots in the town of Deerfield which was to be given for building a house or cabin is now complete, there being twenty-five houses or cabins finished and thirty-five lots taken that we first proposed as an encouragement to form the settlement. We hereby forbid all persons whatever from entering upon, cutting down timber on any lot or lots in said town except they purchase. - John S. Gano, & Co. Cincinnati, Jan 25, 1796."

Deerfield, at the turn of the last century, was the most important place on the Little Miami above Columbia. It was a stopping and gathering place for many of the early settlers of the Miami Valley.

Many family heads often left their families at the newly found town while they traveled on and made improvements on their recently purchased lands.

The earliest execution of deeds in Deerfield were initiated by John Stites Gano, and were dated April 14, 1797. They were assigned to: John Kreker, two lots; Peter Keever, two lots; Elnathan Cory, two lots; and Thomas Cory, two lots. The money consideration for these properties was $2.00 per person.

Gano executed deeds the same day to Isaac Lindley, two lots and one outlot of four acres, consideration, $10; Martin Keever, two lots and two outlots, consideration, $10.

James Cory received a deed for three lots on June 20, 1797, consideration, $5.00.

Deerfield hosted the first sermon in Warren County by a regularly ordained Methodist preacher, Rev. John Kobler, on August 9, 1798. (Francis McCormick, a local preacher from the area of Milford, may have preached within the limits of the County before this occasion.)

Rev. Kobler kept a journal of an account of

his first visit to Deerfield and the difficulties he encountered in obtaining a place to preach. His journal is dated August 8, 1798. He writes:

"In the afternoon rode some miles up the Miami river to a small village called Deerfield, where I suppose there might reside ten or fifteen families.

"On arrival there I was invited into a house to see a sick man, whom I found to be a Quaker. Asked if I should pray with him and his family. He said 'No.'

"Reasoned with him on the necessity and propriety of prayer, and enforced the words of St. James - 'Is any afflicted, let him pray;' but he would hear no reason, said he was raised among the Friends and that I should not pray.

"Had with me a letter of introduction to a man who resided in the place who was supposed would receive the Gospel in his house. When this was presented to him, he treated both the message and messenger with utter contempt, saying his house was no place for preaching. Here I went from house to house making inquiry; at last heard that the man above mentioned had a son living in the place, and that his wife was actually a Methodist - hastened on to the son's house, but found that the old man had been there before me, and given them their charge, by using his utmost influence to bolt and bar every door and heart against me.

"Indeed this son had sent word, I afterward understood, that if any of our preachers came through these borders, he wished them to be sent to his house.

"Finally I heard of a Baptist in the place to whom I applied, who received me cordially - his name was Sutton. Lord grant that he and his family may find mercy at that day for when I was a stranger he took me in hungry and he fed me, I was thirsty and he gave me drink. Next day, at an early hour, his house was filled with attentive bearers to whom I shunned not to declare the whole counsel of God."

Gen. David Sutton was one of Deerfield's first

settlers, and for years one of its best known individuals. He was a native of Hunterdon County, N.J.; the date of his arrival in Warren County is unknown.

He was known to have kept a tavern in Deerfield. At this house, elections for Deerfield Township were held under the territorial and early state governments.

Warren County was organized in March 1803, and Gen. Sutton was appointed its first Clerk of Courts, a position he held for twelve years, from 1803 to 1815.

He was a representative to the State Legislature in 1816, 1818 and 1823.

He left his political post of Clerk of Court at the beginning of the War of 1812, raised a company and was given the rank of captain in the first army that was raised in Ohio.

He was sometime later elected colonel at Urbana and was for many years a general in the Militia.

His political stature was originally associated with the Anti-Federalists or Jeffersonian Democrats. However, with the formation of new parties in 1828, he became a member of the Jacksonian Democratic party.

At the time of his death, September 15, 1834, in his sixty-eighth year, he was the democratic candidate for State Senator from Warren County.

Chapter III

TRANSPORTATION

LOCAL SETTLERS DEMANDED ROADS THROUGHOUT WARREN COUNTY

After General Anthony Wayne's victory over the Indians, in 1794 (the Battle of Fallen Timbers), and the Treaty of Greenville was signed in 1795, the settlers made a demand for roads. Mere paths were the only form of roads. The land was bought by the early settlers and found no way of clearing or farming because of constant Indian attacks.

The Act of 1792 was the first provisional act for the construction of highways in Ohio. This act gave the Governor and judges power to begin programs for roads. Under this act, all able-bodied males, 16 years and over, should work on the roads not more than ten days annually.

A man could hire a substitute or send a team of horses. Refusing to work meant a fine of $.50 per day to be paid to the supervisor. If a minimum of twelve persons, who lived in a county or territory petitioned for a road, the petition could be granted.

A surveyor was appointed at the petitioners' expense. The above was recorded in the County clerk's office. The supervisor was responsible for building and maintaining his own roads.

The Act of 1792 was little touched in-so-far as road building was concerned. Another road amendment was to take place, the Act of 1799.

This act changed the minimum age to 21 years, instead of 16, to do labor on the roads. A fine of $.75 per day was leveled on those who refused to work. A road tax, not to exceed one-half of the tax levied to defray territorial or county expenses, was ordered by the County Commissioners.

All public roads or highways were to be kept in repair according to the statutes of law. A notification of twenty days in advance to all owners of improved property whose land the proposed road was to go through was mandatory.

In 1803, Congress set up what was known as the "Three Per Cent Fund," which said in certain terms, that this amount was to be set aside from the net proceeds of the sale of all public lands for the building of public roads and that two per cent was to be set aside for roads leading up to the states boundary. This money was spent to lay out roads rather than for the building of the roads.

The road law of 1804, or the Sheepskin Code, said in effect: "Labor was required of all males between ages of 18 and 50, who were residents of the townships through which the road would pass, each man to work three days or be assessed a fine of $1.00 per day."

A highway supervisor was responsible for the roads in his respective township. These supervisors saw that roads were kept in repair; the funds came from the fine fund.

The law stated that: "All the road commissioners should make certain that all the roads were properly surveyed and plainly marked to a width of 56 feet."

The money to be spent on each road was specified in the Act of 1804, and to assure fair distribution of the fund, each road was divided into sections from 5 to 30 miles with an equal amount appropriated for each.

A description of the road construction is "that all timber and brush should be cut and cleared off at least 20 feet wide, leaving the stumps not more than 1 foot in height [merely for the wagon axles to clear], wet and miry places shall be made of timber covered with earth; small streams that are difficult to be passed shall be bridged."

The Legislative Act of 1817, provided: "Right of way width-66 ft.; cleared of brush and logs-33 ft.; At least 18 feet to be made an artificial road composed of stone, gravel, wood or other material well compacted together in such manner as to secure a firm, even and substantial road, rising in the middle with a gradual arch, and in no case shall the ascent in any turnpike road be greater than 5 degrees."

The Legislative Act of 1824 fixed width of state roads at 66 feet, county roads at 60 feet, and township roads at 40 feet.

Turnpikes

The first law governing turnpikes in Ohio was in 1817. This law said that the right of way shall be 66 feet. It should be cleared of brush and logs to 33 feet. At least 18 feet is to be made an "artificial road" composed of stone, gravel, wood or other material well compacted together so as to secure a "firm, even and substantial road, rising in the middle with a gradual arch, and in no case shall the ascent in any such turnpike road be greater than five degrees."

Tollgates were to be located every ten miles, but no gates were to be erected within two miles of the centers of the terminal towns.

Toll rates were varied, depending on the companies who built the turnpikes. Some charged only $.12 1/2 for two-horse wagon, while other companies charged as much as $.25.

Rates scaled as low as $.01 per head of cattle and $.10 for a score of hogs or sheep. Men on foot paid no toll. Also exempt from toll were those who traveled to church, to funerals, elections, or militia musters. A fine of $5 was levied upon those persons who tried to evade payment at the tollgates by passing them.

Each company was responsible for the maintenance of its own roads. A fine was imposed if the company was found in neglect, such as the condition of the road.

A complete account of the monetary payment was required. Also an account of the receipts from the toll gates was mandatory.

The County or State might at any time purchase a turnpike by paying a sum which, together with the tolls received, would equal the original expenses, plus 12 percent per year. It was under this and similar arrangements that the roads became public property.

In 1826, only one turnpike in Ohio had been completed. This was a turnpike from Warren, in Trumbull County, to Lake Erie, a distance of 48 miles.

The Cincinnati, Lebanon and Springfield Turnpike (U.S. 42) was subscribed for and passed in 1828 and extended to 1830.

Meetings were held at Lebanon by the citizens of four counties. The fifteen miles from Cincinnati to Sharonville, completed in 1833, were very heavily traveled. Two toll gates were installed on this completed section.

With the State's interest in the road by conscription to its capital stock in 1837, the work was pushed forward. The eight and one-half miles from Sharonville to Palmyra (Mason) were completed in 1838 and a third toll gate was erected.

The road was completed through to Lebanon in 1839. The line of the road was changed from the original plans. These plans called for the road to come in on the west side to Main Street. An agreement was made that a southerly route would allow the road to come in on Broadway.

On December 1, 1839, a fourth and a fifth toll gate were erected to the completed section from Cincinnati to Waynesville, a distance of thirty-eight miles. By December 1841 the road was nearly completed to Xenia.

The Dayton, Centerville and Lebanon Turnpike (S.R. 48) was the main artery from Lebanon to Dayton. The road stretched to a distance of a little less than twenty-three miles. In August 1839, only ten miles was completed of which toll was collected.

A description of this turnpike in 1839 is described as such; "This road leads out of Main Street, Dayton, passing over an undulating country. It is well constructed of stone and gravel, and the grades are in all cases easy, with the exception of a hill near Dayton which it becomes necessary to encounter in order to reach Main Street."

The total cost of this road was about $100,000.

The Montgomery Pike (S.R. 3 & U.S. 22) was the road constructed by the Cincinnati, Montgomery, Hopkinsville and Clarksville Turnpike Company.

This company was incorporated in 1834. The charter called for the road to be completed to Roachester within ten years.

At Fosters, a toll bridge was built over the Little Miami. As of November 26, 1839, ten miles of the first portion was finished and tolls were taken in two locations.

The State paid for this portion of the road more than $28,000, and individuals the same amount.

In 1840, the State withdrew its aid and the company was thrown into a financial bind. Because of this embarrassment many farmers who had worked on the road received no pay.

EARLY CANAL SYSTEM PLANS BEGAN IN LITTLE MIAMI VALLEY

After the defeat of the Indians and the Statehood of Ohio was conceived, transportation was the next goal for the early settlers. The canal system was deemed the first major building enterprise within the new State, turnpikes and railroads being the next major improvements.

The canals sparked possibly more public enthusiasm than any other venture the State has ever undertaken, before or since.

These silent waterways provided transportation facilities which in turn transformed the State into a leading industrial entity. Manufacturing, mining, and agriculture were quickly ushered into a competitive atmosphere that helped shape the Buckeye State into what it is today.

What is probably not known to many of the readers of this column is that plans for the first canal in the State were incorporated in the valley of the Little Miami.

Imagine this valley being a huge lake from the Ohio River to Waynesville! Yes, this was the plan.

The first legislation for the first canal in Ohio was formed on the 25th of October, 1816. This organization was called the Little Miami Canal and Banking Company.

A special act was passed December 29, 1817, with eleven commissioners or managers named to head the project, the names being: Abijah O'Neal, John Satterthwaite, Richard Mather, Thomas Graham, Isaac Stubbs, Ralph W. Hunt, Jeremiah Morrow, John Elliot, Patterson Hartshorn, Zachens Biggs and John Armstrong.

Most of these men were owners of mills on the Little Miami and a majority of them resided in Warren County. Any four of them could conduct the affairs of the company until the election of the first board of directors.

The function of the company was "to construct such dams and locks and to open such canals as may be necessary for a practical ascending and descending boat navigation on the Little Miami river from the confluence of said river with the Ohio river to the town of Waynesville."

Another authorization which the board had was "to erect and establish waterworks and to carry on manufacturing and banking."

The dams were to be constructed "in such a manner that the river should not be obstructed in any way different from the obstructions occasioned by the dams already constructed on the river."

Article I of the charter called for the sale of ten thousand shares at twenty-five dollars each, total monies set at $250,000. Books for the subscription of stock were to be opened on the first Monday in March, 1818, at Cincinnati, Milford, Gainsborough, Lebanon and Waynesville.

The Cincinnati and Lebanon newspapers were chosen to announce a notice prior to the time of payment of any installment of stock. A twenty-five year time period was the restriction for the charter to run its limits, or until January 1, 1843.

Construction of the canal was to begin at a point nearest the Ohio River.

Early development of many river waterways was accomplished by building dams across them to increase their depth. In these dams were placed locks through which the boats could pass.

A requirement of the charter stated that the "private property of stock holders in proportion to the stock they held was liable for the payment of all debts of the company, and if the work of canalizing the river from the Ohio to Waynesville was not completed in five years, or if after the completion of the work the company should suffer the navigation of the river to remain obstructed for more than fifteen months at any time, the charter was to cease and determine and the stockholders were to be liable for all debts of the company."

Apparently the project of the Little Miami Canal and Banking Company never got off the ground, although it was granted full powers under the banking law of 1816.

While roaming through my papers, I ran across an article written in Waynesville's **Miami Gazette**, dated April 12, 1933, by A.C. Thompson which parallels the aforementioned subject.

Mr. Thompson mentions that before the depression of the 1930's, occasional rumors were heard of something going to be done in the Little Miami and Great Miami Rivers concerning the dredging and the building of dams, the idea being to canalize the rivers and thus create a water route to Lake Erie.

His summation was that an all water route from Cincinnati to New York could be established much like the old canal systems.

He also stated that sometime later he read a news item from Washington, D.C., in which an order had been given for a survey of the Little Miami River, "with a view to dredge and canalize the stream."

Mr. Thompson's calculations were that "taking the volume of water and the head that can be procured in the stream at points above the mouth of Caesar's Creek, from ninety to one hundred horse power can be developed for each unit of power, and below Caesar's Creek 125 to 150 h.p. can be developed for each unit.

"Or by installing one water power electric unit at Oregonia, one unit at Waynesville, these three units combined will develop 300 h.p., and, by installing one of the direct connected hydro-electric units at several different points between Waynesville and the mouth of the stream, one thousand horse power can be procured in the distance of forty miles."

Thompson, in his article, suggests that a bear-trap type dam could be utilized if the purpose of the river were to be used only as a source of power. He says these dams should have a roof shape bracket, the peak of the bracket to be lowered to the low water level of the stream and raised to the desired height by hydraulic power.

Thus, on account of the low banks of the stream, the head of water could be held for developing power. At times of flood stage or ice gorges, the bracket could be lowered, leaving the stream to flow clear.

The damming of the Little Miami in this day and time seems preposterous, but, look what happened to Caesar's Creek.

DO YOU REMEMBER THE D. L. & C. RAILROAD?

The County of Warren, with its rather flat lands, and need for railroads, was perfectly situated for the advance of the mode that is still very much in existence.

One railroad that certainly made its own way was the Dayton, Lebanon & Cincinnati Railroad.

On December 20, 1887, the Toledo, Delphos & Burlington Railroad Company, a narrow gauge system, completed a road from a point on its line between Xenia and Dayton, through Lytle and

Dodds to Lebanon, between the last two places using the old grade of the defunct Miami Valley road.

At Lebanon, connection was made with the Cincinnati, Lebanon & Northern, (C L & N) and for a while, trains were operated through from Cincinnati to Dayton and Toledo. The company met with financial reverses and the road, in time, was sold to the Lewis estate and changed to a standard gauge. The name was changed to the Dayton, Lebanon & Cincinnati Railway.

The Dayton-Lebanon-Cincinnati Railroad (D L & C) was called the "rapid transit" (sometimes called "The Damn Long Comin") of its day. This railway company was organized January 29, 1889.

On June 1, 1892, it was leased from the Cincinnati, Lebanon & Northern, (C L & N) which was the successor of the Cincinnati Northern. The line ran from Dodds to the corporation line at Lebanon, a little more than six miles of road.

This property was taken upon a lease of 99 years, renewable forever. The lease provided that the C L & N Company might have the joint use of the lease track upon the payment of a part of the maintenance.

A contract was also entered into by which the D L & C had a right to entrance into Lebanon. At the time of the organization of the D L & C, Henry Lewis transferred to that company the 17 miles of road owned by him.

An article found in the Warren County Historical Society, written by Mr. Walter Kenrick, describes the method of construction used in the building of the D L & C Railroad. It is as such:

"A contract was entered with Frederick B. Douglas, a railroad contractor, to build said road. This road was to be a narrow gauge and was constructed the following year.

"In building the grade Mr. Douglas used a machine, which was called a grader. This machine was constructed mainly of wood; was a framework 8 ft. wide and at least 20 feet long. In the center was a huge plow that could be raised or lowered by chains.

"This plow delivered the dirt on an endless

belt, which deposited the dirt on the bank or on the fill, as the case might be. It was powered by mules or horses, 8 to 10 in front pulling and 4 to 6 in the rear pushing by means of a long tongued cart attached to the rear.

"As the machine was rather cumbersome to turn, they would drive as far as possible on the right-of-way before turning; first on the fill, and then thru the cuts.

"In laying the track first the ties would be carried by a workman on their shoulders to the grade; these would be placed about 8 ft. apart and then the rails spiked down. Over this the men would push small cars loaded with ties and afterward rails.

"Then the work train would be run forward after more ties had been placed under the rails. In this way the work moved forward until the trestle was completed."

The D L & C Railroad was a narrow gauge railroad whose rails had a width of three feet. (Standard gauge of rails is four feet eight and one-half inches.)

Among the other narrow gauge railroads were The Cincinnati Northern Railway Company and The Toledo, Delphos & Burlington Railroad (which owned a narrow gauge road from Delphos to Dayton and one from Dayton to Ironton).

The connecting link between the Lebanon road and the Toledo road, a distance of 17 miles, was made by the T D & B Railroad, which constructed a road from the Lebanon junction on the D & I division to the northern end of the Lebanon road.

The completed road from Dayton to Lebanon was then in operation, and for a time daily trains were run from Toledo through Dayton, and Lebanon to Cincinnati.

Afterward, the C H & D (Cincinnati-Hamilton & Dayton) acquired the Dayton and Ironton division and the 17 miles of connecting link were sold by the receivers of the T D & B Company to Mr. Fairbanks, of Indianapolis, afterwards vice-president.

The property was not used for three or four

years, when it was purchased by Henry Lewis, of Cincinnati, who widened the track to standard gauge. With this move the running of trains to Lebanon was started.

The D L & C started its northward journey from Cincinnati with the main stops at Norwood, Lebanon, Dodds, Centerville and on to Dayton.

Stops in between included Kitchner, Venable (Lower Springboro Road), Edgewood (S.R. 73), and Lytle. Many farmers and individuals appeared along the line to create unscheduled stops. They simply motioned for the train to stop and they merely "hitched a ride."

This was the official announcement given by Vice-President Frank Brandon in **The Western Star** Thursday morning [date unclear]. He said:

"The construction work is just about complete, and were it not for the fearfully cold weather trains would now be running over the new connection.

"The line has been built in a most substantial manner and will carry the heaviest traffic. Contracts for local stations at the various street crossings in the city of Dayton will be let early in the coming week, so that passenger traffic can be established immediately upon the construction trains being removed from the work, and the line is now surfaced so that traffic can be handled with speed and safety."

Continuing and in a retrospective mode Mr. Brandon said:

"The Dayton, Lebanon & Cincinnati Railroad was organized in the year 1889 and operated a line when completed during the following year, from Lebanon Junction to Lebanon, a distance of 23.1 miles.

"The road was never completed or operated in anything like a satisfactory manner until the year 1902, after the property had been taken over by Mr. Appleyard.

"During the years 1902-3, a large amount of money was spent on the main line, and in acquiring the right of way and additional terminal properties in Dayton, and under the Appleyard management, the cut-off line was built from

Hempstead to the Dayton State Hospital."

Nothing further was accomplished in completing the property until after the receivership and reorganization of the property in June of 1907, when the Dayton, Lebanon & Cincinnati Railroad and Terminal Company was organized and took over the property,

The same was operated by this corporation, a reorganization of the bondholders of the old company, until the stock of the corporation was taken over by the present holders early in the year 1908.

However, through the cooperation of the Chamber of Commerce of Dayton, the National Cash Register and many of the enterprising citizens of Dayton, including the city press, the franchise to cross the streets of that city was obtained.

In April 1909, actual construction of the line into Dayton was begun. Work was very tedious and slow in the expansion of the railroad in this region.

The building of the bridges and other specific work delayed the completion for some time. However, the drudgery paid off. The line was completed to the National Cash Register in September, 1909.

The officers of the D L & C were M.I. Sternberger, President; Frank Brandon, Secretary and Treasurer; H.S. Willard, Secretary; Howard W. Ivins, Asst. Secretary; H.C Mordue, General Freight and Passenger Agent; and E. Kahoe, Superintendent.

The D L & C made its first trip over the line from Lebanon to Dayton on Thursday, March 10, 1910.

The train left Union Station at Lebanon promptly at 7:00 o'clock a.m. The crew of this first run was composed of: Engineer, Will S. Thompson; Conductor, Herbert Kennedy; Fireman, Ray Schwartz; Brakeman, Frank Hill; and Master Mechanic, Byron Wright.

The official body was made up of Vice-President Frank Brandon; Superintendent, E. Kahoe; General Passenger Agent, H.C. Mordue; and Assistant Secretary Howard W. Ivins.

The first ticket was purchased by Tom Spencer, president of the Oregonia Bridge Company, the ticket being number "0."

He had choice of any of the seats of the three coaches, however, he picked a seat in the rear of the last coach.

Not too many people showed up for the exiting of the first excursion. The first stop was made at the Main Street station and, the first stop to discharge people was made at Deland.

However, many farmers and their families lined their doorways to cheer the new rail line. Large crowds had gathered at Lytle and Centerville to greet the train.

The narrow gauge was to be up-dated by the assemblance of a wider gauge. This would standardize the railroad system to be more adaptable to other railroads in the area.

Converting the narrow gauge track to a standard gauge was an achievement undertaken by many. On a Sunday morning in 1889, farmers, railroaders, stockholders and businessmen by the hundreds, responded to a general all out call to help widen the railroad. All along this line they simply "heaved-to" and moved the rails apart.

The 1913 flood did not stop the D L & C. It was the only train with through traffic from Cincinnati to Dayton.

The D L & C ran passenger trains as late as 1930. The freight carriers were discontinued in the depression years, about 1936. The automobile was taking over. The diminishing of the passenger numbers and the daily trips took its toll on this excellent line.

TRACTION LINE ONCE LINKED ALL CORNERS OF WARREN COUNTY

The Cincinnati and Miami Valley Traction Company

The Cincinnati and Miami Valley Traction Company ended at midnight May 13, 1939. This ended a means of transportation which had successfully carried the population of the Miami Valley for a period of over forty years. The economic interests of the communities that it served had seen no better means of progression in the whole history of the valley.

The first section of the interurban line was built from Fifth and Jefferson streets in Dayton to Carrmonte in 1894.

A year later a discussion was settled that a realization of a connection from Dayton, through Franklin, to Cincinnati was inevitable. In 1896, a dream came true with the connection of the two cities.

The traction company experienced a problem with considerable difficulty in obtaining a permit to cross the Cincinnati, Hamilton & Dayton tracks south of Middletown near Trenton.

A much publicized court battle ensued in which public sentiment was definitely against the railroad company. The permit was finally granted and the final link in the line was completed on August 24, 1897.

The traction line schedule allowed regular cars each way every thirty minutes for about 18 hours a day.

Up until 1913 the traction line through Franklin experienced little trouble. However, the flood of 1913 washed out much of the track and many of the bridges over the Great Miami were washed away. Repairs were quickly made and service was resumed in record time.

The company had many name changes. The Cincinnati and Miami Valley Traction Company's name existed until 1902 when several Ohio interurban lines consolidated to form the Cincinnati, Dayton and Toledo Company.

Included in the merger were the Southern Ohio Traction Company, the Cincinnati and Northern Railroad Company, The Miamisburg and Germantown Traction Company, and the Hamilton and Lindenwald Electric Company.

Six years later, in 1908, the lines were known as the Ohio Electric Railway Company which operated the traction company until 1918, when the Cincinnati and Dayton Traction Company took over the business.

In 1926, the name was again changed to Cincinnati, Hamilton and Dayton Traction Company. The final name change came in January 1930, when the traction line was taken over by the Cincinnati and Lake Erie Railroad Company.

From the beginning, the speed of the traction cars had been increased as the demand for faster transportation became evident. The original cars, were able to average between 35 and 40 miles per hour.

In 1903, the interurbans were traveling at a maximum speed of 50 miles per hour and the cars used at the time of termination of the line were capable of traveling, on straight stretches, speeds up to 70 miles per hour.

The Lebanon & Franklin Traction Company

The Lebanon and Franklin Traction Company was a very reliable transportation system from Lebanon to Franklin, and vice-versa.

Obtaining the property rights for this line was fairly easy because the farmers saw the need to transfer their products. These products such as vegetables, fruits, and even animals were shipped via this route.

This line was used mainly for passenger service, and also for transfer of students attending the different schools in Lebanon.

The route was finished in July 1903. The actual grading started at the Rhoades hill south of Franklin on what is now S.R. 123. There are still traces of the old line at the top of the hill, and the old line is still fairly visible traveling toward Franklin.

The traction line ran on the west side of S.R. 123 from Franklin to Red Lion. It then was laid out to proceed in a straight line to the junction of Kirby Road and S.R. 123.

The line then proceeded on the east side of S.R. 123 to Markey Road, and then south and east of the latter road to S.R. 63; thence east on S.R. 63 to Lebanon with the line running on the south side of the latter highway.

There are still many signs of the Lebanon-Franklin Traction line that can be seen from S.R. 123, and also some visible signs on Markey Road.

The traction line purchased two cars built by the Barney & Smith company, the dimensions being 40 feet long, 8 feet 4 inches wide and 12 feet high. The car numbers were 103 and 104.

Charles Kohr was the conductor for the entire lifetime of the line. Other employees were Will Whitley, Fred Bluss, William Swink and Perry Schwartzel.

Standard gauge of the line was 4 feet 8 1/2 inches which is considered uniform in modern times. The electric generator was located at 1122 South Main St. in Franklin. This generator was shared with the Miami Valley Traction Company.

Franklin's office was at Brubaker's restaurant on the corner of Sixth and Main Streets. The stop in Lebanon was in front of the library and the tickets could be purchased at the Lebanon Hotel (now The Golden Lamb).

Because of the financial woes of the line, which was constantly in monetary trouble, it was forced to cease operations December 31, 1918.

The Interurban Railway and Terminal Company

A company was formed in 1900 which was named The Interurban and Terminal Company. This was another traction line that was to eventually run through Warren County.

During the first two years of its operation a division named the Cincinnati and Eastern built a route to New Richmond from the Queen City paralleling the Ohio River most of the way, with its route passing by Coney Island.

The Suburban Division was another branch which had its terminal at Bethel.

The Rapid Railway was a division of the line that extended from Cincinnati to Lebanon. The line reached Mason in May, 1902; it reached Lebanon September 26, this date being the last day of Lebanon's Centennial commemoration.

The route of the Rapid Railway was north from

Cincinnati to Mason, Kings Mills, South Lebanon and on to the "City of Cedars."

The office in Kings was located on King Avenue. The main attraction for this stop was the Kings Mills Powder Company and the Peters Cartridge Company.

Workers from the entire area used the line for transportation to and from work.

A double deck bridge framework, 60 feet high and 330 feet long, was located coming east from Mason over Dawson Street to Kings Mills.

The late Marion Snyder stated in one of his articles concerning an item in the Street Railway Journal, dated November 21, 1903, that "near this hillside (at one end of the trestle) has been cut and a solid stone retaining wall erected."

The projection of the line ran a short distance south of the Kings Mills Road from Mason to Kings Mills.

South Lebanon's ticket office was located at Victor Van Riper's store. Mr. Snyder relates that Saturday nights found the cars filled to capacity to and from South Lebanon.

This last night of the week found the cars packed out, initially for special events up and down the line, plays, dances, parties and the like.

One very special person to ride the line was Warren G. Harding, many years before his Presidency.

Standing room only was generally the rule on Saturdays. Crowding onto the open area of the cars on the back was a reality, or occasionally a courageous person would stand on the step rather than wait for the next car.

Mr. Snyder relates an incident which occurred to one Bob Klick, a Kings Mills resident. As was stated, Saturday night was a gala time and the cars were full of frolic-makers. He writes:

"One had neglected to turn the switch back at the Opera House so that the car, instead of going on down the hill towards the railroad suddenly swung left onto Main Street and around the block again.

"The swerve caused Bob to lose his balance, fall off the car (he was hardly on it) and he started rolling down the hill where the car was supposed to go. Of course the car got back where it belonged and Bob rode home."

Mr. Snyder also discloses that French Smith recalled riding the traction from Mason to Kings Mills so he and three other teenage boys could play pool. Mason's rules applied for pool playing only if you were eighteen. As he recalled, the fare from Mason to Kings was ten cents one way.

The Rapid Railway was not only a passenger line. It was also, like the Lebanon-Franklin Traction Line, a rail for farm produce and the like. This particular division of the Interurban Railway and Terminal Company operated for twenty years, from 1902 to 1922.

FLATBOATS BROUGHT EARLY SETTLERS DOWN RIVER TO OHIO VALLEY

The closing of the French and Indian War can be said to perhaps have triggered the migration to the West. At this time the English took permanent possession of the Ohio valley.

Traders and private individuals were preparing to invade the lands along the Ohio with purpose to trade with the Indians. George Crogan, an early explorer of the Ohio country, was permitted to negotiate with the Indians.

The Illinois country was considered the most profitable trade territory.

Fort Pitt, which was positioned at the head waters of the Ohio, was in a fine situation to prosper as a boat-building center.

Boat building was set up as early as 1765 at Pittsburgh. Materials were hauled in by way of Philadelphia in wagons and by packhorses, timber being excluded. The firm of Baynton, Wharton, and Morgan employed six-hundred wagons for this excursion.

The Treaty of Fort Stanwix, in 1768, opened up an entirely new era in river transportation. The

Spring and Summer of 1770 saw a great tide of river travelers. From 1768 through 1770, an aggregate count of river passengers was between four and five thousand settlers.

The greatest interest for the settlers in the new territory was to begin a new life with more favorable living conditions. The lands on the upper Ohio were not best suited for these conditions, so their course was turned toward Kentucky.

With the arrival of the new adventurers at Pittsburgh, a craft that would accommodate the pioneers and allow for the proper transportation down the Ohio was needed. Advertising for sale "boats of every dimension," was the occasion at Elizabeth, Pennsylvania.

The evolution of the flatboat was at first canoes, piroques and rafts. The original flatboats were at first only from four to six feet in width, but soon were made much larger.

The construction was of green oak plank. No nails or iron was used in building them. The heavy oak planks were fastened by wooden pins to still heavier frames of timber.

The seams were at first closed with pitch or tar, but this being very expensive, tow or some other pliant substance was afterward used in caulking. Because of its construction, descending the river was the only practical way of navigating.

There is a record of a semi-mechanical boat that was built at Fort Pitt in 1761 by William Ramsey. This apparatus consisted of two small boats joined together by a swivel in such a way as to make one.

The boat was propelled by wheels attached to a treadle which was moved by the feet of the operator. As impractical as this boat was, it could turn in a shorter space than could smaller boats and that it could rise over falls with great safety.

Flatboats in this period of time were of different varieties, they being named ark, barge, broadhorn, Kentucky boat, and New Orleans boat.

These craft were useful in their own way, but the standard flatboat had preference over the others because of its size and practicality.

These rectangular shaped craft had generally boarded up sides from two to three feet high. The width and length had no standard size. The family generally set size preference.

The lesser sort had no covering, but were provided with a shed in the rear for horses and cattle, and a cabin forward for the use of the owner and his family.

The craft that was used for shorter trips were called Kentucky boats or broadhorns. The boats that were used for longer trips were called New Orleans boats and were covered throughout their entire length.

The propelling of these boats was a task in itself. All flatboats were propelled by "sweeps" which were mounted on the sides. They also consisted of a rudder and a short oar in front known as the "gouger."

A "hawser" was a strong rope which was mounted to a reel on board that could be attached to a tree stump on shore, which in turn allowed the boat to be wound ashore.

The flatboat was designated as "the boat that never came back." It was broken up at the end of its journey and the lumber used for building houses, furniture, etc.

The first parties to reach Columbia (now a part of Cincinnati) used the planks for construction of sheds and camps, this being the only form of habitable quarters erected at the close of the year 1788.

By the close of February 1789, four cabins had been erected at Cincinnati, and ten or twelve camps or shanties had been built with the materials from the flatboats.

A lady told of her first residence at Cincinnati which was a log cabin. The furniture consisted of one bedstead, one table, one chair and several wooden stools. The flooring was of boat plank which was better than that of most of her neighbors, who had for floors logs split in two and laid flatside uppermost.

General Josiah Harmar had noticed the large number of flatboats descending the Ohio and ordered the officer of the day to take an account of the number of boats which passed the garrison.

From the tenth of October, 1786, until the 12th of May, 1787, 127 boats, 2,689 souls, 1,333 horses, 756 cattle and 102 wagons passed Muskingum bound for Limestone (Maysville, Ky.), and the Rapids (Louisville, Ky.).

An average of 3000 flatboats descended the Ohio River every year between 1810 and 1820.

At Limestone the boats became so numerous that they frequently were set adrift in order to make room for others.

General Harmar noted that he had purchased at Limestone from 40 to 50 flatboats at the moderate price of from $1 to $2 each, to be used in the construction of Fort Washington at Cincinnati.

In the winter of 1799, David Lowry loaded a flatboat at Dayton with grains, pelts and five hundred venison hams. The trip proceeded down the Great Miami in the spring. With the raising of the waters at this time of year, a two month trip to New Orleans was accomplished.

Lowry's cargo was sold, along with his boat, and he returned by horseback. This was the first recorded trip from Dayton thru Franklin to New Orleans.

Warren Countians were instrumental in building flatboats. These boats were made as cheaply as possible.

John N.C. Schenck, of Franklin, in 1812, moved his trading post and home to the north of the bridge where a pier was erected at the rear of the building to the river's edge so flatboats could dock. Free rooms and plenty of food was available for travelers. Schenck retired a wealthy man after 35 years with his store.

William Crosson, an early citizen of Harlan Township, was employed by William Paxton, a miller on the Little Miami, to travel on a flatboat to New Orleans.

In 1818, Crosson loaded a flatboat at Stubbs

Mill with produce and went with it to New Orleans. He disposed of his cargo and walked home, making the journey from New Orleans to Cincinnati in twenty-one days. Crosson engaged in this vocation for several years afterward.

In Dayton, on March 26 and 27th, 1825, a fleet of thirty or more boats were waiting for the river to rise because of a rain that had occurred a few days before.

The people of Dayton were anxiously awaiting, shouting and hurrahing the gentle rise of the river. On the 26th, Saturday, many wagons were nervously being unloaded to the waiting boats. Flour, pork, whiskey, etc., was being loaded for the eventual trip to New Orleans.

An estimate of the worth of the goods was set at approximately $100,000. On Sunday, the 27th, the water slowly began to fall and the boats got underway. Most of them finished their journey.

THE CINCINNATI, WILMINGTON, AND ZANESVILLE RAILROAD

As we all know the Little Miami Railroad ran through the historic town of Morrow. But did you know that another line also ran through the town in the same time period?

This line was named the Cincinnati, Wilmington & Zanesville Railroad. It was more commonly known as the "Sheepskin Line" by local residents.

It fell by the wayside as did many other lines in the early days of railroading. Only so much traffic in the middle of the 19th century was available because of the lack of dollars in which to invest in new railroads.

The late Marion Snyder wrote in his article on this subject that "the first plans called for the line to come as directly west from Clarksville as possible and connect with the Little Miami at Hammel, a small way-station a couple miles north of Morrow."

He also wrote that William H. Clement, President of the Little Miami Railroad, might have possibly used his influence to bring the C. W. & Z. R. R. directly into Morrow and build the village up as a railroad town and shipping area.

According to the 1903 Atlas map of Salem Township, six bridges were built over Todd's Fork in order to bring the line into Morrow. However, if the line had proceeded to Hammel, only bridge would have been built.

The Hon. R.B. Harlan, Representative from Clinton County in the Lower House of the Legislature, introduced a bill asking for a new railroad line so-named the Cincinnati, Wilmington and Zanesville Railroad. The charter was granted February 4, 1851.

(The route of the line ran from Morrow in Warren County through the counties of Clinton, Fayette, Pickaway, Fairfield, Perry and a portion of Muskingum to Zanesville.)

The name of Wilmington was added to the name in honor of the County in which the bill was introduced. The 1882 Clinton County history expressed that the line would be a great through trunk line.

But the mistake, according to the history, was made in connecting it to the Little Miami Railroad at Morrow, and using its facilities thence to Cincinnati.

Surveys and estimates were completed from Morrow to Lancaster, a distance of 90 miles, in November 1850.

The building contract was awarded to A. DeGraff, with Clinton County subscribing $200,000 for its construction. Actual work was commenced in December 1851.

Actual track laying began at Morrow in the latter part of March 1853. A certain amount of delay was at first sustained due to bridge building and the terrain.

In August 1853, the road was completed to Wilmington. On the 11th of that month a grand celebration was held in honor of this momentous occasion. From 10,000 to 15,000 folks were present, including about 2,000 who arrived on the 11:15 a.m. train of 20 cars.

Five oxen and a quantity of sheep were barbecued; enough food was left over to feed a regiment. The table arrangements were assembled in the form of a square 1,200 feet long. Many adjoining counties were represented; a fine brass band was present from Cincinnati. Men of prominence made speeches commemorating the event.

The main event train departed at 3:30 p.m. and by six o'clock all was again quiet in the village.

On August 15, 1853, trains began running regularly between Cincinnati and Wilmington, one a day each way, the fare being set at $1.60 per trip.

Mr. Linton, a Representative of the Ohio Legislature from Fayette County, requested that the town of Washington Court House be included in the charter, but "this the gentleman from Wilmington refused to do."

Judge Daniel McLain was employed as representative of the people of Washington C.H., to go to Columbus and express their interest. He eventually succeeded in securing the preferred change.

Judge McLain was elected one of the directors of the new railroad. He took a number of trips to the East, and by November 1852, over two thousand tons of Swedish made iron rail had reached New Orleans headed for Cincinnati.

With the terminus of the road being at Morrow, instead of Cincinnati, the earnings of the road were insufficient to meet the expense.

The road to Washington C.H. was completed November 24, 1853, and the trains started their run on that day.

Regular trains began running through to Zanesville in 1856, the total accumulative mileage from Morrow being 132.

Opening of this railway unveiled communications between Cincinnati and all eastern seaboards, by connecting with the original Central Ohio Railroad.

Fairfield County commissioners subscribed $250,000 for the payment of which bonds were issued bearing seven percent.

These bonds were sold throughout all the counties in which the line operated. The allotted funds were used for bridges, tunnels, ties and the essential part of the iron.

The original charter of the General Assembly of 1850 approved authorization of taking a certain amount of stock in the newly-formed railroad, provided a majority of the people favored the measure and would so vote at a specified general election. All approved of this measure except Perry County.

Two principal routes were favored in Perry County; New Lexington or Rush Creek Valley, and the Somerset Route. Each raised about $100,000 with stipulations that the road be made on a specified line.

It was not until September 1852, that a decision was made at Zanesville to locate on the New Lexington or Rush Creek Valley route.

In the summer of 1854 the citizens of Perry County and New Lexington witnessed the first train from the West. For several months the train stopped at this place for the transfer of passengers and mail from railroad car to stages bound for Zanesville; the reason for this maneuver was because of the construction of a tunnel, located three miles east of New Lexington.

The railway began to have financial difficulties almost from the beginning. The company was unable to comply with the conditions of the mortgage, having taken out first, second and third mortgage bonds.

The monies were expended in the construction and equipment of the road.

On February 22, 1857, a court decision was made through a Receiver in the case, to exercise authority to take possession of the road and property, and to "operate the road for the interest of all parties concerned."

The road was operated under this decree until a plan of reorganization was perfected. The court ordered on June 10, 1863, that the mortgaged property be sold, with such sale to go toward all debts and liabilities.

The sale was confirmed October 17, 1863, the

buyer being Charles Moran of New York.

Stipulations were made that the creditors and stock holders should be made "recognizable as a body corporate," and the railroad should be run under the charter.

A name change was made to the railway on March 10, 1864, under the new title of the Cincinnati & Zanesville Railroad Company.

It was still to be operated under the original franchises of the Cincinnati, Wilmington & Zanesville Railroad. Moran deeded property to the operation held by him in trust.

Erasmus Gest was selected as the new President and Superintendent. The newly organized company now saw daylight at the end of the tunnel. In a period of 26 months a balance of $80,000 was placed to the credit of the road and invested in rolling stock and improvements.

In due time a failure in the payment of its obligation caused its downfall. On December 1, 1869, the road with all its franchises, real estate, machine shops, depot buildings, and rolling stock was sold at auction at the door of the Cincinnati Court House, the purchaser being Thomas L. Jewett, President of the Pennsylvania Central Company. The purchase price was $1,004,000. (One source says "$1,400,000.")

Jewett operated the road under his complete control until September 1, 1870, when the Cincinnati & Muskingum Valley Railway Company came into possession of it.

On May 1, 1873, the road was leased by the Pittsburgh, Cincinnati & St. Louis Railroad Company under lease for 99 years.

The old railway has since gone into oblivion. Some of the names mentioned by Marion Snyder as working for the road were George Shawhan, Vess Zentmeyer, Clyde Miranda, Harry Drake, Byron Hartsock and Charles Durig.

HISTORIAN DETAILS EARLY CANAL CONSTRUCTION

In 1822, Governor Allen Brown of Cincinnati succeeded in setting up a Canal Commission. An act, called the Enabling Act, was started which established the construction of the Ohio and Erie Canal. This became law February 4, 1825. The proposition also provided for the building of the Miami-Maumee Canal from Cincinnati to Dayton and thence to Toledo.

Creation of the Miami Canal was to help move the produce and commodities to and from the leading area cities of Dayton and Cincinnati. The canal could create a new market for the farmers and the businessmen. With the Ohio and Erie Canal completed from Cleveland to the Ohio River, a link to the lakes from Cincinnati via Dayton would serve the purpose.

The first spadeful of dirt for the Miami Canal was dispersed of by New York Governor DeWitt Clinton on July 21, 1825, at Middletown, Ohio. The second was by Governor Jeremiah Morrow of Warren County.

A choice to follow the Great Miami River from Middletown to Hamilton was made by the Canal Commissioners.

The route from Hamilton to Cincinnati was to cross the ground to the Mill Creek Valley where the ground was low and at that time very swampy. Across this plain the canal was from six to ten feet above the level of the surrounding country.

Leaving the plain and stepping down two locks, the canal followed the western bank of the east ford of Millcreek to Lockland. There it crossed the west fork of Millcreek and dropped four locks to the nine mile level leading into Cincinnati.

The upper sill in the second of these locks was strangely on the exact level of Lake Erie - 573 feet above tide water. Continuing three miles to Carthage, the canal crossed to Millcreek's east bank, and from there it emerged into the heart of Cincinnati.

The locks from Middletown to the head of Millcreek were; one at Rockdale, two at Hamilton, two at Amanda and one just below Middletown. Lockland had four locks, thus the name Lockland.

The Middletown-Hamilton section was completed on September 26, 1826. The resevoir for this section was a dam built about two miles north of Middletown. Eight thousand cubic feet of water per minute was provided for the canal.

On July 1, 1827, water was released into this section. In August 1827 the first trip on the canal was made.

In 1827, the upper line was completed to the head of Main Street in Cincinnati. Lines of people gathered to see the rush of water into the canal. However, a disappointing occurrence happened; there was no rush of water! The canal bed had set so long that the water just soaked in. It was almost four months before the water sufficiently filled the channel enough to allow for travel.

Canal laborers were men who came from near and far. The newcomers that worked on the canals were mostly from Germany and Ireland. During the first few years laborers were paid thirty cents a day with plain board and were lodged in a shanty. During the first four months they also received, in addition to board, a "jiggerful of whiskey."

In the summer of 1828, work was continued on the northern section up the valley of the Great Miami; four locks to Franklin, two to Miamisburg, two to (West) Carrolton and three to the Mad River above Dayton.

The canal bed was 40 feet wide and 4 feet deep, the towpath being 10 feet wide for the horses or mules which drew the boats.

The Miami Canal was not all business ventures. Cincinnati had a swimming club called the Canal Swimmer's Society. Many happy days were spent by the young and old alike in their summertime frolic. One happy youngster relates that while living in Cincinnati, he used to dive from shore to shore underneath empty sand boats.

He says he used to also stand in the middle of the canal, wait for the moving canal boat, jump and catch the bow bumper made of rope, climb to the top of the bow beam and dive off the beam while the boat was moving to the front, come up and climb to the top and dive off again and again.

Winter time created excitement because of the frozen conditions of the canal. Ice skating was very popular. One man relates that he skated from Cincinnati to Hamilton and back in one day.

The canal boats were in the general range of 78 feet long, and 14 feet 10 inches wide. The cost would usually range in the $2,000 figure.

Packet boats were the exception to canal travel. It accommodated the statesmen, financiers, and in general, the wealthy seekers of pleasure. These pleasure boats consisted of a "diner, sleeper, smoker, parlor car, baggage and mail coach" all into one enterprise.

From one to four mules were used to pull the canal boat. This was the only method that could be used because machinery in this era was practically nonexistant.

A stronger current flowed in the southward direction so therefore more mules were used to pull the boat in the northerly direction. Housing of the extra mules in the southerly direction was on the canal boat.

Along side of the canal was a dirt towpath, with a slight elevation from four to ten feet wide. A path of this type was used for the mules or horses to travel on. These animals were fastened to the boats by towlines which were seventy to ninety yards in length. The poles used to maneuver or simply "unstick" the boats were of an irontipped sort.

Meeting of two boats along the towpath took drivers of tremendous skill to actually allow for the passing of these two craft.

When the boats met, the team of the downstream boat stepped to the outside of the towpath and stopped, letting the towline lie on the ground and sink into the water. Meanwhile, the boat steered to the opposite side of the canal, away from the towpath.

The upstream boat and team passed between the other boat and its team, the mules stepping over the other's towline, the boat passing over the line in the water. A similar procedure took place when one boat passed another going in the same direction, as packets did the slower freight boats.

The towpath, being only on one side of the canal, frequently changed sides in which a bridge was required. The mule consequently had to change from one side to the other. The mules would go under the bridge, and with promptness, cross over the bridge with the boat slowly moving. The change of this sort had to be made with complete accuracy or the mule was abruptly yanked into the canal.

Life on the canal boat was a mere adventure in itself. The crew normally consisted of from two to six men and very possibly included one woman.

The staff of the freight and line boats were comprised of a driver, or mule manipulator; a steersman who guided the boat; most certainly the captain who was possibly the owner; and a cook, customarily a woman who did "boat domestic work." A handy man, called a bowsman, was generally employed in the more prosperous boats.

The captain's stature was one of "truly American" distinction. He was set up as a hero type in the early transportation of the canals. He was always the master of his "ship." His leadership quality was one to be respected by all concerned, especially the crew.

The social life of the canal crew rested on the fact that they made their stops at the canal houses, locks, taverns and mule/horse stations.

These stops allowed the crew to fraternize or engage in the immediate attention of the locals. Fighting, drinking, wrestling, foot-racing, smoking and a general all-out release of tension was exercised by all.

The captain sometimes chose his crew with respect to their fighting ability. More than once quarrels or squabbles led to fights between the crews of two different boats. Sometimes boats were pulled over and brawls included the use of fists, clubs and stones; tow lines were cut and many men found out the condition of the water.

Of course wages played an important part in

the life of the canal personnel. Before 1860, bowsmen and steersmen were comfortable with their wages of twenty dollars a month. The drivers normally received from eight to twelve dollars per month, and the cook from five to ten dollars per month. These earnings included lodging and board.

After the Civil War, wages rose sharply with a driver receiving twenty dollars per month, the steersmen thirty-five dollars per month, and the captain fifty to sixty dollars per month.

The canal boats were not the only boats on the canal. People localized along the waterway had their own sort of craft, especially farmers. Many used these boats for pleasure or simply to make extra money, or perhaps a living.

Chapter IV

AMERICAN CIVIL WAR

CIVIL WAR: THE FIRST DAYS IN THE COUNTY

The American Civil War (1861-1865) was long in coming. With the bombardment of Fort Sumter, April 12, 1861, President Lincoln called on the States for 75,000 volunteers for three months service.

The regular army, as of January 1, 1861, had a small force of 16,402. This figure was reduced due to the resignations and desertions of officers loyal to the Southern cause.

The President's proclamation calling for three month volunteers was read April 15, 1861. The states of Kentucky, Virginia, Tennessee and Missouri refused to answer the President's call.

However, the Legislature of the State of New York chose to raise $3,000,000 for unlimited support of that State.

Ohio, because of its geographical location, was the centerpiece of the Union. A call by Governor Dennison for thirteen full regiments was received and answered so rapidly that a total complement of twenty-two regiments was filled.

At the end of July the three months service was over. The returning volunteers from the Battle of First Bull Run sought their pay. The original thirteen regiments received their pay as United States volunteers; the remaining nine were considered State Militia and received no wage.

However, Governor Dennison had originally obtained pledges from the United States Government that all volunteers would receive their earnings.

Pay eventually came and several companies/regiments were reinstated into their original outfits, thus signing for three more years service to the Union.

Ohio's Legislature immediately went into session and within less than 24 hours after the President's call, the State Senate carried through the three readings and passed unanimously a bill appropriating one million dollars.

The House immediately went into action declaring a unanimous vote for the passage of the money appropriation.

Within 48 hours after the call, two Ohio regiments were on their way to Washington.

President Lincoln's call for volunteers was received in Warren County at the premises of Washington Hall on the evening of April 16. This was the County's first war meeting.

It was marked with a boldness of general enthusiasm and spirit. The enemy had turned their cannon on the citizens of the North and the flag of the United States was threatened.

With A.H. Dunlevy presiding, a resolutions committee was formed. The panel consisted of George R. Sage, Durbin Ward, James M. Smith, J.D. Wallace, William Crosson, Simon Suydam, and John C. Dunlevy. Addresses of sincerity were given by the president, Judge Belamy Storer, Durbin Ward and J.D. Wallace. Resolutions were adopted as follows:

"Resolved, That we, the citizens of Warren County, most cordially endorse the action of the Government in its energetic measures to execute the laws, and to preserve the institutions of our country.

"Resolved, That we stand by and support the Administration in the most vigorous efforts to put down rebellion and punish treason at whatever expense of men or money.

"Resolved, That we recognize no party in the present crisis, but the party of the Union.

The band played "**The Star Spangled Banner,** "**Yankee Doodle,**" and "**Hail Columbia.**"

Professor William H. Venable, then a young man, described in his address at the 1902 Lebanon Centennial the meeting as such:

"I shall never forget that meeting. It was a gathering of men, some in the flower of their youth, others verging on four score, but the oldest felt young and the youngest suddenly grown mature, was eager to prove his manhood by relinquishing all that youth values, most ease, pleasure, home – to take upon him the soldier's burden, to fight, and if need better die for the Union.

"Durbin Ward made a brief, terse speech, eloquent for its simplicity. He was the first man in the congressional district to enlist. A paper he had drawn up, pledged those who signed it to the service of their country.

"This paper was passed from hand to hand and many names were written upon it. There was no noise, no shouting, the still white heat of patriotism consumed all smoke of outward demonstration. The meeting was solemn thruout and at its close the audience dispersed as quietly as a congregation leaving a church after listening to an impressive sermon."

Every day life of Warren Countians changed from one of habit to a rising "war spirit." The flag of the United States was flown from the courthouse, from stores, work shops and residences. Military preparation had consumed the whole nation.

The county soon raised three companies commanded respectively by Capt. Rigdon Williams, of Lebanon; Capt. John Kell, of Franklin; and Capt. J.D. Wallace, of Morrow.

The sight of real soldiers to the residents of the County was new. The marching away of their loved ones, neighbors and friends instilled into the remainder a silence never before experienced.

On Tuesday, April 23, Capt. Williams' company marched from Lebanon to the railroad with the assumption that the departure for Camp Jackson at Columbus would be swift.

Stores and shops were closed; the public

turned out in great numbers to say their farewells. The procession of soldiers and citizens stretched for nearly a mile between Lebanon and Deerfield. Lebanon had no railroad at this time and the station at Deerfield was the closest depot.

At the railroad station, the Captain received a dispatch that Camp Jackson was full. Consequently, the company returned to Lebanon and encamped at the fair grounds.

Captain Williams' company was mustered into the service of the United States for three months service at Columbus on May 5.

It was reorganized and mustered into service for three years at Camp Dennison on the 19th of June, as Company F, Twelfth Regiment, Ohio Volunteer Infantry.

The first man to lose his life in the War of the Rebellion from Warren County was Jabez Turner from Harveysburg. He was killed at the Battle of Scarry Creek, (West) Virginia, July 17, 1861.

Turner faced the engagement with an emotional tenderness. He went into battle with the feeling that he would not return alive. It was his first conflict with the enemy. He entered into the fighting line and fell at the first fire.

In a letter to his widow, Captain Williams said that on several occasions Turner had related his premonitions to him.

Although these instincts were strong they made no gloomy impressions upon him. He had offered his life for the service of his country. He died with glory, his face to the enemy. A ball struck him in the forehead and death was instantaneous.

His body, along with others, was left to be buried in Virginia soil.

John Kell's company, before the war, had been formed as a militia company. It was called the "Franklin Grays." (Captain Kell had served in the Mexican War, 1846-1848, and had been appointed postmaster of Franklin by Buchanan.)

It was the first company to leave the County for service and it became Co. F, 1st Ohio Volunteer Infantry, in the three months service. The service date is recorded as of April 16, 1861. With drilling experience before the war, most of the company volunteered.

Durbin Ward was the first man of the County to sign an enrollment paper for troops in the Union cause. When the President's call reached Lebanon, Ward was holding court.

He immediately drew up a paper saying in certain terms that, "We, the undersigned, hereby tender our services to the President of the United States to protect our national flag." He signed it and proceeded with his case.

Ward was a Democrat along with about two-fifths of the eligible men of the County. A question arose as to whether these opposing party members would relinquish their politics and join with the Republicans and other political affiliations and take a stand to preserve their country.

Ward declared many times over that politics had no bearing in his effort to reunite the Union.

Political party lines melted in the County and seemed to have no consequences as patriotic feelings ran deep.

A HISTORY OF THE THIRTY-FIFTH OHIO VOLUNTEER INFANTRY

The Warren County Historical Society will again host the Thirty-Fifth Ohio Volunteer Infantry reenactors on July 20th and 21st, 1996, at Glendower. The writer has attended several of these presentations and has found them to most informative and enjoyable.

These volunteers are dedicated to their work, and indeed their exhibits and demonstrations display a remarkable resemblance to the actual war, the Civil War, where over 600,000 Americans lost their lives.

We shall now venture into the history of the 35th. It was organized at Camp Hamilton, Ohio, during the months of August and September, 1861. Companies A and F were mustered in from Warren

County, H from Montgomery County; E and part of G from Preble, County; and B, C, D, from Butler County.

The original members (except veterans) were released from duty at different dates, from August 26 to September 28, 1864. The veteran recruits were then transferred to the Eighteenth Ohio Volunteer Infantry.

At its organization, its original strength was 812 men, and at time of mustering out, 510. Company A had a total of 113 men mustered in while Company F had 115.

The regiment left Camp Hamilton on September 26, 1861, and mobilized at Covington, Kentucky. General O.M. Mitchel, from Warren County, ordered the regiment to board a train at the Ohio River town on the Kentucky Central Railroad.

Some soldiers were ordered to leave the train and were placed at all bridges along the railroad through Harrison and Bourbon Counties.

It was implied that the Confederates would burn these bridges before the 35th could reach them. But by capturing the telegraph offices along the line, all communications were cut off. The Southerners were totally surprised when they discovered that the Union guards had custody of every bridge.

The regiment next moved to Paris where it was housed until the first part of December; it then proceeded on to Somerset.

By orders of General Thomas, the regiment did not participate in the battle of Mill Springs. Thereafter, the 35th marched to Louisville, and then traveled by steamer to Nashville.

Under the Army of the Ohio, organized by General Don Carlos Buell, the regiment marched to Pittsburg Landing, better known as Shiloh. General Thomas' division was placed as the rear guard and did not arrive in time for the battle.

The regiment was involved in some of the skirmishes at Corinth, and was one of the first to enter into that battle.

Later the 35th marched to Tuscumbia, Alabama, and toward the end of July 1862, they pushed on to Winchester, Tennessee.

The setting for the battle of Perryville, Kentucky (October 8, 1862), was commenced with the unforgettable race for that place by Confederate Gen. Braxton Bragg and Gen. Buell.

From Nashville the 35th marched about 28 miles per day and made a gallant showing in the engagement.

Gen. Buell was then relieved of this assignment by Gen. Rosecrans, the division next being commanded by Gen. Speed S. Fry. It then marched to Bowling Green, Kentucky, and on to a camp near Gallatin, Tennessee.

During the skirmishes previous to and including the battle of Stone's River, Tennessee, Company A operated a grist mill near Castillian Springs, while Company F, together with the balance of the regiment, searched the country for grain with which to make flour for the army. (This battle took place from December 31, 1862, thru January 2, 1863.)

The campaign which began at Murfreesboro (Stone's River) and ended at Chattanooga, found the regiment at the front marching and fighting the opponent before them.

In February 1863, Col. Ferdinand Vanderveer, from Middletown, was assigned as brigade commander, and Lt. Col. Charles L'Hommdeieu Long, from Franklin, assumed command of the 35th.

In July of that year, Lt. Col. Long resigned and Col. H.V.N. Boynton was chosen to fill his vacancy. Joseph L. Budd was appointed Captain of Company A and Oliver H. Parshall as Captain of Company F.

The battle of Chicamauga, Georgia, was a fierce engagement that saw the 35th lose fifty percent of those engaged, with just a few being captured. Col. Boynton was recognized for his gallantry and leadership during the battle. (This engagement took place on September 19th and 20th, 1863.)

During the first day of fighting, on the 19th, the 35th and Col. Vanderveer's other regiments of the brigade were positioned on the outermost left of the Union line.

They engaged the enemy and, after many hours

of action, beat back several attacks of Hood's division of Longstreet's corps, which was the finest of the Confederate armies in the West.

Early on the 20th, the next day, the 35th was again called into action and, with the rest of the brigade, instructions were given to advance against Breckenridge's division, which had revolved completely around the left of the Union line.

This clash was extreme and severe. It took place in the open field and without any protection. The two armies charged each other at the same instant. The Union brigade moved forward with outstanding skill, while the Confederates seemed to participate in a disorderly fashion.

The soldiers had been moving through the woods in two lines; the first line was the Second Minnesota and Eighty-Seventh Indiana, and the second was the 35th and Ninth Ohio.

Suddenly, while advancing into an open field, the troops were exposed to a destructive discharge of artillery and musket fire. They were immediately ordered to lay flat on the ground, the Confederates being a mere 150 yards from them.

When within a range of 75 yards, the command was given to the first line: "Thirty-Fifth and Ninth, pass lines to the front! - Brigade, charge!"

With orders promptly executed, the Confederate line was thrown back for almost half a mile into the woods where they congregated with their reserves.

For about an hour the contest loomed, after which ended the flanking of the left.

About 2:30 in the afternoon, the brigade reported for duty to General Thomas. His men were holding a ridge to the rear and right of the line of the morning battle. The 35th was then positioned in the front line where it constructed a wall of logs and stones less than a foot in height.

Repetitive lines of Confederates charged this position, always being met and beaten back by members of the 35th and accompanying troops.

Late in the day ammunition supplies were running low, the wagons having been ordered to Chattanooga.

Several officers and men, among which included Joseph L. Budd, Charles L.H. Long, Lewis F. Daugherty, and James H. Bone, were busily searching the cartridge boxes of the dead and wounded.

Small amounts of ammunition were uncovered and three rounds were distributed to each man; soon this supply was exhausted. Col. Vanderveer then placed an order for the men to hold their position with fixed bayonets.

At nightfall the 35th was employed on the left of the line. It was then too dark to recognize their own companions, and during this occasion, the enemy charged. The ones who had again secured small amounts of ammunition quickly fired upon the Confederates and scattered them. These were the last shots fired on the battlefield of Chicamauga.

Afterward, the entire army marched toward Rossville, with Col. Vanderveer's brigade being the last to leave the field.

Casualties of the 35th during this fierce battle included: Captain A.J. Lewis, Company E, wounded severely in the bowels; Captain Joel K. Deardoff, Company K, suffered a severe wound in the leg; and Lt. L.P. Thompson, Company E, receiving a flesh wound in the leg. (1st Lt. James H. Bone, of Company A, was saved injury by his belt buckle which was twisted out of shape by a ball, and in the same battle a ball struck his gold watch without injury to the owner.)

Captain Oliver H. Parshall, Company F, was killed immediately on the right of the line on the first day. He had only the day before returned from home and was detailed upon the staff of Col. Boynton. It was stated by the Colonel that the Captain acted with much coolness and gallantry, and that he always instilled and displayed a confidence amongst the men.

Also killed in action from Company F during the first day of fighting were Privates David Smith and Patrick Walsh.

The regiment went into battle at Chicamauga on the second day with a total of 280 men and officers. Men killed in action on this day from Company A were: 1st Sgt. George W. Keever, Pvt. George Bate, and Cpl. Thomas G. Strickler.

Killed on the second day from Company F were Lt. Thomas H. Harlan and Pvt. Thomas J. Bloss.

The regiment lay at rest near Chattanooga during the Fall of 1863, where they were frequently engaged in skirmishes.

The 35th was engaged in the battle of Missionary Ridge in Tennessee on November 25, 1863, and was among the first to reach the enemy's position on the pinnacle. They helped drive the Confederates back and captured three pieces of artillery.

Col. Boynton was severely wounded while leading the charge up the steep incline. The command then changed to Major Budd. The next morning, having been defeated, the foe was forced back to Ringgold, Georgia.

In other battles, Lt. James Sabin of Company A, lost his life at Big Shanty, Georgia (the battle of Kennesaw Mountain), on June 16, 1864. Also, Captain Lewis F. Daugherty of Company A was killed July 20, 1864, at the battle of Peach Tree Creek in Georgia.

Total number of soldiers to lose their lives while serving in the 35th O.V.I. was 183, with 40 lives being lost from Warren County Companies A and F.

WARREN COUNTIAN McLEAN LED CIVIL WAR OHIO BRIGADE

From time to time this writer will insert into this column a brief history of a Warren County Civil War participant. This particular article will focus on Nathaniel Collins McLean, the son of Honorable John McLean, of Ridgeville, past Associate Justice of the Supreme Court of the United States.

Nathaniel Collins McLean was born February 2, 1815, near Ridgeville. Graduating from Augusta

College, Kentucky, at the age of 16, he went immediately to Harvard College; he attended the senior class as a resident graduate, and then entered law school.

He married, in 1838, the daughter of Judge Burnet of Cincinnati.

While practicing his profession of law, his health failed. Upon the advise of his doctor, he took a sea voyage and visited Europe. His health not fully restored, he decided to take employment in the business field.

This decisive action fully restored his health, and after a number of years he resumed his law practice.

Not too many months later, his wife suddenly became ill and died, leaving four children.

He again married, in 1858, to the daughter of Philip R. Simpson of Louisville, Kentucky.

At the breaking out of the Rebellion, McLean and Colonel Robert Riley, under the authority of General Fremont, commenced the organization of the Seventy-Fifth Ohio Volunteer Infantry.

The Regiment was organized at Camp John McLean at Cincinnati. On September 18, 1861, McLean was commissioned as its Colonel.

In January 1862, under the command of General Milroy, the Regiment was ordered to Western Virginia. This stint fairly hardened the men into what a soldier's life was to be.

Their first excursion, after a long trek over the Allegheny and Cheat Mountains, was at Huttonsville, at the foot of Cheat Mountain.

On April 12, 1862, the enemy made a gallant attack against the brigade, but with the 75th in the lead, the Confederates were pushed back with tremendous force.

Colonel McLean commanded the regiment personally in all its operations under Generals Milroy, Schenck (Robert C. Schenck from Franklin), and Fremont.

At the battle of Cross Keys, he was promoted to the command of a brigade, consisting of four Ohio Regiments.

Colonel McLean was now assigned to General Pope's army in which he commanded his Brigade through all its campaigns in Virginia. With this command, he led his brigade at the battle of 2nd Bull Run, and on the 29th of November, 1862, he was commissioned a Brigadier General.

He remained with his command in the Army of the Potomac, under Generals McClellan, Burnside, and Hooker, in which he participated in all the active operations through the battle of Chancellorsville, Virginia, it being fought May 2, 1863.

McLean's Brigade was now part of the Eleventh Corp, the commander being Oliver O. Howard.

During the battle, the Eleventh Corp was completely surprised and overwhelmed by the Confederates and fell back in complete disarray. Yet McLean's Ohio Brigade merited the highest praise under the difficult circumstances.

The Seventy-Fifth charged the enemy, but the enemy's fire being too severe, and the odds being too great, the Regiment was forced to fall back to the Chancellorsville House.

In the short space of half an hour, the Seventy-Fifth lost one-hundred and fifty men killed and wounded.

At this battle, General McLean's Corp commander, Oliver O. Howard, was upset with the General's alleged inability to reorganize his troops promptly after Stonewall Jackson's flank attack.

Several weeks later, General McLean was shunted off to the Ohio Valley in a staff position. A year later he was allowed to hold a field command.

He led a brigade in the Atlanta campaign, and again came under fire from General Howard for alleged failures at the Battle of New Hope Church.

The General once again found himself in a rear position. He was later transferred to North Carolina where he served as part of Sherman's Carolina Campaign. General McLean, thinking the war was about over, resigned on April 20, 1865.

During the whole war General McLean was off duty for the space of thirty days, having had leave of absence once for twenty, and again for ten days. After the war he relocated to the

State of Minnesota, where he retired to the quiet occupation of a farmer.

OHIO'S SQUIRREL HUNTERS DEFENDED CINCINNATI

The Squirrel Hunters were Ohio's salvation of the State. They were so named for their dress and mannerisms.

These Civilian soldiers were called up in response to Governor Tod's plea for a defense of Cincinnati.

On August 29-30, 1862, Confederate General E. Kirby Smith and his army completely destroyed a segment of the Union army at Richmond, Kentucky.

Not until late Saturday night, August 30, did Cincinnati receive word of this defeat. News spread to this northern city that Smith was to invade and distress signals rang out. Ohio's Governor Tod issued this proclamation:

"Our southern border is threatened with invasion. I have therefore to recommend that all the loyal men of your counties at once form themselves into military companies and regiments to beat back the enemy at any and all points he may attempt to invade our State. Gather up all the arms in the country, and furnish yourselves with ammunition for the same. The service will be of but a few days duration. The soil of Ohio must not be invaded by the enemies of our glorious Government."

There was no defense of Cincinnati pertaining to a large force. The only obstacle in the Confederate General's way was a few unmanned guns in back of Covington and the crossing of the Ohio River.

An immediate response was answered through the State by volunteers anxious to preserve their part of their Union. Men of all walks of life answered to the call of the defense of Cincinnati.

Laborers, farmers, mechanics and many other occupational skilled men were to drop their labors and heed to the call. A total of 15,766 men responded from the Buckeye State. Warren County had a total of 436.

"From morning till night the streets resounded with the tramp of armed men marching to the defense of the city. From every quarter of the State they came, in every form of organization, with every species of arms. The 'Squirrel Hunters,' in their homespun garments, with powderhorn and buckskin pouch.

"Half-organized regiments, some in uniform and some without, some having waited long enough to draw their equipments and some having marched without them; cavalry and infantry; all poured out from the railroad depots and down toward the pontoon bridge.

"The ladies of the city furnished provisions by the wagon-load; the Fifth Street markethouse was converted into a vast free eating saloon for the Squirrel Hunters; halls and warehouses were used as barracks." (Taken from Reid's, Ohio in the War.)

The battle fatigued Smith and his army were recuperating and regrouping. A prolonged delay of about two days allowed the Squirrel Hunters to gather under their General Lew Wallace.

Cincinnati was swelled to the brim with all types of men who were very well mannered and were fully acquainted with the martial law that had been activated.

Governor Tod insured Secretary Stanton that Smith's force would be met and indeed turned away.

The Little Miami Railroad was protected as far away as Xenia.

The surrounding communities and counties were, because of their geographical location, the first to respond to the call of the "Seige of Cincinnati."

Preparing for war was the upbeat attitude of the Squirrel Hunters. Molding bullets, cleaning rifles and a general all-out readiness was the spirit the men had.

Let them come, we're ready, generalized the feeling. Where were they?

The men had built a pontoon bridge across the

Ohio and had taken a position below Covington and Newport. Still no General Smith.

Had Smith heard of the defense of Cincinnati and turned away or was this just a big scare? Beginning to recognize the happenings that were not visible, the towns people of Cincinnati demanded that martial law be lifted.

After two days of this peculiar situation, many restrictions were lifted. Certainly Cincinnati could not be taken now.

On September 10, 1862, General Smith's army moved close enough to the Covington outposts to actually feint an attack. With this move, Cincinnati was again in a panic.

However, just a few skirmishes occurred and the real threat was the appearance of General Smith's army.

Totally outnumbered, Smith's army retreated. Governor Tod wired Secretary of War Stanton, September 13, 1862, stating:

"The minute-men or Squirrel Hunters responded gloriously to the call for the defense of Cincinnati. Thousands reached the city, and thousands more were enroute for it. The enemy having retreated, all have been ordered back. This uprising of the people is the cause of the retreat. You should acknowledge publicly this gallant conduct. Please order Quartermaster Burr to pay all transportation bills, upon my approval."

Warren County's list of Squirrel Hunters is not complete. Many of the participants did not list their name with the Adjutant General's office. (A roster of the Squirrel Hunters can be found in this writer's book, "Warren County's Involvement in the Civil War.")

LOCAL CIVIL WAR VET REMEMBERED

This week we will feature another Civil War veteran, namely W.A. (Andy) Hathaway. Andy was a veteran of the War between the States and served with the 35th Ohio Volunteer Infantry. He was born in Warren County, Ohio, December 21, 1840.

Mr. Hathaway was serving on the skirmish line near Corinth, Mississippi, when he was shot through the right shoulder, the ball passing clear through.

He was mustered out and returned to the Warren County area and began a career on the railroad that lasted until his death.

For forty years he pulled the throttle on a railroad engine. His first stint was working on the "Sheepskin Road," along with the Zentmyer boys, the line running between Morrow and Zanesville.

His next employment was in Indiana with the Lake Erie & Western R.R., the assignment lasting more than fifteen years; thence on to Moberly, Kansas City and St. Louis, Mo.

During his profession he was involved in many exciting and dangerous events. Several times he was forced to jump from the cab while the train was at full speed. Once he was blown out bodily by the explosion of the boiler.

His age forced him to give up his active life on the railroad. He therefore was employed by the Wabash Company in a position around the shops and yards. During the last year of his life, he was unable to work because of a heart ailment. He died December 14, 1913, in St. Louis, Missouri.

The following is a copy of a letter taken from **The Western Star**, written by Mr. Hathaway during his service in the Civil War.

Camp near Corinth, Miss.
March 23, 1862.

Dear Mother, I received your letter this morning and will hasten to answer. I have met with a little misfortune since I last wrote to you. As the Rebels keep falling it has kept us on the skirmish line and picket fighting for the past two weeks. On last Saturday, May 17, we were called early in the morning to go on the skirmish line. We soon found the enemy.

About 11 o'clock I was shot through the right shoulder, the ball striking on the center, glancing around the bone and coming out on the center. I have suffered considerable but at present my arm seems to be improving and the opinion of our doctor or surgeon is that I shall not be disabled, but they can not always tell as the bone may be slightly fractured. Very poor accommodations here for wounded men, have but one blanket and lay on the ground.

Soldier life is quite a prison life; there is no thought taken for the private soldier, there is too much old Brittain yet in the American people. Think perhaps I will have an opportunity to get leave of absence and go home while I am disabled for duty.

I would have written sooner but couldn't on account of not having use of my arm.

Andy Wilson was buried yesterday. He died Wednesday, May 21st. I was in to see him in the morning, he was very low, requesting me to see if I could not get him home. (He was laying in an old house the regiment was using for a hospital.) In a few moments after he spoke to me he became unconscious.

I went to camp, found all the boys of our company had gone on picket except Mort Eby. He had a fellon on his hand. We went back to the hospital but for no good, he (Andy) died in a few minutes after we arrived. His death was caused by the phthisic; he was buried yesterday with all the honors and respect that we were able to furnish under the circumstances. Col. Vanderveer, Maj. Boynton and Gen. McRooks Ades were present. Maj. Boynton read a chapter in Bible and performed the burial ceremony. Boys took great interest and pains in making head board and in putting picket-fence around his grave. Mort Eby informed his brother John in regard to this. Would have written to him long before his death but no letters are allowed to depart until after the battle here, may be some time before you receive this.

There is a report that we have the Rebs surrounded and expecting a fight any minute. I am getting terribly blood-thirsty and would like to have revenge, nevertheless I would "just as leave stay in the rear."

Tell sister Navine I received her letter, also one from brother Perry; will answer whenever an opportunity presents itself.

Received a letter from Neal and John Conner; they are much pleased with soldier life. Never mind, they have not seen the elephant yet.

I have twenty dollars that I have no particular use for and would send it to you, but think it would not be safe at present, as it is doubtful about the mail reaching you. We are going to be paid soon and if I do not get a furlow I will have an opportunity to send by some one as there is someone detailed expressly to take money to the homes of the boys of our regiment.

You spoke about some of the boys drinking; I have not seen a drop of liquor since I was at Louisville. Our commissary receives whiskey sometimes but the officers generally gobble it up. Privates do not get a smell.

Soldier life is rough and there are great temptations to resist and few inducements to live a moral life, but I can say that soldiering has made but few drunkards, "comparatively speaking with civil times," as they have no opportunity or privileges to get it.

I will bring my letter to a close. The boys from Freeport are all enjoying good health with few exceptions. Tell the Connor girls I am all right on a goose. Received a little jolt in the right shoulder is all.

George Hide is the hardiest one in the regiment, seldom ever complains. Tell Wm. Goes' wife he is well and doing fine. George Bates has not yet arrived. Tell Frank I consider myself slighted; she never gave me an invitation to that party. Give my respects to all enquiring friends, a share of my love to you and sister.

Hoping I may have an opportunity to visit you soon, I am your affectionate son,

ANDY H.

GENERAL R.C. SCHENCK EARLY MILITARY HERO

General Robert Cumming Schenck was born in Franklin, Warren County, Ohio, on October 4, 1809. His father, Gen. William C. Schenck, co-founder of Franklin, Ohio, was an officer in the Northwestern Army under Gen. William Henry Harrison, and afterward served as a member of the General Assembly of the State.

After his father's death in January, 1821, Robert was placed under the guardianship of Gen. James Findlay of Cincinnati, but continued to live with his mother at Franklin until his fifteenth year.

He entered the sophomore class at Miami University in November 1824. He graduated in September 1827, and remained at Oxford extending his studies. He was also employed part-time as tutor of French and Latin until 1830, when he received his master's degree.

In November he entered into the practice of law at Dayton, Ohio. He was elected to the Ohio Legislature in 1840, and was two years later elected to the U.S. House of Representatives, serving four terms.

Resigning this position in 1851, our subject accepted, under President Fillmore, the position of Minister of Brazil, this tenure lasting two years.

During his term in Congress, he was soon recognized as an anti-slavery Whig. The ability to speak his mind of other opponents allowed many avenues in which he could attack his political foes. Being of a proud nature, Mr. Schenck was too tempered to adapt to the already proven political ring.

In September 1859, a meeting was held in Dayton to discuss the political views of the period. Earlier that day Abraham Lincoln had made a speech at the same location.

The evening was Robert C. Schenck's time to back Mr. Lincoln's bid for the Presidency. This was the first time the future President spoke before any large assembly concerning the nation's highest office. Schenck referred to Mr.

Lincoln as an honest, sensible man, and said that a nomination should be at hand.

At the beginning of the Civil War Schenck immediately offered his services to the Union. He was commissioned Brigadier General of volunteers by Lincoln.

His Washington enemies immediately pounced upon this selection as a political appointment. Their quarrel was that the Indian fighters in the West were better suited for a command than a politician. News sources wrote that one who had no military experience should start at the bottom and work his way up.

General Schenck's first test came on June 17, 1861, when he was ordered to take possession of the Louden and Hampshire Railroad as far as Vienna, Va.

With the odds against him, he acted with so much coolness that the Confederates were impressed with the belief that a heavy force must be in reserve, and accordingly they withdrew.

At the battle of First Bull Run on July 21, 1861, Gen. Schenck commanded the First and Second Ohio (both had companies from Warren County), the Second New York, and a battery of six-pounder cannons.

He was stationed on the Warrenton Road near the Stone Bridge. About 4 p.m., being left in command by Gen. Tyler, he determined to clear the abattis from the bridge and march to the relief of some of the Union forces that were severely pressed. He quickly moved forward two twelve pounders and a company of men, the obstructions being promptly removed.

At this moment the order came to retreat and Gen. Schenck, forming his brigade, brought off the only portion of that army that was not absorbed in the element of mob retreat.

General Beauregard, in his official report, gives as one of the reasons pursuit was not made was that he was satisfied large reinforcements held the Warrenton Road. He had no evidence of this other than Gen. Schenck's bold demonstration and orderly retreat.

A brigade assignment was next in store for

Gen. Schenck, who was commanding in western Virginia under Gen. Rosecrans. He was actively engaged in several campaigns on the Kanawha and New Rivers.

Due to the death of Gen. Lander, the General was ordered to Cumberland, Md., and upon arrival found everything in a state of confusion. The town was crowded with the sick and wounded, the troops being in a serious degree of disorder. The administrative abilities of the General soon restored order.

General Schenck successfully defeated the Confederates on several different points such as Moorefield, Petersburg, Franklin and other important junctures.

At the battle of Cross Keys, he was assigned to the right of the line, and the Confederates in heavy force immediately tried to flank his position. This attempt was met promptly and was repulsed, the enemy falling back in confusion under well-directed artillery fire.

Until about 3 p.m., the right continued to press the enemy, in no instance giving back or losing any part of the field assigned it.

After the left gave way, Gen. Fremont ordered Generals Schenck, Milroy and Cluseret to fall back to the position first occupied in the morning. This was done slowly and in good order.

General Fremont, upon being relieved of his command, turned the duties over to Gen. Schenck. During the absence of Gen. Sigel, he had command of the First Corp of Virginia.

At the battle of Second Bull Run, Gen. Schenck suggested to Gen. Sigel that good water could be found at Bull Run rather than at Manassas. Upon this suggestion, Gen. Pope directed the army to Bull Run instead of Manassas.

In the two days fight that followed, Schenck's division took an active part.

On the second day of the battle, the General suffered a crippling wound to the right wrist, his sword being thrown quite some distance from him. With the battle position clearly exposed, the General refused to be carried off the field until his sword had been recovered.

He was removed to the hospital in Washington, his right arm being impaired the rest of his life.

Shortly thereafter he received an appointment to Major General of volunteers.

On December 5, 1863, Gen. Schenck resigned his commission to take a seat in the Lower House of Congress. He had been elected from the Third Ohio Congressional District in 1862, defeating Clement L. Vallandigham, the famed Copperhead.

Gen. Schenck continued his political career in Washington and was involved in the impeachment procedure of President Andrew Johnson.

The General died in the District of Columbia, March 23, 1890, and is buried in the Woodlawn Cemetery in Dayton, Ohio.

Chapter V

BIOGRAPHICAL SKETCHES

EATON FIRST COUNTY RESIDENT

There were many early pioneers to venture into Warren County shortly before Statehood and after, and from the many histories of these settlers, it seems the County got the cream of the crop. However, the writer shall focus on its first occupant, his life and residence. His name is Jonah Eaton.

This story is taken from a paper written and read by George T. O'Neall at the annual meeting of the Miami Valley Pioneers Association in 1889. Its title was, "The Oldest Inhabitant."

Jonah Eaton was reported to have been born about 1735 in New Jersey. His family moved to Pennsylvania when he was a mere child.

Young Eaton was amongst a hunting party near Fort Bedford in the summer of 1750 and was captured by a band of Iroquois. He was taken to Presque Isle in Lake Erie where he was totally accepted by the Indians.

He was treated kindly and even joined in the hunting parties of the Indian tribe, traveling to New York and occasionally into Pennsylvania.

The French commandant requested all his Indian allies assemble and march to deter General Braddock's march to capture the French encampment at the site of present Pittsburgh. Eaton was engaged in this fateful battle on the side of the French.

In 1758 the English marched against Ft. DuQuesne and Eaton again joined the Indians and the French army.

The fort was vacated on November 25 of that

year, and Eaton was later transferred to a band of Shawnees, and departed for central and southern Ohio.

The Shawnee Indian leaders seemed to admire young Eaton. He became a favorite of the Shawnee Indian Chief, Red Hawk, and was adopted into his family where he was treated with the utmost kindness.

He joined their hunting parties and felt at ease to travel, his exploration taking him to the extremes of his new land. These journeys took him from the Ohio River on the South to the Lakes in the North; from the Muskingum River in the East to the Great Miami River on the West.

Eaton spent six years in this drifter type life. During this time he learned the customs, language and manners of the Indians.

Eaton's Indian family life was to end with General Bouquet's victory in November of 1764.

At this time the Indians were forced to accept, against their will, a treaty that included the surrender of all white prisoners.

A total change of presence from that of a nomad in the untamed wilderness, to that of civilization, proved disturbing to Eaton. He was now about thirty years of age.

A story goes that while Eaton was considered a captive of the Indians, his only white friend was murdered by the Indians. This event turned the tide and Eaton returned to the white society.

He soon quested for action and joined General Dunsmore at the Battle of Point Pleasant in 1774.

He later traveled to Kentucky and served as a guide for General John Bowman in his battle against the Indians on the Little Miami (Battle of Oldtown).

He next served as a guide for General George Rogers Clark in his expedition against the Shawnees at the Battle of Piqua in 1780.

He spent the next three years hunting and roaming over southern Ohio and down into Kentucky. He also spent some time amongst the settlers, however, he desired the peace and contentment of a nomadic life.

While at Fort Pitt, in 1784, he met General Richard Butler who asked him to be an interpreter at the Treaty of Fort Stanwick. Butler was one of the three peace commissioners, while the Indians were represented by Red Jacket and Cornplanter.

Two years later, he was asked again for his services as an interpreter, this time at the Treaty of Fort Finney at the mouth of the Great Miami River.

General Butler, General Clark and Samuel Parsons were in attendance for the white nation, and representing the Indian nation were the heads of the tribes of the Delawares, Wyandottes and Shawnees.

The treaty relinquished the rights of all lands by the Indians east and south of the Great Miami River.

The opening up of the Northwest Territory by land speculators initiated a further need for Jonah Eaton's expertise in his land savvy. Eaton became acquainted with Colonel Richard Anderson who employed him to create topographical maps of the Little Miami Valley.

He assisted in drawings of rivers, creeks and landmarks. The drawings were excellent as a resource pertaining to drawing up land warrants without official surveys being drawn.

Eaton explored the next fourteen months what are now the counties of Warren, Greene and Clinton. He restricted himself mainly in Warren and Greene opposite the portion forming the Virginia Military Purchase located east of the Little Miami.

Eaton ventured to Louisville, Ky., in 1787, and rejoined Colonel Anderson. He took with him his rather crude maps and a verbal description of his venture. The colonel at this time had been engaged with land handling in Kentucky, but the lands were being settled with such great vigor that he turned his total attention to land later to be named Ohio.

(One source said that 40,000 acres were deeded to Eaton for his services. He was given Survey

1732 lying on Anderson's Fork, which empties into Caesar's Creek at New Burlington in Greene County.)

The Louisville endeavor brought more than a huge land acquisition; it brought Jonah Eaton a wife. In no time, he found he had been duped by the woman of his choice.

His disposition was greatly wounded, and he left with his gun and dog for the life he so long adored, the wilderness.

He again returned to this area, the land he so loved, and from 1789 to 1802 he occupied his time hunting and trapping.

He was advancing in age at this time, being well into his sixties.

He settled in Survey 57 and prepared himself an unusual home. The site was located in a small valley through which a stream flowed, and which ultimately joined the waters of Caesar's Creek.

(It should be mentioned the little stream is known today as Jonah's Run. There is also a church, Jonah's Run Baptist Church, which was in all probability named for Jonah Eaton. It is located two miles east of Harveysburg.)

The dwelling consisted of a hollow sycamore tree of extraordinary proportions. The tree was a double one, actually two trees joined to make one.

The two elements joined at a height of about seven feet when they then ascended in the form of two separate trunks. The site of the home overlooked a beautiful valley lined with sycamores, elms and oaks.

Vines of wild grapes climbed gracefully on the assorted trees. The undergrowth added to the spectacular view from his isolated tree-house.

Jonah Eaton's tree-home was located on the north bank of the stream. It was about a half-mile from Caesar's Creek and established in an inlet to shield him from the cold, wintry blasts.

The entrance to his home was from the west and stood not more than three feet from the ground.

A heavy slab of hewn timber was used for a door; it could be closed and barred from within.

The interior of his home was of unusual design; it was about ten feet by seven feet while it varied in heights ranging from five feet at the lowest to seven feet at the highest point.

As time moved on, Eaton made improvements in his tree-home. He structured an addition in the form of an open shed of poles over the front of his residence and covered it with bark. This formed a resting place in which he could merely relax and view the surroundings.

His age simply would not let him lead the active life he once so loved. Peace and contentment were in order.

Eaton sought the solace of a retired man, but as the emigration of the population called out, he answered with his explicit knowledge of the land and surroundings.

He lived in his tree-home until 1795, and was periodically frequented by people asking advice.

It is believed that Eaton Township was named for him. It was a township created in Warren County, located on the extreme eastern portion, and afterward canceled out.

It was established June 28, 1806, and in 1815 was made a part of Clinton County.

The retaining of this township would have been a great tribute to Warren County's "first resident."

REV. JAMES SMITH HAS MANY DESCENDANTS IN COUNTY

Rev. James Smith was a traveling minister of the Methodist faith during the last half of the eighteenth century. He wrote journals of his travels pertaining to the years 1783, 1795 and 1797. These were recorded in the July 1907 issue (Vol 16) of the Ohio Archaeological and Historical Quarterly Publications. His journals were entitled, "**Tours into Kentucky and the Northwest Territory.**" This is certainly highly recommended reading.

These journals were used by Theodore Roosevelt while collecting materials for his "The Winning of the West." He mentions them in footnotes, and also makes several references to these manuscripts. He furthermore makes mention of them in his preface.

Since Rev. Smith has many descendants in Warren County, the writer feels it relevant that a sketch of his travels and family be written.

Rev. Smith was born in Powhatan County, Va., September 17, 1757, and died near Columbia (now a part of Cincinnati) July 28, 1800. He was the son of Thomas and the grandson of George Smith, who were believed to have been born in England.

Tradition has it that George Smith moved from Virginia to the valley of the James River, in his possession taking only a gun, tomahawk and buffalo robe.

He was a hunter by trade, but he acquired great wealth and left a large estate to his son, Thomas. The farm was located in Powhatan and Chesterfield Counties, Virginia, about twenty miles above Richmond.

Thomas Smith also accumulated great wealth and consequently left to each of his six children a fine farm and a number of slaves. He was married three times, and by each marriage had one son and one daughter. His third wife, Mrs. Margaret Guerrant, her maiden name being Trabue, was the mother of our subject, James.

Oddly enough, the two elder sons were named George and each carried as a middle name, the maiden name of his mother. The eldest was George Rapin and the second George Stovall.

During Rev. Smith's first journey into Kentucky, he was accompanied by his half-brother George R. to Jessamine County to visit their half-brother, George S.

George R. also kept a journal of his travels, but it was unfortunately destroyed in a fire at the home of his son, Gen. George R. Smith, founder of Sedalia, Missouri.

Thomas Smith instilled deep religious beliefs into his family and all three of his sons became preachers.

He had belonged to the Church of England. Discovering the preaching of the Baptist faith, the two elder sons were converted and became Baptist preachers.

James, at about the age of ten, was introduced to the theology of Methodism, and father and son were among the first disciples of the Wesleyan Reformation in Virginia. Thomas resigned from the established church and became a Methodist.

The Republican Methodist Church was organized in 1792 by James O'Kelly. This occurred after an unsuccessful attempt to limit the power of the Bishop in the Methodist Episcopal Church. James Smith became a preacher of the former. This organization numbered in the thousands in Virginia and North Carolina.

Rev. Smith has no record of being a preacher in the M.E. Church, but it is believed in his later years that his intentions, because of his close and friendly relations with the pioneer preachers of the M.E. Church, were to be united with this church.

He, unlike many other Methodist preachers who were poor, had great resources, among which was a large plantation and Negro servants. However, he continued to preach the Gospel until his death, whether in a cabin, by the side of the road, or before a church congregation.

Rev. James Smith, because of his convictions concerning slavery, although he owned slaves, decided to rid himself of this tragic human bondage theory that had been so instilled into the Southern States, and move to the Northwest Territory.

He writes in his journal of 1795: "I determined if God spare my life to visit the western country, if haply I might find a place answerable to my wishes."

His journal in 1797 stated: "A wish to provide a place to carry my family to."

Among his journals, referral is made concerning his route from Virginia, through the Cumberland Gap, overland through Kentucky to the land north of the Ohio River.

Landing in Clermont County, along the Ohio between the Miami Rivers, he traveled northward and discovered the beautiful lands of the Miami

Valley.

He journeyed up the Great Miami as far as Ft. Hamilton, and traveled up the Little Miami for a distance of sixty miles from its mouth. (This venture also included the exploration of the wilderness from the Little Miami to the Scioto.)

Liking what he saw, Rev. Smith brought his family permanently to the Northwest Territory in 1798. He purchased a tract of land on the Little Miami at the mouth of Caesar's Creek. This tract was in the Virginia Military District and was purchased as 1,666 acres, but was surveyed as 2,000 acres.

He bought this tract sight unseen, the purchase being nothing but uncleared wilderness. He consequently took up residence at Newtown (then called Middletown Station), near Columbia, until at a future time when he could clear the land.

He had no permanent church in his newly-found lands. He preached where and when he could, the means of support of his family not depending on preaching.

His life was ended short, his death coming in 1800 at age 43. A bout of bilious fever had proved fatal. The establishing of his purchase was not realized by Rev. Smith.

He had previously married Elizabeth Porter (a daughter of John and Sarah Watkins Porter) while she was still in her teens. After the Reverend's death, she moved from Newtown with her nine children to the newly purchased lands at the mouth of Caesar's Creek.

We shall now highlight the family of Rev. James and Elizabeth Smith, it being one of the most prestigious in Warren County history. Among the grandsons were Hon. John Quincy Smith of Clinton County; Judge James M. Smith of Lebanon; Judge James S. Halsey and Judge James S. Goode, of Springfield; Judge J. Kelly O'Neall, of Lebanon; and Judge Ignatius Brown, of Indianapolis.

Sarah, age 19 at her father's death, was the oldest child, she being born in 1781. Tradition has it that Ichabod Halsey was standing on shore when the Smith family arrived at Columbia.

Little did he know that he was encountering his bride-to-be for the first time.

Thomas Smith, the second child of James and Elizabeth, was 17 years of age when his father died. He was the one in command when the family moved to the newly purchased lands. He was born in 1783 and married Mary Whitehill in 1817. He died in 1843.

Elizabeth, the third child, was married in 1807 at the age of 20 to Burwell Goode, a neighbor. Their son, James S. Goode, was a renown jurist and one time mayor of Springfield, Ohio. Elizabeth died in 1863.

John W. Smith was born in 1785 and passed away in 1843, the same year as his brother, Thomas. He married Sarah Evans, daughter of John and Elizabeth Browning Evans of Gloucester, N.J. They had several children, one of which, Philip, married and moved his family to Guymon, Oklahoma.

The fifth child, Magdalen, was born in 1789 and married Robert Sale in 1808.

Martha Smith married William O'Neall in 1816 at the age of 25. She died in 1873, surviving all but her youngest brother, George James.

Judith Smith was born in 1794 and married Hiram Brown in 1817.

The only child who did not marry was Cynthia, who was born in 1796. She died 13 years later.

Judge George James Smith was a mere infant in arms at his father's death. He was born in 1799 and was the only child that was born in the Northwest Territory.

He married, in 1822, to Mrs. Hannah Whitehill Freeman. Two sons, James S. and John E. Smith, followed in their father's footsteps and distinguished themselves in the law field.

It might be said of Elizabeth Porter Smith that she was an exceptional mother. Almost single-handedly she raised her family, and stood back and watched as they gained prominence in Warren County and beyond.

She died in 1825 at the age of 62 and was interred in the family plot, but, in 1867, the remains of she and James were removed and placed in the Miami Cemetery in Corwin, Ohio.

There is a much greater history of this family and its offsprings in Beer's 1882 History of Warren County. Also, the Mary L. Cook Public Library in Waynesville has much history on the Rev. James Smith family.

ABOLITIONIST BUTTERWORTH HELPED SHAPE WARREN COUNTY

"He was somewhat eccentric, but his peculiarities of thought and action generally attracted attention and sometimes ridicule simply because he was in advance of his generation, and it learned in time that he was right."

The above statement is how a late journalist described Henry Thomas Butterworth. The description is in direct relationship regarding Mr. Butterworth's work in the abolition movement. Hundreds of runaway slaves were sheltered and assisted by him in their flight to Canada and free soil territory.

Mr. Butterworth was born on the Fincastle Road, six miles south of Lynchburg, Virginia, on the 4th day of June, 1809. He was the son of Benjamin and Rachel Butterworth, and the youngest of five sisters and eight brothers.

In the year 1812 his father exchanged his Virginia farm for a tract of wild land of one thousand acres, lying between what is now Foster and Loveland on the Little Miami River.

At this time his father moved his family in wagons to the new country, which was at the time called the "far west."

Benjamin's newly acquired land was a wild and unsettled tract. Seeing no immediate future improvements, he established a home near Waynesville.

Gradually, his attention turned toward his acreage along the Little Miami, and in due time all the family settled there.

The only improvements on the land, previous to Benjamin Butterworth's acquisition, was a log cabin structured by a squatter named Cook, who for 20 years prior had cleared and cultivated about five acres.

Henry Thomas Butterworth's life was one of toil. The densely packed forest, the habitation of bears, panthers, wildcats and wolves, the constant deadening, grubbing and clearing of the forest, all took its toll on his physical being.

His opportunities to excel were centered around a log cabin school house. The puncheon floor, greased paper for window glass, fireplace for heating, children studying aloud, the teacher hardly unable to control the students, was an almost negative environment in which to advance.

At the age of twenty-one, Henry married Nancy Wales, six months his junior, at the Grove Meeting House of Friends near Harveysburg. The wedding was a double one with Nancy's sister, Jane, uniting in marriage to Valentine Nicholson.

Henry and Nancy, after the wedding, resided at the old homestead caring for his parents until the day of their death.

Henry Thomas and Nancy were the parents of eleven children, seven of whom survived him. They are: Jane W.B. Foster, Mary, Ann B. Thatcher, Isaac W., Emma B. Danforth, Rachel M.B. Bayless, and Caroline B. Lawrence.

Mr. Butterworth was a mechanic by trade, but his circumstances caused him to be a farmer. Nevertheless, he was a success in all his undertakings.

He had some peculiarities which tended to make his mannerisms of a somewhat skeptical nature. This trait often handicapped him, thus giving a wrong impression of his real character.

His deeds toward the public were one of the improvement of the country or community. One such accomplishment was his interest in the Montgomery Pike in which he gave his undivided support.

Another undertaking was his interest in the building of the Little Miami Railroad. His offer of giving the right-of-way through his farm, and the use of his water tank was another public minded effort.

The new railroad had its difficulties in the beginning, but Mr. Butterworth stood by the company and watched it flourish. For his part in the venture, he and his wife received life-time passes over the road and all its branches.

He was instrumental in building the Foster's-Loveland pike. His school promotions and his interest in higher education led to his founding of the Maineville Academy.

The Butterworth's continued in the abolition movement until the Fugitive Slave Law of 1850. His upholding of the anti-slavery movement was, in his opinion, a right that without question was a proper moral judgment.

Henry was brought up as a Friend in its strictest belief, however, he was disowned by the church when he witnessed the marriage of his eldest daughter performed by a "hireling minister." The event was considered contrary to the rules of the Quakers.

He was thus freed from the Quaker's belief and allowed to think and act for himself. His belief wandered toward the so-called modern spiritualism.

A strengthening of his own convictions and a belief encouraged by many of his own experiences never wavered for the remainder of his forty years of life.

JEREMIAH MORROW SHOULD BE CALLED THE FATHER OF OHIO

George Washington has been called the "Father of our Country," and, in this writer's opinion, Jeremiah Morrow should be called the "Father of Ohio." As we read on, we shall examine the political life of this pioneer and his contribution to the State of Ohio and the country.

In the early days of statehood, Mr. Morrow's accomplishments were awesome. He held the office of Representative for a longer period than any other. He was Governor four years, Senator six years, and Congressman-at-large ten years.

Ohio has had only one Congressman-at-large. (A member of the lower house of Congress who represents an entire State is called a Congressman-at-large.) This was Jeremiah Morrow of Warren County. He was for ten years the first and only representative of the State in Congress.

He moved from Pennsylvania in 1795 and located in Columbia, where his stay lasted two or three years. He, for a time, taught school and worked in the surveying field.

In 1798, Morrow moved to Warren County, cleared his newly purchased land, and lived here until his death.

When first elected to this prestigious post, he was a resident of Deerfield Township where he made his home in a modest log cabin. His dwelling was midway between the present site of Foster and Twenty Mile Stand, situated not far from the Little Miami River.

His first election to public office was in 1800 when he was elected as a member of the Territorial Legislature. In 1802, he was a member of the convention which framed the first Constitution of Ohio.

In 1803, he became a member of the first State Legislature. The center of the State Government at this time met at its first capitol, Chillicothe. Mr. Morrow attended all these meetings.

Ohio's first ten years as a State had only two officers chosen by a public vote, the Governor and a Congressman-at-large. Judges of the Supreme Court, U.S. Senators, and other officers for the State were selected by the Legislature.

Under the laws of the new State Constitution, the first election was held January 11, 1803, in which a Governor, members of the Legislature and county officers were elected. The first Governor was from Chillicothe, Dr. Edward Tiffin.

The Legislature designated the date for an election of Congressman-at-large as of June 21, 1803.

Morrow's name was brought up by many Jeffersonians as a candidate. Two of his principal opponents were William McMillan of Cincinnati, and Michael Baldwin of Chillicothe, both well known lawyers.

The official returns of the leading contenders for the first election of a U.S. Congressman from Ohio were: Jeremiah Morrow, Warren Co., 3701; Wm. McMillan, Hamilton Co., 1873; Michael Baldwin, Ross Co., 902; Elias Langham, Ross Co., 615; and Wm. Goforth, Hamilton Co., 313.

The results of the election of the opposing sides were: Jeffersonians, 5558; and Federalists, 1960.

Morrow was a well known and well liked Congressman, being elected to four successive terms, each by a greater majority than the previous.

In 1810, he was elected without an opposing candidate. All five terms incorporated a period in which only one representative from the State was comprised.

He was asked to serve as Governor of the State of Ohio. In September 1812, during his last term in office as Congressman-at-large, he published in several newspapers in Ohio that he would not be a candidate for Governor because of his commitment to Congress.

Ten years later he was elected Governor and served two terms. In the meantime, he had served one term in the United States Senate.

Morrow's record of sixteen years in his service to the country and Congress was elevated to high standards partly because of his journeys to and from Washington City.

Many times his attendance was asked for in special sessions held in the summer, and he responded diligently.

His trips over the mountains were made on horseback along with a complement of necessities. He forded many bridgeless streams, and sometimes swam his horse through the treacherous surges.

His most outstanding work in Congress was related to public lands, in which he served for a long period of time as chariman. Jeremiah Morrow was credited by Judge Joshua Collett (also from Warren County) as a proven land laws expert. He speaks highly of him by writing:

"He may, with propriety, be called the father of the land system of the United States. Being chairman of the committee on public lands he originated the land system and drew all the laws on the subject.

"No man ever possessed the confidence of the national legislature in regard to his public duties in a higher degree."

Henry Clay spoke of Jeremiah Morrow in a speech in the Senate in 1832, with regards to his great service as head of the land committe. He said:

"With the existing laws, the great state of the west is satisfied. During the long period in the house of representatives and in the Senate, that her upright and unambitious citizen, the first representative of that state, and afterwards successfully senator and governor, presided over the committee of public lands, we heard of none of these chimerical schemes.

"All went on smoothly and quietly and safely. No man in the sphere within which he acted, ever commanded or deserved the implicit confidence of congress more than Jeremiah Morrow. There existed a perfect persuasion of his entire impartiality between the old states and the new.

"A few artless but sensible words pronounced in his plain Scotch-Irish dialect were always sufficient to ensure the passage of any bill or resolution which he reported. For about twenty-five years there was no change in the system."

Morrow, while serving in Congress, did not waste much time in debate, his speeches being short, possibly never surpassing twenty minutes.

His elegance of manner tended to carry forth his message more than any other aspect in the business of national interests.

A work edited by General A.W. Greely, entitled, "Public Documents of the First Fourteen Congresses," carried a list of early Senators and Representatives who made the greatest number of reports in Congress.

Of the half dozen men whose names were highlighted were: Jeremiah Morrow of Ohio, 74; John

Randolph of Virginia, 66; Nathaniel Macon of North Carolina, 50; William B. Giles of Virginia, 48; Joseph B. Varnum of Massachusetts, 39; and William Findlay of Pennsylvania, 39.

There is much more to be said about this outstanding citizen. Perhaps at another time another article will appear in this column that tells more of his personal life.

It is well that we read and perhaps eulogize one of the finest men that Warren County has produced. Rarely do we find one who has served the people and his country with such great esteem.

JOHN MORROW INSTRUMENTAL IN WARREN COUNTY

John Morrow, at the time of his death, was the oldest citizen in Deerfield Township, and was also one of the oldest native born citizens of Warren County.

He was the eldest and last surviving child of Governor Jeremiah and Mary Parkhill Morrow.

His two brothers and four sisters reached maturity and died in middle age of pulmonary diseases.

John Morrow was born in the pioneer cabin of his parents November 28, 1800, and died within a half mile of his birthplace November 26, 1887.

His funeral took place, which if he had lived, on his 87th birthday. He had complete control of his mental faculties until his last brief illness.

His father died in his 81st year and his mother died in her 70th year. They were first cousins.

He was but one year old when his father took his seat in the Territorial Legislature. The next year Governor Morrow became a member of the convention which formed the first Constitution of Ohio.

The third year John's father was called to Washington City as the first Representative in Congress from the new State.

He journeyed to Washington with his wife and their two children as far as the home of his wife's parents in Fayette County, Pennsylvania, the journey being made on two horses. John Morrow, in his fourth year, remembered the trip home, the journey being made on the Ohio River.

He remembered being on a large boat with his parents, several other persons, and a collection of horses.

John's education was achieved in the log school houses of the pioneers.

One of his memories was attending an old log school house directly east of the site of Twenty Mile Stand.

The facility was burned to the ground during a holiday celebration when the larger boys barred out the school master.

His youth was one of hardships. Pioneer life not only affected the older generation, but also the youngsters.

His father traveled back and forth to Washington as a Representative for sixteen years without missing a session. John, being the eldest, was depended on by his father for the support of himself and the family.

In the meantime, Governor Morrow built a mill on the Little Miami River which was completed about 1812.

John was also instrumental in the operation of the mill at different times. He engaged himself in hauling flour from the mill to Cincinnati over the ungraveled and bridgeless roads, which at times were virtually impassable. Commonplace at that time, the teamsters who did not bring market produce were to remain overnight on the public landing at the river.

Rather than spend a night at the river, John preferred to stay at Walnut Hills, which at the time consisted of only one dwelling.

When a little boy, he was frequently sent to the nearest post office which was at the time located in Lebanon.

The post office in Montgomery was opened in 1812, which made the trip much closer. Twenty Mile Stand established a post office in 1819.

It was this year that John and his eldest sister made a horseback journey over the Allegheny Mountains to the home of his ancestors near Gettysburg, Pennsylvania.

John Morrow married Nancy Espy, daughter of Thomas, on March 14, 1822. Mr. Espy was one of the early pioneers of Warren County.

Nancy Espy Morrow was born within a half mile of the birthplace of her husband; they were childhood playmates. Their marriage lasted fifty-nine years. Mrs. Morrow died January 6, 1881, aged 82 years.

Morrow, in 1825, became Major of the First Battalion, Second Brigade, First Division of the Ohio Militia, and afterwards was known as Major Morrow.

In May 1825, Major Morrow traveled with his father to Cincinnati to officially welcome LaFayette to the State of Ohio.

Major Morrow was never a contestant for high politics, although he did serve as Township Trustee, Justice of the Peace, and was one of the early directors of the Warren County Agricultural Society.

He was a supporter of John Q. Adams against Andrew Jackson. He was a Whig during the total existence of the party, and afterwards became a Republican in 1856.

His first time voting was in October, 1822, when his father was first elected Governor. His religious faith relied upon the United Presbyterian Church.

He was revered by his fellow man as one of high standards and honesty. His judgment was sound, and he was one of the most respected men in his community.

He was not a man of wealth, but always had enough to pay his debts. He always gave generously to educational and religious causes.

He assisted in the erection of Maineville Academy and was the last president of its board.

WILLIAM HARMON LEGACY LIVES THROUGHOUT
LEBANON AND BEYOND

The people of Lebanon and the County of Warren have given so much to the State of Ohio and boundaries beyond, but one name that stands out as having "given" of himself and shared his wealth is none other than William Elmer Harmon.

Our story begins this week many years before the birth of Mr. Harmon. We shall now venture back to a pioneer Warren Countian named Jedediah Tingle.

Mr. Tingle was a native of the State of Delaware, born in 1767 and lived for a period in the Redstone country of Pennsylvania. He settled in Columbia at the mouth of the Little Miami River about 1791.

Later, in 1797, he established a home about a mile and a half west of Lebanon; his deed called for a total section (640 acres) of land.

Sometime later he sold one-half of his section to David Reeder for $213.33, the price being 66 2/3 cents per acre, the exact amount Judge Symmes paid for the land in his original patent. Mr. Reeder established his home on the southern half while Mr. Tingle settled on the northern segment where he died in 1827, age 61.

Jedediah Tingle married Elizabeth Reeder, a native of Virginia, the relationship producing fifteen children. The last survivor of these children was Mrs. Asenath Wood, widow of William Wood.

Mr. Wood was a successful businessman, his endeavors including a woolen factory (located on Mulberry Street and operated by horses walking on an incline plane), and mercantile business. The Woods were the grandparents of William E. Harmon which in turn made the pioneer, Jedediah Tingle, the great-grand father of William E. Harmon.

William Elmer Harmon was born in Lebanon, March 25, 1862, on the northwest corner of Mechanic and New Street. He died July 15, 1928, at his home in Southport, Connecticut.

His parents were Lieutenant William R. and

Mary Wood Harmon. He had one brother, Clifford Burke Harmon, who was born July 5, 1868.

Their father was stationed at several remote garrisons which was an unsuitable place to raise children. The boys were subsequently raised mostly in Lebanon.

Young William's early Lebanon memories inspired his motivations which led to his many generous philanthropic ventures. His memories and experiences of the old reservoir, the swimming, boating, fishing, and skating were deeply etched into the mind of the youth.

He attended Lebanon public schools and graduated in 1881. His stint at the National Normal University was interrupted by his ambition of becoming a physician, later transferring to Jefferson School of Medicine in Louisville, Ky.

The financial difficulties of his father interrupted his medical schooling, and so he was forced to take a job as a salesman.

His marriage to Corrine Lado in Louisville in 1883, ended in tragedy; his wife died in childbirth fifteen months after their wedding.

Still another tragedy: Mr. Harmon's mother died in August, 1884, and his father succumbed less than a year later. The misfortunes of the family set heavily on him, and with no professional job stability, and a minor brother to care for, great stress was placed upon him.

Sometime later, William and his brother, Clifford, worked together with their uncle, Charles E. Wood, in the real estate business. Their first joint undertaking was the development of a subdivision of Branch Hill in 1887.

Expanding to Cincinnati and Dayton in their new business proved to be a successful and prosperous move.

Further expansion included twenty-six Midwestern cities which encompassed Pittsburgh, Chicago, Boston, Brooklyn, Midwood and Flatbush on Long Island, their organization developing dramatically.

Mr. Harmon again married, this time to Catherine F. Griffiths on October 1, 1890. They made their home in Lexington, Massachusetts. To this marriage was born one son and two daughters. Catherine Harmon died October 5, 1948, and is buried on Staton Island beside her husband.

The Wood, Harmon Company, in 1900, was acclaimed the largest real estate operation in the world.

The Wood, Harmon Company real estate operation was concluded as such in 1907. William Harmon continued in his capacity, maintained the operation and took complete control of the organization.

Mr. Harmon never forgot his birthplace of Lebanon. Through his real estate profession he accumulated a fortune. His generosity and a well developed philanthropic plan allowed him to distribute his monies for many public needs.

If such a financial shortcoming was evident, a mysterious check would find its way to the source. For many years checks would arrive from New York which were endorsed by a mysterious "Jedediah Tingle."

The checks were sent to writers of prose and poetry who were thought to be in need of funds, to the aid of poor children, and many hundreds more. The Children's Aid Society received many donations from this intriguing person.

The receiving of these many gifts from a person unknown was often questioned as to whom the benefactor's identity was. This "Jedediah Tingle" at one time announced he was carrying on a mission "to bring smiles and tender thoughts to the great in heart in high and low places, to comfort and cheer those who do exceptional things or suffer."

On July 19, 1928, soon after Mr. Harmon's death, the New York Times announced to the world the mysterious benefactor was none other than William E. Harmon himself, assuming the name of his maternal great-grandfather.

Mr. Harmon retired at the age of sixty from active work in his real estate business in New York and devoted the rest of his life to the solution of social problems.

His generosity gave more to his home town than any other location. One of his gifts went to the

Mechanics Institute Library of his home town; the donation being a large collection of new and valuable books. The books were much read by the young people.

He proposed to set up a free public library in Warren County which was to be centralized in Lebanon. He agreed to give in cash a sum of $3,000 and $100 annually for ten years, with a provision there be added by the citizens of the County $2,000 in cash and $100 annually for ten years. This was the first such proposal in the State of Ohio.

The library located in Lebanon removed much hope of Warren Countians contributions left by Mr. Harmon. Times being what they were almost ruled out county wide donations for providing financial upkeep of the new venture.

After a period of time and hashing over the issues by the Lebanon Carnegie Library trustees, the town accepted a gift of $10,000 from the Carnegie Fund, the deal being finalized by a gift of $3,000 from Mr. Harmon.

The future site of the library was a part of the public square so the town paid nothing either for the building, furnishings, or the site.

Harmon Park, a tract of 88 acres, was conceived and given to the citizens of Lebanon in 1912. The park was so well received by the residents that a program was set up on a national and world wide park system that was so named, "Harmon Playgrounds."

The many sites were located in Texas, Michigan, Utah, Oregon, Kentucky, Minnesota, West Virginia, Georgia, South Carolina, Maryland, the Dakotas, Florida and Washington; one hundred and nineteen facilities were established in thirty-two states by 1926. Ohio had its share, too many to mention in this article.

Mr. Harmon had discussed with many residents and friends of Lebanon the feasibility of a building in which athletic and indoor events could be performed.

The corner stone of Harmon Hall was laid December 12, 1912. Within this stone was a copper box lined with asbestos which contained many papers and objects of the time. The hall was dedicated on November 6, 1913.

Harmon Hall is located at 105 S. Broadway, the present home of the Warren County Historical Society.

Through his Harmon Foundation, he established the Religious Motion Picture Foundation for producing films especially designed for church services, Sunday schools and young people's Sunday meetings.

Four such films had been distributed and received favorably. These films were not intended as a substitute for the formal service, but as an additive.

There had been much opposition to the portrayal of Jesus in motion pictures up to this time, but in these films he is depicted as a "living, active being, performing his mission on earth and the portrayal arouses in the spectator feelings of reverence."

The Harmon Foundation is still active, some seventy-three years after its creation. Through his many social gifts, William Elmer Harmon simply returned what he had received from life.

HISTORICAL FIGURE EVANS HAD ROOTS IN WAYNESVILLE AREA

A Warren County man who is seldom mentioned went on to become one of the most distinguished gentlemen from the County. His many accomplishments far exceed that of modern day adventurists. His name is John Evans.

He was a physician, teacher, writer, governor, railroad builder, founder of a city and two universities.

John Evans was born March 9, 1814, in Waynesville, Ohio, to David and Rachel Burnet Evans. He was the oldest of 13 children.

The first of the Evans family to move to Warren County was Benjamin and Hannah Smith Evans, the grandparents of our subject, the time being October 1803, shortly after the organizing of the State and County.

The Evans family were devout Quakers. In 1811, a decision was made to build a house of worship by the Friends. By 1812 the lower section of the brick structure was completed. In 1813, an upper portion was added.

The relevance to this building is that the marriage of David and Rachel Burnet Evans was the first to be performed in the new structure.

David Evans owned 640 acres of good land in Wayne Township. John, being the eldest, was to acquire the land and holdings of his father.

But John's mind wandered toward the aspects of a medical career. He was destined to be a friend to humankind.

In 1833, when only a lad of 19 in Waynesville, he wrote his cousin: "It is the imperative voice of the Almighty that we shall do all the good we can."

John was apparently prodded along in his medical career by his mother. He entered Clermont Academy in Philadelphia, but was graduated in 1838 from the medical department of Cincinnati College.

With his father's forgiveness and a gift of a pony, saddle, bridle and ten dollars in cash, John ventured West to gain his personal undertaking.

He spent about a year roving and finally settled at Attica, Indiana, in which he spent nine years. He proceeded to leave his mark in the State.

Dr. Evans and others grappled with the State and finally persuaded them to build the first school for deaf mutes. He and his accomplices petitioned for the insane and the outcome was a new institution called the Indiana Lunatic Asylum.

He was made superintendent and director of the building project. In this particular era the procedure was that the insane and the hardened criminals were housed within the same establishment.

One year later, in 1845, he was assigned professor of obstetrics at Rush Medical College, this being a dual role while overseeing the building of the Lunatic Asylum.

In December 1848, the Asiatic cholera was spreading like wildfire. No cure was available at the time. Dr. Evans surmised that it was a transmutable disease that followed the shipping routes and rail lines.

Many medical authorities seemed amused at the Dr.'s idea, however, his perspective was accepted and laws of quarantine were initiated nationally.

From 1848 to 1852, Dr. Evans edited "The Illinois and Indiana Medical Journal," his subjects being limited not just to medicine.

Aside from his editorialization he was an inventor of sorts. Among other inventions, he invented an extractor which he considered superior to forceps.

Dr. Evans removed to Chicago and again made his mark. He served on the city council and was responsible for the establishment of the first high school in Chicago, the years being 1853 to 1855.

While serving on the council, he brought up an issue for the adoption of an ordinance in which all the low-lying streets and sidewalks be elevated for health as well as traffic purposes.

Perhaps his most notable accomplishment was the founding of "Northwestern University," the name being derived from the Northwest Territory. As he stated it, the establishment of a Christian college would "mold minds and characters for good."

The university was located amongst a wild and wooded portion of land along Lake Michigan just north of Chicago. The Illinois Legislature granted a charter for the university January 28, 1851. Immediately a community sprang up which was appropriately named "Evanston."

It seems odd that Dr. Evans was a born Quaker; apparently the turn to the Methodist faith was inspired by Bishop Simpson's preaching.

Dr. Evans had much influence in creating the Hospital of the Lakes, later known as Mercy Hospital.

His father sent substantial sums for purposes of investment in the expanding Chicago area. Using these funds wisely, Dr. Evans ventured into real estate. Some of his holdings were: the Methodist Church block, which was one of Chicago's first office buildings; the Methodist book concern; and the "Northwestern Christian Advocate."

Filling in his spare time, he managed to take charge of a rail line from the Indiana border to Chicago. The line was the western end of the Fort Wayne & Chicago Railroad, it being part of a system that extended from Pittsburgh to Chicago.

Politics was the next move for this man of many vocations. He was a great admirer of Abraham Lincoln, thus becoming a member of the convention of Mr. Lincoln's nominating committee in 1860.

President Lincoln remembered Dr. Evans and in 1862 convinced him to become Territorial Governor of Colorado.

He moved to and resided in Denver, which at that time was a "shanty town of twelve or fifteen hundred inhabitants."

After Lincoln's assassination, President Andrew Johnson vetoed the Colorado Bill which caused the doctor to leave politics, but he diligently remained in Colorado for the next 35 years.

While residing in Denver, Dr. John Evans founded the Colorado Seminary, first school of higher education in the State. Out of this venture grew the "University of Denver."

His accomplishments in Denver included: a business block, the Evans school, a station on the Denver and Pacific railroad, the first cable car, and a mountain peak in the Rocky Mountains appropriately named "Mt. Evans."

Dr. Evans donated enormous sums to the universities he founded. Being an extremely generous man somehow seemed to reap rewards far beyond our imagination.

This man of personal enormity was married twice, first to Hannah Canby, December 11, 1838.

The union saw the birth of four children, three of which died, while a daughter, Josephine, married Samuel T. Elbert, who was Governor of Colorado in 1873-74. Hannah Evans died in Chicago on October 9, 1850.

His second marriage was to Margaret Gray in August 1853. Four children were born to this wedlock.

Dr. John Evans died July 3, 1897, his physical being surely missed, but his deeds will always live on.

HON. JOHN McLEAN FOUNDED THE WESTERN STAR

There is so much to be written about one of Warren County's finest men that only books could record his superior achievements. However, with just a few words, the writer will humbly try to review the life of one of the County and Nation's finest, John McLean.

John was born in Morris County, N.J., March 11, 1785, the son of Fergus McLean, an immigrant from the north of Ireland. Fergus was of Scotch descent and John's mother was of Dutch descent.

Fergus was determined to locate with his family to the Ohio Valley. He was delayed for a short time in western Virginia, later moving to Jessamine County, Ky., and thence to the neighborhood of Maysville, Ky.

He purchased and opened a farm in what is now Clearcreek Township. He later laid out the town of Ridgeville in 1814.

Fergus and his eldest son, John, visited their newly purchased land as early as the spring of 1796. Together they cleared a parcel of ground, planted it in corn, and returned to their family in Kentucky.

John occasionally made the journey from Maysville to the clearing in Warren County on foot, packing his supplies with him.

The McLean family was large and very poor. This situation caused John to endure many hardships. Nevertheless, he had acquired a keen sense for education and sought to pursue it.

There were no high schools nor any good elementary schools near his home. In 1802, he traveled two miles up the Licking River in Kentucky to study Latin under Robert Stubbs.

To pay for this education he sometimes chopped down trees and helped clear the land for his neighbors.

At the age of 19, John was apprenticed to John Stites Gano, Clerk of Common Pleas of Hamilton County. An agreement was made that Fergus was to supply all wearing apparel and account for all sickness, accident, or disasters incurred by young John for a period of two years. He was also restricted from marrying during this period.

Gano in turn was to educate him in the duties of clerk and provide him with comfortable lodging.

John studied law under Arthur St. Clair, Jr., at Cincinnati. For self support, he wrote in the courthouses at Cincinnati and Lebanon.

While a law student in the small town of Cincinnati, he found there were no social functions nor evening recreations. He joined a society that had a great number of outstanding members, one being Dr. Daniel Drake, then a young physician.

His energies were so great that on one occasion, when he was to participate in a debate, he questioned himself about the subject and sat up all night in preparation. His extra effort paid off, for the next evening he was well rewarded for his nights toil.

In 1793 an old press of the Ramage pattern was floated down the Ohio River to Fort Washington, now the site of Cincinnati. On this press was published the Queen City's first "recognized" newspaper, **"The Liberty Hall."**

In 1806, McLean learned the old Ramage press was for sale. Racing against time, he caught the first stage to the Queen City for the express purpose of purchasing it.

He loaded the press and type into a cart and borrowed a yoke of oxen from Judge Gano. He drove the oxen himself to the home of David Fox at Deerfield. Here he remained overnight and the next day proceeded on to Lebanon.

His success was assured, and in a few weeks, the primitive old machine was installed and running in the City of Cedars.

That following year, the press began striking off the first edition of **The Western Star**, a newspaper that still carries the excellent tradition it was founded on. It is at present time the oldest weekly newspaper in Ohio, the first issue being published February 13, 1807.

Fergus McLean aided his son in the distribution of the newly established newspaper. He rode many miles on horseback throughout the countryside delivering the paper and taking subscriptions.

Mail delivery was disgusting at this time, and it was possible that during this dilemma, young John got some ideas regarding the reconstruction of the postal department, a service he later provided.

It was a good year for McLean. At the age of 22 he had started a newspaper, was admitted to the bar, and took a bride, Elizabeth Edwards.

After a short time, he sold his newspaper to his brother Nathaniel, who operated it until he entered the War of 1812.

John was converted to the Methodist faith about 1811 by John Collins. He was active in this denomination the rest of his life.

In 1812, he was elected to public office, being chosen a Representative to Congress. The State was at this time divided into congressional districts, the first district consisting of Warren, Hamilton, Butler and Preble counties.

Jeremiah Morrow had been a Representative to Congress in this district the previous ten years.

McLean ran for reelection in 1814 without opposition, and it is reported that he received the vote of every voter who went to the polls.

While serving in this capacity, he was a leader in Congress that appropriated funds to rebuild Washington after its burning during the War of 1812. He also introduced bills to pension the widows and families of non-commissioned men killed in the war.

The Thirteenth Congress assembled in the old post office and patent building until Washington was rebuilt.

Federal troops had been occupying the Cincinnati courthouse during the war and, due to carelessness, a fire was started and the facility burned. McLean secured passage of a bill to compensate Cincinnati for this loss.

In 1816, he was unanimously elected a Judge of the Ohio Supreme Court. With this new post he was forced to resign his seat in Congress.

His new position lasted six years until President Monroe appointed him Commissioner of the General Land Office.

The following year, in 1823, he was appointed Postmaster General of the United States.

The postal department had been mismanaged by the previous parties. Order was restored and supervised with such great precision that Postmaster McLean and his department met with eminent praise.

A deficit of $150,000 was facing him when accepting this assignment. Under him, new postal routes were established and modern offices were built. In 1827, through his reorganization, it had attained a balance of $100,000.

By unanimous vote both Houses of Congress voted to raise his salary from $4,000 to $6,000 a year. John Randolph voted against the pay raise, stating his belief that it should be reduced to $4,000 should McLean leave office.

John Quincy Adams was next elected President and agreed to allow McLean to serve in the same capacity, his total tenure being six years.

Andrew Jackson, as President, offered the jobs of Secretary of War and Navy to McLean. He refused the request because of the former's plan of removing political opponents from office.

Jackson then asked McLean to be an Associate Justice of the Supreme Court of the United States, a position he accepted and held for 31 years until his death, April 4, 1861.

From 1834 to 1841, tragedy darkened his personal life. Three of his daughters, his mother, his father, his brother William, and his wife Elizabeth, all died.

In 1843, he married Sarah Belle Garrard, the widowed daughter of Israel Ludlow, one of the founders of Cincinnati. A son, Ludlow, was born to this union but lived only a few weeks.

Sarah accompanied her husband in his job assignment and soon became well known in Washington and Philadelphia circles.

McLean was continuously in high political or judicial office for forty-nine consecutive years. He was distinctively identified with the party opposed to the extension of slavery.

Possibly John McLean's most important and long-lasting moment was when he dissented in the vote regarding the Dred Scott case. His judgment has gone down in history as a monumental stride toward human rights.

In 1856, he was a presidential candidate in the first Republican convention ever held. He received 196 votes to 396 for Fremont. He was also a write-in candidate for the same office in 1860.

He became ill in 1859, but through a committal to his work load, he continued until the close of that session of court.

He became very sick due to a cold during Lincoln's inauguration and returned home to Cincinnati on March 22, 1861. He contracted pneumonia on April 3 and died the next day.

Fifty carriages gathered at the Cincinnati courthouse on the afternoon of the 6th. Together they drove to his funeral in a pouring rain almost at the same moment guns were being fired at Ft. Sumter, marking the beginning of the Civil War. He is buried at Spring Grove Cemetery in Cincinnati.

Many American history books contain excerpts concerning John McLean's aspiring lifetime. In this writer's opinion, he has without a doubt achieved the highest honors of any fellow Warren Countian.

GENERAL WILLIAM CORTENUS SCHENCK WAS FRANKLIN FOUNDER

In commemoration of Franklin's 200th birthday this year, 1996, the writer will sketch a short history of its founder, General William Cortenus Schenck.

Franklin is one of the oldest settlements in the County. It is easily identified as the city that lies in the valley of the Great Miami River.

It was founded in part by General Schenck and Daniel C. Cooper, both surveyors from New Jersey. The new settlement was not recorded at Cincinnati until 1800.

Cooper, in September 1795, marked and laid out a road from Ft. Hamilton to the Mad River. In 1796, he, along with other proprietors, settled Dayton. In 1800, he sold his interest in Franklin to General Schenck.

The treaty with the Indians was not signed until August 1795. Schenck was commissioned, at the age of 20, a Lieutenant of the Hamilton County Militia of the Northwest Territory on February 6, 1793. (Hamilton County originally consisted of all of Hamilton, Warren, Butler and part of Greene and Montgomery counties.)

While a part of the militia, Lieutenant Schenck, along with others, traversed the lands north of the Ohio, traveling on the east side of the Great Miami. No doubt he evidenced on this trip the magnificent site along the river that was later to become Franklin, for late in 1795, the town was platted. After a long hard winter, spring abounded and the building began.

Schenck was born near Freehold N.J., January 11, 1773, the son of Rev. William Schenck. The latter was ordained a minister of the Presbyterian denomination in 1771, and a year later was found to be serving a church in Allentown, N.J.

This era was marked with the beginnings of the American Revolution. Rev. Schenck served the American cause as an army chaplain.

In 1777, the family, which included four year old William, were driven out of New Jersey by the British and removed to Bucks County, Pa. Here Rev. Schenck served as pastor of the church of North and South Hampton.

William received his first schooling from his father. He later lived with his uncle, General John N. Cumming, and attended school at Princeton College. Undecided as to his vocation, his studies included both law and medicine.

Gen. Cumming was associated with land deals in the Ohio country, along with Judge John Cleves Symmes and a Mr. Burnet from New Jersey. Possibly the General instilled an interest in William to travel west into the unexplored frontier.

After young William's first explorations in late 1795, he became ill and returned to Huntington, Long Island, where his father was ministering a church.

Gen. Cumming thought it would be better for William's health if he were to return to the Ohio country. On April 26, 1796, a letter was received by William from Uncle John which stated that a compass, a chain and mathematical instruments, along with land warrants, would be supplied him by Israel Ludlow and Jacob Burnet.

Never having an interest in surveying procedures, he was now in a position to do what was possibly in his heart for some time, explore the great unknown lands north of the Ohio.

Through this godsend William C. Schenck would become known as the most proficient draftsman and capable surveyors in the West. (Ohio was then the proving grounds for the most elaborate surveying system in the world. The rectangular surveying system in Ohio included both five and six mile townships.)

At age 23, he was employed as a surveyor of the Virginia Military Lands, which lay between the Little Miami and Scioto Rivers.

He returned to his father's home at Huntington, Long Island, in 1797. It was here he took as his bride, Elizabeth Rogers, daughter of Captain William Rogers. The new couple set out for Cincinnati in the spring of 1799.

Schenck was elected Secretary of the first Territorial Legislature in Cincinnati on September 26, 1799.

He was away on business during the winter of 1801 and '02, having traveled to the area of Licking County where only a few families had settled. He surveyed a tract of 4,220 acres owned by Uncle John and G.W. Burnet, and was given a one-third interest in the lands due in part to his surveying. While in this undertaking he laid out the town of Newark, Ohio, designed from the same town in New Jersey.

He moved his family, which at this time included two children, to his town of Franklin in 1803. It was here that he would father eight more children, which included Admiral James Findlay and General Robert Cumming Schenck. He spent the rest of his life in the town that he founded and was buried in the Woodhill Cemetery.

His home was built along the river on Front (River) Street between First and Second. He had picked out a spot that comfortably fit in with the scheme of the beautiful river.

The unsettled country apparently attracted family members from the old homeland, for John Noble Cumming Schenck, William's younger brother, followed him to the Miami country in 1799 or 1800. He first worked for Martin Baum, a well known marketer from Cincinnati. His work was of such quality that he was sent to Franklin and became its first Postmaster and a successful businessman.

Other family members to follow William were brothers Garrett and Peter. Both portrayed the family name in Franklin.

General Schenck was very comfortable with his brothers near him. He was now content and proceeded with the business of the town. He donated lots for public buildings, a church, a school and a park along the river.

(In 1814, a governmental body was organized and, in 1837, Franklin's incorporation charter was finalized. It became a city in October 1950.)

Schenck advertised on August 31, 1803, in the Cincinnati newspapers, **The Western Spy** and **The Hamilton Gazette**, that "a person qualified to teach an English school will find employment."

His interests were directed toward higher education, and in securing this concern, he was appointed to the original board of trustees of Miami University in Oxford.

He was also elected to two terms in the first Ohio Senate.

William received his second military assignment on November 17, 1807. He was selected Captain of a Battalion in the 3rd Regiment of Hamilton County. It was either prior to, or during the War of 1812, that he received the commission of General.

General Schenck founded the Eastern Star Lodge of the Masonic Order on December 17, 1819.

While serving in these capacities, he still worked as a surveyor and was engaged in selling lands mainly for General Cumming and Mr. Burnet.

By an Act of Congress, in 1816, an area of 12 square miles on the Maumee River, near its mouth, was surveyed and sold. The General surveyed the tract and laid out a town, Fort Lawrence, which later became known as Toledo.

Part of this land he acquired for himself. This area, infiltrated with swamps, caused Schenck undue sickness. He later sold his part for a thousand dollars.

A canal project was being discussed that would link Lake Erie to the Ohio River by way of Toledo to Cincinnati. William C. Schenck was one of three commissioners appointed by Governor Ethan Brown for this undertaking. His part as commissioner was to survey a portion of the lands.

On January 11, 1821, General Schenck delivered a speech in the Ohio Legislature encouraging the construction of the canal. He was suddenly stricken ill, and within seven hours of the address, he died, age 48.

He had suffered many hardships in the wilds during his stint as surveyor. His dream of seeing a canal arriving in Franklin did not become a reality, for in Middletown, Ohio, on July 21, 1825, the first spadeful of dirt was removed for the beginning of the Miami Canal.

HISTORIAN FINDS GUSTIN A FAMILIAR WARREN COUNTY NAME

"What's in a name?"

This is a familiar old saying that has been handed down through generations. We all know that our name is our only possession that cannot be taken away from us.

I found while researching my genealogy that my surname originated in Ireland. It came from the word "bog" which was derived from the people who worked the bogs in the old country.

The origin of many of our American family surnames has been lost forever. Many of these surnames can be traced to the European countries and points beyond.

The population of the United States has so many nationalities represented, and has had so many name changes since our forefathers arrived in this country, that tracing one's own name can be very challenging.

A grand old Warren County surname, "Gustin," actually originated in America.

It was at one time more common in the County than any other place in the United States.

The name has been traced back to the latter part of the 17th century.

The origination of the Gustin family came from the Island of Jersey where the language and descent of the people was French.

The family name in Jersey was Jean, the French version of John.

Edmond Jean lived in the Parish of St. Owen, Isle of Jersey, where he married Esther Rossignon on April 25, 1638. This marriage had a number of children, one of them being baptized January 9, 1647, and christened Augustin.

Augustin Jean came to America about 1674. Possibly his first residence was at Reading, Massachusetts. He was a soldier in the Indian war known as the King Phillip War. His name was written in the roster of soldiers as Augustin John. The transition of his name was easily changed to John Gustin in which he was customarily known in his later years.

A deed was signed by John transferring land and houses left to him by his father. It reads as such:

"As the name was given or left or otherwise ordered unto me, the said Augustine John by my father and mother, Edmond Jean and Esther, his wife, late of the Parish of St. Owen, in the island of Jersey."

After King Phillip's War had ended, John received a tract of land at Falmouth (now Portland, Maine), after which he later purchased more land.

He married Elizabeth Brown on January 12, 1678, and resided at Falmouth for several years, until this small town was destroyed by the French and Indians in 1690. This incident caused him to move away for a spell, but returned at a later date where he died in 1719.

His will named six children, four sons and two daughters. As generations passed, the Gustin family was found not only in Portland, Maine, but in many surrounding states and in the Province of Quebec, Canada, and after 1798, in Warren County.

The first Gustin found in the County was Jeremiah, a grandson of John. He was born July 1, 1740, possibly in Glastonbury, Connecticut. He moved with his parents to New Jersey, and later to Pennsylvania in 1798, when he was 58 years old.

His family was fully grown, and with them he moved to the Northwest Territory, finally settling in Clearcreek Township in Warren County. The family was among the pioneers of the area.

He purchased a full section (640 acres) just east of Red Lion. Jeremiah, along with his family, settled in the middle of the woods and built a home.

He died August 31, 1823, and was buried, along with his wife, Bethany, in the Kirby Cemetery (now called the Turtlecreek Cemetery) just north of Lebanon.

MELVA BEATRICE WILSON

Women in recent decades have received their share of recognition in the many professional fields, and rightly so. One career in which one would not expect a woman to excel in is the art of sculpture.

A Warren County woman achieved honors as one of the greatest sculptors in the world: her name is Melva Beatrice Wilson.

Miss Wilson came from a long line of distinguished ancestors, one of whom, James Wilson, was a signer of the Declaration of Independence.

She was born in Morrow, Ohio, the daughter of John Lafayette and Mary Brooks Wilson.

She was said to have "not only been born with the proverbial silver spoon, but that the spoon was diamond studded."

At an early age, instead of making mud pies with her playmates, she began to model in clay. Her favorite spot was a quiet hillside overlooking Morrow, where as a child she used to dream of her future life's work.

Miss Wilson, at the age of 15, accepted a scholarship for the art of sculpturing at Adrian College in Michigan.

She graduated from Morrow High School at the age of 17, applied for, and for three successive years, won the $100 prize for superior sculpture at the Cincinnati Art Academy. In addition to the prize money she received free tuition for these years.

Her first instructions at the Academy were received from the famed Rebisso. While at the Institute she sold her models and received orders for her works.

She next traveled abroad and then to New York. While in the countries of Europe she made a thorough research of the raw materials of the marble quarries. Into this segment her creativity was to be developed.

She decided that New York was the best location for the quality advancements she needed. To supplement her income while pursuing a career as a sculptress, she reverted to writing poetry.

Melva Wilson's artistry in the field of sculpturing was soon known throughout the world. Possibly one of her best known creations is the outstanding statue of Christ which tops the mortuary chapel at Calvary Cemetery on Long Island.

It was erected by Cardinal Farley as a suitable burial place for his clergy. This figure of Christ typifies the Christ of the second resurrection, the only one that any artist had ever created. A period of five years was needed for this magnificent undertaking.

On many of her works this lady of creativity actually supervised the construction of the scaffolding. She would mount the structure and, with chisel and hammer in hand, fashion the marble and stone in her own artistic manner.

One writer says that "Miss Wilson has made a profession of architectural sculptured figures, patriotic and ecclesiastic, for Country and for God, and many of her works adorn public buildings in this country."

She worked for years on sculptures for the new Saint Louis Catholic Cathedral. This display consisted of large porcelain panels for the walls of the cathedral, they being the largest such panels in the world. They had to be turned in large sections, each weighing 400 pounds. "Everything must be done for the first time, even in art," said the fine sculptress.

Her two largest panels were in Byzantine sculpture displaying seven archangels. Most meaningful were two very large angels, with five being grouped in the background, and two cherubs as attendants. The panels measured 13 feet 6 inches in height by 4 feet 10 inches in width.

The primary feature of these panels consisted of two statues, one of St. Michael and the other, St. Raphael. Each figure measured 10 feet high and were placed on opposite sides of the altar.

Miss Wilson's work was highly commended by art connoisseurs and Fathers of the Church as refinement in the highest fashion.

Included in her work at the Cathedral was a

series of 400 figures, which measured 200 feet long and 8 feet deep, entitled, "The Way of the Cross."

In 1913, she traded in her sculptor's tools for a whole new way of life, that of a nun. Her entire life had been one of personal accomplishment. Asked as to her reasoning, she replied:

"I have thought it out, and I know where my best happiness will be found. I am through with art and the world. I have accomplished what I most desired. I believe that I am called to the church."

She became a Sister of Charity in the convent Mount Saint Vincent, on the Hudson in New York, one of the most meticulous orders of the Catholic Church.

Her last works were entitled, "Stations of the Cross." She completed over thirty figures, all in Parian marble for the Saint Louis Church. She had turned down offers for a long period of time knowing of her new venture into the church.

She vowed to serve the poor and devote her every waking hour to works of charity. She never again took up the sculptor's chisel, the mission that made her world famous.

Melva Beatrice Wilson died in 1921. She was brought back to her birthplace and buried in the family plot in the Morrow cemetery. Her burial place is marked with a large angelic form at the top of a monument shaft that lies in the northeast section of the cemetery. It is an outstanding exhibit to the memorial of one of the world's finest in the field of sculpturing.

LT. CHARLES L. EARNHART: LEBANON'S WAR ACE

Down through the years Warren County has produced many men and women of the Armed Forces who have excelled in times of battle. One such person was Lt. Charles L. Earnhart, Lebanon's World War II flying ace.

Lieutenant Earnhart was born Nov. 6, 1919, in Lebanon, Ohio, a son of Walter and Sarah Guttery

Earnhart.

He entered the U.S. Air Force at the beginning of the war and took his training at Curtis Field in Texas. He was later shipped overseas and served as a pilot in the Twelfth Air Force in North Africa.

From the beginning he was engaged almost daily in combat with the German Air Force. At one point, Lt. Earnhart was shot down in enemy territory, escaped German machine gun bullets, walked back to his burning plane to pick up his jacket, and then made his way safely back to his home base.

He was credited with damaging four enemy planes before losing control of his own.

Mrs. Earnhart received a letter from Mrs. Frank Mullinux, Jr., of Watertown, Tennessee, telling of the experience her husband had with Lt. Earnhart. Mullinux was in the same squadron with Lt. Earnhart and was shot down. The Lieutenant saved his life, although he was captured later.

She also disclosed that Lt. Earnhart had six Messerschmidts and one Junkers troop plane to his credit.

In the March 20, 1943, issue of the New Yorker an unidentified reporter, who had visited troops in Tunisia, wrote of his meeting with Lt. Earnhart.

The reporter obtained a piece of paper that contained direct accounts of pilots that had filed claims for shooting down a German plane. He copied part of a report written by Lt. Earnhart of whom he thought showed a form of academic finesse.

The Lieutenant wrote that he had shot down a Junkers 52, a German troop carrier, and at the same time had been attacked by several enemy fighters.

"As I was climbing away from them," he wrote, "a 20-millimeter explosive shell hit the windshield and deflected through the top of the canopy and down on the instrument panel. Three pieces of shell hit me, in the left chest, left arm, and left knee.

"I dropped my belly tank and, having the ship under control, headed for my home base.

"On the way I applied a tourniquet to my leg, administered a hypodermic, and took sulfanilamide tablets.

"I landed the ship at my own base one hour after I had been hit by the shell. The plane was repaired. Claim: one Junker 52 destroyed."

Word was received in February 1943 that Lt. Earnhart had been missing and was last heard from on January 28, 1943.

A telegram addressed to Mrs. Earnhart read: "Your son, Lieut. Charles L. Earnhart reported prisoner of war of the German Government. Letter Follows."

Mrs. Earnhart received letters from folks in many parts of the country revealing that her son was a prisoner, according to German radio broadcasts. Many letters referred to him as the "Ace of Africa."

Lt. Earnhart praised the Red Cross for the part they played in the welfare of the soldiers during his capture by the Germans. He wrote that the men were well clothed and fed. He said most of his time was spent playing bridge, a favorite pastime.

He was released at the end of the war, spending over two years in confinement.

Awards for his part in the service were given by Maj. Gen. James H. Doolittle. First Lieutenant Charles L. Earnhart was awarded the Distinguished Flying Cross, the Silver Star, and Air Medal with oak leaf clusters,

Shortly after the war, in 1947, he moved to Masury, Ohio, and purchased a pharmacy. In June 1974, during a hold-up in his establishment, he was shot four times by his assailants. He died in route to the hospital, his death being ruled a homicide.

SERGEANT RALPH P. SNOOK DIED IN WORLD WAR I

"I do solemnly swear that I will bear true

allegiance to the United States of America, and will serve them honestly and faithfully against their enemies, whomsoever."

These words were repeated by Ralph P. Snook as well as by millions of men and women who have honored our country by serving in the Armed Forces.

Sergeant Ralph P. Snook served in World War I in Company E, a unit of the First Regiment Ohio National Guard. It later became a unit of a Depot Brigade and was merged into Company E, 147th Infantry, 37th Division, at Camp Sheridan, Alabama. It was here that Ralph trained and became a true American soldier.

After basic training Sgt. Snook traveled to Camp Lee, thence to Hoboken, N.J., from which point he sailed with his company to Brest, France, June 22, 1918.

The 37th Division was next assembled in the Beaumont area with preliminary plans to go to the front. The Division next traveled to Southern France, Alsace Lorraine, into the Baccarat Toul sector.

Sgt. Snook and others of the 147th, on July 25th, were engaged in trench warfare. Ralph, along with others, was often requested to do outpost duty, always with the enemy close-by.

German prisoners were taken and handled by Company E, and because of his excellence in the performance of this duty, Ralph was promoted to Sergeant.

On September 23, the 147th moved north of Ricourt to Boisede Parois in anticipation of the Argonne Forest campaign.

On the 25th the men advanced toward Avicourt, a German held fortification. Attacks of a large measure were evidenced with the line of battle extending from the English Channel on the north to Belfort on the south.

The engagement of the greatest battle of the war was now underway. The Allies, with their multi-sized guns and cannon, were relentlessly fighting for their lives. It is sad that this battle was fought, for within a little over a month the Armistice was signed.

On September 28, with the battle raging to an unheard of degree, the opponent persistently delivered fierce resistance. Men were being gassed, shot and falling in droves, many being mortally wounded. However hard the enemy fought, it was not enough to stop the onward march of the Allies.

Among those wounded heroes on this day was Sgt. Ralph Snook. He was immediately carried off to a field hospital, thence to base hospital No. 31, where he was received by the Red Cross.

On October 9, 1918, Sgt. Snook died of his wounds. A Higher Power had now taken him to report up There.

The local American Legion Post, which was named in honor of this fallen compatriot, was in charge of the service. It was conducted at the South Lebanon cemetery by Chaplain Wm. R. Hughes of Miamisburg on June 5, 1921.

This was said to have been one of the county's largest funerals. Folks from all parts of the county and country arrived to show their respect to this fallen defender of the flag of the United States.

Most deserving of praise was the manner in which the ex-servicemen paid tribute to a dead comrade. They not only presented themselves in grand fashion, but provided funds for the day's service.

One-hundred and twelve men, most of whom served in Company E with Sgt. Snook, were in parade dress, while twenty or thirty marched in civilian clothes.

Also present were three or four Spanish American War veterans; the Civil War veterans were too feeble to march and occupied seats reserved for them at the church.

A special space was reserved for Major Earl McCreary, Ralph's Captain in the service.

A select railroad car transported most of the ex-servicemen to South Lebanon, while many found it more practical to make the trip by automobile.

Citizens from Morrow and Mason were also present under the direction of Post Commander

Paul Kemper. Headed by the Harmon Hall band, they marched to the residence of Sgt. Snook's father, Mr. R.D. Snook, and escorted the body to the church.

South Lebanon neighbors in large numbers tipped their hat as the funeral procession passed. The Lebanon Boy Scouts controlled the crowd until the relatives could be seated.

A lasting tribute was paid to Sgt. Snook by Chaplain Hughes. Members of Company E served as pall bearers and firing squad personnel.

Ohio's Senator, Warren G. Harding, later to be President of the United States, wrote to Ralph's father. In his letter he offered his condolences:

My dear Mr. Snook,

I have just noticed the name of Serg't Ralph Snook among those who have given their lives in the service of their country.

I know how futile it is to attempt to lighten your sorrow by any words of sympathy, but I do want you to know of my interested share in your grief and my pride in the sons of Ohio who have so gallantly made the supreme sacrifice in the great cause of the Republic in this epochal conflict to maintain our ideals of liberty and civilization. May this knowledge serve to temper your great sorrow.

Very truly yours,
Warren G. Harding.

GLENDOWER WAS HOME TO
J. MILTON WILLIAMS

Glendower is one of five stately homes situated in old Floraville, just off U.S. 42, south of Lebanon's business district. It was built by Amos Bennett about 1838, and was considered the finest home in the County.

Glendower's first residents were the family of J. Milton Williams. Here the Williamses had their six children and opened their home to many important guests.

J. Milton Williams was born December 17, 1807,

within the corporate limits of the city. He was the son of Enos Williams, who held the position of County Recorder many years, as well as other public appointments.

Young Williams helped his father in the recorder's office, and also wrote in the office of the Clerk of Court. His handwriting was described as "legible, bold and rapid."

This early training primed him for a career in the law field that he pursued and accomplished with great vigor.

He was dreadfully poor, but, with a great amount of energy, and a full slate of ability, he succeeded to great heights.

He wrote: "When I went out into the wide, wide world in business, on my own hook, I had two dilapidated shirts and a poor suit of clothes to match them. I opened my office in a cellar, with three musty old Ohio statutes, given me by my old father, which he had held as a public officer. This was my entire stock in trade."

He was admitted to the bar, at age 23, on June 7, 1831, at a term of the Supreme Court held at Lebanon. He was received the same day and place as was Hon. Robert C. Schenck of Franklin.

Williams immediately secured for himself a place at the bar, and at once gained a large and rewarding practice.

For several years he had more cases on the dockets of the courts than any other lawyer in the County. His fees charged were less than other lawyers of the same stature.

He was elected Prosecuting Attorney of Warren County in 1833, succeeding Hon. A.H. Dunlevy, a position the latter held for 12 years.

In 1850, Major Williams, as he was called because of his status in the Militia, was elected a member of the convention that devised the second Constitution of Ohio.

He was elected, in 1857, to the House of Representatives in the General Assembly of Ohio as an independent candidate.

His capacity to sway jurors was the result of his superior intellect of human nature. He maneuvered within himself a personal charisma perhaps foremost in the history of Warren County.

He was considered one of the leading lawyers of southern Ohio, and was virtually connected to every case in Warren County. His honest ways exhibited a semblance that no client would be cheated or misrepresented in any way.

Thus far, he had effectively moved from a cellar to a mansion high atop a hill, not only in accomplishments, but in life.

All stories do not end in such a fashionable and respectable way. Such was the case of J. Milton Williams.

He married the daughter of Dr. Rigdon, of Hamilton, in which they had six children. The marriage was quite a happy one for several years.

Through his good years, the Major had picked up the habit of intemperance. At some time he separated from his wife and family which caused him great distress.

About the year 1854, he deeded his property to Robert Boake in trust for his wife and family. He was at this time a complete wreck of his former self, and was the target of pity and charity.

He had totally lost his sense of stability and was burdened by his loss of family and property.

He was in fragile health, both in body and mind for several years. On July 13, 1871, he was able to take his meals, walking a short distance from his room.

Two days later, it was essential that a nurse be employed for his care. An appeal was made to the ones handling the property, which consisted of several thousand dollars, to give him support concerning his condition. It was refused.

He was consequently taken off in an express wagon, an object of public charity, to the infirmary where he died on July 21, 1871. He was buried in the Lebanon Cemetery.

J. Milton Williams was at one time the ablest lawyer at the Warren County Bar. In a time of need he was shunned by his friends as just another case for the unfortunate. From a cellar to a mansion on a hill, his life ended as "a man without a home."

HISTORIAN TELLS STORY OF WAYNESVILLE RESIDENT ALLEN BROWN

Allen Brown was born four miles north of Waynesville, near Lytle, in 1808.

He was the son of Asher Brown who had emigrated from New Jersey to the Waynesville area in 1804. Asher and his family moved into a log cabin which had been occupied as a dwelling for hogs during nights; it had no floor and no doors. A new puncheon floor and other improvements were realized and it was later transformed into a desirable home.

Asher Brown later purchased 500 acres in Clearcreek Township. To pay for the new property, he bought a large number of hogs, drove them to Philadelphia, and sold them at a large profit.

Allen lived on the land originally purchased by his father. He declared that he was born in a sheep-house, his brother John, in a hog-house, and his brother Asher in a hen-house.

Allen's explanation of this was that "the increases in the family census occurred in detached portions of the house, which were afterward appropriated to shelter the several creatures by whose names they were thenceforward known."

The population of the area was slight to say the least. The closest mill at this time was three or four days ride, the only paths being bridle paths through the forests; the horse had to carry grist and rider.

Sometimes events popped up that prevented the families from going to the mill. When the meal barrels became exhausted, makeshift mills were held in a hollowed out stump.

The corn would be placed in the stump and be treated with a wooden pestle. The finest of the meal was sifted through a sieve, and what would not pass through the sieve would be served to the chickens.

Mr. Brown was interviewed by a reporter in 1884. I shall now transcribe the discussion. It goes as such.

Mr. Brown was asked what they did for clothing. He said: "We raised our flax, and, when spun, took it to the weaver's, a man named Thomas Stephenson, who lived some distance southwest of our place. Most of our small spinning-wheels have disappeared, but I believe the large one is still in existence out at the old place."

"And as to Schools."

"We only went to school in the winter. There was an old log school near Aaron Chandler's which we used to attend. George Ward and Owen Evans were teachers when I was a student there.

"By the way, Maria Ohio Ward, Aaron Chandler's second wife, was given her middle name because of her having been born on the Ohio River, near Wheeling, [West] Virginia, while her parents were coming down the Ohio in an ark."

"Do you mean something which looked like an ark, or one of the flatboats used in those days."

"No; arks were arks, and flatboats, flatboats. One was used for traveling and the other for freight, lumber, stock, etc. Maria Ward was born on an ark."

"The old meeting-house we had was a log building which stood on the present site of the Orthodox Friends' meeting-house in Waynesville.

"This was, of course, before the separation when all the Friends hereabouts were Hicksites, or followers of Elias Hicks.

"But, speaking of mills, John Jennings built a mill down here on the Little Miami, I think just about where Wright Brothers saw mill now stands.

"That was a great convenience, saving my father many long and wearisome journeys, not to say dangerous ones, for there were plenty of bears and wolves in those days. The latter would often come into the yard, and make night hideous and our blood would run cold with their howlings, and my father would not shoot at them, because of the difficulty in procuring ammunition, which could not be got nearer than Cincinnati.

"They were dreadfully destructive to hogs and sheep, and, of course, we could ill afford to lose any of them, for meat was scarce, especially fresh meat. I remember, once, my father bought a cow with a calf by her side, and when he brought them home my mother was very anxious to raise the calf, it being a heifer.

"But father objected. He said the men were working hard, and he thought the calf would make nice meat, which they ought to have. It was very hard for mother to forego her pet scheme, but she would have been compelled to had it not been for a fortunate interposition of luck.

"My father went into the woods for some purpose, and three deer made their appearance before him. He had his trusty flintlock gun, an inseparable backwoods companion, with him, and, stationing himself behind a tree, he made a careful aim, pulled the trigger, there was report, and he saw a fine buck give a few plunges, and then stretch himself prone upon the ground.

"Father could not, of course, shoulder Mr. Buck, and carry him to the house, so, making a slit in the deer's hamstring, and bending down a strong young hickory sapling, he hung the deer to the tree top, and swung it back to its former altitude, placing the venison far out of reach of bear or wolf.

"Then he started for home, making his way by breaking and bending down twigs and branches of the trees, so he might be able to find his meat again.

"Finally reaching home, he returned on horseback, and supplied our larder for many a day with venison which would make the modern epicurean's mouth water.

"My mother, however, was the one most gratified, because now there was no obstacle in the way of her keeping the little calf.

"Stoves were unknown then, and our cooking was

all done by the great fire on the hearth. The crane and the Dutch ovens were the nearest approaches of stoves, and there never was any sweeter bread or any better meat than my mother used to cook in those days.

"I still have an old Dutch oven, which is now used as a whitewash kettle.

"People would not so nowadays, but to my mind there is no comfort like that of the old fireplace, with the immense logs throwing out their heat over all the room. The fireplaces were very large, and the back-logs, of which you have record or heard, were usually brought into the room in this way; if there were two doors, one opposite the other, and opening out-doors, the log would be brought up to one door, outside of which would be a horse, to which the rope would be attached, and the horse, well acquainted with his business, would pull the log into the room, and it would be rolled to its place in the cavernous chimney. We used the tinder-box to strike fire with when we had them, but it has often happened that the fire went out, and there was no other way to start it again but by sending across woods and clearing to one of the neighbors to procure a pan of coals."

"What were the wages paid in those days for farm labor, Mr. Brown?"

"Thirty-seven and a half cents a day was considered good pay, and when people got fifty cents a day they thought they were coining money.

"By the month, eight and nine dollars was the general price paid for farm hands. And we didn't saunter into the field at 7 o:clock, and hasten out at 6, either.

"In those good old days it was from dawn till dark. We were up when the birds were just beginning to rustle their wings and whisper their first waking notes; had breakfast before sunrise, and were up and away to the field or woods.

"And, after supper, out we went again, and worked generally until bed-time. Oh, I tell you people worked in those days, and, as far as I can judge, they were healthier, if not happier, than people now, who do not work so hard or so long.

"Of course, we had not the facilities then for doing work, either; just think of the mold-board plows of those days, and compare them with the riding plows of the present.

"They were made of almost any kind of hard wood, such as hickory or oak, and hewed out into shape with an ax. This is what we had to plow the ground with.

"How many farmers of Warren County now would be content to till the soil the old way? Not many, I guess."

UNION TOWNSHIP'S WILSON FAMILY
KNOWN ACROSS U.S.

The Wilson family was a very distinguished family of Union Township. Robert Wilson was born in Rockbridge County, Va., November 10, 1797. A significant number of the inhabitants of that county were of Scotch-Irish descent and were Covenantors in religion.

Among others which were from the Virginia County to settle in Warren County, were the Hopkins and Hart families, settling near Hopkinsville.

These families assisted in the organization of an Associate Reformed Church, a denomination formed in America by a union of the Scottish Covenantor and Seceder Churches. Robert Wilson was a member of this church most of his adult life.

Robert Wilson II was eleven years of age when his parents emigrated to Ohio and established a home at Hopkinsville.

He, like many other children of emigrants, was brought up on limited means. However, he tended to the necessity of acquiring the best education the country schools could offer. His education excelled in comparison to many other emigrant children.

He later taught school at Hopkinsville and was

elected to township offices, being assessor, and for a number of years Justice of the Peace of Hamilton Township. He was also County Treasurer and was elected as State Representative.

In 1843, he relocated from Hopkinsville to a farm he had purchased at the "ridge" in Union Township. The location was about three miles below Lebanon where he lived until his death on November 15, 1854.

His intellect and ability allowed him to become a very successful farmer. Throughout his life he acclaimed "industry, education, morality and religion" as a practice of life.

Robert Wilson II, on August 25, 1825, married Martha Smith, daughter of James and Nancy Smith, who were pioneers of Hamilton Township. Robert was survived by his wife by 27 years who died at Lebanon in 1881, aged nearly 80 years. Eight children were born to this marriage.

Elizabeth H., the only daughter, was married to Allison L. Scott; she died in 1859.

Judge Jeremiah M. Wilson (named for Jeremiah Morrow) was the eldest son. He was born at Hopkinsville, November 24, 1828, and died at his home in Washington D.C., on September 24, 1901.

He received his education in the common schools and the Lebanon Academy. He was possibly one of the most successful lawyers from the County of Warren. He studied law under Durbin Ward in Lebanon and later located at Connersville, Indiana.

Jeremiah was a judge when the Civil War broke out. He was the only one of his father's sons that did not enter the service. He was twice elected to Congress as a Republican from the Connersville area.

At the close of his second tenure he made Washington his home and practiced law with such success that at the time of his death, he was one of the most acclaimed lawyers in the nation's Capitol.

Among his many distinctions was that at one time he was the attorney for the Union Pacific Railroad.

He became a very wealthy man and was president

or director of some of the large corporations in Washington.

Judge William W. Wilson was the second son of Robert and Martha Wilson. He was also born at Hopkinsville and made Warren County his home nearly his entire life.

He attended the Lebanon Academy and studied law under Judge John Probasco. He practiced his profession at Keokuk, Iowa, but was later called home because of the death of his father. He afterward made Lebanon his home.

William enlisted in the army as Captain of Company A, 79th Ohio Volunteer Infantry, and was made Major of his regiment from August 1862 to November 1864, being discharged for disability from an occurrence in Sherman's Atlanta Campaign.

Returning home, he was elected mayor of Lebanon in April, 1865. He was elected Probate Judge of Warren County in October 1865, an office he held until October 1869, when he was elected Representative in the Legislature, this tenure lasting only one term, thence resuming his law practice in Lebanon. He died at Lebanon, March 8, 1885, being only 54 years of age.

James S. Wilson, the third son, was employed as a clerk in a commercial venture in Hamilton, Ohio, when the Civil War broke out. He was mustered into the 3rd O.V.I.; he served as Lieutenant and Captain, and as Assistant Adjutant General of his brigade throughout the war. He served in the Army of the Cumberland, having seen action under Buell, Rosecrans and Thomas.

Providence M. Wilson was employed in the mercantile business in Franklin. He enlisted in the 2nd Ohio Militia, thus serving at First Bull Run.

Robert Bruce Wilson enlisted in Captain Rigdon Williams' company, the first company to leave Lebanon. He saw action the entire war, serving in the eastern sector of the country.

He was a Captain at the close of the war. Robert was the third son who became a lawyer, his practice being located at Cincinnati.

Marshall L. Wilson was a mere boy at the start

of the war. He served, in 1862, in the area of the Cumberland Gap. After the war he was employed in the railroad and telegraph service.

Americus Wilson, the younger son, enlisted in a 100 day regiment and served in West Virginia.

MOSES MILLER EARLY LEBANON RESIDENT OF NOTE

Moses Miller was born in Bridgetown, Cumberland County, New Jersey, April 11, 1812. His parents were Joseph and Charlotte Miller, who were of German Descent. He died in Lebanon, Ohio, January 1, 1885, aged 72 years, 8 months and 20 days.

A common practice in the early days of our country, was to train boys at an early age to learn a trade; such was the case of Moses Miller.

He was apprenticed to be a wagon maker. Having served his apprenticeship he moved, at the age of 21, to Franklin in Warren County. He remained but a few weeks and then moved to Lebanon, which he made his permanent home.

His first employment in the new town was with the firm of John P. March, then a prominent carriage and wagon maker. Mr. March passed away and Moses remained in the employ of the sons, George R. and John W. March.

While working for the brothers, Moses was appointed janitor and Court Constable in 1839. (Previous to this, Mr. Miller was elected Town Marshal for three years, and reelected for a fourth.)

After receiving his newly appointed jobs, he still retained his tenure of wagon maker until the March brothers went out of business in 1862. He worked at his trade and attended to his duties of the courthouse morning and evening, except during terms of court.

He was united in wedlock to Catherine Smith August 11, 1839. To this union three children were born, namely, Matthias, Matilda D., and Moses S. Miller.

On August 23, 1848, he was activated into Lebanon Lodge, No. 15, I.O.O.F. He at once became an active, hard-working and honored member. He was elected Secretary July 1, 1854; Vice Grand, January 1, 1855; and Noble Grand, July 13, 1855. On April 21, 1870, he became a member of the Encampment.

For several years he was Out Side Guardior and janitor of the Odd Fellows' building. He was always faithful in his attendance and service to the Lodge until his age and health slowed him. He was still a frequent visitor and never failed to attend the night the dues were taken.

In 1865, business was a bit slow in Lebanon so he went to Cincinnati to work. While there, he encountered a fall which was almost fatal. He was confined to his home for several months.

In 1876, Moses took his entire family to visit old friends and relatives in his native State of New Jersey. His stay lasted several weeks; he always referred to this trip as one of enjoyment.

His work in the courthouse was one of excellence. His salary came from the public treasury, but his time was his own to manage.

Moses was never idle. He was described as "one of the most industrious men that ever lived."

Before daylight, he would be at his work, scrubbing, sweeping, dusting and mending. Darkness fell and he would often be detained by a session of court or in completion of his work. His labor of work would extend from the top of the dome to all property associated with the courthouse.

His training and mechanical ability allowed him to do all chores called upon without any outside assistance. Visitors to the courthouse would constantly comment on the orderliness and cleanliness. The credit always went to "Uncle Moses Miller."

Being wasteful to the public charge was not allowed at the courthouse. Miller was extremely alert to all the rogues who attempted to mark the wall, scar the benches, or mistreat the beautiful lawn.

He was sometimes thought to be too severe in the protection of the premises, but he was being paid by the taxpayer, and he set out to protect their interests. His iron constitution was a part of his nature. He would rather have suffered dire consequences than to alter his character.

He was not a user of tobacco or alcohol. He loved the right and hated the wrong.

Not being a respecter of persons, Moses would accommodate the poorest and humblest who had business in the courthouse, to the wealthiest.

It had been commented many times that Moses would work as long as he lived.

He had long been suffering poor health, but he continued at his labor of work until less than a week before his death; he died as he desired, at his post of duty. It was said, "He idled no time away."

DEY VENTURED TO LEBANON FROM JERSEY, MET JACKSON, CLAY

Among the many pioneers of Warren County was a well known gentleman named John E. Dey.

He was born in Monmouth County, New Jersey, in 1791. He was the only child of William and Phoebe (Ely) Dey, natives of New Jersey.

His grandfather, John Dey, was a surveyor and an extensive real estate dealer who moved from New York to New Jersey.

At the age of two John moved with his father to Kentucky, the trip he well remembered. It was down the Ohio River. The Indians were still hostile and the flatboat was fired on several times.

After living in Kentucky two years, the family returned to New Jersey, where he grew to manhood and learned the carpentry trade.

In January 1818, John married Sarah Mount, and in May they moved to Cincinnati. A short time later they settled in Lebanon.

In 1822, he ventured through the South spending his winters first working at his trade, and afterward selling plows, which he, along with a gentleman named Hackney, manufactured in Lebanon. (The firm's name was Hackney & Dey.)

The plow was of an improved sort and was the first of its kind manufactured west of Pittsburgh. His business trips covered the rivers of the Ohio and Mississippi from Cincinnati to New Orleans. His trips would start in the fall and end in the spring, the last one being made in 1845.

When he first made his treks south, Memphis had a total population of just one white man, who was living with a tribe of Indians. Vicksburg was represented by a single blockhouse.

Dey's winters were spent at Bruinsburg on the plantation of Judge Bruin, who afterward became the first Governor of Mississippi. Andrew Jackson, years before when he was just a Colonel, lived at this place. Colonel Jackson quite often frequented the plantation and Mr. Dey became well acquainted with him.

He remembered that he was a tall, slim man, with a nervous manner. He used to carry a pocket full of shelled corn and play with the grains at the dining table.

Dey told a story about Andrew Jackson that was more fact than fiction. He said Colonel Jackson, soon after he came to Mississippi, went back into the woods about four miles from the river to a noted meeting place of the hunting gentlemen of the country.

Here he started a saloon which he continued for many years. He never appeared behind the bar, but the establishment was his and he was responsible for it.

Dey's first trip to Lebanon from Cincinnati was by stagecoach, the trip taking a day and-a-half. The roads were so atrocious that the route was taken through the woods rather than by road. The appearance of Lebanon was nothing like it is now.

There was a sugar camp where the present courthouse now stands. The total east end was planted in corn.

The first businesses he remembered in town

were a grocery operated by William Lowry; George Foglesong had a pottery just below Broadway; a man named Nixon operated a tannery; and a saddler shop was kept by John Reeves.

There were two taverns, one managed by Mr. Corwin and another whose owner was called Parcell. Phineas Ross was cashier of the Lebanon Bank and his brother, Thomas, was a lawyer.

Lebanon was on the regular stagecoach road from the South and West to the East. All the Southern and Western Senators and Representatives passed through here.

Mr. Dey remembered many, but the one who stuck out most was Henry Clay. He recollected him very well, describing him as a tall, heavy, loosely jointed man.

One story told by Dey was the occasion of Thomas Corwin's change from farmer to politician.

Young Thomas was a stout, robust farmer and he was never to be outdone. At one of the corn huskings a few of the men were bragging of what they could do.

Young Tom, committed not to be outdone, exclaimed, "Pshaw! fellows, that's nothing. Why, I can kick the moon out of its socket. Look here."

With no regards to his safety, he made a herculean spring into the air, but, losing his balance, came down on his knee-caps, thus injuring them so that he was unable to walk for some time.

With this venture, he was forced to give up all thoughts of farming and turn to law.

WILLIAM H. CLEMENT: ONE OF MORROW'S FOUNDERS

Our story this week will focus on one of the founders of Morrow, William Henry Clement. The settlement of the town, in 1844, centered around Mr. Clement's direct involvement with the Little Miami Railroad.

Prior to his residency in the County, Mr. Clement had been engaged in several different engineering projects.

A sketch of Mr. Clement states that he attended the village school in Saratoga Springs, N.Y., his birthplace, and afterwards entered the Rensselaer Polytechnic Institute at Troy.

During school vacation of 1834, he joined the engineering corps of William C. Young, then engaged in surveys on the Saratoga and Whitehall Railroad.

After his graduation at Troy, in 1835, he was identified with the engineering party supervising the construction of the Utica and Schenectady Railroad. He was appointed superintendent of track laying and finalized the project at Little Falls in 1836. (He was but 21 years of age at this time.)

He next traveled to Canada, where he devoted several months to the construction of railroads.

The year 1837 finds Clement in Ohio where he was engaged for a brief time on a line south of Sandusky, the Mad River Railroad.

The next year he became engaged with the Little Miami Railroad, in which he took great interest. He was brought along by one of the supervisors of the former line and made chief engineer. By the time the line had been completed to Springfield, he had been appointed General Superintendent, a position he held until 1857.

Clement was known to rule with an "iron hand." One writer says that work under him "was like military service; he developed the character of his men by strict discipline so that they felt the pressure of his reliance on them to properly discharge their duties."

During the coal shortage of the severe winter of 1856, the Little Miami was about the only railroad in Ohio with access to the mines. Work continued day and night to restore operations, and, despite this, "no man left his post."

His positions on the Little Miami Railroad included that of engineer, superintendent and president. At the time of his death he was a director. Under his guidance, the railroad was known as the best managed and safest railroad in the United States.

Clement's contributions to the village of Morrow included the donation of a lot to the first church in Morrow. It was known as a Union Church and built previous to 1847 by private subscription.

He also donated a lot in 1848 for the construction of the Methodist Episcopal Church. The congregation commenced building soon after their organization, and, until it was completed, held their services in the Union Church.

He was attracted by the layout of the land surrounding the present site of Morrow. He purchased a tract of land and erected a house known today as Oak Hill.

From 1857 to 1860 he was vice-president and general manager of the Ohio and Mississippi Railroad, a long trunk line running through Southern Ohio, Indiana and Illinois to St. Louis.

At first the Little Miami officials refused to release him, but buckled under after a couple of months. He spent three years in St. Louis as president and general manager of the Union Depot and roads connecting there.

From 1877 to 1882 he was president and general manager of the Cincinnati Southern Railroad, which ran directly through Kentucky and Tennessee for a distance of 336 miles.

Although his time in his later years was spent in the West, his leisure time was devoted to his farms near Morrow, one of which he lived on for a period of forty-five years.

Clement was the eldest child of Joel and Aurelia Putnam Clement of Saratoga Springs, N.Y. He was born July 30, 1815, and died on January 17, 1887.

He was married twice, first to Elizabeth Steiner, which bore him two children, Henry S. and John B. Clement. His second wife was Mrs. Caroline Smith, by which he also had two children, Mrs. Caroline Watson Soteldo and Miss Florence Putnam Clement.

Clement retired in 1882. While wintering in Florida in 1885, he fell and sustained a severe knee injury. He never fully recovered.

A visit from his son, Col. H.S. Clement, on January 8, 1887, found him in poor health. On January 17 of that year, he passed away.

LEBANON RESIDENT LINCOLN BEACHY WAS AVIATION PIONEER

In the early part of the 20th century, aviation was viewed as a new experiment in transportation.

Certainly everything as far as aerial navigation at this time was perceived as tentative. It took a Lebanonite to take hold of this new craze and elevate it to his/her standards. This man's name was Lincoln Beachy.

He was born in 1887 and was the grandson of Thomas Beachy of Lebanon. Lincoln was known in the City of Cedars as Professor Beachy.

He was an inventor and pilot and was described as one of the "most coolheaded and nervy men in a work that required the greatest self control, and steadiness of hand and eye."

His aerial debut involved the operation of small airships for Thomas Baldwin.

In the early part of this century, the dirigible was coming fast in America.

Beachy flew one of Baldwin's airships at the St. Louis Exposition in 1904, creating a sensation with his daring exhibitions.

On June 13, 1906, he made a spectacular flight around the Washington Monument in Washington, D.C., in full view of Congress.

In 1906-07, Beachy flew two airships on an international excursion which extended from Montreal, Canada, across the United States, and down to Mexico City.

The dirigible was a popular attraction at many fairs and exhibitions.

A rivalry between Roy Knabenshue and Lincoln Beachy was the main attraction at many of the larger meets. The latter beat the former in an air match of the St. Louis Aero Club, October 4-9, 1909. Beachy won $1,000 for his efforts.

With a wandering eye, he soon gave up ballooning and moved on to Curtiss pushers and ultimately received his aviator's certificate in 1911.

Lincoln became a pilot as well as a stockholder for Curtiss and flew for his exhibition company.

In this venture he was often known as "The Flying Fool." He eventually capped a reputation as "America's greatest aerial exhibitionist."

One of his most sensational flights was made in a Curtiss biplane on June 27, 1911. The fearless aeronaut rolled through the mists of Niagara Falls, descended down to within 30 feet of the thundering river below, glided under the International Bridge, and proceeded down the deep gorge. Fifty thousand onlookers were held spellbound. He received $5,000 for this remarkable stunt.

Beachy performed with so much skill in his 80 h.p. aircraft, that, as he buzzed around race tracks, he would casually drop the planes' wings to the ground and sling up dust for the audience's entertainment.

He teamed up with the famous race driver Barney Oldfield in another extraordinary stunt.

One source says that with car and plane speeding along at 60 m.p.h., Beachy would position his plane just over the speeding racer and carefully settle a front wheel on Oldfield's head.

His most breathtaking feat was to cut his engine at 5,000 feet, and dive headlong toward the ground, pull out at the last minute and negotiate a perfect landing.

Another rather dramatic stunt was that he once roared down Chicago's Michigan Boulevard, just above the heads of the dazzled pedestrians, scaring the daylights out of them.

At Ascot Park in Los Angeles, he spotted a number of people who had gathered in a tree to beat the admission charge. He immediately dropped his plane, and, with his unusual, uncanny accuracy, just sheared off some of the branches. Panic arose amongst the spectators as they scrambled to get away from this flying machine.

The end result was that three spectators received broken arms and one a skull fracture.

At Hammondsport, New York, in 1913, Beachy flew too close to a hangar roof and killed one spectator while injuring three.

He retired in 1914 and was still treated as a hero. Up to his retirement, he was paid as much as $1,000 a day to fly.

As one sometimes flirts with fate, thing often happen. Such was the case of Lincoln Beachy.

In March 1915 he came out of retirement and performed his last stunt.

Lincoln Beachy, a native of Lebanon, plunged to his death in San Francisco Bay at the age of 28. He fell 2500 feet and dived 40 feet below the surface. Thousands of stunned and terror stricken citizens watched in horror. His home made plane was still in experimental stages, and, while doing a loop, the wings fell off. The plane struck the water tail first.

An autopsy performed later showed evidence of the struggle the aviator had made in his efforts to get free. The safety belt he had relied on so much in his performances now held him captive until the end.

CEPHAS HOLLOWAY A PROMINENT SHAKER LEADER

The Shakers of Union Village had amongst its longtime members a very prominent gentleman named Cephas Holloway. He was described as a "genial old man with a pleasing countenance."

He spent most of his years of manhood in the Shaker denomination and held almost all the important offices of the Society.

A history of the Society recorded that on July 26, 1868, Cephas Holloway was released from the ministry to take the Eldership of the First Family. In 1882, he was classed a Deacon.

He was but five years old when the first Shaker sermon was preached in the Turtlecreek Presbyterian Church on March 22, 1805.

His father was a member of this church from which most of the members had been transformed to the Shaker faith after the great Kentucky Revival.

Cephas was baptized into the Presbyterian Church as a youth, although his father was amongst the first Shaker converts at Turtlecreek.

His faith, however, was united with the Shakers ever since he was old enough to form his own opinions.

Success of the Shakers formed them into their own independent community.

In 1819, the population was given at 600. Among them were blacksmiths, masons, stonecutters, carpenters, tanners, carders, spinners, etc. All that were able found employment.

The former Presbyterian preacher, after his conversion to Shakerism, found employment in making chairs and spinning wheels. Cephas entertained the trade of shoemaking and for ten years operated a shop.

Holloway took great pride in his part in the improvement of the many breeds of cattle, horses, hogs and sheep.

The Shakers of Warren County, with their large land holdings, took the lead amongst other county farmers in these achievements.

The Shakers are most noted for their development of the Poland China hog (created in 1816), which had originally been called the "Shaker Hog," and the "Warren County Hog."

He yearned to produce the finest breed of horses in the world. His ambition was to produce a horse of speed and ultimately asked for a "training track."

He was rejected by his brethren because of the mere suggestion of a race track. He next asked for a "training road," but again was refused. His quest for a fine breeding horse was unsuccessful.

Cephas Holloway was born in Turtlecreek Township, December 29, 1800. He was the son of Jacob and Hannah Cory Holloway. Both were natives of Morris County, N.J.

His parents were among the many families that

emigrated from New Jersey to the new land called Symmes's Purchase.

The family arrived before Wayne's Treaty of Peace with the Indians in 1795, first settling on a farm four miles from Duck Creek in Hamilton County.

The family in about 1799 moved to a farm about a mile and three-quarters northwest of the site of Lebanon. Cephas, being the first child born in the new home, said: "I was born in a thicket and had to chop my way out."

The locality in which Cephas was born was an unbroken wilderness. His birth cabin was surrounded with thick spice-wood and underbrush.

His cradle consisted of a sap trough, made out of timber about two feet long, split into halves and dug out into a trough for catching sugar water.

All the early schools were made of rough logs. The school that Cephas attended was no exception. It was made of buckeye logs, which, during the first summer of existence, grew green sprouts eighteen inches long.

The schoolhouse consisted of only three study guides; a primer, Webster's spelling book, and the New Testament. Geography, grammar or arithmetic were not taught at the time.

He taught himself the skill of arithmetic by gathering daily a bundle of hickory bark on his way home from school. As he would throw a piece in the fireplace at night he would count and calculate the pieces. The light from the fire would serve as a light for his study.

It could be said that Cephas was self-taught. If not for his expertise and ability he would not have risen so far into the Shaker community.

JAMES E. MURDOCH WAS CELEBRATED ACTOR AND PUBLIC READER

Murdoch is located on Route 48 in the southern portion of Warren County, less than two miles from Maineville and about two miles northeast of Loveland.

It was never considered a village, just a group of houses. It was founded and named after James E. Murdoch, a most celebrated actor and public reader.

Murdoch called his hamlet "Hamstead Grove," but with the establishment of a post office it was renamed Murdoch. (The name is often mistakenly spelled Murdock.)

Murdoch acquired a farm here in 1851 and planned to make a living at his new vocation. He lived in a neat frame cottage very well landscaped. Near the cottage was a log cabin which served as his study which he called his den.

He was at this time forty years of age and had reached his popularity as an entertainer ten years previous. Country life was favored over city life by Mr. Murdoch, thinking his sons should be raised on a farm.

He had no formal training for this new occupation which produced many failures over the years. His spirit was never mentally broken. He achieved through perseverance what many thought a great success.

He was instrumental in making a turnpike out of the dirt road leading from his farm to Loveland; introduced an improved breed of cattle from Kentucky; and mildly dedicated himself to grape culture. However, the actor had to support the farmer.

Murdoch, as an inhabitant of Philadelphia at an early age, did nothing to prepare himself for farm life. He was the son of a bookbinder and worked as a boy at his father's trade.

As a youth he displayed a talent as a public reader and speaker. Consequently, he became a member of a debating society and an amateur dramatic organization. His later experiences in the theatrical field were achieved as an actor, stage manager, teacher of elocution in Boston, and lecturer on Shakespeare.

Being involved in the agricultural profession did little to alter his theatrical career. Soon after removing to his farm he traveled to California and fulfilled a successful theatrical engagement.

In 1856, he made a trip to Europe and performed successfully in London and Liverpool.

His readings were generally accepted by Warren Countians, although drama presentations had virtually disappeared a generation before, especially in the rural areas.

His background in his readings had usually been before large audiences on opera stages well lighted with gas, but he was just as much at home with the rural gatherings.

A little village, a country church, all occasions seemed very pleasing to Mr. Murdoch. If for a good cause, no payment was accepted.

Possibly his first reading in the County was in the summer of 1852, the year after he moved to his farm. The Maineville Academy hosted the first teacher's institute of Warren County and he was asked to read at one of the five evening sessions.

This was the first time the County school teachers and residents had the privilege of hearing him and learn what the finely trained voice of Mr. Murdoch was capable of.

He performed at many different locations in Lebanon which included Washington Hall, the Baptist Church, and the Opera House. His longest selection was the Trial Scene, Act IV of the Merchant of Venice, which he often placed on his program.

Murdoch scheduled a series of vocal lessons at his farm home beginning July 9, 1862. He had a number of circulars printed and the demand was so great that he had a second edition printed.

He was met with disappointment; on the first day less than a dozen were present. The class included four preachers, two teachers of elocution, a law student and some young students. Every member of the class was well satisfied with the results achieved.

The Civil War was in full progress at this time. Murdoch was purely devoted to the Union effort.

His speaking abilities lent to his patriotic feelings. He gave readings in all the larger cities of the North. He read to the soldiers in camp and in the hospitals. He raised money for the sanitary commissions, soldiers and societies.

One writer estimates that he read to more than 250,000 soldiers and citizens. His many readings were of a patriotic nature which were designed to boost the morale of the soldiers.

The Bethel Church in Murdoch was badly in need of a new building. Mr. Murdoch unselfishly offered to raise one-half of the cost of a new building if the members would do likewise.

The funds were raised and the new church was dedicated in November, 1872, with Rev. Dr. J. G. Monfort preaching the dedication service. (Much of the money was raised by Mr. Murdochs' readings on Sunday evenings in different churches.)

The cost of the building was a little more than $4,500. Not being a man of wealth, his sacrifice was fulfilling to the members. Mr. Murdoch was not of the faith of the Bethel Church, which was Presbyterian; his religious views were of the Unitarian faith, which makes his gesture that much more admirable.

CINCINNATI'S CROSLEY FAMILY HAD CLOSE TIES TO WARREN COUNTY

Many of us folks can call upon our memory, and with a little nudge a recollection of things past suddenly become numerous. The subject of our article this week is the Crosley family.

The name Powel Crosley, Jr., tends to jog the memory which brings back a reminiscence of old Crosley Field, home of the Cincinnati Reds for many years; the Crosley refrigerator, the Crosley car, the Crosley radio, and of course, radio station WLW.

The Crosley name, sometimes spelled Crossley, from which Powel (one "l") Crosley, Jr., was descended, has its Ohio origins in Clear Creek Township, Warren County.

The origin of the Crosley family goes back to the fourteenth century in England to the vicinity of Lancashire and Yorktown. The name at that time was spelled "Croslegh," but a hundred years later, it was changed to "Crosley."

The family started immigrating to America as early as 1660, settling first in New Jersey, and later were found to be living in Pennsylvania, and still later, in Maryland.

Moses Crosley was born in 1764 and died in 1843. He was the first of the family to come to Ohio, first settling in Mason County, Kentucky (Maysville), and later in Warren County. He served in the Revolution from Maryland.

Moses was married to Rachel Powell; their son, William, born in 1785, migrated to Ohio from Kentucky in 1810. He settled in the northern section of Warren County and the southern sector of Montgomery County.

William was a manufacturer of gunpowder which enabled him to acquire considerable wealth. He was involved in politics serving in many township offices.

He moved to the Centerville area in 1834, becoming a commissioner of the Dayton and Lebanon Turnpike, and serving as its president and treasurer.

William also served in George Rogers Clark's army in his Vincennes expedition.

Powell Crosley, Sr., was a descendant of Moses and Rachel Powell Crossley. He was born on a farm in northern Warren County and resided there until he was seventeen.

His older brothers, William J., and Luken S. Crosley, served in the Civil War. William was captured at the Battle of Fisher's Creek and spent time in Libby Prison in Richmond, Virginia.

Powell Sr. attended school in Springboro, Ohio; next he taught school at Clarksville, Ohio; afterward he became manager of a commercial house in St. Joseph, Missouri.

He later gave up business to study law. He was graduated from Ann Arbor Law School in 1876, and later made his residence at Cincinnati to begin his practice of law. He was associated with Congressman Benjamin Butterworth.

Powell Sr.'s interests in wireless and radio

began at the birth of these two man made miracles. He bought some stock in Marconi's original company after the first signal was flashed across the Atlantic Ocean.

Crosley Sr. was born Christmas Day in 1849 and died at Cincinnati's Christ Hospital, September 13, 1932.

A tribute to him was written by Attorney G. Albert Rummel which stated: "He ranked with and was recognized as one of the best lawyers in Ohio during the last half century. He had the genius to see 'all around' and the common sense to consider all sides of a question of the law, made him remarkably successful in trial work, as well as mediation in having adverse interests unite in harmonious action."

Powel Crosley, Jr., was born on September 18, 1886, in Walnut Hills in Cincinnati. In 1893, the family moved to College Hill. He was educated in the Cincinnati public schools and enrolled in the Engineering College at the University of Cincinnati.

He was married four times, his first marriage was to Gwendolyn Aiken on October 17, 1910. They had two children, Martha and Powel Crosley III.

Powel Jr. acquired an early interest in automobiles. When he was 13 years old he had rigged up an electric car for his own use.

He had built, in 1907, his first six-cylinder engine and his interests were directed toward the Indianapolis Speedway.

He built his first marketable car in 1939. The convertible coupe sold for $325 and the convertible sedan sold for $350. The weight was less than 1000 pounds. It encompassed an air cooled engine that delivered 12.5 H.P. at 4000 RPM.

Much skepticism was tossed around concerning the small car. The fuel efficiency of 50 miles per gallon was apparently stirring up much interest, but the public was not quite ready for it. Crosley was several years ahead of his time.

He displayed the compact car at the Indianapolis Speedway on April 28th, 1939.

Powel Jr. was a common man with a keen sense for business, an entrepreneur whose sights were set not on wealth. He possessed an almost inborn sense to help others. His credo was that "He who serves best profits most."

Crosley Sr. lost most of his money through unfortunate investments. Powel Jr. says of his father: "My father left nothing in worldly things. Looking back now, I am much more grateful for his moral legacy: a philosophy of perseverance, a gratitude to a bountiful country, a knowledge that my future was my own to forge the way I would."

One day Powel III asked his dad for a new wireless outfit. Powel Jr., seeing his son's jubilance over the thought, purchased a one-tube set for $150, quite a price to be paid for a nine year old boy. The elder Crosley left the store with a 25 cent book called the ABC of Radio.

After reading the book, he became somewhat intrigued. Making another trip to the store, he asked where he might buy parts so he could assemble them himself.

For a minimal cost of $20 or $25, he returned home with headphones, tuning coil, a crystal detector, a condenser, along with other gadgets, and built a set. This was the beginning of the Crosley Radio Corporation.

Absolutely fascinated with the venture, he was sure it had a future. He went to another shop and had them build a 3 tube set for something like $200. He then ordered a 2 watt transmitter and started sending out recorded music over the air.

Crosley hired a couple of University of Cincinnati engineering students and built the Harko receiver which sold for $35, much less than anything on the market.

In 1921, he secured an experimental broadcasting license for a 20 watt transmitter which was to be used in his home. From that he expanded to a small commercial station.

So successful was this station that in 1935, with a 500,000 watt transmitter, WLW was the most powerful radio station in the world. The station was making plenty of money, but it was all poured back into the enterprise.

Crosley was very successful in the advent and sale of radio parts, too many to mention in this article.

Other Crosley gadgets were: he devised a strip of material for calking draft leaks at the top of the windshield; he marketed "TREDKOTE," a patch for auto tires; and "DRIKLENIT," an auto polish. He built phonographs and marketed them under the trade name of "MARION."

He conceived the idea of a walker for babies and called it "GO-BY-BY." He sold the combination kiddy car and baby stroller, and consequently the new owner used the name "TAYLOR-TOT."

Crosley devised the first refrigerator. It was shaped like a dumbbell. He later conceived the "KOOLREST" refrigerator which had an electric motor that cooled.

He also came out with the first Shelvador; a refrigerator with a door used to store food.

Powel Jr. contrived a "hair growing machine" called "X-ER-VAC." It was a floor type apparatus much like a hair dryer that fit over the scalp.

He pioneered with a "SNOW VEHICLE" which the Army used to haul sleds.

He also built washing machines, dryers, kitchen equipment, etc.

Baseball was born in Cincinnati in 1869. In the early 1930's, the Cincinnati Redlegs were having financial difficulties. Powel Crosley, Jr., had no inclination to get into the baseball business, but the ball club had gotten into difficulty and was in the hands of the Central Trust Co. in Cincinnati.

Crosley, in 1934, invested $200,000 and received complete control of the Redlegs. He announced that in 1939, $163,000 had been repaid him.

He paid team manager, Bill McKechnie, and Warren Giles, business manager, $30,000 a year each.

A taxi driver mentioned to Crosley that the publicity of him buying the Redlegs would be a great advertising venture. He immediately changed the name of the baseball park from Redland Field to Crosley Field.

Larry McPhail had arc lights installed in Columbus, Ohio. In his first talk with Crosley concerning night lighting, McPhail described the remarkable powers of night baseball. His hope was to persuade the major league tycoon to use the power of artificial light.

The first night game in major league history was scheduled in Cincinnati for May 23, 1935.

However, it was postponed 24 hours because of rain. Franklin Delano Roosevelt, seated in the White House, pressed a button, and by some long distance method, the 632 lamps lit and Crosley Field was illuminated.

Philadelphia was the visiting team and Ford C. Fricke, president of the National League, threw out the first ball.

The attendance (20,422) that night was ten times greater than it would have been for an afternoon game with the Phils.

HOLLINGSWORTH AND HAMILTON EARLY WARREN COUNTIANS

She was described as a "bright and shining example of a meek and lovely Christian." Her religious belief was that of the Friends doctrine, having adhered to that faith since childhood.

Rhoda Whitacre Hollingsworth was one of the lady pioneers that made her mark in Warren County.

Rhoda was born March 12, 1802, the daughter of Robert and Patience Mckay Whitacre, who were both natives of Virginia.

Robert was born in 1758 and Patience in 1763. Patience was Robert's third marriage. To this union was born seven children, namely, Andrew, John, Priscilla, Jane, Aquilla, Rhoda and Moses.

In the early part of the Nineteenth Century they traded their farm in Frederick County, Virginia, for a military claim of four thousand acres located on the Little Miami River and

Todd's Fork. The land purchase was known as Military Survey No. 1494.

They migrated to their new home in the wilderness in 1805. Rhoda at this time was but three years old. They established their home on a beautifully elevated spot which now overlooks Morrow.

They merely existed in an unbroken wilderness and suffered the many trials and hardships that went along with securing a new home in a wild and untamed land.

Roads were practically nonexistent in this time period which made the thirty mile trip through the woods to the markets in Cincinnati a struggle beyond belief.

Sometimes they would load their produce onto the flatboats and float them down on a rise in the Little Miami River to Cincinnati, and sometimes to New Orleans.

Robert at one time drove his own hogs, along with his neighbors, to Baltimore, Maryland, starting in August and arriving in the small city in time for the fall market.

Patience would ride on horseback to her old home in Virginia (a journey of several hundred miles), and visit her friends and relatives. Here she would receive encouragement which would strengthen her to renew her work in the wilderness.

Patience, with her three daughters, Rhoda, Jane and Priscilla, contributed to the comfort and the welfare of the family.

In this day and time, clothing was a main factor for the family. They picked, carded, spun and wove the wool for winter clothing and the flax for summer. Under these circumstances, Rhoda was raised.

At the age of eighteen she was united in marriage to Joseph Hollingsworth (born in 1786), a native of Frederick County, Virginia. He migrated to Ohio in 1816, first to Centerville, Montgomery County, and from there to Waynesville.

Here he worked for a time in a flouring mill. From there he went to Stubb's Mill, which was a short distance west of Morrow.

Joseph and Rhoda were married in 1820 and settled on a farm near Beech Grove Schoolhouse, about two miles from her father's home.

They had several children, the last survivors being Moses and Ruthanna. With hard work and a straight forward course of life, they succeeded in establishing themselves a comfortable home and an excellent farm.

Joseph was a miller by trade and was instrumental in forming a company with his brothers-in-law. Together they built what was known as the Whitacre Mills on the Little Miami River near the mouth of Todd's Fork in the years 1832 and 1833. (The skeleton of the old mill is still standing at this printing.)

About the year 1851, they sold their farm and moved to near Harveysburg, where Joseph died in 1853.

Soon after, Rhoda and her son Moses moved to Springboro. Ruthanna had been residing with them since the death of her husband, Nathan Hunt.

Rhoda, at the time of her death, lacked but a few days of being eighty-two years old. She died February 25, 1884. She was the last of her family, all her brothers and sisters died years before.

A writer once wrote of her: "There are, perhaps, but few people who have lived to her advanced age that have lived during the entire time a life more consistent, or one worthy to be more praised and held up as an example to future generations. Her loving friends were only limited by the circle of her acquaintance, for none knew her but to love her."

CAPTAIN WILLIAM H. HAMILTON

One of the many early Warren County residents to make his imprint on the County was Captain William H. Hamilton. He was born in Greene County, Pennsylvania, October 31, 1795. He was the son of Robert Hamilton, born in Bainbridge, County Down, Ireland in 1760.

Robert came to America when a young lad of fourteen. He sometime later became a soldier in the Revolution. He served throughout the war much of the time under the command of General Anthony Wayne. He was with him at the invasion of Stony Point, and was one of the men to lift him up when a glancing bullet had toppled him.

He was afterward captured by his brother, a British officer. Refusing to go home to Ireland if set free, he preferred to fight for his newly adopted country.

Robert's first wife was Susannah Kean. He worked as a blacksmith in Lancaster County, Pennsylvania, and about 1791 moved to Greene County, Pennsylvania. Here he married Ann Hays, a native of Berkeley County, Virginia. In 1797, he moved to Morgantown, Virginia, and in 1803 to Trumbull County, Ohio.

This part of the country was wild and crude. William spent his early years experiencing the hardships of pioneer life. Dwelling in log cabins and living in the simplest manner developed into him an iron constitution with which he retained throughout his life.

After living in Trumble County twelve years, he moved with his father to Warren County in 1815, where he resided until his death.

Possibly his first paying job as a tradesman was that of a blacksmith. He soon changed his profession to carpenter and builder, which he followed for about forty-five years. His building expertise consisted of bridge and mill structures.

He was for a period of four years superintendent of carpenter work on the Little Miami Railroad from Columbus to Cincinnati.

He afterward was employed on the Marietta Railroad from Loveland to Marietta. On the latter road he superintended the construction of thirteen important bridges.

He was an officer of militia from 1815 to 1822, his assignments being Ensign, Captain, Adjutant and Lieutenant Colonel; he was known familiarly as "Captain."

He was several years appointed County Commissioner of Warren County. In this capacity, being the only mechanic on the planning board, he superintended the construction of many bridges and buildings, among them being the first infirmary. It was commenced in 1867 and was the largest of the County buildings; the total cost was $51,459.

His residences in the County included the thriving villages of Millgrove, and Oregonia. (He was appointed local postmaster of the former December 13, 1833, and the latter February 5, 1846.) He lived on a farm near the mouth of Caesar's Creek, on a farm near Genntown, and in 1871, moved to Lebanon where he resided until his death.

Captain Hamilton was married to Elizabeth Schrack September 23, 1819. She was born in Frederick Co., Virginia, December 18, 1800. To them were born 10 children.

He died on Thursday, June 30, 1887, aged 91 years and 8 months. His health had been failing for some months. He left five sons and three daughters. His wife of sixty-five years died in 1884, aged eighty-four years. Two children, a daughter, Mary, and a son, John, had preceded them into eternity.

His character was one of high standing. He was one of the best-known and highly respected men in the County at this time. His education was one of wanting, but his sound judgement and high moral standings overrode any obstacles. His declining years were comforted by his son William and daughter Maggie who lived with him until his death.

GENERAL O. MITCHEL WAS A TRUE RAIDER

General Ormsby McKnight Mitchel astronomer, renowned lecturer, engineer, teacher and Civil War General, was born in Morganfield, Ky., July 28, 1809. At the age of four, General Mitchel moved, with his widowed mother, to the village of Miami in Clermont County, and shortly after to Lebanon in Warren County, Ohio.

Ormsby, during his youth devoted himself to books. At the age of 12 he thought it was time to support himself. He moved to Xenia, Ohio, and was placed in a country store as errand boy and clerk. He worked for twenty-five cents a week.

After an incident in the clerking trade, he talked his way into becoming a teamster.

Teamster life was not for a boy who had read Virgil at the age of nine and knew something of Greek at the age of twelve.

His mother was a relative of Judge McLean of the Supreme Court of the United States, who was at the time a resident of Lebanon.

Through the pressure of his mother, Judge McLean and John Ross of Lebanon secured an appointment to West Point for young Ormsby, not yet fifteen.

Mitchel graduated in the class of 1829, ranking fifteenth. Among this class was Robert E. Lee, second; Joseph E. Johnston, thirteenth; both who would become famous Confederate generals. Our subject was also a very good friend of Jefferson Davis, who later became President of the Confederate Nation.

In 1833, he moved to Cincinnati and began the practice of law with Edward D. Mansfield, the vocation paying very little at that time. Arriving in Cincinnati, he was appointed professor of Mathematics, Natural Philosophy, and Astronomy in the College of Cincinnati.

At the age of 26, Mitchel was called upon for his engineering expertise. A railroad was needed to open up a path from Cincinnati to the North. With a loan of $200,000 secured from Cincinnati, the Little Miami Railroad was underway; professor Mitchel was its chief surveyor.

Through his teachings of astronomy, his mind wandered in the direction of an observatory. No one had at that time in the United States an observatory; why should a back-woods town like Cincinnati have one?

Through his endless lectures and speeches, he was at last able to organize a company, a joint stock company in which the shareholders would buy at twenty-five dollars each share a part of the venture.

Professor Mitchel traveled the world finding

parts and lenses in which to build his controversial telescope. In March, 1845, this giant venture was finalized. Only the Russians had this caliber of telescope.

The Spring of 1861 was the end of a career for the man of genius. His days of lecturing, railroading and oratorical skills as a civilian were over. The fall of Fort Sumter aroused the patriotic pride in a man that was really too old to endeavor in a war. However, he felt the freedom of the country was at stake.

The ninety days war was not a reality. Bull Run was a tragedy to the North. This was a major setback for the Union troops.

On August 8, 1861, Mitchel was appointed Brigadier General of volunteers. He was assigned to command the Department of the Ohio, with headquarters in Cincinnati.

Gen. Mitchel was first assigned to the Cumberland Gap area. With this order countermanded he was relieved of his position, and the Department was put under the command of Gen. Buell.

Gen. Mitchel was then put in the command of a division in the army then organizing at Bacon Creek, between Louisville and Bowling Green, Ky. Working with raw recruits, he worked frantically to bring his command into shape.

His nervousness and eagerness to confront the enemy was a pitfall as jealousy sprung up amongst his superiors. Mitchel was the opposite of Gen. Buell who had replaced him. This instilled jealousy in the latter.

Gen. Mitchel was not in any major battles, but his raiding parties in Alabama, in which he seized the Memphis and Charleston Railroad at Huntsville, cut Confederate lines of communication, and harassed secessionists in northern parts of the State, were fore-runners of the strategies of Sherman and other generals of note.

Two years before Sherman, Mitchel showed how armies might depend on single lines of railroad through great tracts of the enemies country for supplies. Eighteen months before Rosecrans, he secured the essential point of the whole central half of the Southern States.

He was ordered from his command in Alabama on the 2nd of July, 1862. He was assigned to command the Dept. of South Carolina on the 12th of Sept., 1862. Gaining success in this venture was a reward for the Union troops.

Confederate railroads were destroyed, salt works were burned at Bluffton, and the general instilled confidence in all.

Five weeks after his arrival in the Department, on the 26th of October, 1862, General Mitchel contacted yellow fever. He died October 30, 1862.

General Mitchel is probably best known in the circles of war as the man who gave the O.K. to the "Andrew's Raid" or in literary circles, "The Great Locomotive Chase."

Chapter VI

NATIVE AMERICANS

WARREN COUNTY ONCE HOME TO TWO OTHER "ANCIENT FORTS"

We have all heard of Fort Ancient and most of us have visited it, but, did you know Warren County had two other prehistoric forts within its boundaries? There is one in the northwestern corner of the County, partially in Warren and Montgomery, called Carlisle Fort or Fort Carlisle.

The other one existed on the hill opposite Foster on the west side of the Little Miami. It was in one respect the most remarkable one in the country.

In this area the river flows south through a deep gorge. On the west side of the river a steep accent led to a high narrow plateau. This plateau was bounded on the west by a tributary known as Cline's Run. Thus, the plateau was surrounded by the river and creek on all but its northern portion.

Around the steep sides of this hill and cutting across the northern and part of the southern portions, there was a singular structure of burnt clay and stones which had long been an object of interest in the neighborhood.

Many tons of burnt clay and slag were to be found in the walls. An exploration was made in August 1890, by Professor F.W. Putnam, of the Peabody Museum in connection with Harvard University.

Helping the professor with the project was a Mr. Crosson and a Mr. Dorsey. A camp was set up within the enclosure in a group of oaks, maples and other trees, which had long been preserved.

Mr. Crosson was placed in charge of the exploration with Mr. Dorsey as chief assistant. The work was carried on until the end of September with interesting results as to the formation of this singular structure.

The structure was in the form of a circumvallation over half a mile in length. The height of the northern portion was nine to twelve feet high above the level of the field, and was about forty-five feet in average width.

The area across the south-eastern portion of the bank, though partly destroyed, was still several feet high.

Around the edge west of the hill, the rise above the level of the enclosed portion was hardly noticeable, but the structure extended into the sides of the hill about fifty feet, and from ten to twenty feet down the sides.

The whole structure was made up of a carefully laid wall of flat stones along the outer side several feet to height. Behind this were loose stones, both large and small, making up nearly half the structure. Behind and over these stones was a mass of clay burnt to all degrees of hardness.

Only slightly burnt to great masses of slag displayed that the clay had been subjected to much heat. In some places it formed a surface over the slag which resembled a blast furnace.

In many places the limestones had been burnt in varying degrees. Here and there, large quantities of pure lime were found.

Large pieces of charcoal and beds of ashes were discovered in many parts of the structure.

At one place on the north side, the burnt material ran out in the form of a low mound nearly one hundred feet long and eighty feet wide. At this point there was a larger quantity of charcoal and ashes than in other part of the works explored.

Here was also uncovered a singular wall of stones about six feet long and two feet high.

All throughout the excavation, with the digging of a trench, burnt stones and clay, ashes and charcoal, and a mass of stones was faced on the other side by a good stone wall.

In the northern portion a few potsherds, two flat points and a few flint flakes were found. Tthis was the only evidence discovered of the work of man, except the singular structure itself.

Several trenches were made within the enclosure. The plowed portion was carefully examined for traces of former habitation and for burials.

But with the exception of a few arrow points found on the surface, not a thing was discovered to indicate that the place had ever been occupied.

The extreme labor in this project must have taken a great period of time. The enclosure itself could have possibly been a habitational location. It is a possibility that the burials took place in the surrounding perimeter.

The burnt clay enclosure was known locally as "the fort." With the absence of tools, burials, etc., a knowledge of the builders is left unknown, a mystery left unsolved.

A structure of this kind could have been of regular clay, why burnt clay?

Mr. Crosson made numerous sketches and a Mr. Savill took a number of pictures. A thorough investigation was made with no clues as to why a prehistoric civilization would take up such an undertaking.

With little evidence of antiquities, and certainly no evidence of any battles, history will have to write this "fort" off simply as a great archaeological find.

CARLISLE FORT EXISTED ABOUT 2,000 YEARS AGO

In a previous article Carlisle Fort was mentioned as being a prehistoric find within the confines of Warren County. As was mentioned it was located in the extreme northwestern part of the County, a portion in Warren and part in Montgomery Counties.

Carlisle Fort, or Big Twin Works, is a hilltop fortification which lies on the west bank of Big Twin Creek, about 2 1/2 miles south of Germantown and about one mile west of Carlisle.

The creek empties into the Great Miami River about four miles to the south. The name of the fort was suggested by C.E. Blosser in regards to its location near Carlisle.

Hilltop fortifications were thought to be of a later time than the mounds and hilltop enclosures.

The ancients, to whom these works are attributed to, are the Hopewell Indians who lived within the bounds of Ohio nearly 2000 years ago.

Carlisle Fort was thought to have been built from AD 1 to AD 300. Historians thought this type of defensive fortification was a reflective measure concerning a declining cultural race.

The first survey of the site was by S.H. Binkley and C.E. Blossom in 1835. They returned to the site in 1875 for further examination.

Carlisle Fort is different in respect to other earthworks located along the Scioto, Ohio, Great Miami, and the Muskingum Rivers, because of its location along a secondary waterway.

The actual site is located on the peak of a hill a short distance west of Big Twin Creek. On the north and south side of the hill are deep ravines; on the east of the extensive bluff is a sharp declining drop of from one hundred and twenty-five to two hundred feet. On the east of the bluff is a terrace leading to Big Twin Creek.

J.P. MacLean, an early archaeologist, writes in 1885 in regards to the layout of the fort:

"The terrace is separated in two parts, an upper and lower, formed in the direction of the stream. On the west the hill is connected with the level lands by a broad peninsula. The wall is not accompanied by a ditch, and is situated on the brow of the hill, except on the northern side, where it occurs a little below.

"The wall, for the most part, is made of surface material although limestone is found in the southwestern gate. On the west, where the enclosure is most exposed, are discovered three walls. The entire length of the wall on the direct line of the middle wall, is three thousand six hundred and seventy-six feet, and encloses an area of from twelve to fifteen acres. The length of the wall on the Twin bluff is eleven hundred and ten feet."

Within the enclosure two stone mounds and one stone circle was originally located, the circle being near the center of the enclosed area. The stones within this enclosure were of such great abundance that when the first white settlers first saw the enormity of this find, they hurriedly made a makeshift road.

With many hundreds of wagons they removed the stone contents which were used in building dwellings, houses, barns, wells, etc., leaving only depression marks where the stone and circle mounds once stood.

S.H. Binkley wrote in 1889 that the stones previously mentioned "may" have been laid out by the Hopewell Indians for building a shelter. He explains a method of five lines of posts being erected, regarding height, notched for a reception of plate, and being securely fastened to the posts.

The posts were to be held together by pole ties and rafters, secured by thongs, tough bark or cordage of a type. Binkley suggests that the outer lines of posts were low, probably not extending more than six feet from the ground, while a height of fifteen feet would be enough for the central line.

To preserve the structure in its upright form, the great ridge of stone was heaped around the low posts as a support. (The Lake-dwellers of Switzerland practiced this method in early times.)

Binkley also suggests that the construction of a roof in which would be waterproof could have possibly been made from thatch.

Bark was used by the Indians as a roofing material for their huts, but its tendency to roll up at the sides would make it impractical on a large scale.

Carlisle Fort was in the headlines in early 1990 concerning the installation of a 36 inch natural gas pipeline from Indiana to Lebanon, Ohio, by the American Natural Resources Pipeline Company.

The Miami Valley Council of Native Americans made claims that the pipeline would interfere with the Indian burying sites.

An agreement was made to install the pipeline at least 600 feet outside the Carlisle Fort border. (The boundaries of the fort consist of two areas, one fifteen and one twenty-two acres.)

Carlisle Fort was added to the National Register of Historic Places concerning its safekeeping for future generations and further study.

THE MOUNDS OF OBSERVATION IN SOUTHWEST OHIO

The mound builders have left monuments of their works in the form of huge heaps of dirt that were basically shrines to their dead ones. With no record of their culture, other than what archaeologists, amateur and professional alike have excavated, a puzzle was left for the curious to solve.

In our article this week we shall highlight the "Mounds of Observation." The writer will attempt to guide you through a short session of the "signal mounds" in Southwestern Ohio and beyond, and their reasoning.

These extremely high mounds were possibly built for the purpose of signaling, or informing neighboring tribes of certain events. An event of war could be passed on to neighboring tribes, or a Chief of a nation could be announcing the birth of a child.

Various ceremonies could be relayed, revealing a season of plenty for a tribe, or one of disparity. These signals could also announce the surrender to an enemy, or perhaps a victory.

This method of communication was in the form of a huge fire that was built on top of these mounds. Puffs of smoke were made by placing a wet blanket or mat, made of corn husks, over the fire and throwing a small amount of water onto the flame.

Our trail through these mounds shall begin at Miami Fort at the mouth of the Great Miami, located in Hamilton County. (This should not be confused with Fort Miami at the foot of the rapids of the Maumee.)

The Great Miami flows southwest and empties into the Ohio at a sharp angle. An elevated peak of some two hundred feet or more lies significantly in this land angle, separating the two rivers. Within this angle lies Miami Fort. This is our first observation mound, as we shall call it.

From this elevation a line of signals could be conveyed which would cover the southwestern portion of the state.

Three mounds, one at Miami Fort, one at Colerain, and one at Hamilton, combined with mounds up the river to Dayton and Piqua, were all designed as signaling objectives with each other. These mounds were considered a connected line of defenses along the Great Miami River.

Fort Ancient on the Little Miami stands as a fortress in the rear of the center of this line of mounds. A mound at Norwood commands a view eastwardly to a mound in the valley of the Little Miami, then traveling northwardly through the valley of the Millcreek and the depression in the land, and on to the mound at Hamilton.

A chain of signal mounds, about twenty in number, along the Scioto from the northern boundary of Franklin County to the Ohio River, could transmit by signal fire, an alarm from the small mound at Worthington, Ohio, through the entire length of the valley to the earthworks at Portsmouth.

Some archaeologists say these particular mounds were not specifically used as signal mounds.

Many of them contain human remains, most assuredly that of the mound builders. Whether they were built as observation mounds or burial sites, one has to accept his own theory, as no evidence of this period's culture exists except the physical findings.

J.P. McLean writes of the mound builders in 1891.

"On the hills they erected mounds for posts of observation, and when a war party came down upon them, the fires were kindled, and the people thereby warned sought their shelters of refuge."

These signal mounds were not only related to the rivers of Ohio, but they could also have been spread over any number of Ohio counties. From any point in these counties a signal fire could be relayed from one mound to another in almost any direction.

From the Piqua area to the mouth of the Mississippi, these mounds of observation could transmit signals with the utmost speed.

From the mound at Hamilton let us now travel to the "Great Mound" in Butler County. Along Wayne-Madison Road is a landmark that has been known to county residents for years. It, like the previous mounds named, was built by the Adenas. They occupied the Ohio Valley dating approximately from 800 B.C. to 700 A.D.

The Great Mound was first measured in the 1800's with its height given as 43 feet and 511 feet circumference at the base. Through erosion and farming near its base, it has now been reduced to about 34 feet in height with its base at 178 in circumference.

Our next observation mound is located about a mile southeast of Miamisburg in Montgomery County. It is likewise called "The Miamisburg Mound."

This mound is the second largest in the United States. It was originally about 85 feet in height and its base measured about 300 feet in diameter.

There has been some diggings into the mound but few human bones were uncovered. It too was figured to be a signal mound.

Located just off Deardoff Road in Franklin lies the "Kinder Mound." It is closely related to the Miamisburg Mound, lying just a few miles south. It is reportedly the last of the chain of signal mounds from Lake Erie to the Ohio on the east side of the Great Miami.

From this mound signals could be seen from Carlisle Fort near Carlisle, and from the hills of Oregonia where messages were conveyed on to Fort Ancient.

Digging into this mound has been prohibited by the owners, because they thought it to be a place of worship.

In March 1990, a theory was tested which was to prove whether or not signals could be sent to nearby mounds. It was organized by The Archaeological Conservancy and experimented on three Adena Mounds, namely, The Miamisburg Mound, The Great Mound in Butler County, and The Kinder Mound in Warren County.

The test was originally to be at night, to see if road flares could be detected.

E.G. & G. Mound Laboratory is situated next to the Miamisburg Mound, and it was thought that the lighting effect of the laboratory would prove negative in that situation.

Consequently, the test was changed to daylight. The usage of large mirrors, measuring 36 by 42 inches, was suggested and adopted.

Much concern was raised as to whether the mirrors would work because of the trees on the mounds which could block the sun's reflection.

Field glasses and compasses were equipment used for the experiment, along with radio operators using their communication network. The mirrors were positioned so as to catch the sun at just the right angle.

Cheers went up as bright flashes were seen from one mound to another. Radio communicators sent word from mound to mound as the success of the experiment began to unfold.

The signals had worked magnificently and all were very pleased with the experiment.

OHIO MOUND BUILDERS NOT AS ADVANCED AS HISTORIANS THOUGHT

The ancients who built the mounds were, according to some early writers and archaeologists, of an advanced race, or descendants of the "lost tribes of Israel."

These writers wrote of the advanced technology of the first inhabitants of the continent and their culture. The publications have yet to prove the existence of superiority amongst the mound builders.

Ohio has the largest accumulation of mounds in the nation. The most noteworthy in this area are Fort Ancient near Oregonia, and the Miamisburg Mound near Miamisburg. These two earthworks have been explored and excavated and no trace of a "superior race" and their works has been found; only old relics have been unearthed.

The relics of these two earthworks, along with thousands of other works, have been scientifically digested with the conclusion being that they were the work of a rather crude people.

The original writings professed that the mound builders consisted of a mathematical knowledge and engineering skill. This theory was widespread for many generations, but has since been proven a falsehood.

Some early archaeologists, using inadequate measurements and observations, overstated that the mound builders geometrical figures were precisely laid out, that the circular works were perfect circles and the rectangular works perfect squares.

Modern instruments of precise measurements and surveys have disrupted that theory. Not a single discovery has been found that shows the earthworks to be built on a perfect scale. The culture of the mound builders was no further advanced than that of the Indians Columbus discovered.

The conclusion that the builders were without architectural science or engineering skill, is one of scientific advancement.

The stones in their walls were without chisel marks. They had no mortar or cement. Their embankments were practically absent of stone in which to prevent them from sliding down hill. They used fire, but had no chimney to carry away the smoke. No evidence of a walled up cistern or dug wells has been found.

The mounds were and still are an amazing feat, but compared to the building of the great Pyramids, they are feeble in their construction. They are merely structures of earth in which mere aborigines could dig and carry materials in baskets for their configurations.

Fort Ancient is acclaimed the most studied of the archaeological forts in the United States. The accumulative amount of earth in its 3 1/2 mile structure would hardly equal just one of the great pyramids of Egypt.

The dirt of the fort was carried up from the sides of the hill a distance of about 20 or 30 feet, while the huge 40 cubic feet blocks of the Great Pyramid were carried to a height of more than 400 feet.

An opinion of many was that a mighty race once dominated the Mississippi Valley which predated the American Indian. This population was supposed to be racially distinct from the Indian. They were called the lost race, and it was believed they disappeared before the arrival of the Indian.

The scientist has found no proof of such a race. No distinction has ever been made between the ornaments, utensils and artifacts that the mound builders and Indians made.

The Indian tribes at the time of the discovery of America were mound builders. When DeSoto wandered through the Gulf States in 1540-41, several tribes were using mounds, and articles found in the mounds were indications that the Indians had erected them since the coming of the white man. David Zeisberger, the Moravian missionary, writing in 1779, wrote:

"Underground dwellings, there were also of which here and there traces may be found, particularly along the Muskingum, in which region one may find many places where embankments, still to be seen, were thrown up around a whole town.

"Here and there, furthermore, near the sites of such towns there are mounds, not natural, but made by the hand of man, for in those days the natives carried on great wars within one another, the Indians being formerly according to their own testimony far more numerous than at the present time.

"At the top of these mounds there was a hollow place in which the Indians brought their wives and children when the enemies approached and attacked them, the men ranging themselves round the mound for defensive action.

"Their weapons were the bow and arrow and a wooden club, this last a piece of wood of not quite arm's length, having at the end a round knob about the size of a child's head and made of very hard wood. In such attacks both sides usually lost many men, which were often buried in one pit and a great mound of earth raised above them, such as may even now be seen bearing in these days great and mighty trees."

BOW AND ARROW GREATEST LABOR-SAVING INVENTION FOR FLINT-USERS

In this particular article, the writer will elaborate on "flint" and its various uses concerning the first inhabitants of the North American continent.

Bone and wood were not suitable for the construction of hunting implements of the early aborigines. The North American Indians, in existence long before the first white man appeared, relied on no type of manufacturing facilities as far as every day life was concerned.

Stone tools of various kinds are still being found, but these were used mainly for grinding corn and utilized in various other fashions.

The bow and arrow, being the most important Indian implement, was his greatest labor saving invention. It was made from the three kingdoms, animal, vegetable and mineral; animal intestines for the string, wood for the bow, and flint for the arrowhead.

Some flint products are classed as arrowheads

or spearheads, however, with some study, the shape of these objects, in regards to the size, are quite identifiable.

The larger of the two was simply too heavy to be used as an arrowhead. The smaller arrowhead was about two inches in length with the larger points being used as javelin or spear heads, or some had handles attached and were used as knives.

The Mound Builders, and still later Indians, made these implements of flint. The characteristic of this culture and the flint tool is indistinguishable.

There were no settlements in the lower Miami Valley when the first white man arrived, but flint, as well as stone tools, has been found in abundance.

Huge quantities of flint must have been used because the chipped implements are widely scattered and are found in large quantities year after year in the same plowed fields.

A large portion of the flint was wasted because of broken implements in the crafting procedure. Large blocks of flint were sometimes rejected because of poor quality standards.

We have talked so far of the basic use of flint, now where did the flint come from? About midway between Newark and Zanesville, Ohio, lies an eight mile stretch of land called Flint Ridge.

This area was undoubtedly the source of flint for the early Ohio natives. The entire distance of the ridge was scarred with the trenches and pits left by the ancient diggers.

Stones suitable for flint products were of top priority with the quarrying of the stone being one of the great industries of the native tribes.

The distance between the quarries were great. Two other locations of quarries were Millcreek, Union County, Ill., and in the vicinity of Hot Springs, Ark.

W.C. Mills, an early archaeologist, made quite an extensive study of the different kinds of flint and the evolving of the flint explorations.

A layer of flint is often covered with earth many feet in depth. The Indians made hundreds of excavations in order to find flint suitable for their cause.

Their exploration of Flint Ridge, Ohio, stretched over thousands of acres, but the most valuable quarries were located within perhaps a 100 acre tract.

After finding the flint and clearing away the earth, a layer of solid flint several feet in thickness would be found. The stratum was broken into slabs in order to be carried away.

Mr. Mills believed the flint "was quarried by the use of heavy stone hammers or mauls for breaking off large slabs and perhaps wooden wedges for prying, tho no wedges of any kind were found."

Hammerstones were found in small abundance, one which weighed 25 pounds.

These hammers were mostly made of flint or granite which were used without handles as no evidence of grooves for the attachment of a handle was evident. Only one such hammer was found at the Flint Ridge location.

One test performed by Mr. Mills was that he experimented with the splitting of the top layers by fire.

A hot fire was kept burning over the rock for a period of two hours. Removing the fire, water was thrown on the heated exterior. The experiment was not successful; a large piece was split off, but the flint was cracked into small pieces to a depth of only half an inch.

The first step consisting of the retrieving of the flint was perhaps the most laborious for the Indians.

Often large blocks were quarried and brought to the surface, which led to the second step, the blocking out the flint into such forms and sizes as to be easily carried. This work was carried on in perhaps a five or ten acre plot.

The third step was the shaping of the blocks into segments in which could be transported to the many locations. Not all workshops were set up in the immediate vicinity for this task, some being as far away as one-hundred miles.

The next challenge for the Indians was a way to fashion and shape the flint into a useful implement. The popular belief for the early archaeologists was that a type of metal tool was used to fashion and shape the arrow and spearheads, however, no evidence of this type has been found.

It is a fact that a file, the hardest of our tools, will not make an impression on some flint.

Some authorities suggested that the early inhabitants had a way of hardening copper to the necessary degree, but nothing of the sort has ever been discovered. It can be said that if a knowledge of metals were indeed an early art form, more physical evidence would have been uncovered.

The making of heavy articles, such as axes, pestles, etc., which did not require accuracy in the work, was done with a hard, tough pebble, the preference being some form of quartz.

The purpose of this was to knock off all the large chips of flint and to form his choice of tools. With the useless portion knocked away the Indian then pecked very lightly over the entire surface until an effective outline was visible.

He then used a gritty sandstone to remove the hammer marks, and a still finer grained sandstone was used to create a smooth surface. All instruments for cutting or splitting customed the edge which made it sharp and smooth by rubbing. If a groove was needed, it was made as early as possible.

Fashioning an arrowhead or a spear point relied mainly on the tribes doing the crafting.

Gerald Fowke, an early archaeologist, says the Mexicans held a piece of obsidian (volcanic glass) in the left hand, and pressed it firmly against the point of a small goat's horn held in the right. By moving it gently in different directions they chipped off small flakes until the arrow was complete.

The great plains Indians used buckskin and a

point of bone or antler to knick off the edges. They later laid the flat side of a flake on a blanket or another surface and knicked off the edges with a knife.

The arrowhead had two basic forms - the triangular, and the pointed oval or leaf-shaped, though both could have straight edges and a curved base. The arrow point of the smallest size to the larger spear type appear to have the same general shapes.

When going to battle the Indian had two forms of arrow points, both small and sharp. The first, of triangular pattern, was lightly attached, so that it would remain in the wound when the shaft was pulled out, and consequently work deeper in.

The other, with long, sharp barbs would be securely held so that it would pull out with the shaft, lacerating the flesh as it came.

Axes were sometimes made flat or grooved lengthwise on one side, so that a wedge could be driven in to tighten the handle.

Tomahawks, or "celts," were set in a split stick, and firmly fastened. Another method was the head being set into a hole cut in a stick, and some form of glue or gum used to secure it.

The use of stone implements by the Indians was one of amazement. White man, with all his mechanical skills and tools, would marvel in astonishment if he could witness the precision and accuracy the aborigine showed in his repertoire.

When the Indian wanted a log for his house, or simply to make a canoe, he depended on the amazing rock called "flint."

He dressed deer and other skins with a small celt, one side being often flat or beveled, to secure better results.

His larger celts made good wedges when he wanted to split out boards; also they were good to strip off bark when he wanted to deaden trees for a clearing.

Very small celts were set in the end of a bone or antler and used as knives and skinners.

Square or rounded arrow points were used to wound or kill small game without puncturing the skin.

The Indian's spear was designed so as not to leave his hands, the head would be made without barbs so that it could be easily withdrawn. His spear for war, however, might be barbed for the greater pain it would cause.

There are many other uses and applications for the use of flint that the Indians employed, but due to space the writer cannot continue.

HISTORIC OLDTOWN HOSTED TECUMSEH, DANIEL BOONE

Allow us this week to take a short trip to visit our neighbor to the North, Greene County. In our midst lies the most historic town in the State of Ohio.

About three miles north of Xenia, on U.S. 68, lies Oldtown, long before called Old Chillicothe. Many years before the Boston Tea Party, long before Washington's great army defeated the English, this grand town was existing in a peaceful fashion.

It was 215 years ago (1778) that Daniel Boone first became acquainted with the Shawnee Indians of Old Chillicothe. Boone recorded his historic experiences while sitting in his crude log cabin in Harrodsburg, Kentucky. He writes:

"January 1, 1778, I went with 20 men to the blue lick on the Licking river to make salt for the different garrisons. On February 7 I was hunting by myself to procure meat for the company and I met a party of 102 Indians and two Frenchmen marching against Boonesboro. They pursued and took me and that day I capitulated for my men, knowing they could not escape. They were 27 in number, three having gone with salt. The Indians used us generously. They carried us to Old Chillicothe, on the Little Miami river.

"On the 18th of February we arrived there after an uncomfortable journey in very severe weather. On the 10th of March I and 10 of my men were taken on to Detroit. On the 30th we arrived there and were treated by Gov. Hamilton, the

British commander of the post, with great humanity.

"The Indians had such a fondness for me that they refused 100 pounds sterling if they would leave me with the others that he might send me home on my parole.

"Several English gentlemen there, sensible of my life and touched with sympathy, generously offered to supply my wants, which declined with many thanks, adding that I never expected it would be in my power to repay such generosity.

"The Indians left my men in captivity at Detroit, and on April 10, after a long and fatiguing march, they brought me back to Old Chillicothe."

Oldtown is dotted with just a few dwellings and is easily passed by. However, if one were to park their vehicle and walk this historic ground, a vision of long ago would begin to grasp their inner being.

Possibly the greatest event in the history of Old Chillicothe was that Tecumseh was born within a few rods of the town. This occasion itself is a distinction of sufficient historical interest.

On the street of Old Town the greatest Indian warriors of the time sat around the council fires and planned their many campaigns against the white man.

Years before the birth of Tecumseh the village was considered of great importance.

Tecumseh was not the only notable personality to grace the land of the Shawnee. Others included Gen. Josiah Harmar, Col. John Bowman, Simon Kenton, George Rogers Clark, Simon Girty, General Arthur St. Clair, and numerous others.

The village consisted of one main street, then as now, which was approximately one-fourth of a mile in length. No regularity was used in the positioning of the huts and tepees. Most of the huts were located in the vicinity of the old school house.

The common Indians had their huts along the banks of the Little Miami. The council house was a long, narrow building, roughly made, and scarcely waterproof.

In the shelter of this committee house, plans were possibly made to a degree that made every white man shudder for a circle of two hundred miles.

The old council house served in many capacities. Simon Girty and the Scotch renegade, Dixon, came on the scene, and volunteered to aid Chief Blackfish, then in command of the village, to construct a more permanent structure. This new building stood in Oldtown until as late as 1840.

The Shawnees caused the white man more trouble than any other tribes in the vicinity. Their initial village was located at Chillicothe on the Scioto River.

Second in importance was the village at Old Town. There was a constant communication between the two villages. The Shawnees, being excellent walkers and runners, allowed the 70 miles distant to be common ground.

They were constantly in contact with the other Indian tribes, the Miamis, the Wyandottes and the Delawares; these latter settlements being farther to the North and West.

When the alarm sounded for war, their primitive methods of communication reached out and a response was immediately answered by the neighboring tribes.

There is much more to write about Old Chillicothe, but if one were to visit and keep in perspective the history of this area, a more common knowledge would become visible.

There are no less than eight markers in the proximity. The most prestigious marker is located in the Oldtown Reserve which is situated on the east (right) side of U.S. 68, just north of Xenia. It marks the birthplace of Tecumseh, the great Shawnee Chief.

WARREN COUNTY HAD ITS OWN SERPENT MOUND

Warren County has within its boundaries many

archaeological sites, some of which have been examined and some which have not.

A site, which no longer exists, was originally called the "Kingsnake Mound," or in later years, "The Warren County Serpent Mound."

The Warren County Serpent Mound was first discovered in 1839. It was thought to have been built by the Adena Indians about 2000 years ago.

Only three other serpent mounds have been uncovered in the world: one each in Canada and Scotland, and the other, the Great Serpent Mound in Adams County, Ohio.

The Warren County effigy mound existed in a small loop of Baker's Creek, just south of the Little Miami River, off Stubbs Mill Road. It has since been consumed by a gravel company.

Dr. S.S. Scoville, a student of archaeology, in the spring of 1892, was passing through the woods near the town of Morrow. He came upon a peculiar elevation which attracted his attention.

He found on top of this elevation a growth of immense trees which were many centuries old. The remains of other large trees and foliage were found rotting on the location.

He worked his way through the mass of entanglement and traced the ridge to a clearing. The work of the American Indian had again been uncovered.

A once dominant race had indeed left its work behind, and was rediscovered by the trained eye of Dr. Scoville. His discovery was all too symmetrical to have been an incidental fluke.

Over the years the plow and the machinery of man had taken its toll on his findings.

Dr. Scoville for some time studied the mound and had carefully taken into consideration the many cuts and gaps that were missing in the configuration.

He concluded that they had mostly been made by roadmakers cutting through it and had consequently used the materials for roadbeds.

He suggested that if the gaps were filled in, the snake-like mound would be a total of 1900 feet long, some 400 feet longer than the Serpent

Mound in Adams County. The serpent was measured at 15-20 feet wide and three to five feet high.

It did not take him long to discover that the "head" of the effigy had practically been destroyed.

The body was still enveloped in the virgin forest. He retraced his steps along this giant mass and found the tail section had also been destroyed by the plow.

In 1892, Professor Putnam, of the Peabody Museum of Harvard College, was called on by Dr. Scoville to examine the mound.

After a brief examination, the professor called for and supervised an excavation. (The actual excavation was carried on by Dr. C.L. Metz and Dr. Scoville with the results being conveyed to Prof. Putnam at all times.)

The professor stated that it was a rare find and was constructed in the same manner as the Serpent Mound in Adams County, and the fact that a second effigy mound was uncovered, was proof of the existence of a densely populated Indian culture.

Cross sections were cut into the mound, and a line of flat stones standing on edge, on each side, was found to extend along its whole course, somewhat representing a back bone. The bulk of the mound was found to be made of clay, with ashes along the edge.

The exploration was carried on by digging trenches into the body at short distances apart.

Graves of the ancient people were found which contained skeletons and certain articles of household goods.

What happened to the serpent mound? As was stated earlier, a local gravel company bought the property on which the mound existed, the year being about 1961.

On September 24, 1950, an eight member board had been appointed for the purpose of looking into the present status of the effigy earthwork.

It was named "The Warren County Serpent Mound Committee." A meeting was held on October 15, 1950, at the site of the mound concerning its findings. Between 1927 and 1950, the matter was allowed to lie inactive.

Through much effort, the committee presented its final report to the Ohio Indian Relic Collectors Society on the afternoon of November 18, 1951.

A statement was made that the matter of the mound had been settled forty years previous. It was at this time concluded that an exhaustive investigation should be made.

(The Ohio State Archaeological and Historical Society had officially recognized the earthwork as an authentic effigy since 1909. The Society, between 1914 and 1927, had repeatedly tried to acquire the site as public property. A committee was formed to inquire into the ownership of the farm with a notion of purchasing the site. It was not for sale.)

Two sides, negative and affirmative, were brought up regarding the mound. It was suggested to the committee that no more than three men had ever written anything about the subject which would be considered relative to its restoration prior to 1938.

Colonel Charles Whittlesey had drawn a map of the earthwork in 1839, and published the same in 1853.

Harlan I. Smith, in 1892, a young man considered to be an inexperienced student of Dr. Metz, carried on some explorations of the earthwork under the Dr.'s guidance.

Smith was not convinced that the effigy was a work of another culture, contrary to the belief of Dr. Metz. Smith's inexperience and untrained eye were in question concerning his decision.

Scores of persons were interviewed on the affirmative side. All data was compiled along with affidavits from individuals concerning the mound.

All data was made public: aerial photographs were produced; written statements from archaeologists were obtained; and countless statements were signed by prominent laymen who had seen and had direct personal knowledge regarding the earthwork. The document contained approximately 350 pages consisting of the above.

The committee's findings were made public in the form of a resume.

It said in certain terms that all information contained in the 350 pages of the resume related directly to both the negative and the positive findings as to whether the Warren County Serpent Mound was an authentic effigy.

All knowledge of the mound was to be based upon the facts prior to the restoration of the earthworks previous to 1938. It was restored under the direction of Senator John Holden of Morrow.

In 1933, Senator Holden used his political influence and got the ancient works declared a worthwhile project for the Works Project Administration (WPA). In 1934, a crew of workmen, along with their mechanical giants, moved into action.

A question arose in 1964 when the Cincinnati Enquirer charged that the Warren Serpent was the result of a WPA project, in which bulldozers had transformed a "linear type mound and several small mounds into a serpent with a head, five convolutions type forms and a coiled tail."

In 1951, Mr. Schuchter, the owner of the land, offered to sell the "Little Serpent Mound" at a price of $10,000.

Until this time he had failed to put a price tag on it. Because of all the controversy, no one at this particular time seemed interested.

In time interest in the mound faded away. It disappeared in the early '60's with the question of authenticity still unresolved.

Chapter VII

RELIGIOUS DENOMINATIONS

THE FIRST BAPTISTS IN OHIO AND WARREN COUNTY

Organization of the people and the church was the first attempt to form some sort of stability in the Miami Valley once the migration started arriving. The writer will now attempt to profile some sort of history involving the first Baptist organization in Ohio and the Miami Valley. Material for this article was taken from the very distinguished writer, Josiah Morrow.

Evolving of the first Baptist Church in Ohio was formed at the house of Benjamin Davis at Columbia (now a part of Cincinnati) on the last Saturday in March, 1790, some five years before the Indian peace treaty. The membership was made up of nine people.

The following Sunday, Rev. Stephen Gano, a prominent Baptist minister from Providence, R.I., preached at the home of Major William Goforth, one of the pioneers of Columbia. The sermon created three new converts which were baptized in the Ohio River.

The first house of Christian worship built in Ohio, except for the Moravian Missionaries, who preached among the Indians in the northeastern part of Ohio before the Revolution, was built in the years 1792 and 1793 at Columbia, by the Baptists. The building was thirty-six feet long by thirty feet wide.

It is believed that the first structure was made of logs. A sketch of the church was given by O.M. Spencer when a boy living in the area about 1790. It goes as such:

"Fresh in my remembrance is the rude log-house, the first humble sanctuary of the first settlers of Columbia, standing amidst the tall forest trees on a beautiful knoll where now (1834) is a grave-yard and the ruins of a Baptist meeting house of later years.

"There, on the holy Sabbath, we were wont to assemble to hear the word of life; but our fathers met with their muskets and rifles, prepared for action and ready to repel any attack of the enemy. And while the watchman on the walls of Zion was uttering his faithful and pathetic warning, the sentinels without at a few rods distance, with measured step, were pacing their walls."

A.H. Dunlevy, son of Francis Dunlevy, tells that on the opening day for the new house of worship, that Col. Spencer, the father of O.M. Spencer, visited the service and afterwards addressed the militia present on the importance of the presence of arms at the gatherings.

At a later gathering at the church, two men appeared carrying an Indian's scalp they had just taken. Still within the same period two members of the church, Francis Griffin and David Jennings were killed by the Indians, and the boy, O.M. Spencer, was taken prisoner.

A meeting was held at Columbia on September 23, 1797. Attending were seven ministers and twenty-three lay members of the Baptist Church. (Two of the ministers were from the Kentucky area.)

The purpose of this meeting was to form some type of organization of associations of churches. Francis Dunlevy, his place of residence being at the time the Miami Island, was one of the laymen attending.

A second assemblage was gathered on November 4, 1797, with the same body of men, and an additional ten more in attendance. A further exchange of organization was discussed, the conclusion being that the first meeting of the Miami Baptist Association be held June 2, 1798. At this time four churches were represented, viz: Columbia, Miami Island, Carpenter's Run and

Clearcreek.

A third meeting was held at the Miami Island on Saturday, October 20, of the same year.

The first Baptist body in the area of Ohio was formed in 1798, regardless of whether the membership was called association, conference, council, etc.

The first meeting, with statistics being recorded by the association, was begun at Columbia on Friday, September 6, 1799. Six churches were represented and reported their membership. These churches were: Columbia, 35; Miami Island, 62; Carpenter's Run, 32; Clearcreek, 20; Middle Run, 15; Straight Creek, 21; total, 185. Elder James Sutton was moderator and Francis Dunlevy, clerk.

A great majority of the churches in the new country took their names from streams, not towns. The increase in population of the towns caused most of the churches to move to these areas, and consequently new names were chosen.

When Columbia's population started to decline, the church was moved about two miles north. In 1808, the church was named Duck Creek.

The State of Ohio was not formed until 1803, but the Baptist organized a church in what is now Warren County in 1797. It was named Clearcreek Baptist Church. It is said to have been the first church organized in the County, and the fourth Baptist Church in the Miami Country.

Its first building stood a little north of the present site of Ridgeville. Elder James Sutton was its first pastor, later being succeeded by Elder Daniel Clark.

In 1798 the church was represented in the Miami Association by James Sutton, Ebenezer Osborn, Thomas Kelsey and Francis Dunlevy.

Fergus McLean, father of United States Chief Justice John McLean, was an early pioneer in the Clearcreek area. He was a declared Presbyterian, but his wife was a Baptist; their three sons all became Methodists. It is a possibility that Mr. McLean assisted in the building of the church.

At this early time in the State's history, transportation to and from the new Clearcreek Church was a chore to say the least. Members traveled from great distances to attend the services. Many members lived in the Turtlecreek area and they had themselves created a church service on a once-a-month basis.

In 1798, the Turtlecreek members organized a branch of the Clearcreek Church. They secured land and constructed themselves a meeting house of hewed logs. It was located just east of the present site of Lebanon. The building stood near the northwest corner of the Baptist Cemetery.

The new Baptist meeting house was being used before construction was completed. Its floor was not laid and the log joists on which the floor was to be placed was being used as seats by the worshipers.

Leaders of the new church were: Matthias Corwin, father of Governor Thomas Corwin, his two brothers, Ichabod and Joseph; Francis Dunlevy, Col. Lewis Drake, Peter Drake, John Osborn, Thomas Lucas and Peter Yauger.

The Turtlecreek branch was solvent with the Clearcreek branch until 1802, when it was declared an independent congregation. The now independent Turtlecreek Church held its first official meeting on Saturday, December 11, 1802.

Minutes of the first meeting shows the choosing of Brother Daniel Clark, who was formerly pastor of the Clearcreek Church, as its first pastor. Brother Matthias Corwin was chosen as its first Deacon.

The minutes stated that the time of the meetings shall be "On the Saturday before the second Sabbath in each month and the Sabbath following."

Elder Daniel Clark continued in the capacity of pastor until 1830. His dedication to the church came to a halt in 1834 due to his death.

In 1815, Elder Stephen Gard was called upon to be assistant pastor. In 1819, he tendered his resignation and Elder Wilson Thompson assumed the position of assistant pastor for a five year term. Elder Thompson later became pastor of the Turtlecreek Church. Elder Hezekiah Stites was also assistant pastor for a time.

Meetings at the new site continued until 1811

when a new brick meeting house was erected on the West side of Lebanon. The name of the new church was changed from Turtlecreek to Lebanon.

Organization of the Turtlecreek Church seemed to surpass its parent church in membership. It soon became one of the largest and most important churches of the Baptist denomination in the Miami Country.

Before being organized into an independent church, the membership, in 1800, held a meeting with the Miami Association. Elder John Smith was the moderator and ten churches were represented.

From 1798 until 1835, when the church was undergoing changes from the Old School and the New School branches, the Miami Baptist Association held seven of its annual meetings at the Turtlecreek/Lebanon Church, the most held at any other given place. Clearcreek only hosted one meeting of the organization, this being in 1825.

The Miami Baptist Domestic Missionary Society was organized in 1816. The Ohio Baptist Education Society was conceived in 1830. Lebanon had the distinction of hosting both meetings. This small town had within its ranks some very influential people in the Baptist organizations.

Not quite so fashionable now as back in the early beginnings of the church, the pastor received for his compensation basically the fruits of the land. Salary compensations for the pastor were not noted in the Lebanon Church until 1827, when Elder Wilson Thompson's salary was fixed at $500 annually.

The pastors generally had some other means of support other than preaching. Some of them were farmers or farm hands. Elder Thompson practiced medicine during his tenure as pastor.

Responsibility for the division into branches of the Old School and New School appears to have been a publication entitled "Simple Truth," authored by Elder Thompson.

Another book written by Elder Thompson was entitled "Triumph of Truth." He became a leader of the Old School Baptists and opposed all religious and moral associations except the church.

A meeting of the Lebanon Baptist Church was held on Saturday, October 1, 1836. With this gathering a decision was made to divide the church into two distinctive branches.

The Old School branch with sixty-one members formed the West Baptist Church. The New School branch with forty-two members formed the East Baptist Church.

JONATHAN TICHENOR: A PRESBYTERIAN PIONEER

Jonathan Tichenor's name goes down in history as one of the founders of the first Presbyterian Churches in the Miami Valley.

He was born in Essex County, New Jersey, in 1741. He lived for a brief period in Kentucky and he later emigrated to the Ohio Valley about 1786.

He next located on the north side of the Ohio in or near Columbia, the oldest town between the Miamis, now a part of Cincinnati.

In about 1796 or '97, he moved to Turtlecreek and bought a tract of 120 acres lying north of the former Shaker Hill school house. He received a deed April 21, 1802, the purchase price being $360, or $3.00 per acre.

His son, David, also bought land in the same section: 160 acres at the purchase price of $400, or $2.50 per acre.

Jonathan Tichenor, Daniel Reeder, Jacob Reeder, Joseph Reeder, Annie Reeder, Samuel Sering, Sarah Sering and Isaac Morris, on October 16, 1790, joined in an effort to establish a Presbyterian Church in the settlements of Columbia and Cincinnati. This was the first such effort to organize a Presbyterian Church between the Miamis.

Rev. James Kemper, a pioneer minister, recorded that he formed an unorganized church of six males and two females at Columbia and Cincinnati. The church served as one for the two places.

He says he was ordained its pastor in 1792, even though the organization was not completed;

the reasoning being "that they thought the number of male members was too small to select a promising session."

The church membership progressed very slowly. There were only nineteen adult members recorded on the 5th of September, 1793. Out of this number they unanimously elected five ruling Elders and two Deacons.

The names of the five Elders first elected in the Miami Valley were: Jonathan Tichenor, Moses Miller, Joseph Reeder, Daniel Reeder and David Reeder.

In the forming of the church, Rev. Kemper wrote:

"I had a few objections from the beginning tho I past them over. The chief of these was, they were formed on a written agreement only expressing the name of a church and church government, in a compendious way, without any reference made in it to the confession of faith, and I think without the members having a sufficient knowledge of that book."

With Wayne's Treaty of Peace in 1795, many families moved from the early settlements of Columbia and Cincinnati up the Miami Valley and began to establish their own settlements.

Five of the aforementioned names followed this trend, thus settling in Turtlecreek on the west side of Lebanon. Their names were: Jonathan Tichenor, Moses Miller, Isaac Morris, Samuel Sering, and one of the Reeders.

The Turtlecreek Presbyterian Church was formed one mile south of Union Village. It was the first of the denomination in Warren County and soon became the strongest in the Miami Valley, Jonathan Tichenor being was one of its Elders.

In 1799, Rev. James Kemper became the pastor of the Turtlecreek and the Dick's Creek churches. He purchased a farm at Turtlecreek, but he remained on it only one year.

Rev. Richard McNemar, of Kentucky, visited the Turtlecreek Church in November 1799 and preached.

Of this milestone he wrote: "On this occasion I found a large and respectable congregation;

had an interview with their pastor, James Kemper, at the house of Jonathan Tichenor, one of the Elders, where I had an evening meeting and we lodged together. Kemper was about to move his family from the vicinity of Cincinnati and take charge of the Turtlecreek congregation."

Richard McNemar moved his family, in the spring of 1802, to Turtlecreek, purchased a farm and was settled as pastor of the church.

His eloquence as a preacher in the great Kentucky Revival had preceded him. He brought to the Turtlecreek Church his methods and principles of the revivalists later to become the Newlights.

Nearly all the Presbyterian churches in the Miami Country had been disturbed by the Kentucky Revival.

It seemed that all of McNemar's congregation followed him into Newlightism. Tichenor was one of the elders at Turtlecreek to object to McNemar's philosophies. He did not go the way of the Newlights.

In the spring of 1805, one year after the organization of the Turtlecreek Newlight Church, McNemar converted to the Shaker religion. He took with him a large part of his congregation, including three of his elders, Samuel Sering, Francis Beedle, and Malcolm Worley. Shakerism claimed four Presbyterian preachers from Ohio and Kentucky which were involved in the Kentucky Revival.

The organization of the Lebanon Presbyterian Church was about 1805. Its members consisted of the Turtlecreek Church west, and the Bethany Church east of town. Both were disrupted by the Newlight revival.

A deed dated September 7, 1806, from John Shaw to Jonathan Tichenor and Abner Smith, places the first Presbyterian Church one mile west of town. The consideration for the land was recorded at $40.00, "for the only proper use of the Lebanon Presbyterian congregation forever."

This acre became the Presbyterian Graveyard in which are buried Jonathan Tichenor and Abner Smith.

The first session of the church was not selected until December 3, 1807, when Jonathan Tichenor, Abner Smith, James Gallagher and Silas Hurin were chosen ruling Elders.

On October 22, 1808, there were 46 members.

Jonathan Tichenor's accomplishments in the Presbyterian Church was to be praised. He was one of eight persons to sign the first agreement for the organization of a Presbyterian Church in the Miami Country, the church for Columbia and Cincinnati. He was elected as one of the first Elders of the church.

He was later elected the ruling Elder at Turtlecreek, the first church of the denomination in Warren County.

He, almost alone, defied the teachings and doctrines of the Kentucky Revival preached by Richard McNemar, which tended to destroy the church and leave in its place the first Society of Shakers in the western country.

Judge Francis Dunlevy said that Tichenor was one of the best men he ever knew. He settled more cases of disagreement between his neighbors than the courts of the County.

One such case was that while plowing one day he was told that a member of the church, living east of Lebanon, was about to be converted to Newlightism. Dropping his working apparatus, he rushed to the man and persisted that he remain in the church.

Jonathan Tichenor resided on his farm west of Lebanon until his death in 1815.

His son, David, left no children. Five of his children survived him: Daniel, Aaron, Catherine, Hannah and Susannah.

MAINEVILLE CHURCH CELEBRATES INTERESTING HISTORY ON 150TH BIRTHDAY

The Maineville Methodist Church is presently being redecorated for the sesquicentennial event of July, 1994. Among the many guests will be former preachers of the congregation. The writer thinks some form of recognition should be in order for a church of such high standard and longevity.

The Maineville Methodist Church has a very interesting history attached to it. While rummaging through my papers, the writer found a sketch of the early history of the church that was submitted to **The Western Star** in 1944, in observance of its 100th anniversary. The writers were: Ruth Roosa, Mildred Blickensderfer, Lillian Stotler, Helen Duncanson and Robert Conover.

The first congregation was organized by Sarah Tufts in 1842. It was a testimonial class consisting of two males and nine female members, the group meeting at the different homes for worship. There was a Baptist log church building near the Maineville cemetery which was used by many of the Methodist members.

One year later, in 1843, as the membership grew, a revival was launched. Two ministers were asked to preach, Rev. W.H. Fyffe and Rev. Moses Smith.

The revival lasted several weeks which resulted in forty new members.

Among the new converts were Seth, Moses and Benjamin Tufts, brothers of the founder, Sarah.

Little interest was shown by the trio in the church until the revival took place. Afterward they vigorously joined into the activities and affairs of the House of God.

A building committee consisting of Samuel Knowlton, Moses Tufts, and Benjamin Tufts, Jr., was assigned to create plans for a new church building. The brick for the church came from a kiln owned by Samuel Cain, located on the Cain farm.

The bricklaying was done by Eliphelat Stevens and Samuel Cain with the aid of Benjamin Tufts and other members. Sarah Tufts gave one-twelfth of the cost for the building.

Completion of the church was in 1844 and dedicated in the fall of that year. It was named Smith Chapel, possibly in honor of Rev. Moses Smith, a circuit rider.

The building remains the same today except the

entrance doors. At the time of the early opening there were two front doors, the purpose being that the men and women sat on different sides of the church. The disciplinary rules forbade the men and women sitting together.

No one could enter the church after the services began because the doors were locked. Sunday morning services lasted until afternoon.

After dinner the congregation would go to the Negro church to help. Returning to their own church, late in the evening, often resulted in a lengthy meeting.

Services were absent any musical instruments, only singing "by the pitch" given by the choir director. The song was sung in verses one line at a time or "lined out."

An organ was purchased from the John Church Company, of Cincinnati, in 1869 for $135.00. The council, which included Frank and Belle Tufts, Jane Tufts and Julia Tufts, traveled to Cincinnati on February 25 to acquire the music piece.

The long seven hour journey down the Three-C Highway was in a peach wagon. The Tufts' family returned several days later, after spending some time with relatives.

A special dedication service of the organ was given, with Rev. Quarry preaching the sermon.

Circuit riders were roving evangelists who periodically checked on the congregations in their district.

Another of their functions was to hold communion services, to perform weddings, funerals, and baptisms which had gathered.

Rev. Quarry was probably a circuit rider for there are no records of regular ministers until 1877, when Rev. C.T. Crum became the preacher. Burials were held frequently, but services were regularly held by the preacher.

Once a preacher was found to lead the assemblage, the follow-up was to send out special formal invitations to friends and relatives ascribing the occasion.

Circuit riding preachers were always welcome at the Tuft's home. There was a room set aside for the event called the "Preacher's Room."

In 1877, the membership of the Methodist Church stood at 150, and still growing.

Another revival was started in 1884 which saw the church grow by an additional forty members.

A new belfry and bell were installed in 1925.

Names of the early builders of the church are placed in memorial plaques on beautifully stained glass windows on the interior. These names are: Benjamin and Permelia Tufts, Moses and Jane Tufts, Seth and Eliza Jane Tufts, Eliphalet and Mary Stevens, John and Sarah Ertel, Drew Ertel, Mabelle Lewis and Lillian Lee Lewis.

SHAKERS MADE THEIR IMPACT ON WARREN COUNTY ALMOST 200 YEARS AGO

Warren County had during its early history a religious group that was the first of its kind in the West. The Society of Believers, or Shakers, preached their first sermon on Sunday, March 24, 1805, just two short years after the formation of the County.

The first Shaker assembly in the world was established at New Lebanon, N.Y., located about twenty-five miles southeast of Albany N.Y. It was founded by Ann Lee, who, with nine others, had immigrated from England in 1774.

A great revival amongst the Shakers, in 1787, revitalized the church and many were led into the new denomination.

Until 1805 there were 13 Shaker settlements, all located in the eastern states.

The formation of the Turtlecreek Presbyterian Church was founded about 1797 and soon became the largest church in Warren County. Rev. James Kemper was pastor for a period and was followed by Rev. Richard McNemar. The latter was a leader in the "Great Kentucky Revival."

Why was the Turtlecreek Church selected as the first sermon on the western side of the Alleghenies?

What had prompted the three Shaker missionaries, John Meacham, Benjamin S. Youngs and

Issachar Bates to travel from their New York home to the lands of Warren County?

Again, I will refer you to the "Great Kentucky Revival." Nowhere on either side of the Ohio River was a greater effect felt than at the small Turtlecreek Church.

The remarkable physical manifestations were expressed more-so at this church than at any other.

The Shakers in the East had heard and read numerous accounts of the happenings due to the Revival.

An account of the convulsive body movements had been received by the Shakers, and indeed, an investigative team of missionaries was sent to the scenes of the Kentucky Revival.

Their long journey from New Lebanon, N.Y., was started on New Year's Day, 1805. The excursion began in a sleigh of 60 miles, the rest on foot. One horse was used for carrying their apparel.

Long journeys on foot were customary for the missionaries. Issachar Bates relates in his journal that, ten years previous to 1801, he had traveled as a Shaker missionary about 38,000 miles, mostly on foot, and contributed his part in converting about 1,100 persons.

Their journey took them through the cities of Philadelphia, Baltimore and Washington. Their arrival in Kentucky allowed the threesome to frequent the sites of the great revival.

They traveled across the entire State of Kentucky and down into Tennessee. They met with the preachers who had instrumental in the revival and inquired into the events.

Heading north they crossed the Ohio River on March 19, and were received by Rev. John Thompson, pastor of the Springdale Church in Hamilton County.

On Friday, March 22, 1805, they arrived at Turtlecreek after a venture of 1,233 miles since the first day of January.

The Shaker missionaries were described as "grave and assuming men, intelligent and prepossessing in appearance."

Their dress was plain and neat and perhaps of

the old Quaker style. They wore white fur hats with brims five and a half inches wide and crowns five inches high. Their coats were grey, waistcoats blue and overalls brown.

On Friday they frequented the home of Malcolm Worley. He was a man of good education and had large land holdings. His activity in the Kentucky Revival was described as "one of wildness."

The next morning, Saturday, they visited Rev. McNemar, who made claim that he had never heard of the Shaker faith before. He proclaimed that the strangers seemed to be of honest integrity, and had a deep understanding of the things of God, though some of their discussions were not well understood.

Permission to speak in the church on the next day, Sunday, was asked and given. The first convert was Malcolm Worley, who adopted the faith on Tuesday after the sermon.

The second transformation to the faith was Ann Middleton, a Negro woman. On April 24, Rev. McNemar and his wife officially joined the denomination.

David Hill hosted the first regular meeting of the new denomination on May 23.

Dancing was instilled into the meeting as a part of the Godly worship, one missionary "striking up a step and the other two beginning the dance."

The Society of Believers in the township had at the beginning one ordained preacher, two licensed exhorters, two ordained ruling Elders, two physicians and about thirty additional members.

Public meetings were soon held in the old log church where "they preached and sang and danced and shouted until the opposing party withdrew and left them in peaceful possession."

New settlements were quickly organized out of the followers of Shakerism. These new communities had been channeled out of the Presbyterian organization by the revival.

Two of these were: Eagle Creek in Brown County, June, 1805; and Beaver Creek, southeast of

Dayton, in the spring of 1806.

Four Presbyterian preachers who had been active in the Kentucky Revival, and had joined the Shaker faith were: Rev. Richard McNemar, April 24, 1805; Rev John Dunlavy, July 29, 1805; Rev. Matthew Houston, February, 1806; and Rev. John Rankin, October 28, 1807. All four lived the Shaker faith until passing on.

Rev. Dunlavy was pastor of the Eagle Creek Church. This congregation numbered in 1807 about twenty or thirty families. The members lived in different localities and met on Sunday for worship. The Brown County community was relocated to different settlements about 1810.

Rev. Dunlavy was long associated with the Shakers at Pleasant Hill, Ky. Reverends Houston and Rankin were pastors of churches in Kentucky with Shaker communities expanding from their congregations.

Union Village was always considered the parent community of the Shakers in the West. The number of members in 1812 were given as 370; in 1839, about 500; March 17, 1859, 255; January 1, 1865, 167; and the close of 1867, 152.

SHAKERS FACED SETBACKS WHILE IN COUNTY

The Shaker sect, namely the Society of Believers, is full of rich history. There is so much written about this subject that this column can hold just a portion of the many happenings. An account of some of the setbacks embarked upon by the Shakers will be our subject for this article.

The direct results of the "Great Kentucky Revival" caused the Mother Church of the Society of Believers in Lebanon, N.Y., to send three of its missionaries to the Miami Valley, namely, John Meacham, Benjamin S. Youngs, and Issachar Bates. (They arrived in Turtlecreek Township on Friday, March 22, 1805.)

Rev. Richard McNemar was a principal player in the revival. Following this momentous event, Rev. McNemar was found preaching at the Turtle

Creek Presbyterian Church at Beedle's Station.

Through his conversion to the Shaker faith, he became a great leader in a movement that was to last for over 100 years in Warren County.

The first convert to the Shaker faith was Malcolm Worley. His lands became the site of the newly formed Society. He was recognized as the first Shaker convert in the West.

He had previously been involved in the Kentucky Revival, which had so affected him that the ways of the Shakers totally embraced him.

Worley entered Shakerism at the age of 43; he lived 39 years after becoming a member, and died August 3, 1844, at the age of 82.

His family had converted with him. However, his three children, Rebecca, Joshua and Joseph, at a later time withdrew from the Society.

They went through legal channels in efforts to try to reclaim the land he had deeded to the Shakers. Their claim was that their father was not sane at the time of the transaction.

The Supreme court heard the case and a decision was made in favor of the Shakers. A sum of $1,200 was spent in legal actions by the children, but to no avail.

Another decision by the Supreme Court was rendered in 1811, again the Shakers being the defendants. Robert Wilson sued Elder David Darrow for $250, and again the Believers were victorious.

Court action was brought against them in 1816 by Jonathan Davis, but again proved unsuccessful. They were also involved in court proceedings as a result of the 1817 mob.

Elder Solomon King became the new leader in 1829. Joshua Worley was second in the ministry to Elder King, while his brother, Joseph, was an Elder at the North House.

The year 1835, near the end of Elder King's reign, saw a financial reverse which totally shocked the Society. Nathan Sharp, the Society's primary trustee, departed with a valuable horse along with an unknown amount of money and valuable papers.

The new converts were astonished at this act,

who were at this time trying to establish the character of the Ministry and Elders.

The same year other disasters to the organization were experienced. On June 9, close to nine inches of rain fell in a very short period of time. Damages incurred amounted to about $25,000 when all the mill-dams were swept away. The tail race had been filled with gravel and stones. Other noted damage included clothing, fulling and coloring shops.

The lowlands to the west of the community were many feet under water and large trees were uprooted and carried away. The crops in this section were also damaged.

An abundance of caterpillars caused significant damage that year, eating away the foliage on the forest trees and killing many of them.

In October of the same year, Elder King returned to the parent home in New Lebanon, N.Y., and while there resigned his position at Union Village.

In succession to the leadership, David Meacham was next and served a short time. In 1836, Freegift Wells took over. At this time Joshua Worley's name was still entered as an assistant to the ruling Elder of the Society.

Joshua's name does not appear again in the legislative committee. A thought was passed on that he might have been disappointed for not having been chosen as the head of the settlement, even though his faithful service merited it.

In July 1859, a gang of organized thieves from Indiana made arrangements to burglarize the sect. The plot was unveiled by a gang member and all appropriate steps were taken to prevent an occurrence.

A large amount of wheat and clothing was stolen in March, 1860. The thieves proved to be renegades.

A fire that completely engulfed the old North House occurred on March 4, 1865. In this enclosed building was a tin shop, broom factory, carpenter shop, shoemaker room, and sarsaparillas laboratory. A total loss of $10,000 was experienced. To add to this tragedy, they already had an indebtedness of $12,000.

By 1875 the debt added up to $20,000. A reform of sorts was called for, and instead of paying a rate of eight or nine percent interest, money was borrowed from other Shaker communities. Consequently, $2,000 was paid on the debt the first year. Elder William Reynolds was the appointee handling the finances.

A cow barn and 39 head of cattle were lost by fire on January 2, 1876.

Further losses to the Society were felt in 1877 because of a bank failure in Lebanon. The Shakers suffered a loss of $7,468.

On January 22, 1884, the Elder at the West Family fled with $500 belonging to the family.

The Society had begun loaning money in 1885 in which a Dayton business (the Dayton Furnace Company) had collective loans of $16,000. This venture proved to be a total loss, the culprit being a shrewd lawyer.

A tornado struck the village on May 12, 1886, which caused havoc to several buildings, uprooted many of their fruit and forest trees, and blew their wooden fences over.

In 1890, the Farm Deacon sold about $700 worth of livestock and disappeared with the money.

On April 12, 1890, the two-story wood shed at the South House was destroyed by fire.

Just seventeen days later the dwelling at South House, wash house, and laundry equipment were destroyed by fire. The homeless quickly took up residence amongst the other families.

An investigation by a detective was called for by the Elder which revealed that one of the Shaker inmates was the rogue. He was sent to the penitentiary for a period of four years.

THE PASSING THROUGH OF THE PILGRIMS

A radical sect of religious extremists, organized about 1817, passed through Warren County, their projectory extending from the Eastern States to the vicinity of Arkansas. Their leader and Prophet, Isaac Buller, was a native of the New England States.

Mr. Buller had a spine injury which was caused from the effects of a fall which in turn caused partial paralysis. He was confined to bed for many months because of the painful effect.

His devout neighbors had repeatedly met in his room and had prayer concerning his recovery. During one of these episodes, he immediately stated his pain was gone and he was restored to complete health. With absolute pain-free insistence, he was now able to walk with two canes.

An announcement was made that the Lord had healed him, and made him His Prophet. Many of the prayerful had believed this act was the intercession of Providence.

The new Prophet, now pain-free, told his flock that through the intervention of the Lord, he would lead them to the Promised Land.

This new religion was embraced not only by the common folk, but by the wealthy, and people of high social standing.

The Prophet positioned his cane in an upright position and let it fall. This was a sign of the path the new sect would take. The cane always fell in a southwest direction.

Loading of wagons, teams, a minimal supply of clothes, beds, food and cooking contrivance was for their journey. First, they made their way from New England to New York, and, a year later, they reached Lebanon, Ohio.

Their journey was full of revelations by the Prophet, presumably from the Lord, directing the followers to change their way of habit of dress and manner of life.

Bathing was outlawed as was washing their clothes. No allowances were made concerning excessive material objects. Their clothing was very minimal, only enough to keep away the cold. The only meat allowed was raw bacon. "Filth, rags and wretchedness" were a need for them to reach the Promised Land.

Their arrival in Warren County was a despicable sight. Some of the more intelligent members of the band had quite readily figured Prophet

Buller for an impostor. They in turn returned to New England, or picked out spots along their route to make their homes.

The remainder, who stayed in Lebanon, held public gatherings for worship. At these meetings, the Prophet and other speakers warned the people to avoid all pride and everything worldly in dress and food.

The speakers at the meetings would utter these words: "Oh-a, Ho-a, Oh-a, Ho-a - My God, My God, My God!" The congregation would in turn repeat the words.

The Prophet and his people traveled from Lebanon to Union Village and remained several days. The Shakers remarked in their notes that the first time they heard of the clan was at Xenia. Two of the Shakers ventured to see them on the 19th of February, 1818.

The Pilgrims, on the tenth of March, being only fifty-five in number, reached Union Village. The brethren kindly received them and fed them and their horses. A meeting was called at the church; it was held by five of the Pilgrims of which three men and two women preached. After the preaching the strange clan quickly withdrew.

They had been assigned a single room by the Shakers, in which to lodge, and sent some of their preachers to speak to them, but to no avail, they were shunned by the leaders of the Pilgrims.

The next day, their gratitude was expressed and they set out again for the Promised Land.

Mason was next in line for the visitation of the sect. While in this neighborhood, the small-pox broke out and caused many deaths among them.

Still following the direction of the falling cane, they arrived in New Madrid, Mo., where the Prophet became ill and died. Before his death, he promised to return to them in two years, and for them to continue their journey.

The frail band at last found the Promised Land which was located on the west bank of the Mississippi, not far from the mouth of the Arkansas River.

In 1824, Hon. John Hunt traveled to New Orleans in a flatboat, accompanied by two other flatboats along with their crews. They stopped at the mouth of the Arkansas to inquire about the fate of the Pilgrims.

The Promised Land consisted of a narrow ridge of dry land, almost surrounded by a swamp; a most decrepit place for habitation.

The remainder of Buller's clan consisted of two ladies living in a wretched tent, made with forks and poles, reed cane and bark. They were neatly dressed and spoke with a very intelligent keenness; still they claimed the reverence of the Prophet's religion.

Mr. Hunt offered a sum of money for their transportation by steamboat to Cincinnati, but they thanked him and refused his service.

Mr. Hunt, during a later trip down the Mississippi, learned that one of the ladies had died and the destiny of the other was unknown.

Chapter VIII

LEBANON, OHIO

TAKING A PEEK AT LEBANON IN THE 19TH CENTURY

Lebanon has long been an historic town dating back to September 1802, when Ichabod Corwin, Silas Hurin, Ephriam Hathaway and Samuel Manning laid out the town into 100 lots.

It has always been fixed into the hearts of those who were born here, or to the ones who have been fortunate enough to have had the privilege of close association with it.

Over the years Lebanon has been cast into the national limelight through many of its famous citizens; it has also been highlighted as the site of the making of two recent movies, "Harper Valley PTA," and "Milk Money."

Let us now travel back to another time when the City of Cedars was a place of residence for the pioneers who have since passed on their inheritance and culture to the community of today.

One in that time would experience the old wooden stoops which stretched far out onto the sidewalks. These little structures were nothing but wooden platforms, two or three times as wide as the doorways, and flanked on either side with benches, sometimes with backs and sometimes not.

These configurations were not fitted with roofs. They faced only the open skies and the houses opposite, the latter possibly exhibiting their own opposing stoops.

They were charming locations and were considered the gathering place for the older folks. Here they would spend the afternoon, or early evening hours, reveal the days' events, or possibly spin a yarn of the old days in the old country, or perhaps early Lebanon.

Sitting far out onto the sidewalk gave one a sense of closeness which in turn made the whole neighborhood seem more friendly.

One could possibly envision the residents relaxing on the home-made chairs, or the self-fashioned benches, chatting and greeting the passersby in the open air. And, of course, a good cigar or a rather large plug of tobacco would be in accord with the gentlemen.

This good old Dutch custom made the town residents feel eminently close. When the old folks left the old town, they always expressed delightedness about returning to the scene of the ever present stoops.

Many of the early citizens of Lebanon built their houses up to the sidewalks. Front yards were often not thought of because the remainder of their land was devoted to gardens.

This practice of house building brought about a custom, among those who did not have stoops, of placing chairs and other sitting arrangements on the sidewalk, and making a spot for family members and visitors.

One resident remembers passing up Mulberry Street and seeing the familiar figure of Jimmie Hayes as he sat in his chair on the sidewalk in front of his residence, his cane in his palsied hand shaking violently.

He also recalls that farther down on Broadway there was an old Dutch stoop, and an all too familiar sight was the figure of Mr. King sitting on one of the multi-fashioned benches.

The Lebanon House had an old wooden shed that extended over the pavement in front. Located at the curb were wooden pillars of a rather odd architectural design which supported the roof structure.

The arrival of Dickens found the framework filled to capacity with the prestigious and the curious alike.

Ira Watts, a one-legged man, whose home was at the tavern in the days of the shed, spun yarns and sometimes truths of the old times which intrigued the many who gathered to hear. With his cane in hand and his crutch stretched across his remaining knee, he enjoyed telling the inquisitive his favorite story of how a calf once bit his leg off.

Another distinction of the town of Lebanon was the memory of the old town pumps. They provided fire protection, watered the great stock herds, and the just plain thirsty. The woodland springs brought forth a flavor in which no sweeter taste of water could be found.

The long-armed handles of the pumps were kept constantly in motion as the passersby quenched their thirst, drinking from home fashioned tins or iron dippers.

As modern water-works crept in, the last of the old pumps were replaced, not to the liking of the older residents. A feeling of sorrow was experienced at the removal of the ever-so-present wooden spouts. They had hung for years so gingerly over the horse-troughs which had been for so long a part of everyday life.

Land bordering Silver Street, east of Broadway, was a swamp in early times. Children of that day had quite a time amongst the reeds and wet mosses on that plot of land.

Although wells were not sunk in this portion because of poor drinking qualities, accounts of good times were recounted on the low-lying wet plains.

Tanyards were plentiful in the early days of Lebanon. A youth often found himself ingrained in the somewhat aromatic fragrance of the fresh-ground tan-bark before it was put into the vats, which were placed all about.

Tanning of the different animal hides was probably first created in Egyptian times, at least 5,000 years ago. Paintings of that time have been depicted showing tanners at work with their tubs and mixing vats.

Prehistoric people used the hides of animals to clothe themselves. Untreated hides would have been too stiff and crack easily; also, decomposition would ultimately set in.

The American Indian used animal brains to soften the hides and make it more water resistant.

Smoking, soaking in urine, and rubbing with plant or animal oil, were procedures that the pioneer first used when treating the hides.

Bark-mills were used in the olden times to chip the oak bark into small chips. The small chips were then placed into the vat along with a mixture of rain water, in which tannic acid was derived. The skins were then soaked until the tanning process was finished.

Tanyards were commonplace in each community. One such enterprise was located in Lebanon on Main Street, near Cherry. Another was located on Mechanic, and still another at the corner of Silver and Broadway.

The boys and girls would go and watch the blind horse in the bark-mill make his rounds, and quite often would ride the broad beam that went around with the horse, the first version of the merry-go-round in Lebanon.

This was just another attraction that caused the Lebanon youth to reminisce and meditate upon their reflections regarding the old town.

Early sidewalks of the town were constructed of creek-stone, gravel, or tanbark.

Lighting was supplied by the light of the lantern which was punched full of holes.

James Turner supplied the tallow candles by which the early folks read and found their way to bed. Church, prayer meetings, and public entertainment always began at early candle-lighting.

The era of camphene, coal oil and gas for lighting, have since passed and the period of electric lights is now upon us.

In the days of the early church, musical instruments were not allowed; the choir director acquired his pitch by means of a tuning fork, and the preacher always "lined" off the hymns.

From the melodeon to the pipe organ, advancements in church services have progressed, and our puritanism has disappeared.

A recall by the children of the early days

details with enthusiasm the games about the old market-house on South Broadway. This house stood for years until it was replaced by the market-house located on Silver Street. The latter was eventually torn down and Washington Hall was built.

Lebanon still has many of its early homes still standing. The interiors with their high mantel shelves, the broad fire places, and the impressive chimneys still stand as a reminder to the past.

The wood fires in the great hearths were a symbol of pioneer life as the flames so romantically pranced their way up the ever-so-present chimney.

Cooking over these great fires was not only a way of life, but a treat to those, family and visitor alike, who recollect that community life was centered around the great hearth in a way that cannot be forgotten.

The smell of freshly roasted apples, the scent of fresh-baked cornbread spreading its aroma throughout the home, an everlasting taste of home-made breads that will linger on for a lifetime, all beckoning to the tired and hungry to sit, relax and enjoy these delicacies in the comfort of his or her own home.

The old ways, the old streets, houses, creeks and creek banks, the many games, all held a certain place in the hearts of the Lebanon pioneer.

If the past could only speak, volumes would be filled which would impress the visitor as to why Lebanon is so renowned.

LEBANON ALMOST HAD ITS OWN "REDSKINS"

With the controversy over the changing of the name of Miami University "Redskins" because of alleged racial discrimination, the writer feels it appropriate to insert an article on the history of the founding of Miami University.

The College Township Road was an old Indian trail that started at Chillicothe, passed through Lebanon and then extended to Oxford in Butler County. This road was established by the Legislature of Ohio, February 18, 1804.

It ran from Chillicothe through Clinton County to a point west of Cuba, and a mile and a half southeast of Clarksville.

It next ran through by Smalley's cabins and Fort Ancient to Lebanon, crossing Todd's Fork at Smalley's. (Smalley's cabins were located between two trees which exist in a now-cultivated field on the northwest side of Route 350, 0.5 of a mile from the intersection of Route 350 and the Pennsylvania Central Railroad tracks in Clarksville.)

Fort Ancient-Clarksville Road, which runs through Turtlecreek and Washington Township (S.R. 350), is part of the College Township Road. (Part of the road is now vacated in the vicinity of Lebanon.)

This road picks up at Greentree Road in Turtlecreek Township and extends into Butler County on Oxford State Road, which ultimately leads to Oxford, home of Miami University.

George Crout, Middletown area historian, says that in some parts the road must have run north of the present S.R. 73 in Butler County, which seems to be a shortening of the original road. It seems to have followed the Middletown-Oxford Road at some points. State Route 73 has been rebuilt in places, especially near Oxford.

There is quite a story surrounding the name of this roadway.

When John Cleves Symmes made his acquisition of land between the Miamis, an agreement was made to set aside an entire township in which a commitment was made for an institution for learning.

Symmes failed to locate the township and the consequence being that, when Ohio was made a State in 1803, Congress granted another township in-lieu-of for the same purpose, which was to be located west of the Great Miami.

In February 1809, the Legislature passed an act "to establish Miami University," proclaiming that the institution should be established "within that part of the country known by the name of John Cleves Symmes Purchase, which university shall be designated by the name and style of Miami University."

This act appointed three commissioners, Alexander Campbell, Rev. James Kilburn and Rev. Robert Wilson to locate grounds for the institution with their meeting place at Lebanon. These men were, after taking an oath of affirmation, to seek a positive location within the Symmes Purchase.

Cincinnati, Hamilton, Dayton and Yellow Springs, along with Lebanon, contested for this institution. All were within the Symmes Purchase at the time.

The first Tuesday in June 1809, was the schedule for the three commissioners to meet and decide upon the location of the school. One commissioner was absent due to sickness (Rev. Mr. Wilson). However, a decision was made. Lebanon would get the new university. This action being confirmed by Judge Burnet, concreted the decision.

Icabod Corwin donated a parcel of land, being 40 acres, at the western edge of Lebanon. A large walnut tree was marked, as stated by A.H. Dunlevy, on the western portion of the grounds to designate the area of ground on which the main college building was to be erected. (Supposedly, this spot was the grave site of Thomas Corwin, Ohio Governor, Senator and United States Minister to Mexico.)

Many of the residents of the different selected cities were disgruntled over the decision to locate at Lebanon. At the next meeting of the Legislature, after Lebanon had been selected, a Mr. Cooper of Dayton suggested that lands upon which had been selected, "in lieu of," be designated as the location for the college. This property, chosen in 1803, was located in western Butler County.

The township of Oxford, yet to be named, was a wild and untamed area with just a few squatters as residents. It took two days through the woods for the residents of Cincinnati to reach this locations for a look-see.

The Ohio General Assembly on February 6, 1810, instructed the trustees to lay out a town to be called Oxford, and to choose a campus site within the college lands. This land, being filled with forests, now had a definite foothold on civilization.

The changing of lands definitely, according to Lebanon residents, tended to violate the original law providing for the residency of Miami College. No attempt was made, however, to relocate the college.

LEBANON'S FIRST GRIST MILL ON TURTLE CREEK

Warren County, with its great abundance of free-flowing water, had many mills in its early days. This greatly eased the pioneers' trials for their food source.

The first mill in Lebanon, if not in the County, was Taylor's mill, situated on the west branch of Turtlecreek.

Samuel Gallaher was born in Monmouth County, N. J., September 16, 1769. When a mere lad he was taken to Allegheny County, Pa., where he learned the millwright trade. It was at this location he was united in marriage to Sarah Holcraft.

His son, Carvel, thought Samuel emigrated to the Northwest Territory about the year 1795. The family floated down the Ohio to Cincinnati and stopped for a time at Ludlow's Station.

Beedle's Station was located in the fall of 1795. The next spring the future site of Lebanon was being established with the families of Henry Taylor, John Shaw and Ichabod Corwin.

Henry Taylor had lived in Cincinnati for some years before moving to Turtlecreek. His claim was that his oldest son, William, was born March 20, 1791, and was the first white male child born in Cincinnati.

Flour and meal were two essentials the pioneers counted on for their daily meals. Waldsmith's mill, near the site of Camp Dennison, was the closest mill in the vicinity of Deerfield and Beedle's Station, the only settlements in the County at the time.

Taylor bought and located on a section of land on Turtlecreek, the tract being situated on the southwest portion of where Lebanon was laid out. He resolved to build a mill on his land to be run by this stream.

Millwrights were hard to come by in this day-and-time. Taylor was told of a millwright at Ludlow's Station, Samuel Gallaher. He summoned Gallaher and asked if he would be interested in erecting a mill on Turtlecreek.

An agreement was made. The condition was that Gallaher was to be paid, not in money, but land after the mill was completed.

Arrival of the millwright at Turtlecreek was gleefully met by the area folks. Immediately they combined their efforts and assembled a log cabin home for the new arrivals.

Gallaher was regarded as a public champion as the building began. This mill would increase the value of the surrounding land and promote emigration.

Settlers for miles around willingly helped assemble and raise the mill framework. Some even assisted in building the dam.

Indians were still marauding at this time and, although no murders were committed, horse stealing was still an unsettled issue.

Mrs. Gallaher one day, in the absence her husband, spied an Indian sitting close to her cabin door, his face painted in a most frightful fashion. He was casually smoking a long-stemmed pipe and appeared calm.

Mrs. Gallaher instinctively screamed. The family dog instantly ran out and attached itself to the Indian's shoulder. The intruder in turn shrieked in pain and ran away in total agony. The woman called off the dog, the unwanted caller fleeing to be seen no more.

Carvel Gallaher seemed to think the mill was completed in 1796. A.H. Dunlevy gave the date as about 1799. If Carvel was right, this mill was the first built in Warren County. William Wood's mill, at the site of Kings Mills, was not completed until 1799. In all respect, Taylor's mill was either the first, or one of the first, built in the County.

After completion, Taylor gave Gallaher a deed for 100 acres. But afterward, by mutual consent, the deed was destroyed and another given in its place. It is possible that a smaller tract of better land was traded for.

(A deed is found on record from Henry Taylor to Samuel Gallaher for 81 acres in Section 5, T 4, R 3, dated January 25, 1800.)

The mill was probably a one-story log structure with a single pair of stones used primarily for grinding corn. It is not known where the millstones came from. Some of the earliest stones were formed from boulders found in surrounding neighborhoods, the diameter being sometimes less than eighteen inches.

Turtlecreek's supply of water was more abundant in early days as compared to now. However, during the dryer seasons, the water supply was not enough to run the mill. The settler who took a sack of corn to the mill would have to wait quite a spell for his grist.

Taylor sold his mill about 1803 and moved to Butler County. It was abandoned so early that its site cannot be located.

Gallaher farmed the greatest part of his life after the building of Taylor's mill. He was said to have assisted in the erection of a sawmill on Clearcreek, and sometimes worked in repairing mills.

About 1808 he traded his farm for one purchased by Jonas Seamon northwest of Lebanon. Here he resided until his death December 14, 1833, aged 64.

Samuel Gallaher and his wife are buried in the old Baptist graveyard in Lebanon.

BARRING OUT THE SCHOOLMASTER WAS A FAVORITE PRANK OF PUPILS

Many customs of old still continue to be used

although just as many have disappeared.

Our subject this week shall be the barring out of the schoolmaster. This custom certainly is not used today, but in olden days it was considered traditional.

The first school house in the Lebanon area was built in the spring of 1798. It was a rather low, rough log cabin, constructed in one day with nothing but an axe. The first teacher at the school was Francis Dunlevy, later Judge Dunlevy.

A.H. Dunlevy was a son of Judge Dunlevy, who at the age of only five years old, attended the school. An account of the first Christmas after the opening was recorded by A.H. and preserved. I shall now use his own words.

"As the cold weather of 1798 commenced, this school was crowded with young men of a much larger size than had attended during the summer.

"At Christmas it was determined to bar out the master, according to the custom of the times. The object in part was a mere frolic, in part to secure the holidays free from school, and sometimes the master was required to treat.

"When the barring out was successful, there was a regular and sometimes a tedious negotiation between the scholars and teacher, and the terms of pacification were required to be stipulated with precision.

"But the teacher was not easily thwarted. He was opposed on principle to treating and he had served in so many campaigns against the Indians that he had imbibed a spirit which knew not how to submit to or suffer defeat.

"After having been driven from the windows by long handspikes, with which he was several times severely struck, he retired for a time.

"Returning, he ascended, unobserved by the boys, to the top of the chimney, made of cat and clay, and very large. He suddenly descended down the chimney, though a brisk fire was burning.

"The boys astonished at his appearance from this unlooked for point, capitulated with as much coolness as, under circumstances they could command.

"Defeated in their Christmas frolic, on New Years Day the boys gathered recruits from the young men who did not attend school, and took much pains to secure every possible point of ingress. The fireplace was well guarded, the windows secured and the door barricaded with large logs piled against it to the top.

"As the master approached, a loud note of defiance went up from the inmates. The scene was the more exciting as many of the neighbors had come to witness the siege, which was to result in the triumph or defeat of the young men.

"After surveying the field as well as he could from the outside, Dunlevy soon determined on his mode of assault.

"Taking on his shoulders a large green log which had been brought for firewood, he stepped off some ten paces from the door, and then rushed with his utmost speed, bringing the end of the log against the top of the door.

"The concussion was so violent as to break the door and displace the logs on the inside so as to open a hole, through which he instantly entered to the terror and consternation of the boys.

"For a moment, there was some show of resistance notwithstanding the fort had been captured. But this soon subsided. There were no more attempts to bar out Francis Dunlevy."

The barring out of the schoolmaster was rather common in the Northwest Territory. In Judge Dunlevy's case the custom had apparently been brought by the larger boys from the older states. The origination seems to have stemmed from an old English custom.

It was commonplace in the old country for the scholars to take custody of the school room and to lock out the schoolmaster.

A rule of the day was that "the scholars could sustain a siege against the master for three days and were entitled to dictate terms to him regarding holidays and the hours of recreation."

If the master triumphed in forcing an entry before the three days were up, the students were at his mercy.

James Harris, a former teacher, relates in his history of Washington Township, that he suspicioned the boys intended to bar him out. His skepticism prevailing he remained in the schoolhouse the evening before until he presumed all the students had gone home.

He then took down the door, carried it away and hid it in the nearby bushes. The larger boys were aware of this act and watched from some distance; they simply replaced the door. The next morning Mr. Harris found himself barred out.

Not to be defeated, he climbed to the roof, removed some clapboards, laid them on the chimney top and consequently smoked the boys out.

THE BUILDING OF THE FIRST SCHOOLHOUSE IN TURTLECREEK TOWNSHIP

This week's column takes a page from the writings of Josiah Morrow.

The first school in Turtlecreek Township was established within two years after the Lebanon pioneers built their first homes. In many localities, schools were not built until ten years or more after the first settlements.

Emigrants from New England were normally the first to build schools in the Northwest Territory; those from the middle and southern States last.

The first settlers in Warren County were primarily from New Jersey, Pennsylvania and Virginia. Many of them settled for a short time in Kentucky before coming to the land north of the Ohio.

Education in the aforementioned states was not given top priority. In Virginia, one might travel a hundred miles without seeing a schoolhouse.

The first towns in Warren County were: Deerfield (South Lebanon), 1795; Franklin, 1796; and Waynesville, 1796. Morrow stated that the first school in the County was opened in the spring of 1798 near where Lebanon was laid out four years later.

The first teacher at Turtlecreek, five years previous to Ohio becoming a state, had been to college and was an exceptionably fine Latin scholar. His name was Francis Dunlevy.

It is not known whether Dunlevy purposely came to Turtlecreek to establish a school, or whether he was convinced by the early leaders to continue his occupation of school teaching in the vicinity.

The location of the first schoolhouse stood a little west of the present site of Lebanon (along the bank of Turtlecreek) and on the north side of the road to Shakertown (St. Rt. 63).

It was built on an elevation close to a marshy low ground known as Big Springs; possibly this water supply saved the active pioneers the labor of digging a well.

A description of the first schoolhouse is detailed as "a low rough log-cabin put up in a few hours by the neighbors who formed the little settlement and stood on the north side of Turtlecreek about a half a mile west of the place where Lebanon now stands."

It was a typical design in comparison to schoolhouses built in this time period. All were constructed of logs, and in the early ones, the logs were unhewn.

The construction of the pioneer schoolhouses advanced with time, as did the early homes. These first homes were a crude cabin of round logs with a chimney of sticks and clay; next the house of logs hewed inside and out with a rough stone chimney; and lastly, the comfortable frame of today.

Land in the early days was cheap and timber was found in abundance. Because of this situation, many settlers were anxious to donate a parcel of land for a schoolhouse. However, John Shaw, an emigrant from North Carolina, was chosen to give his land for the first educational enterprise in the township.

On a specific date, settlers from miles around gathered at the selected site, most of them bringing with them only an ax, which was the only tool needed for the erection of the walls of the building.

The first building procedure for the structure was the clearing of the land. All the trees on the site of the building were cut down.

Tree trunks of an acceptable size for the walls were felled in the woods nearby. A yoke of oxen was used to drag the logs to the location of the new schoolhouse.

White oak furnished the clapboards (a long board, thicker along one edge than along the other) for the roof.

The blue ashes provided the puncheons (a slab of timber, or a piece of a split log, with the face roughly dressed) for the floor and benches of the interior.

Notching of the round logs at the ends for the walls was essential so as to lie close together. The open spaces left between the logs were filled in with strips of wood and daubed over inside and out with clay.

The clapboard roof was held down by poles stretching across the roof, called weight poles.

An opening of ten feet was cut out of the logs at one end of the building for the installation of a fireplace.

The chimney was made of sticks and covered with clay. Both fireplace and chimney were on the outside of the building. (Most chimneys in early times were built to be physically pulled away from the building when they became too hot and consequently engulfed in flames.)

Winter time found the students laboring to keep the fire burning. Logs as long as the chimney was wide would be dragged in from the woods.

A number of students found themselves standing before the fire to warm themselves. In excessively cold weather, the one-roomed schoolhouse could hardly be comfortable.

Windows were fashioned by cutting out sections of a single log on two or three sides of the building.

Upright sticks were placed in the empty spaces and paper was pasted to them to keep out the cold air and admit the light. The paper was made transparent by hog's lard, and on sunny days, the light cast was a soft glow.

But in contrast, on dark dreary days, the room must have been most dark.

The floor was possibly natural earth or covered with hewn puncheons. The door was made with heavy planks and swung on wooden hinges and was fastened with a wooden latch.

Of course the early school building had to be equipped with furniture. The seats were benches made of slabs split from logs with long pegs installed in them for legs; they had no backs.

The writing desk was also slabs hewn smooth on the upper side and fastened to the wall by pegs driven into augur holes in the log under the window. The pupil in writing would sit facing the light.

What is a school without a teacher's desk? It was a smooth plank some two feet wide and three feet long fastened to the wall by two wooden pegs. Blackboards, wall maps and charts were unheard of.

The early schoolhouse of the Northwest Territory could be erected without cost for the ground; materials and labor was free. It could be built and furnished and ready for occupancy in a single day. Skilled mechanics were not needed and it could be built without the use of a nail, a pane of glass, an iron hinge or lock, or a paint brush.

Twenty-five years passed before a public school system was initiated in Turtlecreek Township.

Early schools were not free schools. The teacher was paid by the quarter so much a scholar. He or she was forced to accept pupils of all ages and degrees of achievement.

Classification of the pupil was almost impossible. Most students were in classes by themselves. They had no printed subject matter furnished by the school. They brought from their homes miscellaneous publications, some of which were badly mangled. The most common reading material consisted of the Bible.

Writing materials consisted of pens from goose and turkey quills which the teacher mended when broken with his "pen-knife." Ink was made at home from oak bark and coperas. Paper at that time was un-ruled, thus the pupils were taught to write in straight lines.

Francis Dunlevy, after some two years of teaching on the bank of Turtlecreek, removed his schoolhouse some two miles northwest nearer his farm. Being known as a defined man of education, his expertise in teaching attracted many quality students, and soon the new school was filled up. Some of the students walked for a distance of four or five miles to receive their education.

He was a member of the Territorial Legislature which began in the winter of the years of 1801-02. The sessions were short and he may have taught school a segment of each year until he was elected judge in 1803.

Many of the early teachers were inappropriately qualified for the teaching trade and students were taught only English. Too often teachers of the pioneer children were wanderers and a worthless lot and were not adapted to any type teaching ability. The classroom was often supervised by a teacher who was ironhanded and cruel.

The pupils of the Turtlecreek school were most fortunate to have such a fine teacher as Dunlevy. A student with natural ability, regardless of the primitive surroundings, could apply himself, and with a desire for knowledge could learn at a rapid pace.

Many students of the Turtlecreek school became good scholars and several of them went on to become citizens of distinction.

Dunlevy is given credit for tutoring Thomas Corwin, the great orator, who became the twelfth Governor of Ohio.

James Q. Howard said of Thomas Corwin: "In the concurrent judgment of all who have felt the spell of his matchless eloquence, the greatest natural orator and the most marvelous wit, mimic and master of the passions of men that the continent has yet known."

Matthias Corwin, Jr., an elder brother of

Thomas, was also a pupil. Receiving a good education, he became a man of intelligence, a member of the bar, and served several years as Clerk of the Court. He died in middle life.

Moses B. Corwin, a cousin of Thomas and Matthias, was also a pupil. He was a well known lawyer in Urbana, Ohio, and was twice sent to the Legislature and twice to Congress.

George Kesling was an older student of Dunlevy's, turning fifteen after entering school. He became an outstanding citizen of Warren County, serving as Captain in the War of 1812, and as a Representative in the Legislature, as well as an Associate Judge. He was appointed postmaster at Lebanon by Andrew Jackson, serving ten years.

Enos Williams taught the first school in Lebanon after it became a town. He also was a student of Dunlevy.

A.H. Dunlevy, the eldest son of the teacher, was one of the younger students in the first school on Turtlecreek. His occupation in life after school conformed to that of a lawyer, an editor at Lebanon, and the County's first recorded historian.

One of the earliest pioneers in the area was Henry Taylor. He purchased an entire section of land in the Lebanon area and built the first mill on Turtlecreek. His two sons attended Dunlevy's school.

One of these sons, William, was said to have been the first male child born in Cincinnati, the date being March 20, 1791.

Two sons of Rev. John Smith, from Columbia, were known to have attended the early Turtlecreek school. Smith, in 1803, was elected one of the first Senators in Congress from Ohio. Rev. Smith preferred this school to any taught at or near Cincinnati at that time.

LEBANON'S OPERA HOUSE WAS A CULTURAL LANDMARK

Lebanon's once outstanding landmark, the old

Opera House, was a beacon of light for the multitude who had the opportunity to frequent it. It served as a cultural center for the elite as well as the interested.

It served as an institution for the betterment of Lebanon citizens as well as for persons in the County of Warren. It was a beehive of activity until its demise, Sunday, Christmas morning, 1932, when the structure was totally destroyed by fire.

It was the scene of many a ball, a holiday gathering, or just a mecca for entertainment. A long list of persons of national and international fame performed for the Lebanon audiences. Dramatic, musical, educational and political events, as well as lecture courses, were the performing highlights of the famed Opera House platform.

Political figures who made their appeal to the public, or those who just simply spoke of the times, were of huge enormity. Many Governors of the State of Ohio, during the Opera House's tenure of some fifty-four years, appeared to reveal their message.

Two Presidents made their appearance on the Opera House platform, President Harding in 1910 and again in 1914. President McKinley solicited his views from the stage during his Governor's campaign of 1893. Other notables of political stature who implemented their skills on stage were Joseph B. Foraker, Frank B. Willis and Nicholas Longworth.

Impressive lectures were given regarding the times by such notables as Frederick Douglas and Henry Ward Beecher.

Local talent who performed at the Opera House in musical and theatrical performances, and who became known world-wide, were James E. Murdoch, E.D. Mansfield, Laura Woolwine Bellini, Dolly Woolwine Nobles and Jane Osborn Hannah.

In November, following the fateful fire of the Town Hall of September 1, 1874, Lebanon council asked for an election concerning a bond issue for a new building.

Authorization was approved by a vote of 197 to

33 to proceed with the bond issue and a new building. The proposition asked for a 3 1/2 mill levy for a period of eight years; a goal of $45,000 was in the plans.

Actual costs of the building exceeded that of the original plans, and architects proceeded to adjust in order to comply with the amount of money at hand. A third floor was eliminated and the building was shortened several feet with other designs altered.

A special legislative act was enacted in March 1877 to issue the bonds. This bond act deleted some of the then existing Burns Bond Act. Actual cost of the building was $36,000.

The Opera House was located on the northeast corner of Broadway and Main streets, where the Town Hall now sits.

Work began on the stone foundation on July 16, 1877. These stones were transported from Dayton, where they had been taken from some old Miami Canal locks.

The foundation wall started from footings 5 ft. 2 in. wide, placed 11 ft. below the pavement, and was 2 ft. 6 in. wide at the top.

Outside dimensions of the building were 132 x 64 ft. The auditorium was 101 x 60 1/2 ft., with the ceiling height 32 ft. above the floor. The spire on the tower was elevated to 132 ft. above the pavement.

Lew Seiker, one of Lebanon's leading merchants in later years, fired the brick for the structure.

Enclosed within the building front were three stone tablets. Berean stone was used to display on either side the seal of the village. On one stone was the number "18," and on the other, "77."

Other decorations included that of free masonry displays, galvanized iron and tin work.

The large roof section was divided by 17 chimneys and 20 dormer windows. The raised cupola corners housed the large tower and steeple into which the clock and bell were installed at a later time.

The main hall could seat approximately 900

persons, and a few hundred more, if needed, by the use of additional chairs. Village offices were housed on the first floor.

The facility was decorated inside under the direction of Josiah Morrow, longtime writer of Warren County history. He was asked by village council to communicate with select artists, scene painters and stage carpenters, and upon his recommendation, "council contracted with the most talented fresco and scene painters in Cincinnati."

The building was completed and opened in September 1878, with Morrow as its first speaker.

Results were so magnificent, according to Morrow, that visiting companies in later years contended that Lebanon had "one of the most beautiful Opera Houses in Ohio."

For the first twenty years the Opera House saw a consistent activity of stage performances. Plays led the list with 309 scheduled. Seventy-one concerts, 65 lectures, 31 minstrels and 58 unclassified performances brought the total to 534.

Fifty cents was the going rate for admission for many years, regardless of seating priority. The first week of operation consisted of six plays, three of which collected over $400 in receipts.

The Fire.

Herb Schwartz well remembers the Opera House fire. He was told to stay in the area of his home on East Silver Street by his father, Harry C. Schwartz, and wet down the roof of the neighbor's small four room house, in the event the fire spread to the locality. All persons who were in the path of the burning embers remained either on guard of their property or on their roofs.

Water pressure from the pumpers could not reach the tower roof because of its extreme height. Herb said much fear had arisen that the clock tower would fall westward toward The Golden Lamb hotel; however, it did not.

Because of the all-wood construction of the interior walls, the building collapsed inward.

From his home Herb said he heard the tower clock fall and hit the basement area. The old clock rang out the hour of four o'clock Christmas morning with flames leaping at the base of the tower. It continued to run until 4:08, and withstood the assault of the flames nearly an hour before it collapsed into the building's interior.

The old clock, along with the accompanying bell, was given by William Henry Newport in 1914. The bell was said to have fallen to the second floor in the center of the front of the building, adjacent to the picture projecting room.

(Some members of the high school graduating classes customarily climbed the inside of the tower near the clock, and inscribed their names on the walls.)

Marion Mulford was on the roof of the Masonic building, and twice he extinguished the menacing embers by using his coat sleeves.

Schwartz's father, having seen the destructive manner and direction in which the fire was spreading, packed and moved the family car into the street in case of evacuation.

Schwartz said that pieces of metal from the roof area, from four to six feet, were so hot that some of them actually floated through the air and landed in the school yard of the Pleasant Street School.

Rolls of movie film were stored in the balcony area; the heat from the fire was so extreme that when it closed in, the film actually exploded, again the water pressure not being enough to reach the area.

Blair Brothers hospital was quickly prepared for evacuation in case the fire spread in that direction. The Oswald and M.E. Merrill Funeral homes had ambulances backed up to the door to remove patients if needed.

All medical records were removed from the hospital and the county health board to safety.

Fire Chief Pfanzer and Officer Ned Ross set up

a patrol of the threatened areas as far away as the French creamery.

No cost estimate was placed on the loss to the building at the time. Members of council who had the responsibility of cleaning up the rubble were: Mayor Ralph H. Carey, Carl S. Bangham, president of council, R. Wilds Gilchrist, J.A. Schilling, Clarence Dunham, O.M. Abbott, Dr. Frank A. Dilatush, W.C. Maple, attorney for council, and M.E. Gustin, clerk of council.

Cause of the fire was first questioned as to Christmas tree lighting to be used for the community Christmas programs. However, Mrs. Edward Blair, chairman of the program committee, said that no tree had been set up for the Monday evening program. Plans called for two small trees without electric decorations to be set up on each side of the stage.

One wise man said: "The curtain has rung down on the last act never to be raised again, but the history of the old Opera House will live forever."

MARY HAVEN HOME HAS LONG HISTORY OF CARING FOR WARREN COUNTY CHILDREN IN NEED.

Many lives have been changed and memories treasured through the efforts of one fine lady, Mary Ann Klingling. With the closing of The Mary Haven Home, formerly known as the Orphan Asylum and Children's Home, one of Warren County's noted landmarks, as we know it, has gone into extinction.

(Mike Coleman wrote an excellent story in **The Western Star** in November 1995, concerning the Mary Haven Home. He explained that a new facility on Justice Drive will now house both boys and girls, whereas in recent times, the old Home housed only boys.)

The timeworn building is located about one mile west of Lebanon on the old Shakertown Pike, now Route 63. It commands a magnificent view that overlooks the Turtlecreek valley.

The original building is a sizable brick

structure, measuring 52 by 82 feet with three stories and a basement. It was constructed in 1874 at a cost of $23,000, furnishings included.

On June 6, 1863, Mary Ann Klingling, a German maiden lady, who resided on Broadway in Lebanon at the time, drew up a will to the amount of $40,000. This fund was to be used for the founding of an asylum "where poor white children, who have lost one or both parents, may receive a sound moral and Christian education, and if necessary, be supported during their minority."

Originally, the monies were not to be used unless they were duplicated by some individual. If no one accepted this proposal, then it was to go to the community of Lebanon with the same stipulation.

If Lebanon failed to take up the matter, the total amount would then be forwarded to the county and put into a trust fund to be used for the support and maintenance of such an institution.

It was stated in the will that the income from this fund was to be offered only for the education and support of orphan "white" children.

It was advised that all provisions for a "like benevolence for indigent children of all classes" be deemed proper.

On February 11, 1869, an Act of the Legislature authorized the commissioners to accept the Klingling fund and to "erect and maintain an Orphan Asylum in connection with a Children's Home."

Two sets of books were to be kept, one for each institution. A just monetary portion was to be divided equally amongst each branch.

We shall now pry into the operation of the institution. In July 1896, a group of local citizens visited the establishment for a period of three hours. It was at that time operated by Rev. and Mrs. R.S. Hageman who were, respectively, superintendent and matron.

The visitors first noticed the condition of the grounds, which were in an immaculate state. They made an excellent place for the children to romp and play.

The interior exhibited a state of cleanliness.

The second and third floor consisted of fifteen or twenty rooms that were used as sleeping rooms for the children.

The beds were smaller than the ordinary, each room containing from three to six. All were nicely made up, as if appearance counted for everything. It was remarked that they looked as comfortable as any "millionaire's couch."

The reception room and the office had just been cleaned and repapered. They were nicely equipped, the furnishings being inexpensive and of a common fashion.

Each story, including the halls, had recently been repainted. No two rooms were painted alike.

Because of the economic factor, few of the rooms were carpeted. Nearly three barrels of paint were used to paint the floors.

The visitors were in the basement area when the supper bell rang. They soon heard the pitter-patter of 36 pairs of little bare feet in the hall above them, and down the stairs they came.

First came the girls, the largest and oldest in the lead, followed by the next largest to a little tot of two years.

Then came the boys in the same order. All proceeded quietly into the dining room and were promptly seated on stools encircling the table.

At the word from the superintendent, each child bowed his or her head and said Grace. The food was said to be fit for a king. Although of a common nature, it was considered most palatable.

Meat was provided once a day and beef two days a week. Chicken was occasionally served, as it required six large fowl for a meal. The size of the flock could not provide this luxury as often as the children would like.

A comment was made that a brighter, more intelligent, or better looking group of children could not be found anywhere, or among any class of people.

Of the thirty-six children housed in the Home at this time, twenty-one were girls and three

Negro boys were amongst the males. The majority of the children were from five to ten years of age.

The older children were taught work around the farm, this being a part of their education.

Children placed in the Home were given up by their parents or guardian. The superintendent had authority to place them in any home where they may be wanted, provided the individuals were respectable and capable to care for and train a child. If they were not properly cared for, they were taken away.

A schoolhouse was provided by the trustees for nine months of the year. The cost of a teacher was $315 per annum.

A laundry was built in 1893, and afterward, no extra help was needed for the washings. The savings on this item paid for the machinery in three years.

Truck patches and farm gardens often yielded more than was required for consumption. Receipts from the excess garden products some years ran as much as $200.

The fifty-three acres required constant care. Wages paid the workers were surprisingly low, but the chores were done is a most professional manner.

Church was occasioned every Sunday in nearby Lebanon. One year they were taken to church in one location, the next year, another.

The summation of the visitors was that the Children's Home was better kept and operated more compassionately than any other in the State.

The Mary Haven Home was operated for more than 120 years. It was a special institution that had run its course, and has nothing but fond memories for its children and administration down through the years.

THE OBSTACLES FACED AS LEBANON TRIED TO LURE A RAILROAD

Lebanon's bid for a railroad goes back to the

early days of the Little Miami Railroad. A direct route over the hills from Kings Mills to Lebanon, Waynesville, Xenia, and on to Springfield would have been 5 miles shorter than the proposed Little Miami River course. This route would put Lebanon directly on the main line.

However, the terrain being too hilly for the smaller engines to pull their train disallowed this venture. Ormsby McKnight Mitchel, being the chief engineer, walked the two tentative routes and made his report, the commissioners consequently choosing the river path. The railroad bypassing the City of Cedars at this time was a practical move, not a snub.

In the early 1840's a group of Lebanon citizens confronted the Little Miami administrators to build an extension line to Lebanon from the site of Gainsborough (Kings Mills). The railroad officials set a figure of $40,000 for the presumed extension. An amount of $46,000 was raised, but to no avail, the railroad backing out of its commitment.

A few years later interest was again stirred amongst the Lebanonites concerning a railroad. A line from Deerfield (South Lebanon) on the Little Miami Railroad thru Lebanon and on to Dayton was the next move.

A survey was taken and the Little Miami was to help in the process of getting started. Another failure ensued and Lebanon wound up paying for the survey.

Still a third move was underway by 1850 with an anticipated effort again being negotiated by the residents of Lebanon and the Little Miami officials.

The line again was to be from Gainsborough to Lebanon with a provision that the Lebanonites would provide the right of way and pay half the cost of construction.

A period of dealings for almost a year passed and again the authorities of the Little Miami broke their promise.

The year 1852 was one of jubilation for the Lebanon citizens. Subscriptions were generously made, a right of way was secured, and actual work on a railway to Lebanon had been started. The name of this renewed project was the Cincinnati, Lebanon and Xenia Railroad.

The town residents started sprucing up the village for the great event. Many substantial houses were being built which included two elegant mansions.

One hundred acres adjoining the town on the south had been acquired and were to be sold as town lots by A.G. & E.B. Wright, Hurin & Co., along with other personnel. On the east the Rev. Charles Elliot had laid out fifty-seven building lots and nine outlots.

The steam mills of Cowan & Co., and Mr. A.S. Bennett were ripping wood to no end. The greatest obstacle was the want of brick and other materials, the demand being so great.

The noise of the hammer, the clicking of the trowel, the constant blazing of the fires in the kiln, and the cry for more materials transformed the community of Lebanon into an industrial entity.

Painting, repairing and a general dressing up was in order for the pioneer town. The "order of the day" significantly waged an all out town remodeling.

Enlarging churches, selling property, projecting plans for future improvements encompassed a generalization of the town.

Land sales were rising and selling almost at their owners' prices. One such sale was G.W. Stokes selling to Edgar Conkling of Cincinnati, the selling price set at ninety dollars an acre.

Mr. Conkling's projection was to erect, by the aid of a joint stock association, a hotel and cottage houses in which the summer residents were to have complete composure and relaxation. Also, a spacious hotel was to be built to accommodate the elite.

From cellar to attic the town was full of people with the grand expectation of the coming of the railroad. A suggestion was that "we advise all who contemplated moving here this fall [1853], to bring their houses with them."

The city was shocked to find their dreams had

again been shattered. Though construction had begun, the contractor went bankrupt and Lebanon was out some $100,000, and still no railroad.

The year 1866 was the year chosen by the Little Miami line to again proceed to Lebanon. A subscription of $60,000 was proposed to the residents of Lebanon, their total donations being $64,000, and again the line backed out with no given explanation.

Plans for a new line from Cincinnati to Springfield were in the making. The rail line officials required the residents of Lebanon to come up with $250,000, in which they assembled and raised $265,000.

Passed up again, the line ran by the way of Middletown, Franklin and Dayton, the originators claiming that an arrangement was made prior to the organization of the new company.

The Cincinnati Northern Railway Company, in 1879, purchased at judicial sale the uncompleted roadbed and right-of-way of the Miami Valley Narrow Gauge Railroad Company from Cincinnati to Waynesville for $61,000, and constructed the first narrow, or three-foot gauge railroad in Warren County.

On May 30, 1881, the road was completed to Lebanon, and on that day the county seat saw its first locomotive. (The road was never completed to Waynesville, although much of the grading and bridge work had been done.)

Later the name of this road became the Cincinnati, Lebanon & Northern, and in 1894 was widened to a standard gauge.

About 1897, the road was purchased by the Pennsylvania Company. Passenger service on this line was discontinued the first week of February, 1938.

THE FIRST BANKS OF OHIO AND
THE CITY OF LEBANON

Most of us have historically invested our money in our local banks for safety purposes and have come to expect a dividend on our savings.

In this article the writer will attempt to outline the early history of the first bank in Lebanon and also, Ohio.

Ohio, in the beginning of its existence, experienced the largest growth of any of the newly formed regions in the Northwest Territory. The Miami Valley, because of its rich agricultural resources, was the most populous and developed of all the lands in the new country.

Cincinnati was the largest city in the West. It is appropriate to think that the Queen City would house the first and most important bank in the State. Such was the case.

The Miami Exporting Company was incorporated April 15, 1803, it being organized at the first session of the Ohio Legislature.

Its duties were organized to facilitate the "exploration of the produce of the Miami Country by boats to New Orleans; and banking it purposed at all originally, was a secondary consideration."

Fifteen men were named to act as first agents, only three living in Cincinnati. The remaining twelve resided in other parts of the Miami Valley. Three lived in Warren County, their names being: Jacob D. Lowe of Deerfield, David Faulkner of Waynesville, and Jacob Reeder of Franklin.

The Miami Exporting Company was the first great corporation formed in the State. The capital stock of the newly formed organization consisted of shares of $100 each, but only $5 was required to be paid on a share in cash at the time of subscribing, $45 by the first of the next March in produce and manufactures, and $50 by the first of March of the succeeding year, also in produce and manufactures.

The business of exporting produce proved to be a failure, however, the early banking policies proved to be a success. It was reported in 1815 that its capital stock was $450,000, its stockholders numbering 190, and its dividends fluctuating between 10 and 15 percent.

Possibly this bank (the word bank did not appear in the name of the corporation) issued more paper money to the settlers of the Miami Valley than any other bank in the early history of the State.

Some of the early banks and their dates of corporation and organization in Ohio were: Marietta and Chillicothe in 1808; at Stuebenville in 1809; at Warren and Zanesville in 1812; at Cincinnati (the Farmers and Mechanics Bank) in 1813, and at Dayton in 1814. Some of the names of these establishments were unacceptable because in some cases they not mention the place of business, nor did not display banking as the business of the corporation.

(The bank at Warren was the Western Reserve Bank; the one at Zanesville, the Muskingum Bank; and at Dayton, the Dayton Manufacturing Company.)

The success of the Miami Exporting Company at Cincinnati may have triggered a swindling scheme. The Scioto Exporting Company may have taken its name synonymous with the company at Cincinnati, which resulted in a counterfeiting ring at Delaware in 1812. Before too much fake currency was circulated, the ring was broken up.

Several banking concerns were being run in Ohio without charters. Some other companies dealt in banking which had purposes other than banking.

Lebanon's first bank was organized early in the year 1814. Of all the counties in the Miami Valley at this time, Warren was third in population, being exceeded only by Hamilton and Butler.

Naming of this corporation was foremost on the organizers agenda. A simple name such as: "The Lebanon Bank" or the "Bank of Lebanon," seemed not to be "high-sounding" enough, thus constituting a long and lumbering name, "The Lebanon Miami Banking Company." The original articles of the association is quoted as such:

"We, whose names are hereunto subscribed, for the purpose of encouraging trade, to promote a spirit of improvement in agriculture, manufactures, arts and sciences, to aid the efforts of honest industry, and to suppress the unlawful and pernicious practice of usury, do mutually covenant and agree with others to establish a banking company for the objects before mentioned, at Lebanon; Warren county, Ohio, to be called and known by the name of the Lebanon Miami Banking Company, which shall continue for the term of twenty years from the commencement of its operations."

The directors board was elected in April 1814, and consisted of: Dr. Joseph Canby, Joshua Collett, Daniel F. Reeder, William Ferguson, William Lowry, William Lytle, Alexander Crawford, Thomas R. Ross and George Harnesberger.

The first president was Daniel F. Reeder and the first cashier, Phineas Ross. Some of the best known and most respected citizens of Lebanon are represented in this list.

An issuance of notes soon began circulating from the bank which included denominations of $1, $3, $5 and $10.

Tickets were issued for sums less than a dollar for circulation.

This operation proved most useful. Silver coins were scarce, and in making change, "cut money" was used. By this method a silver dollar was cut into quarters, and a quarter into 12 1/2 cent pieces.

Shinplasters (a piece of money depreciated by inflation or, formerly, one having a face value of less than a dollar) were also issued by merchants for small sums.

The bank at Lebanon was introduced without a charter, but on August 24, 1816, it became a chartered establishment.

The management seemed to be on track in-so-far as good dividends were declared to its stockholders. On January 1, 1819, it reported its capital stock, paid up as $86,491; notes in circulation, $31,831; and resources as $12,000 more than its liabilities.

A financial crisis struck the banking industry in 1818-19, which led the directors of the Lebanon Miami Banking Company on February 2, 1819, to resolve: "that it is expedient for this institution to close its business as soon as practicable, that it is not expedient that this resolution be now made public." The business of the bank was closed about 1822.

The bank was reopened in 1841 under the same name. Its president was John S. Iglehart with James H. Earl as its cashier. It again issued notes for circulation, but its business lasted only a short while.

LEBANON MARKET HOUSES OF YEARS AGO

Because transportation in the early and middle 19th century was limited mostly to the areas in which the residents lived, the old markets of this era thrived in each individual community, giving to these citizens a great abundance of trade substances.

At this time we shall examine the "old market-house" and Washington Hall on Silver Street in Lebanon.

The old market house was built in the 1830's and stood in the middle of Silver Street, just east of Mechanic Street. It had roadways on each side of the building, as most market-houses had, with the two roadways meeting again near the alley in the block.

The western end of the block, between Cherry and Mechanic streets, was wider than the eastern end to allow room for traffic on each side of the market-house.

It was described as a spacious building, fifty feet long by twenty wide, and had all the conveniences of a greater Cincinnati market-house. It was brick paved with stalls, blocks, and even had a hay scale at the eastern end.

Thomas Best ran a silversmith shop and lived in a small house on the north end of the lot. His property was later purchased by John Drake upon which he erected a carriage shop. (Perhaps some of the citizens of Lebanon now have in their possession some silver spoons with the name, "T. Best," engraved on them.)

On the south side of the market-house was the chair factory of Ezekiel Cretors, father of

George and John Cretors. Ezekiel manufactured the old fashioned split bottomed kind of chair, and it was said that better chairs were not made.

The market catered mostly to folks buying meats and produce. The meat market was run by William Smith, his brother John, and William Marlatt. Beef and pork, then, as now, were the bulk of the meat trade. An occasional roast of mutton, spring lamb and perhaps a veal cutlet were available for the buyers table. Fowl were plentiful, ducks and geese being much more accepted then than now. Rabbits were immediately bought up in the winter time. Squirrels were also in great demand.

The markets were held twice a week during the winter, at 11 a.m., and three times a week in summer, Tuesdays, Thursdays and Saturdays, at 4 a.m.

The rule of the market was "first come, first served." Every householder had his or her large basket, or other type apparatus, which was always set in an appropriate spot the night before the opening of the market. The finest cuts of meats, the freshest vegetables were purchased by the earliest marketer.

It was not unusual to see someone with his hand covering a freshly killed fowl, a prime cut of beef, or a special head of lettuce, waiting for the signal of the opening.

Obidiah McCabe, or "Okey," as he was often called, was given the reputation of the "vegetable gardener par excellence of early days." His market garden was located a mile below town on the Cincinnati Pike.

He was a skilled vegetable gardener with no one to his equal in the Lebanon area. Residents of the vicinity watched with keen interest McCabe's early lettuce and radishes in May; kidney potatoes, beets and peas in June, and especially the ripening of tomatoes by the Fourth of July.

The old market-house was abandoned due to the building of Washington Hall. Plans to construct a new building in 1855 was reviewed by the village council. It was decided that the City of Cedars would build a new facility that housed a fire department and a new town market-house, all under one roof.

The town hall at that time stood on part of the ground that housed the old Opera House on the corner of Broadway and Main Street.

The old hall was a two story building (later another story was added by the Masonic Order) that housed the Masonic lodge room, the Mechanic's Institute lecture room, a public meeting room, a public library and reading room, and a courthouse which housed all the town and county offices. (It was also said that in the early days church was held in the building.)

This crowding of facilities into one building intensified the plans for a new structure.

The idea of a fire department being housed in a new structure for purposes coinciding with a market place did not go over well with the citizens of Lebanon. With this controversy up in the air, council decided to put the proposition on the ballot. The proposal was defeated by 11 votes.

With a defeat at the ballot box, a stock company was formed to raise the necessary funds for the erection of the new building. The town became a stockholder in the new enterprise which amounted to one-half the cost of the anticipated building.

Funds from the village of Lebanon and private funds were to be used jointly in the erection of Washington Hall. This action was against the law, but since no one complained, the building went up.

The structure was about one-third of a block long, two stories high and was constructed of home-made bricks at a cost of $3000. It was located on the southwest corner of Mechanic and Silver Streets. The north half of the first floor was used for the market house, the south side as the fire department headquarters.

The entire top floor was used as a meeting place for the town. Seating arrangements were built to accommodate 500 people.

The market place was terminated soon after the close of the Civil War; businesses were turned over to the local grocers and butchers, which left the entire first floor for the fire department.

Dedication of Washington Hall took place on Christmas Eve in 1856, given by the Franklin (possibly named for Benjamin Franklin) Independent Fire Company. On January 10, of the following year, the stockholders met and named the new structure Washington Hall in honor of our first President.

Many events were given at the new facility, the first being a public lecture on Friday evening, January 23, 1857, by Rev. C.G. Giles of Cincinnati, a Swedenborgian preacher, later an instructor at the National Normal University.

Most lectures up to the Civil War were primarily given by local folks such as lawyers, ministers, physicians and students, many of whom were impatient to spread their reputation.

In 1859, a succession of lectures were delivered in the hall on the "Duties of the American People." The first of these speeches was given by the great orator, Thomas Corwin.

Following the lecture courses, the list of speakers is quite long. Horace Mann, Wendell Phillips, Mrs. Scott Siddon, Josh Billings, John B. Gough, Baylord Taylor, Mrs. Elizabeth Cady, and many others of prominence were heard in the hall.

Some time later the National Normal University leased the hall. It was used by Prof. Alfred Holbrook, founder of the school and its first president, for his grammar classes.

The professor also used the building for general exercises every morning to bring students from various colleges together before the day's work was brought about. Occasional get-togethers and socials were held for the intention of getting the students acquainted with each other.

A custom of the school at the hall was that two young people, male or female, were to promenade around the hall several times until they became acquainted. Next they were to introduce each other to some of their friends, who in turn performed a promenade, thus keeping the dance up until everyone became acquainted.

Rutherford B. Hayes, in 1867, who later became the nineteenth President, opened his first campaign for Governor in Washington Hall.

In 1878, the upper room was turned over to the Granville Post of the G.A.R.

In 1886, the west end of the building was unroofed by a terrific storm, but was replaced by the veterans who afterward received free use of the hall.

In March 1921, the old hall was sold by the Village Council for a sum of $3000 to the County Commissioners. The bid was not accepted until the Commissioners agreed to allow the village to withhold the title until some other suitable quarters could be accessed for the fire department.

In the late 20's, the Ralph P. Snook Post raised $6,000 and installed a kitchen and dining room on the first floor, and added new hardwood flooring on the second floor auditorium.

Sometime later, Washington Hall was renamed Memorial Hall.

In October 1957, a decision was made by the Warren County Commissioners to sell the aging building. An estimate as to the cost of repair ran as high as $50,000. These costs would far exceed its value.

The building had been inspected the previous summer and the conclusion listed 14 defects which included about everything.

In June 1961, workmen began the task of demolition of the building. A landmark that had lasted for 105 years unquestionably had an impact on many generations of Lebanoites and Warren Countians.

WOMEN OF DISTINCTION AMONGST MULTITUDE

This week our article shall be entitled "Distinguished Women of Warren County." It seems as though the writer has been focusing on the men of the County, however, there were many women of distinction amongst the multitude.

Some of these ladies have gone forth and distinguished themselves in a world-wide fashion and some have simply wound themselves into the hearts of Warren Countians.

Catherine Hurin Skinner, daughter of Mr. Silas Hurin, was the first child born within the bounds of Lebanon. Hurin Park was named in honor of this event.

A great benefactor by the name of Mary Ann Klingling has put her imprint on the community of Lebanon. Mary Ann died August 15, 1867, from injuries received in a runaway horse accident.

Her will stipulated that $35,000 be left for a building that would shelter the homeless children, thus an institution named the Children's Home was built.

Mary Ann came to Lebanon from Germany with her brother, John. He acquired a small fortune in the drug business which was located in a room where the Henry Reid drug store was later established.

After John's death, Mary Ann inherited her brother's estate. A story goes that Miss Klingling had a lover of high standards in Germany, but his family disapproved of this relationship.

Vowing never to marry, both parties provided a will which stated that if either dies the monies were to go toward the building of a children's home. The lover died first leaving a will providing for a home for the poor children in his home-land.

Another lady born in Lebanon was Dolly Woolwine Nobles. She moved to Cincinnati with her family while still a young lady.

While in the Queen City she joined the Shakespeare Club. Madame Madjestka, the renown performer, was entertained by the club and was impressed by Dolly's performance. She urged her parents to have Dolly take comprehensive dramatic training.

Dolly later moved to Washington and became a student of Madame Madjestka. She joined the company of Milton Nobles, noted actor and playwright, and later became his bride. They entertained throughout the country, and in later life settled for Vaudeville.

Another lady by the name of Laura Woolwine sought her recognition on the stage, too. Her professional name was Laura Bellini. She has been renowned as Lebanon's Prima Donna.

Bellini first attracted attention while studying with Madame Rive in Cincinnati. Later, after traveling to Milan, Italy, she studied under Lamperti, and it was here that she took the name of Bellini, just before she made her debut in Rigoletto.

She consequently traveled and sang in Italy, France, Trieste, England, Corsica, Havana, Mexico, and New York. She sang with the Conreid and Duff Opera Companies until she was called home by the sudden illness and eventual death of her parents.

Remaining in Lebanon, she made her home at her grandparents, subsequently going into the teaching vocation at Lebanon and Cincinnati.

Jane Osborn Hannah was not a true Lebanonite, having been born in Wilmington, but she came to the city at a very early age to live with her grandparents.

Her career was one of brilliance. She was a concert and oratorio singer, and studied abroad for Grand Opera.

She sang at all the leading opera houses in Germany, later returning to America, and on February 18, 1912, Madame Hannah made her debut at the Lebanon Opera House.

Still another vocalist that sprang from the City of Cedars was Blanche Scoville.

She was graduated with honors from the Cincinnati College of music where she studied under the guidance of Signor Albino Porno.

After graduation, she traveled to New York City and found employment under Anton Seidl in his Opera Company. A prearrangement that she return home to study German for the Opera Company was interrupted by a bout with typhoid fever. She died at the age of 24, never fulfilling her dreams.

Amanda Stokes was the first woman from Warren County to enlist in the Civil War. Selling all her possessions, she used her funds to buy delicacies for the soldiers who were gallantly serving their country.

Her presence in the great war was for a period of about five years. She was present at the battles of Stones River, Chattanooga, Chickamauga and Nashville.

Having spent her entire funds, she left the service penniless. She ultimately found employment at the O.S.S.O. Home in Xenia.

She petitioned for a pension through many channels and none was given, until, by a special act of Congress, a pension of fifteen dollars a month was awarded shortly before her death in 1886.

In recognition of this fine and generous lady, the Daughters of America, in 1906, named their lodge The Amanda Stokes Council, No. 132, in her honor.

Mrs. Mary Proctor Wilson had the distinction of being one of the most prominent newspaper ladies of her day. She was editor/owner of the Warren County Patriot for over twenty-five years.

Among her other accomplishments were: the first Probation Officer in the County; she was a member of the State Board of Visitors for more than eight years; she was on the Board of Lady Visitors for the O.S.S.O. Home in Xenia for twenty-one years; and was Postmistress of Lebanon during the Cleveland Administration.

Grace Margaret Wilson at one time graced the city of Lebanon. She moved to Toledo in her stature as a newspaper woman, and was the Dramatic Editor for the Toledo Times. Her accomplishment in that capacity was that she published two volumes of poetry, and was notable in the literary clubs of Toledo.

L. Ray Balderstone, the niece of Jarvis F. Stokes, received her Master of Arts at Columbia University in 1915.

In 1914, she published her second book on

laundry work which was a guide for both housewife and teacher. She was an ardent lecturer on the subject.

Melva Beatrice Wilson, raised in Warren County, was one of the world's top sculptureres. She was the daughter of Judge John Lafayette Wilson. She received a scholarship from Adrian College, Michigan. For three consecutive years, she won the $100 prize for sculpture excellence at the Cincinnati Art Academy.

This lady of renown first traveled to Europe and then to New York. Possibly her greatest work was a processional of four hundred figures called "The Way of the Cross," crafted for the St. Louis Cathedral.

These were the ladies of another time. Perhaps, in another article, the writer will bring this episode up to present.

'STORM OF CENTURY' ROCKED LEBANON AREA MORE THAN 100 YEARS AGO

"Darker and darker became the sky and louder and louder rolled the thunder-drum of heaven." The preceding was a vivid description of a storm that settled over Lebanon and the surrounding country side on May 12, 1886. This is just a reminder that tornado season is once again upon us.

The "storm of the century," was an event that the Lebanonites had feared for years. Evening was broken by something in the clouds which caused an uneasiness amongst the people.

The crowds gathered and gazed at the heavens in all its majesty. A continual outburst of lightning, the roar of the thunder, and the frightening winds lent a ghostly and somber appearance to all surrounding objects.

The sky lent a dark, eerie feeling as the clouds churned in all their glory. The spectacle of mother nature moved into town about 7 o'clock and continued to roll out of the west for more than two hours; whirling, rolling and blowing itself into a fierce storm that the town folks would talk about for years to come.

About 9:30 the storm threatened havoc on the Lebanonites. Meetings were let out and the folks hurriedly scampered for the safety of their home.

Fifteen minutes later it seemed that all the fury of the heavens showered its ravages on the small town. Men, women and children alike expressed silent concern over the spectacle. For a few minutes it raged most fiercely, filling the hearts of the strong and the weak with fear.

Like a demon from the southwest, it struck the old tannery building on Main Street. It then leaped to the Lebanon House, ripping away the tin roof, rolling it into a huge ball and dropping it in front of John W. Thompson's grocery on Broadway.

The next stop for the storm was the Greeley & Davis Mill which scattered debris on both sides of the street.

It then jumped from this place to a little frame dwelling down in the hollow by the reservoir, splitting it almost into kindling wood. The occupants were two black families, Mr. Sutton and his wife, and a man named Alford and his wife and two children.

By a miracle, they received no injury. Mrs. Alford grabbed her two children, one aged three and the other two, and got into the mill race under one of the foot bridges.

Ed Grimes and Jim Johnson, two young boys, occupied the upstairs. They were blown a hundred yards against the bank at the overflow of the reservoir.

At this point the storm seems to have turned back toward the center of town and the crisis was prolonged. This time it wrecked the Union School Building, the M.E. Church, Memorial Hall and unroofed many private dwellings.

Memorial Hall's west end caved in right on the stage ruining all the scenery, and produced a loss of several hundred dollars to the G.A.R. Post.

The narrow escapes were many as told by the different individuals.

A boarder by the name of Phillips was asleep at Mrs. Waggoner's boarding house when part of the roof of the M.E. Church came crashing in under his bed. The commotion woke him up, but he was not injured.

The streets were full of all kinds of debris from the devastation of the buildings. Shingles, boards, lath, household items, etc., were strewn in a manner of total destruction. Trees were snapped off like straws at the tops. Many were uprooted and countless numbers were twisted like licorice sticks.

Damage in Lebanon amounted to thousands of dollars. The Union School suffered damage between four and five thousand dollars.

Swinging eastward the storm traveled from town toward the river creating havoc on its way; doing damage to the farms in its path.

Damage reports from the individuals was quite extensive, however, because of lack of room in the article, they cannot be listed.

Chapter IX

MISCELLANEOUS ARTICLES

ABRAHAM LINCOLN VISITS SOUTHWESTERN OHIO

When one tends to travel this beautiful county of ours, the thought of a visit from the greatest President, or possibly the greatest American of all times, is far from our thoughts.

However, in the years 1859 and 1861, Warren County was graced with his presence. His name is Abraham Lincoln.

It was in Dayton that the name of Abraham Lincoln was first publicly mentioned for the presidency of the United States.

Lincoln was fairly unknown at this time except for his debates with Senator Stephen A. Douglas, the "Little Giant."

Our setting is the year 1859. An exciting gubernatorial race was being held in Ohio between Republican William Dennison, a native of Cincinnati, and the Democratic contender, Judge Rufus P. Ranney, a resident of Portage County.

The subject matter of this political post was based on the issue of whether the Union could survive half slave and half free.

Lincoln had served his Illinois district in Congress. At this time he became acquainted with Thomas Corwin, from Lebanon, and other dignitaries from this area of the State.

Corwin extended an invitation to the Illinois attorney to visit Ohio because of his commendable presentation against Douglas in debating the slavery question.

While the new party of the Republicans were jostling for outside orators, the Democrats were also on the move.

They had secured the services of Stephen A. Douglas, and in his address in Columbus, Sept. 7, 1859, many highly ranked Republicans were swayed in their beliefs.

Justice could only be served by bringing Lincoln into the picture. On Friday, Sept. 16, he made a speech in Columbus on the east terrace of the State House, and, in the evening, at the City Hall.

The following day he chose to make a stop at Dayton.

Preceding Lincoln's visit to Dayton was a scheduled stopover by none other than Mr. Douglas.

He was received by Hon. Clement L. Vanlandigham, the soon-to-be leader of the famed "Copperheads."

Douglas's appearance of September 8 was addressed not only to the citizens of the Gem City, but to the country as well.

Lincoln was welcomed to Dayton by Robert C. Schenck of Franklin, who had since made his home in the Gem City. Schenck was an old friend of the future President, both having served in the 30th Congress, 1847-48.

He was considered "Lincoln's best friend in Dayton."

Lincoln originally had not prepared a speech for the Dayton residents, but he later changed his mind. On the 16th a message was sent from Columbus that: "Hon. Abe Lincoln will speak in Dayton at 1 1/2 o'clock; let the people attend."

Mr. and Mrs. Lincoln and their party arrived by train, making their stay at the Philips House.

(This fine hotel once stood on the southwest corner of Third and Main, just south of the old courthouse.)

Schenck introduced the speaker with a speech of his own, which consisted mainly of political parties and their beliefs.

Lincoln had been fittingly introduced. He referred to his two previous visits to Ohio, but stated that this was his first trip to Dayton.

His earlier visits were made to Cincinnati in

connection with legal cases in the Queen City, in which he represented clients residing in his own State of Illinois.

His speech was in referral to the often repeated statement by Douglas that the Ordinance of 1787 had never made a free state and that Ohio had been made free merely by the action of its own people.

The main issue of his speech was that getting rid of slavery was a troublesome concern.

He also declared himself in favor of an absolute "Popular Sovereignty." He outlined his belief thus: "That each man shall do precisely as he pleases with himself, and with all those things which concern them."

After his stopover in Dayton, Hamilton was Lincoln's next destination, arriving in the afternoon of Sept. 17, 1859, on the Cincinnati, Hamilton and Dayton Railroad.

Before his scheduled stop, the train arrived at Middletown Station, which was located on the west side of town. (It was at that time called Madison.)

The train was to be serviced and wood and water taken on. This took several minutes.

According to George Crout, Middletown area historian, Lincoln stepped off the train and conversed with the fairly small crowd.

A chance to see the opponent of Stephen A. Douglas, whom most of them supported, was a once in a lifetime experience.

Mr. Crout, wrote that "Lincoln looked to the east across the river, noting a few three-story brick buildings on the horizon."

He also wrote that the Madison House was somewhat new, having been constructed in 1846. Some of the passengers frequented the bar, but Lincoln remained near the engine chatting with the small crowd.

The fireman completed his assignment and complained that his fellow workers were too slow.

He bellowed quite loudly, "Come on, men, we got to get out of here - We've got to have Lincoln at Hamilton on time, for he still has to make Cincinnati tonight."

Lincoln immediately stepped back onto the train, and, in a matter of minutes the C.H.& D. was on its way.

He arrived at the Hamilton Station (the station is still standing and has been placed on the city's Historic Preservation list), and on the afternoon of the 17th, he gave his speech.

It was along the same lines as the speech given in Dayton, which concentrated on Popular Sovereignty.

It started out giving mention to the Miami Valley. He said: "This beautiful and far-famed Miami Valley is the garden spot of the world."

Now it seems all too fair to mention that the procession traveled the Cincinnati, Hamilton and Dayton Railroad. The tracks of this line pass through the corporation of Carlisle, which at that time was called Carlisle Station.

So, according to written tradition, this was the first excursion through Warren County for the soon to be President.

Abraham Lincoln was elected President in 1860, receiving only 40 percent of the votes. His activity on the campaign trail consisted mostly of stump speaking. He was the first Republican to win the nation's highest office.

His opponents on the Democratic ticket were Stephen Douglas, John Bell and John C. Breckenridge. If it were not for the split in the vote of the opposition, he would have been defeated and Stephen Douglas would have been elected President.

President-elect Lincoln and his family stepped off his special train (the Wabash Line) in Cincinnati on his 52nd birthday, February 12, 1861. Cincinnati was honored with the presence of the newly-elected President and his family.

They stepped into a special carriage drawn by six white horses, and rode in a procession that included brass bands and fife-and-drum corps.

The citizens, Democrats and Republicans alike, welcomed them and all plans were carried out as hoped for.

Their stay was the Burnet House at Third and

Vine streets.

As he gazed across the Ohio River into Kentucky, his birth place, he would say: " We mean to treat you, as near as we possibly can, as Washington, Jefferson, and Madison treated you," that "under the Providence of God, who has never deserted us...we shall again be brethren, forgetting all parties - ignoring all parties."

President-elect Lincoln was invited to visit Dayton once again. An invitation was sent by some respected citizens of the Gem City and he answered the request through his secretary, John Nicolay.

"Mr. Nicolay will answer this, that I will pass through Dayton, and bow to the friends there, if I can get to and from Columbus as soon; other wise not. - Lincoln."

The citizens of Dayton were disappointed when news arrived that the C.H.& D. line was not to be used. It was decided to use the Little Miami Railroad as an alternative route, thus bypassing Dayton and taking the trip from Cincinnati to Xenia and on to Columbus.

The President's party arose at 6:15 on the morning of February 13, ate breakfast and were at the Little Miami depot by 8:30.

A lead engine preceded the special train which was made up of three coaches.

The Presidential train was now underway. It moved along at speeds of 30 miles per hour. It slowed for stops at "Milford, Loveland, Miamiville, Morrow, Corwin, Xenia and London."

In an article by the late Marion Snyder, he informs us "that at Morrow, a junction point, Mrs. Lincoln was presented a bouquet of flowers of white camellias on behalf of the railroad president's wife."

Snyder presumed that Mrs. Clement, wife of the president of the Little Miami, made the presentation of the flowers either to Mary Todd Lincoln or to one of her attendants.

Many Dayton citizens, obviously disappointed at the news concerning the change of plans, jumped into their buggies, or took the train to nearby Xenia, and enlarged the crowd there.

Lincoln did not eat from breakfast time until late at night.

The folks at Xenia prepared food for the Presidential train, but it was soon devoured by the massive crowd that had stampeded the depot dining room.

Some of the train party were left behind simply pacifying their appetite.

The Dayton Journal noted on the 14th: "A large crowd of people, some 5,000, welcomed Mr. Lincoln to Xenia yesterday. He spoke a few minutes from the platform of the car. The enthusiasm was great...Mr. Lincoln addressed them from the rear of the car, reiterating what he said before - no speech to make, and no time to make one."

On April 14, 1865, President Lincoln was assassinated. The whole nation mourned for one who was to become the greatest President in the history of the United States.

In accordance with suggestions from the War Department, religions services were to be held at noon on the 19th of April in all parts of the country.

In Dayton, all businesses were closed in honor of the dead President.

A committee of 100 on the 25th was appointed to go to Columbus in respect of the slain leader.

On April 29, Abraham Lincoln's funeral procession passed just north of Dayton, traveling from Columbus to Piqua, on to Greenville and New Paris.

This was the President's last tour through the Miami Valley.

The writer might add that the next time you pass through Carlisle, or cross the Little Miami Railroad (now a bicycle and walking trail most of the way), just look around and you will catch a glimpse of history that was once shared with our 16th President.

LITTLE MIAMI WAS ONCE OHIO'S MOST IMPORTANT MILL STREAM

In the early days of Ohio the Little Miami was the most important mill stream in the State. Cheaper transportation was needed to transport the products from the mills on the river.

Besides the numerous grist mills, and flour mills, there were one or two paper mills, a cotton mill at Oregonia and woolen mills on or near the river. It was thought that the town of Gainsborough, laid out in 1815 (the site of Kings Mills), would be an important factory town.

Oliver M. Spencer, when a mere boy, recorded a situation in which a type of mill (Wickersham's) was used near Columbia, now a part of Cincinnati.

He stated that he witnessed a class of mill that was actually floating on the river. It consisted of a small flatboat tied to the bank, its wheel turning slowly with the natural current and a small piroque anchored in the stream, and on which one end of its shaft rested; and having only one pair of stones, it was at best barely sufficient to supply meal for the inhabitants of Columbia and neighboring families.

At least three mills were in operation on the Little Miami River at the turn of the 19th century. The first mill, known as Waldsmith's Mill, was located at the present site of Milford; the second and third mills, built in 1793 and 1799, respectively, were located near Xenia and Kings Mills.

The county, in 1832, contained 30 gristmills, 44 saw mills, 25 tanneries, 28 distilleries, 6 woolen factories, 3 iron foundries, 3 oil mills, 2 paper mills and 1 brewery.

Also in this year, Todd's Fork, in the twenty-five miles of its course, turned eight saw mills and four grist mills.

East Fork, which feeds Todd's Fork one mile below Clarksville in the thirteen miles of its course, turned two saw mills and two grist mills. Turtlecreek had two saw mills and two grist mills.

Some of the earliest mills in Warren County were constructed on the small streams which feed the Little Miami. The reasoning for this was the greater ease and less cost of constructing a dam across a larger stream.

Directing the water current upon the wheel of the mill consisted of cheap structures of brush and logs. This was done rather than using a reservoir to retain the water.

The water power was converted into energy in which to turn a huge grinding wheel. During the dry season the mill would be idle. The clearing away of the forests caused the smaller streams to be less constant in their flow.

Before the early mills a type of home-made mill was used by the early pioneers. A rather crude method in the process of getting corn cracked into meal is described as such (taken from the 1882 History of Montgomery County):

"Every expedient was resorted to get corn cracked into meal. The 'hominy-block' was unsatisfactory, and grating by hand was worse. The stump-mortar was made by burning a round hole in the top of a stump; a spring pole was rigged over it, with a stone pestle attached. Hominy was first made by hulling corn, soaking the grains in weak lye, then cracking in the 'hominy-block,' or in the improved 'stump-mortar.'

"The hand-mill, although hard, slow work, was a welcome improvement, and soon one stood in the chimney-corner of every cabin. The stones were about four inches thick, and were broken down as nearly round as possible to about twenty inches in diameter.

"On top of the upper stone, near the edge, one end of a pole was fixed, the other end working in a socket in a piece of timber on the floor overhead. One person turned the stone by hand, while another fed the corn into the eye. It took two hours to grind enough meal to supply one person for a day, the operators often changing places in the work.

"Before the cabins were all supplied with

these hand-mills, neighbors sometimes shouldered a peck or half bushel of corn, and carried it five miles to the cabin of a settler who had one, grind his corn, and return with the meal.

"Flour was very scarce, and, at this time, was all brought from Cincinnati, and, as we have said, was very expensive. Most of the settlers kept a small quantity laid by for use only in case of sickness.

"Those who could afford it had biscuits for breakfast on Sunday morning, baked in a spider before the fire. Corn-pone, dodgers and flapjacks, supplied them for the rest of the week. Those who could not afford to buy flour would run the wheat three or four times through these hand-mills.

"The next advance made was when these little mills were rigged to run by horse power, by fastening a pole across the stone, hitching the horse to the end of the pole, and driving him round and round a circle.

"The next improvement was made in running a single pair of stones by water-power. The wheel was a simple paddle wheel, run by the natural current of the stream, and, although not reliable, was good enough to grind all the wheat and corn that the settlement needed."

PRINTING PRESSES CAME EARLY TO OHIO FRONTIER

What would we do without our daily or weekly newspapers? Although television has taken over as a huge media success, the newspaper and its coverage still has a large hold on our lives. The writer this week shall focus on the history of the early printing presses in Ohio.

The large towns of the early Nineteenth Century such as Dayton, Springfield, Columbus and Cincinnati can trace their newspaper publications back to the very early times of the organization of the State, before and shortly after.

Chillicothe has long claimed to have given itself the prestige of publishing the first newspaper east of the Allegheny Mountains. This claim has gone unchallenged.

The Scioto Gazette (first publication in 1792) was in existence when Springfield, Dayton and Cincinnati were but mere trading posts. News of their families and neighbors along the Atlantic seaboard, and news of the events of the old World were printed.

Seven years prior to the appearance of **The Gazette**, Ohio boasted a printing press. The press was used largely for commercial purposes and did not for several years serve as a publisher of news.

A year after the Chillicothe newspaper was founded, Cincinnati took her place in the newspaper field, it having the distinction of publishing the second newspaper in Ohio.

In 1793 an old press of the Ramage pattern (now exhibited in the Smithsonian Institute at Washington) was floated down the Ohio River to Fort Washington, now the site of Cincinnati. On this press was published the Queen City's first "recognized" newspaper, "**The Liberty Hall**."

In 1806, a Lebanonite of the highest distinction, John McLean, learned the old Ramage press was for sale. Racing against time, he caught the first stage to the Queen City for the express purpose of purchasing it.

His success was assured, and in a few weeks the primitive old machine was installed in the City of Cedars.

That same year, the old press began striking off the first edition of **The Western Star**, a newspaper that still carries the excellent tradition that it was founded on. It is at present time the oldest weekly newspaper in Ohio.

Among the first editors of the **Star** which received national attention in pursuance of their editorial work, were the distinguished names of: Nathaniel McLean, a brother of the founder; A.H. Dunlevy, Wm. H.P. Denny, Dr. James Scott, Judge George R. Sage, and Hon. Seth W. Brown.

The revelation of the first printing press in

Lebanon was achieved some time before the appearance of the press in Hamilton, Dayton, Urbana, Springfield or Xenia.

Advertisements and announcements were sent from these cities to **The Western Star** to be inserted for publication. All the "job work" for those towns was struck off on the old wooden Ramage press.

It outgrew its usefulness in time and near the close of the Civil War, it was sold and removed to a western State.

The press was worked with a bar which required a long, hard days labor to print as many as 300 copies of a small-sized newspaper.

Lines of type in those days consisted of thin splints of wood, similar to those used for the seats of chairs. The type was inked with peltballs, since the use of rubber for printer rollers was unknown.

McLean used that pioneer piece of machinery to implement a flourishing business. In 1808, he secured a contract with the Shakers to print a rather large volume entitled, "Christ's Second Coming."

The work was completed by the end of the year and some of the books were bound by hand at Lebanon.

Other early publications off the old press were: an almanac for the year 1812, with weather calculations by Matthias Corwin, Jr.; "The Ohio, or Western, Spelling Book," which was printed by A. Van Fleet in Lebanon in 1814.

The same author printed and published the same year a volume entitled, "The Ohio Justice and Township Officers Assistant."

In 1822, a monthly magazine known as the "Ohio Miscellaneous Museum" was issued from the **Star** office. The first four publications were a valuable relic in the library of the Mechanics Institute in Lebanon.

In 1826, **The Ohio State Journal and Columbus Gazette** inserted in their publication a complete list of Ohio newspapers published at the time. The list goes as such: **The State Journal**, at Columbus; **The Ohio Monitor**, at Columbus; **The**

Western Statesman, at Columbus; **The Ohio Repository**, at Canton; **The Scioto Gazette**, at Chillicothe; **The Western Star**, at Lebanon; **The Patron**, at Delaware; **The Clintonian and Xenia Register**, at Xenia; **The Western Pioneer**, at Springfield; **The Mad River Courant**, at Dayton; and **The Register** at Eaton.

Cornelius Van Ausdale, the first merchant of Eaton, has been given the honor of being the originator of the first newspaper in the county seat and in the County of Preble. **The Western Telegraph** was created in 1817.

In 1819, Van Ausdale made the acquaintance of Judge Samuel Tizzard, who along with Van Ausdale, was a member of the Ohio Legislature.

Judge Tizzard had learned the trade of printing with his tenure at **The Scioto Gazette** office in Chillicothe.

A friendship immediately developed between the two, and at the end of their terms in 1820, chaperoned by Van Ausdale, Judge Tizzard traveled to Eaton and became impressed with the newspaper.

The Judge had been seeking to purchase an enterprise of this sort. He promptly bought the equipment of the then defunct **Western Telegraph**, and published the first number of **The Eaton Weekly Register**.

Dayton was not far behind Lebanon in the journalistic field. The first paper to be printed in the Gem City was known as **The Repertory**, which was printed on a single sheet consisting of foolscap paper, eight by twelve inches. It was printed on a small hand press by William McClure and George Smith.

The first publication was printed September 18, 1808, and the last printing was issued on December 4, 1809.

The press used was considered a marvel for the time period. It was brought from Pennsylvania and its construction was entirely of metal.

The news contained in **The Repertory** consisted of but a few paragraphs, word from Europe being three months old at the time of publication.

Springfield at this time was still making

peace with the few remaining Indians. The wilderness had not yet been conquered and a new townsite was still in the planning stage.

However, in 1817, with growing progress being made in the new town, a newspaper was established, the name of the first publication being, **The Farmer**. Prospering for a brief period, it soon became disorderly.

A temporary break in its publication was reestablished under the name of **The Republic**, and respectively, **The Republic Times**, **The Press Republic**, and the **Daily News**.

Springfield, though being late in the development of a newspaper, had another enterprise that was established as a manufacturer of woolen goods.

The plant suffered financial difficulty and was soon taken over by Jacob W. and William Hill. It was modified and was made into a paper mill.

This change in hands soon implanted Springfield with the first paper mill in all this part of the country. It furnished much of the paper on which our pioneer publications were printed.

The writer has tried to describe in a brief moment the beginnings of the newspaper business in Ohio.

Although many of the leading publications in the United States have combined their efforts because of financial strappings, there will always be a place for printed news and gleanings of local insight.

ELECTRIC MULE COULD PROPEL A CANAL BOAT SYSTEM

We all know what a mule is, but have you ever heard of an "electric mule?" This will be our choice of subjects this week.

Because of the slow demise of the canal system due to more modern transportation methods, such as the railroad and motor vehicles, another method of canal mobilization was established.

An "electric mule" was the name given to a

machine that ran on rails which would do away with the old method of mules and horses that propelled the canal boats.

A company was formed to build and install an electrical system in which a canal boat could be moved through the efforts of electricity.

Such a system was presented in 1901. Introduced into the office of the Ohio Secretary of State was a proposition for reopening the Miami and Erie Canal to commerce. Especially interested were the paper companies along the route from Cincinnati to Toledo.

The corporation was known as the Miami and Erie Deep Waterway Association, and was formed February 16, 1901.

Its principal business residence was at Cincinnati. It was incorporated for the purpose of owning, operating and propelling boats and other craft on the Miami and Erie Canal between the southern terminus of the canal in Cincinnati and a designated point at Toledo.

The new company was to cooperate with the Ohio Valley Improvement Association (which was actively engaged in promoting the canalization of the Ohio River, so as to give it a minimum depth of nine feet the year around), and with the Toledo, Fort Wayne and Chicago Deep Waterway Association. (The latter was associated with the deep waterway construction by way of Fort Wayne and Defiance.)

Members of the new association toured the different cities along the canal line for the purpose of analyzing the old ditch to see if a new method of propulsion could be executed.

The first encounter dealing with the possibility of an "electric mule" was first introduced on April 25, 1898, through an Act of the Ohio General Assembly.

This Act authorized the Board of Public Works to allow experiments to be performed concerning the feasibility of electricity as a reasonable power source for the propulsion of boats and other craft.

On March 26, 1901, the Board of Public Works leased the construction and operational works of the "electric mule" to Thomas M. Fordyce, and his associates, for thirty years after the first operation of boats.

On April 10, 1901, Fordyce and his associates sold and assigned their lease to William H. Lamprecht, who was acting trustee for Cleveland parties. The consideration of the sale from Fordyce to Lamprecht was that the former was to receive $75,000 in cash, and his associates were to receive the sum of $50,000.

Lamprecht assigned to the Miami and Erie Transportation Company all rights granted Fordyce in consideration of $2,990,000 worth of stock fully paid up to the Cleveland syndicate.

Also the company was to issue to Lamprecht and syndicate $240,000 worth of bonds of the company out of a total authorized issuance of such bonds of $2,000,000.

On May 3, 1901, The Miami and Erie Transportation Company was granted all canal rights between Cincinnati and a point in the city of Dayton.

Construction of an electric plant was started several miles below Dayton. (The writer at this time does not know the location of this plant.)

Installed was a standard gauge railroad track of ordinary railroad ties with 70 pound "T" rails, along with the erection of poles and apparatus for an ordinary electric trolley railroad. Much of the original towpath was graded and tracks laid.

In November 1902, a contract between the Miami and Erie Canal Transportation Company and the Traction Terminal Company was ratified with the stipulation that all rights and property of the "electric mule" should be conveyed to the latter for ten years at a price to be agreed upon.

On July 2, 1903, an audit of the company was made and the financial records, along with the minutes of the meetings, were found recklessly kept.

As with any large project, opponents of the enterprise, the most active among whom were the owners of the water right leases, rebelled actively and agitated the whole system.

(One rather large problem was that the "electric mule" just went too fast. The speed of this apparatus tended to pull the canal boat so fast that it simply pushed the water to the edge of the canal and caused the waves to destroy the towpath on which the rails were installed. Another factor was that the excessive speed caused many of the boats to drag the bottom of the passageway.)

With much adieu, the company dissolved and the rails, ties and other equipment disappeared from the banks of the canal.

An article inserted into **The Western Star** in November 1905, referred to the fall of the "electric mule." It reported the tearing up of the tracks and poles after a strenuous running of the gauntlet in the courts, legislature and public opinion.

Tearing up of the tracks and the court fees ran the cost up to $30,000. Mr. Harry Probasco, from Cincinnati, announced the sale of whatever property it held to satisfy its creditors and repay in part the stockholders.

Bond holders of the company resided principally in Cincinnati and Cleveland. A report stated they had sunk $2,000,000 in the project; it was thought that the final settlement will give them from five to ten cents on the dollar.

Felix J. Koch, a resident of Cincinnati, took a ride on the electric mule in 1903. His description of the operation in Cincinnati is as such:

"At that time there were seven electric mules, or motor trucks, in service. These motor trucks were fourteen feet long and were equipped with twin motors equal to eighty mule power.

"Retaining walls of stone were built along the canal in the city, tracks were laid and electric poles with the wires were put up. `Turning bridges' were erected for the `electric mule' at Twelfth Street and Hartwell, and a large headquarters building was erected on the canal between Walnut and Main streets. Construction costs were reported to have exceeded a million and a half.

"On the trip that I made our boat was pulled up the canal at the normal rate of three to four miles an hour. As we reached the suburbs I saw several women working in truck gardens and wearing wooden shoes!"

TREATY OF GREENVILLE EXPANDED THE EARLY UNITED STATES.

I have made mention from time to time the Battle of Fallen Timbers, The Treaty of Greenville, and the Northwest Territory. These three subjects all have one thing in common: the expansion of the geographical United States.

The result of the combination of the three meant the carving out and annexation of Ohio, Michigan, Indiana, Illinois, Wisconsin and Minnesota (the portion east of the Mississippi River) to the United States. The original flag of thirteen stars was changed to the flag of the United States. The success of the Revolutionary War was then assured bringing forth the birth of a new republic.

For 40 years the struggle with the Indians for new lands west of the Alleghenies took precedence over all other issues. George Washington had sent several of his generals, Gen. Bowman, Gen. Clark, Gen. Harmar, and Gen. St. Clair to quell the Indians, but only Anthony Wayne could make a final settlement with them.

His defeat of the Indians at the Battle of Fallen Timbers on August 20, 1794, was a stepping stone for some type of permanent peace.

The actual Treaty of Greenville was signed August 3, 1795, at what is now Greenville, Ohio. The tribes under the Indian leaders Little Turtle, Tahre and Black Hoof had been defeated. Little Turtle, after the Battle of Fallen Timbers, declared that General Wayne "never sleeps; night and day are alike to him."

George Washington knew that the expansion of the original thirteen colonies depended upon defeat and ultimate peace with the Indians. He also knew that the salvation of his plans and the plans of those who had secured their name on the Declaration of Independence, rested entirely on the banishing of all French and British interests in the Northwest Territory.

To do this the colonies resorted to bribery and tempting promises to secure the Indians as allies.

Washington had complete faith in Anthony Wayne and news that peace had been secured was embraced by him and all the colonies.

It was the signing of the treaty that stopped violations of the Paris Treaty of 1783, and forced the British to surrender territory held against the terms of that pact. It was the most momentous event in American history since Cornwallis' surrender.

What if General Wayne had not won his campaign against the Indians? What would be the boundary lines for the United States?

If the British had secured this territory, for which they continued to contest in the face of the Treaty of Paris assigning it to the colonies, the growth of the republic of the United States, as we now have it might have been stopped at the Ohio River.

It would have meant a United States bounded on the east by the Atlantic Ocean, on the north by the Ohio River, and on the west by the Mississippi River, from its junction with the Ohio, southward.

The French, at the time the Treaty of Greenville was signed, owned Louisiana, thus probably retaining that ownership. Great Britain would have had province over the Great Lakes and all that territory including what is now Ohio, Michigan, Indiana, Illinois, Wisconsin and Minnesota.

All the property west of the Mississippi would have been a vast wasteland. With the continuing battle involving the original 13 states, Great Britain and France, the new Treaty averted all possibility of war.

The Ordinance of 1787 was the law that governed the new territory gained by the peace treaty. It was the model for future territorial governments.

This was the third most important document ever written, next to the Declaration of Independence and the Constitution.

In the initial stage the Northwest Territory was ruled by a governor, secretary, and three judges, all appointed by Congress. When the population reached 5,000 free adult males the territory was permitted an elected legislature and a nonvoting representative to Congress.

When the population reached 60,000 a constitutional convention could be summoned and draw up a State constitution. The Ordinance also included a Bill of Rights, promising freedom of worship, the right to a jury trial, and the protection of habeas corpus. Last, but not least, the Ordinance prohibited slavery in the Northwest Territory.

SOUTHWESTERN OHIO TOBACCO GROWERS SAW SOME TOUGH TIMES

We have all heard and possibly discussed the controversy over the tobacco industry and its growing trend toward oblivion. However, rather than getting involved in the politics of the subject, we shall concentrate on the founding and the growing of the product in the Miami Valley.

Tobacco was originally a product of the tropics. Seed was transported to the North American continent by the different Indian tribes. Tobacco was looked upon by the early tribes as a special gift from the Great Spirit.

It was crushed into powder, and in time of drought, scattered to the winds that the Almighty should send them rain. The tribal medicinal trait was that it was taken for periods of pain, sorrow, happiness and gratitude.

A general plan or method of planting tobacco by the tribes was that they planted the seed in the soil of their gardens which were situated near the wigwams. The area covered was from one hundred to two hundred square feet.

When the plants matured, leaves were stripped from the stalks and placed in the sun to dry. After the drying process, the leaves were crumbled together and used for pipe tobacco.

Tobacco was first observed by the early colonist upon their arrival in Virginia. Cultivation of tobacco by the white settlers soon lent to their social, economic and political development.

It appears that growing of cigar leaf in Ohio dates back to 1797, but only small quantities were grown by the settlers for their own use.

About the year 1838, a Mr. Pomeroy brought from his home State of Connecticut to Montgomery County some tobacco seed.

He immediately experimented with his new seed in the vicinity of Hole's Creek, near Centerville. So successful was his achievement that the cultivation of tobacco was gradually adopted by his neighbors.

Until 1850 the crop was confined to Montgomery County, however, in that year it was introduced into Greene County (some farmers in the neighborhood of Alpha began to grow it), and in other surrounding counties such as Warren, Preble, Miami, etc. A small quantity was raised in Butler County in Dick's Creek valley.

The census for the year 1850 reported 2590 pounds for Butler County, 1460 pounds for Clinton County, 135 pounds for Champaign County, 7132 pounds for Darke County, 2500 pounds for Miami County, 50 pounds for Preble County, and 2601 pounds for Warren County.

Montgomery County, for the same year, reported 195,971 pounds, or about 500 cases, which indicated that tobacco had become a staple crop in this district.

The total crop grown in the Miami Valley in 1850 and 1851 amounted to about 2000 cases, and in succeeding years the production had risen to 4000 cases. All the crops were marketed in New York.

Prices in 1850 brought from 9 to 10 cents a pound, but the harvest in 1851 averaged only 4 1/2 cents a pound.

Growing of tobacco in this time period is reported to have been grown on the soils in the river or stream bottoms. There was no effort to grow a fine quality of leaf, the main object being to produce a large yield, which was used mostly for binders and wrappers for cheap cigars.

Ultimately the dealers demanded a more finer leaf and the river bottom lands were eventually given up as producers of tobacco. Consequently, the rolling uplands were used to a large extent for growing the famous cigar filler.

Early Ohio tobacco growers were inferior in their knowledge of curing their crop. They experienced great losses every year due to damage from mold and the pole rot. The reasons were attributed to poor construction of the curing sheds and the lack of sufficient barn room at harvest time.

Nature seemed to have done its job by supplying a suitable climate, excellent ground conditions, a proper growing season, but, due to the farmer's haste in these early times, handling led to insufficient production.

Until 1870 seed leaf variety was about the only kind grown in the Miami Valley. However, some Yara seed was sent to the valley, which, owing to the properties of the soil and condition of the climate, developed into a variety known as Dutch tobacco.

In 1876, a Wisconsin grower secured seed from Havanna and after meeting with success in growing it, sent some seed to a Mr. Zimmer of Miamisburg, who distributed it amongst the growers of the vicinity. Cultivation was successful and Zimmer Spanish was at the time one of the leading varieties.

The crop of 1906, which was of an inferior quality, managed to sell at high prices. At that time the field was flooded with buyers, they being rated as good to poor. Appearance of the crop was one of excellence, but when housed it contracted many diseases, shed burn, black rot, etc.

The buyer was not pleased with what he had

bought; diseases and handling were the direct culprits.

The writer never worked in the tobacco fields, but I can still remember the different locations in which they existed. I'm sure many of the readers can relate to their own growing or working experiences in the yellow fields.

AUTOMOBILES OF YESTERYEAR STILL INTRIGUE

As we gaze at the sleek automobile of today, we tend to forget that they were once looked upon as a mere trial of man's ingenuity. From the single cylinder engine to the massive horsepower of today's racing cars, they are possibly the single-most accomplished mechanical invention of the times.

What has happened since the invention of the horseless carriage? Absolutely nothing, except the greatest change in societal patterns that has ever been witnessed by mankind.

Say goodbye to the reliable old livery stables! Farewell to the sleek, well-fed horses! Hard times concerning the livelihood of the stable owners was now approaching.

How far have we really come? In the latter part of the Sixteenth Century, Leonardo Da Vinci was the first to publicly consider the idea of a self-propelled vehicle.

In April 1740, a Frenchman demonstrated in Paris a contraption in the form of a carriage propelled by a large clock-work engine.

It was suggested in 1760 that by mounting small windmills on a cart-like vehicle, the power could be converted to wind springs that would move the road wheels.

As we wander into the early part of this century, we see automobile agencies springing up in all parts of the State. Lebanon's first agency, and possibly one of the first in this part of the State, was the firm of Kilpatrick-French Company.

Such a prosperous business they had, that while other new agencies were just being founded, their's was flourishing, selling as many as four distinct brands of cars at one time.

I think it only fair to mention that one of the first automobiles in the State was built by this writer's great-great uncle, Richard Turner.

Turner, from Marysville, Ohio, built his automobile in 1900.

He was a successful steel bridge-builder from Union County and he conceived the idea of building a gasoline engine driven vehicle that would more easily move heavy timber to bridge sites than a horse-drawn wagon.

Turner made all the mechanical parts for the motorcar himself, including the engine, which was a two-cylinder water-cooled design.

It was cranked from the right side, just below the step-board. The wooden body was made by an employee.

The transmission is planetary, similar to that used in the Model T Ford.

The car, ultimately called the "Turner Car," was driven for about ten years, and is presently housed in the Marysville Museum.

In the beginning no license plates nor title were required for the auto. It was much like selling or buying a cow or pig, or a farm implement.

In 1907, an automobile division of the Secretary of State was established; it is now called the Bureau of Motor Vehicles. A license fee was set up through registrations which called for a $3.00 fee for electric cars and a $5.00 fee for gasoline cars.

Roads of travel at this time were mere mud holes, causing many horseless carriages to come and go.

Some names of the early autos were the Queen, the Wayne, the Silent Northern, and the White Steamer.

In the beginning, a top speed of fifteen miles per hour was an astounding feat for the new contraption. One exception is given by the air-cooled Logan, which was clocked on the Warren County Fairgrounds race track at a dazzling speed of sixty miles per hour.

Arrival of the two-cylinder machines was approaching in the year 1905 around Lebanon. Buicks were equipped with this larger engine as well as the Ford Model N, which preceded its more superior cousin, the Model T.

John Harding, of South Lebanon corn-canning fame, was one of the first owners of the automobile in the County. Sparking around the County in his new two-cylinder 1905 Queen, he created a sensation unequaled in that time.

Harding's auto cost approximately $800 in 1905. As time passed, and auto production increased, the mechanical machine came down in price. In 1920, the Ford Roadster cost $550, or 20 cents per pound; in 1925 it cost $260.

Similar decreases in prices were seen in the Ford Touring car. In 1920, it cost $575, and in 1925 it cost $290, etc.

I guess one might say that Henry Ford, and his turn around involving the working man and the $5.00 work day in 1909, created more money in the pockets of the family man, which in turn allowed them to buy their own product.

HARRY E. PENCE: LOCAL AUTOMOTIVE PIONEER

Some time ago the writer portrayed in this column (April 9, 1995), Lincoln Beachy, an aviation pioneer from Lebanon, and his part in the advancement of the flying machine. This week we shall recount the adventures of an automobile pioneer from Springboro.

The Pence family has long been known as one of the first settlers in the county, with descendants by the multitude. At this time, I shall now attempt to write a segment on the life of Harry E. Pence, automotive pioneer.

Harry Pence was born in Springboro, Ohio, the son of Charles N. Pence, a prosperous farmer. At the age of 18, at the invitation of his uncle, John Wesley Pence, he traveled to Minneapolis, Minnesota, home of the latter.

John Wesley was prominently identified with the early growth of Minneapolis, his operations including railroad and mining corporations, along with banking and real estate enterprises.

He became so engrossed in his businesses that his health began to fail. He decided that a trip abroad would result in a cure and he invited Harry to accompany him.

They spent five years on a leisurely trip together and made a study of Europe and the Orient.

Returning to Minneapolis, young Harry made a decision to go into business. He foresaw a future in the transportation of commodities between the North and the South on the Mississippi River.

With capital behind him, he purchased six rather large steamboats for both freight and passenger service, which he operated between St. Louis and New Orleans during the winter months. He also ran a packet line between Taylors Falls and Stillwater during the summer months.

Two years involvement in this venture demonstrated to him that returns were too small for larger investments. He sold out and returned to Minneapolis where he became a member of the Board of Trade as a grain commissioner.

Just about the turn of the Twentieth Century, automobiles were beginning to appear. They were at first looked upon as mere experiments, such as was the first flying machine.

In June 1902, Pence attended an automobile race which was run from Minneapolis to Lake Minneapolis and back. Apparently this created a stir in him, and consequently he began to look upon this as a possible new venture.

He had never even owned an automobile when in 1903 he decided to go into the business of dealing in the horseless carriage.

He first made a tour of the cities in which they were being manufactured. He carefully made a study of their construction and decided on the Cadillac made at Detroit. He thought this machine was best adapted for good service and durability.

That year he opened up the second dealership in the city of Minneapolis, handling several makes of automobiles.

The first year he sold 83 motor cars. His business so expanded that afterward he had to move into a larger building into which he made an investment of $40,000.

This building at the time was considered by the public as a reckless venture, and that it could later be made into a store or restaurant. They were proved wrong.

In 1905, Pence thought the motor car should have a two-cylinder engine. He discussed the idea with the Cadillac people and they declined the idea. The Cadillac company's faith in the one-cylinder engine was one of conjecture for the future.

Not to be defeated in his idea of a larger engine, he began to look for a manufacturer that would conform to his idea. He succeeded in bringing the makers of the Buick machine, who had just started out in an insignificant way in Jackson, Michigan, around to his idea.

The Buick company agreed that a larger engine would be feasible and began building them on an extensive scale. Pence ultimately took up this new dealership and sales skyrocketed. His company sold at this time 29 percent of all Buicks that were manufactured. (The Cadillac company started the sale of two-cylinder automobiles within two years.)

He was possibly the first to recognize the fact that an increase in cylinder capacity meant more power and more speed.

Harry Pence popularized the automobile through the introduction of its use for business purposes, a service that cannot be measured.

With his endless energy, and his capacity for dealing with large projects, he started a trend that most certainly advanced the automobile industry to what it is today.

Again, a citizen of the County of Warren contributed much toward the evolving of the greatest country on Earth.

HISTORIAN DISCUSSES SEVERAL HISTORY TIDBITS

War Roads

The first war road which led from Old Chillicothe into Kentucky is believed to have been one which passed down the east side of the Little Miami River to a point about a mile below the intersection of Caesar's Creek, then crossing the river at what is known as "fish pot ford."

The ford was possibly called "fish pot" because John Sublett, who was known for his devices for catching fish, used a contrivance consisting of a stone net which in turn was called a fish pot.

The ford was located at the head of a ripple about a mile below his home. The ford, however, existed long before the first white settlement in the country.

It is believed that an Indian trail from Old Chillicothe (Old Town, located in Greene County), to the Ohio River crossed the Little Miami at this location. The war road passed through Warren and Hamilton counties to the site of Fort Washington (Cincinnati) where it crossed the Ohio.

The first military expedition against the Indians at Old Chillicothe that used this trail was Colonel John Bowman in July, 1779. A version of the battle was taken from **The People's Express**, Xenia, Ohio, dated November 21, 1826. It says:

"THE BATTLE OF OLDTOWN. In the month of May, 1779, Col. John Bowman, with 160 men, marched against the Indian town called Chillicothe, situated about 60 miles from the mouth of the Little Miami and near the head of that river.

"The party rendezvoused at the mouth of the Licking, and on the second night got in sight of the town undiscovered. It was determined to wait until day-light in the morning before they would make the attack, but by the imprudence of some of the men, whose curiosity exceeded their judgment, the party were discovered by the Indians before the officers and men had arrived at the several positions assigned them.

"As soon as the alarm was given a fire commenced on both sides & was kept up, whilst the women & children were seen running from cabin to cabin in the greatest confusion, and collecting in the most central and strongest.

"At clear day-light it was found that Bowman's men were from 70 to 100 yards from the cabins, in which the Indians had collected, and which it appeared they intended to defend. Having no other arms than rifles and tomahawk, it was thought imprudent to attempt to storm strong cabins well defended by expert warriors, in consequence of the warriors collecting a few cabins contiguous to each other, the remainder of the town was left unprotected; therefore, whilst a fire was kept up at the port-holes, which engaged the attention of those within, fire was set to 30 or 40 cabins, which were consumed, and a considerable quantity of property, consisting principally of kettles and blankets, were taken from those cabins. In searching the woods near the town, 130 horses were collected.

"About 10 o'clock, Bowman and his party commenced their march homeward, after having nine men killed. What loss the Indians sustained was never known, except their principal chief, Black Fish, who was wounded through the knee, and died of the wound. Black Fish proposed to surrender, being confident that his wound was dangerous, and believing that there were among the white people surgeons that could cure him; but that none amongst his own people could do it.

"The party had not marched more than 8 or 10 miles on their return, before the Indians appeared in considerable force in their rear, & began to press hard on that quarter. Bowman selected his ground and formed his men in a square; but the Indians declined a close engagement, and only keeping up a scattering fire, it was soon discovered that their object was only to retard their march, until they could procure reinforcements from the neighboring villages.

"As soon as a strong position was taken by

Col. Bowman, the Indians retired, and he resumed the line of march, when his rear was again attacked. Col. Bowman again formed for battle, again the Indians retired, and the scene was acted over several times; at length, John Bulger, James Harrod, and George Michael Bedinger, with about 100 more mounted on horseback, rushed on the Indian ranks and dispersed them in every direction; after which the Indians abandoned the pursuit.

"Bowman crossed the Ohio, at the mouth of the Little Miami, and after crossing the men dispersed to their several homes. Colonel Bowman had nine men killed, and one wounded. The loss sustained by the Indians was never ascertained, except the death of Black Fish."

A "possible" location of the retreat of Colonel Bowman's army and the battle is given by one source as taking place about five miles, a little to the east and north of Waynesville and near the Bellbrook and Waynesville road. Several tomahawks were found in this area, it being in Greene County.

Colonel Bowman's route is given as such: From Fort Washington the trail goes north over the Dixie Highway, Old U.S. 25 to Sharonville; thence, on U.S. 42 through Lebanon, crossing over to the east side of the Little Miami River and following it thru Waynesville, Spring Valley to Xenia, and then on U.S. 68; three miles north to Old Town (Old Chillicothe).

Gen. George Rogers Clark

The second military expedition through Warren County was made by Colonel George Rogers Clark with 100 regulars and 1,000 Kentucky volunteers. They crossed the Ohio River on August 1, 1780. The next day the army started on their way to the Shawnee Indian town of Old Chillicothe. This road was very similar to the one Colonel Bowman took the previous year.

On August 6th, the army reached Old Chillicothe and found a complete obliteration of the town. Apparently an alarm had been sounded that the angry Kentuckians were moving on them. The

Indians had taken all their possessions and proceeded to burn their village.

The town was never rebuilt. This village was considered the central town of the Shawnees west of the Scioto.

On August 8th, Colonel Clark and his army then proceeded to the Shawnee Indian village on the Mad River called Pickaway (Piqua).

This town was completely destroyed by Clark and his avengers. Before the destruction, the Indians fought a vicious battle in defending their homes. Twenty whites were killed.

It has been estimated that approximately five hundred acres of corn and edible vegetables were destroyed in the destruction of the two villages.

On August 10th, Clark and his army started the march home.

They camped at Old Chillicothe that night and soon the army marched back toward Fort Washington. At the mouth of the Licking River, the army was released and each man was free to his own doing.

With his triumph over the Shawnees in 1780, Colonel Clark was again called upon to quell the uprising Indians in 1782. Because of the aiding and murder of the whites in Kentucky, Clark's assignment was to destroy the Indian towns on the Great Miami River.

Clark, with his 1050 riflemen, an estimated number, left the Cincinnati area on November 4, 1782, and reached the Indian towns on the 10th.

(There is probability that this army followed the old Bowman and Clark trail for about two days, diverged from it and passed west of Lebanon, and crossed Mad River near Dayton, possibly using present S.R. 48.)

The principal target for Clark's army on the Great Miami River was Lower Piqua and Upper Piqua. Lower Piqua is the present site of Piqua and upper Piqua was about three miles north.

Viewing the more superior army, the red men fled to the woods, but not without ten killed and seven prisoners taken. Clark suffered only two casualties, one being killed and one wounded.

The soldiers continued to burn and destroy the complete village. A majority of the corn and provisions were destroyed by the ensuing army. The Indians never again congregated a large force to intimidate the Kentuckians after this defeat, although small raiding parties were still to invade and ravage the southern settlers.

Gen. Josiah Harmar

Warren County had yet another leading military man to traverse its lands. General Josiah Harmar was the third Commander-in-Chief of the United States army, Washington being the first and Henry Knox the second. Lieutenant Colonel Harmar was brevetted Brigadier General in 1787.

At the time of Washington's inauguration there was in the United States army only one regiment of infantry, consisting of eight companies and one battalion of artillery consisting of four companies. This was the full strength of the defense of the United States.

Treaties were continually being broken by the Indians and some sort of retaliation was being discussed.

The Northwest Territory needed a station or fort in which to centralize its operations.

Fort Washington was built on the present location of Cincinnati in 1789, this being a very important location for the harboring of the settlers who were continually being harassed by the Redman. The fort was also centralized and an ideal location, between the Miami Rivers, to deal with the defiant Indians.

General Harmar's army consisted of 1,453 men, those being regular army and militia from Kentucky and Pennsylvania.

The militia had been drafted, and many who wanted no part in the proceedings hired substitutes. Young boys and old men were among the ones employed. These paid recruits presented a problem as to how to deal with them. The regulars looked upon the militia with scorn and refused to deal with them.

The supplies were much more in accord than the previous armies. Cannons on wheels were more in style than General Clark's 1780 venture of carrying one cannon on a pack-horse. Fresh beef was also the plan of General Harmar.

Beef cattle were driven along on this expedition to allow the men to have fresh meat. The earlier settlers of Wayne Township reported wild cattle were found grazing in the woods, supposedly from General Harmar's army.

The junction of the St. Joseph's and St. Mary's Rivers, where the Maumee River begins (location of Fort Wayne, Indiana), was to be the point of contact. The Indian settlements in this area were to be destroyed.

General Harmar selected the route best suited, according to his guides, and the shortest. The following was taken from **The Western Star**, dated June 8, 1908. The route was as follows:

"The course of the army from Fort Washington was directly up the Mount Auburn hill. Thence the direction was generally north east to Old Chillicothe. The first day, seven miles to a branch of Millcreek. The second day, eight miles to another branch of Millcreek.

"The third day, fifteen miles, and says Captain John Armstrong's journal, encamped in a rich and extensive bottom of Muddy Creek, one mile from Colonel Hardin's camp and halted at Turtlecreek, about ten yards wide, where we were joined by Colonel Hardin's command.

"Here the line of march was formed two miles.

"The next morning at half past nine the army moved in a northeast direction about eight miles and at 3 o'clock crossed the Little Miami and moved up that river about a mile to Caesar's Creek and there encamped, the day's march being nine miles.

"On October 5 [1790], the army passed Old Chillicothe and re-crossed the Little Miami. [Simon Kenton was a Captain and a scout on this trip. Daniel Boone was also a scout. The place of encampment was about two miles up Caesar's Creek from the mouth of the Little Miami, close to the present dam area.]

"On October 7, the army crossed Mad River and moving northwestwardly crossed the Great Miami on the 10th.

"The Indian towns were reached on the 15th, but the redmen had all disappeared. The General ordered the Indian towns at the head of the Maumee, of which there were six or seven, to be burnt the orchard trees of which there were a great number, to be girdled and the property of the Indians of every description, including 20,000 bushels of corn, to be destroyed.

"Four days were spent in this work of destruction. This was, in fact, the main purpose of the expedition to destroy the enemy's means of subsistence and thus prevent active campaign against the white settlements."

This was an accomplishment without battle. However, some of the officers wanted bloodshed.

General Harmar sent three detachments to find the Indians and were completely surprised.

Being concealed in the high brush, the Indians brought complete disaster to the army. The militia, at the first attack, turned about and ran.

A loss of several officers and men was the result of this massacre. General Harmar's army started its homeward march with only a few Indian reprisals.

The great Indian chief, Little Turtle, had won a decisive victory.

BULLSKIN TRACE EXISTED THROUGH WARREN COUNTY

There is an old trace called the Bullskin Trace which skirts the eastern portion of Warren County. This writer had tried for some time to find its exact location. However, by knocking on doors and asking questions, I located an abstract on the Trace which was written by Norma Lewis and Richard Scamyhorn.

These two energetic people explored the trace from its beginning on the Ohio River to the area of Xenia. I shall now take from this abstract and also from the book "Old Chillicothe," written by William A. Galloway.

The term "Trace" was defined by Senator Thomas H. Benton, son-in-law of John C. Fremont, "the pathfinder," in a speech he delivered to the Senate. He says:

"There is a class of scientific engineers older than the schools...they are the wild animals which traverse the forests, not by compass, but by instinct which leads them always the right way to the lowest mountain passes...and the shortest route between two distant points. The Indian first, then the hunter follows this same trail. After that, it becomes the wagon-road of the immigrant, and lastly, the railroad of the scientific man."

In their quest for a new home by the early adventurers in the Northwest Territory, the Bullskin Trace became an artery for these early pioneers. These narrow path-like trails were followed by every type adventurer and homeseeker.

The steady increase of the population allowed the paths to become a trail, a road, a stage road, and a post road for the delivery of the mail.

Next came the toll-pike, the free turnpike, and finally the Interstate system.

The Treaty of Peace with the Indians at Greenville in 1795, opened up a whole new country in which to explore.

The Bullskin Trace was an essential part of the prehistoric trails which led through Ohio. It extended from the old town of Rural (founded in 1845 and later destroyed by the flood of 1913), located on St. Rt. 133, near the Ohio River in Clermont County.

The entire course wound its way through Ohio to its destination of Detroit, Michigan.

Its southern extension was used heavily as a trail following the high ridges along Locust Creek to the Great Salt Licks, located along the Licking River in Kentucky.

The Great Salt Licks was a northern branch which was connected to the Great War Road that ran south through the Cumberland Gap, and the Scioto Trail which extended southwest from Portsmouth, Ohio.

The name Bullskin was taken from a creek by that name in Clermont County.

A log house in this region was known as Davenport's Meeting House where Thomas Scott, later Judge Thomas Scott of Ohio's Supreme Court, and Edward Tiffin, later first Governor of Ohio, used to preach. The name Bullskin can possibly be linked to this large Methodist migration from western Maryland.

Many prehistoric sites that parallel the trace is certain evidence that it was in use many centuries before the arrival of the white man.

At the mouth of Bullskin Creek is an archaeological site composed of late archaic pre-pottery artifacts dating around 4000 BC to 1000 BC. This site is on the National Register of Historic places.

The line of the Trace is dotted with archaeological finds. The most prevalent exploration is in the Caesar's Creek Reservoir region.

Many names have been associated with the Bullskin Trace such as: the Augusta and Round Bottom Road, the Miami Warrior Trail, Corduroy Road, Detroit Highway, and Xenia State Road.

The Xenia State Road was enacted by the First Ohio Legislature to be selected as an official road the entire length from the Ohio River to Detroit, Michigan.

It was designated a public highway February 4, 1807, being one of the first officially recognized state highways in Ohio.

The Bullskin Trace had an extension which led from Harveysburg to Waynesville. General Charles Scott and his army, led by the Indian scout William Smalley, traveled this trail and occupied a camp at a little creek called Camp Run, which was a mile south of Waynesville.

The nearby hills protected it from enemy approach. Water was found in abundance for the men and the animals at a nearby spring. Smalley is said to have rested his command a day and a night, by which time all stragglers had reached camp.

Smalley's next point of travel was to Fort Jefferson which is located near Greenville. This "van" had already driven the southern Shawnees of the Little Miami country north to points where they were massing their forces for battle.

It has always been rumored that Anthony Wayne encamped in the Waynesville location, but no proof has been found. However, Waynesville and Wayne Township were named for this occasion.

Beer's 1882 Histories of Warren and Clinton County make many mentions of the Trace synonymous with the land owners.

In 1787, George Washington bought four surveys of land which were located in Clermont County on the Bullskin Trace, this acreage totaling 3,051.

The War of 1812 was primarily fought in the area of the Great Lakes. As was stated earlier, the enactment of the Legislature to officially make the Xenia State Road a highway, made an open and usable roadway, from the Ohio River north to Detroit, a military necessity.

The first monies that were to be used for its improvement was $700.00 which was obtained from the sale of public lands. The roadway was cleared to a width of 20 feet. The right-of-way varied from 60 to 66 feet. Logs were laid side-by-side which formed corduroy roads. Frequently these logs were left in place for the next road construction.

It was fortunate that the road was ready when the conflict came, for as soon as the War of 1812 was declared, Perry's fleet on Lake Erie had to be supplied with provisions and ammunition.

Isaac Blanchard, of Edenton, took a contract to furnish these supplies, which were boated down the Ohio River to the mouth of Bullskin Creek.

From there his caravan of fifteen wagons bumped over the new corduroy road on its way to Sandusky. Blanchard hauled supplies on the Bullskin Trace nearly two years.

On our northern journey, from the junction of the Ohio River and Bullskin Creek, the Trace crosses S.R. 52, known by the early settlers as the Atlantic Pacific Highway, the Iroquois Trail, Grants Road, or the Road from Cincinnati to Marietta, depending on the period of time.

An alignment similar to the present St. Rt. 133 intersected a trail at present-day Stringtown, which is now Rt. 222, originating at Chilo. The original Trace mainly follows present-day Rt. 133 through Felicity, Bethel and Williamsburg in Clermont County.

North of Williamsburg, and about one mile east of Monterey in Jackson Township, the Trace intersects S.R. 50.

The Trace then passed Van Camp's corner, known historically as Slab's Camp. It then passes through Edenton. Here, at the intersection of Route 727 and Route 133, a stone memorial was placed by the Daughter's of the American Revolution at a dedication ceremony on Labor Day, 1927.

It then travels north where it crosses Rt. 28 near Blanchester. The Trace proceeded north and crossed over a hill west of Todd's Ford, just to the west of Clarksville.

Proceeding in a northern direction, it then crossed Springhill Road into Clinton County and connected with George Road.

It then entered Warren County and followed the Harveysburg Road to the intersection of Brooks Road, where it followed it for about a quarter of a mile to the west.

It then turned north and crossed over St. Rt. 73 at Hatton's Hill, where the parking lot of the Ohio Renaissance is located. Following a straight northerly direction, it then intersected with Ward Road and ran to St. Rt. 380, passing through where New Burlington was once located.

Following this route it then intersected with U.S. 68 at Xenia and proceeded north through the towns of Yellow Springs, Springfield, Urbana, West Liberty, Bellfontaine, Kenton, Findlay, Bowling Green and Perrysburg.

The Trace branched in the area of Perrysburg; the east branch went directly to Perrysburg and then north along the west side of Lake Erie to Detroit. The west branch crossed the Maumee to Fort Miami, which was built by the British in the spring of 1794, about two miles below the lowest rapids.

Index

----, Auntie Fan 89 Frank 193
ABBOTT, O M 345
ACHTERMAN, Miriam 52
ADAMS, Elva 120 John Q 215 John Quincy 227 Willie 51
ADDISON, 97
ADES, McRooks 192
AIKEN, Gwendolyn 268
ALFORD, 364 Mrs 364
ALFRED, Mr 116
ALLEN, Abram 7 David 7 Estel 51 Jackson 109 Kenneth 51
ANDERSON, Benjamin 70 Col 200 Kinny 114 Richard 200
APPLEYARD, Mr 155
ARCHER, 112
ARMITAGE, Mark 88
ARMOUR, Donald 50
ARMSTRONG, John 150 397
ARTHUR, Albert 43
ASHMEAD, Jacob 88 Richard 88
AUTRY, Gene 10
AYERS, Pollyana 51
BAALS, S S 43
BACHMAN, Charles 62
BACKUS, Eliza 132
BAILEY, Emmor Jr 50
BAILY, 40 Francis 6
BAIRD, 114 Andrew 116 John 76 Samuel 76
BALDERSTONE, L Ray 362
BALDWIN, Michael 211 Thomas 259
BALLARD, Silas 133
BANES, Evan 69
BANGHAM, Carl S 345
BARKALOW, 113 William 114
BARNES, Albert 53
BARNHART, 74
BARR, Albert W 117
BASORE, Mr 117 William 117
BATE, George 185
BATEMAN, Jacob 7
BATES, Evelyn 53 George 193 Issachar 314 316
BAUM, Martin 231
BAYLESS, Rachel M B 208
BAYNTON, 162
BEACHY, Lincoln 259-261 389 Prof 259 Thomas 259
BEADLE, 2
BEAUREGARD, Gen 195
BECK, Samuel 74
BEDELL, 2
BEDINGER, Daniel 8 George Michael 394
BEDLE, 2 William 3
BEECHER, Henry Ward 341
BEEDLE, 2-3 Esther 5 Francis 2 4 309 James 5 John 5 Lydia 5 Mary 5 Mr 68 Phebe 5 Susannah 5 William 2 5 68
BEER, 2 86 88 401
BEGLEY, Mary E 53
BELL, John 369
BELLINI, 361 Laura 361 Laura Woolwine 341
BELSFORD, John 104
BENHAM, Robert 20
BENNETT, A S 350 Amos 242
BENNINGTON, Patricia 52
BENTON, Thomas H 399
BERCAW, Emma May 53
BEST, T 355 Thomas 355
BIGGER, John 20
BIGGS, Zachens 150
BIGHAM, John 127
BILLINGS, Josh 358
BINKLEY, S H 282-283
BIRD, Elizabeth 50
BLAIR, 344 Mrs Edward 345
BLANCHARD, Isaac 401

BLICKENSDERFER, Mildred 311
BLOSS, Thomas J 185
BLOSSER, C E 282
BLOSSOM, C E 282
BLUSS, Fred 160
BOAKE, Robert 244
BOLANDER, George 130
BOLMER, Percy 120
BONE, Frank 134 James H 184
  Kathryn 18
BOONE, Daniel 295 397
BOOTHBY, Timothy 15
BORDEN, John 39
BOUDINOT, Dr 40 Elias 40
BOUQUET, Gen 199
BOWMAN, 393 Col 394 Gen 382
  John 199 296 392 Michael 129
BOWYER, James 133 Levi 129
  Stephen 127 129
BOXWELL, Alexander 56 Mr 57
BOYNTON, Col 184-185 H V N 182
  Maj 192
BRADBURY, John 89
BRADDOCK, Gen 198
BRAGG, Braxton 182
BRANDENBURG, Abe 119 H 119
BRANDON, Frank 155-156 Mr 155
BRANT, Albert 47
BRECKENRIDGE, 183 John C 369
BRENNER, Rachel 54
BREWSTER, 124
BRIGODE, Ace 138
BRINKER, Riley 110
BROOKS, Mary 235
BROWN, Allen 170 245 Asher 245
  David 86 Eda 52 Elizabeth 234
  Ethan 232 Hiram 206 Ignatius 20
  86 205 John 245 Karl M 43 Mr
  246 248 Ruth 51 Seth W 375 T
  T 127
BROWNING, Elizabeth 206
BRUBAKER, 160
BRUIN, Judge 255
BUCHANAN, 179
BUCKLES, James 108 John 108
  Robert 108 William 108
BUDD, Joseph L 182 184 Maj 185

BUELL, 251 Don Carlos 181 Gen
  182 277
BUFORD, Abraham 93
BULGER, John 394
BULLER, Isaac 320 Mr 320 Prophet
  320-321
BURGERS, Moses 54
BURGESS, Elizabeth 54
BURNET, G W 231 Jacob 3 13 22
  230 Judge 186 329 Mr 230 232
  Rachel 220-221
BURNSIDE, Gen 187
BURR, Peter 20 Quartermaster 190
BURROUGHS, William W 139
BURSK, Ole Josie 132
BURSON, David S 100
BUTLER, Gen 200 Richard 200
BUTTERWORTH, Ann 208
  Benjamin 207 267 Caroline 208
  Emma 208 Henry 209 Henry T 7
  Henry Thomas 9 207-208 Isaac
  W 208 Jane W 208 Mary 208 Mr
  9 207-209 Nancy 9 208 Rachel
  207 Rachel M 208
BUZZARD, Elizabeth 50
CADWALLADER, A 40
CADY, Elizabeth 358
CAIN, Samuel 311
CALDWELL, 110
CALVIN, S 76
CAMPBELL, Adam 33 Alexander
  329
CANBY, Hannah 223 Joseph 354
CAREY, 110 Ralph H 345 Samuel
  118
CARLISLE, George 115 Mr 116
CARNEY, W H 78
CARR, Job 7
CHAMBERLAIN, 114
CHANDLER, 39 Aaron 246
CHASE, Mr 116
CHURCH, John 312
CLAP, John 129
CLARK, Betty 52 Billy 52 Brazilla
  137 Brazilla 127 129 Col 395
  Cornelius 99 Daniel 304-305
  Elisha 127 129 Gen 200 382 397

CLARK (continued)
　George Rogers 68 199 267 296
　394 John 127
CLAY, Henry 212 256
CLEAVER, Ezekiel 70
CLEMENT, 258 Aurelia 258
　Caroline 258 Caroline Watson
　258 Elizabeth 258 Florence
　Putnam 258 H S 259 Henry S
　258 Joel 258 John B 258 Mr
　256-257 Mrs 370 William H 166
　256 William Henry 256
CLEVELAND, 362
CLEVENGER, 112
CLINE, Frederick 129 Ida 121
CLINGAN, 110
CLINTON, Dewitt 171
CLUSERET, Gen 196
COBURN, James 12
COCHRAN, Jimmie 50
CODDINGTON, Joseph 127
COFFEEN, Goldsmith 61-62
　Thaddeus 63
COLBERT, James 49
COLEMAN, Mike 345 Nathaniel 72
　Washington 72
COLLETT, Joshua 211 354
COLLIER, William 51
COLLINS, John 226
COLUMBUS, 288
COMLEY, 98
CONKLIN, Samuel 62
CONKLING, Edgar 350 Mr 350
CONNER, Clyde Lee 52 John 193
　Neal 193
CONNOR, 193
CONOVER, 114 Benjamin 115
　George 115 Robert 311
COOK, 207 Mr 110 Stephen 110
COOLING, Albert A 139
COON, Sidney 107
COOPER, Daniel C 1 78 229 Mr
　329
COREY, James 74
CORNELL, 112 William 111
CORNWALLIS, 383
CORWIN, Dorothy 51 Ichabod 9 75

CORWIN (continued)
　79 305 323 329-330 Joseph 305
　Mathias 68 Matthias 305 340
　Matthias Jr 339 376 Moses B
　340 Mr 256 R G 7 9 Thomas 8
　37 68 256 305 329 339-340 358
　366
CORY, Elnathan 142 Hannah 128
　262 James 142 Noah 127-128
　Thomas 142
COUDEN, Samuel 88
COWAN, 350
COZAD, John 82 John A 83-85
　John J 83 John Jackson 82-84
　Robert Henry 83-86
CRADDOCK, Will 92
CRAFT, 110 Josiah 111
CRAIG, Alfred S 117 Lew 116
　Samuel 80
CRANE, Absalom 81
CRAWFORD, Alexander 354
CRETORS, Ezekiel 355-356
　George 356 John 356
CRISPEN, Mr 39
CROGAN, George 162
CROSLEGH, 267
CROSLEY, 266-267 270
　Gwendolyn 268 Luken S 267
　Martha 268 Moses 267 Powel III
　268-269 Powel Jr 266 268-270
　Powell Sr 267 Rachel 267 Sr
　268-269 William 267 William J
　267
CROSSLEY, 266 Moses 267
　Rachel Powell 267
CROSSON, Mr 279-281 William 74
　165 177
CROUT, George 328 368 Mr 368
CROW, Elizabeth 50
CRUM, C T 312
CUMMING, Gen 230 232 John N
　230 Uncle John 230-231
CUNNINGHAM, Richard 74
CURTISS, 260
CUSTER, Gen 12
DALTON, Dennis 74
DANFORTH, Emma B 208

DARROW, David 317
DAUGHERTY, Lewis F 184-185
DA VINCI, Leonardo 387
DAVIS, 364 Benjamin 302 Elijah 5 Jake 119 Jefferson 276 John 5 Jonathan 5 317 Lydia 5 Susannah 5 W 119
DAWSON, Ezra 131
DAYTON, Jonathan 2-3 40
DEARDOFF, Joel K 184
DEBORD, Howard 34
DECHANT, 106
DECKER, Raymond 48
DEGRAFF, A 167
DEHAVEN, Peter 111
DENHAM, Obed 14
DENIS, 114
DENNISON, Gov 176 William 366
DENNY, Wm H P 375
DESOTO, 289
DEY, 255 John 254 John E 254 Mr 255-256 Phoebe 254 Sarah 254 William 254
DICKENS, 324
DILATUSH, Frank A 345
DINE, 64 John 63 John C 63 William 63
DINGLER, Isaac 59
DIXON, 297
DOCZY, Ed 16 19
DODDS, Benjamin 127 William S 132
DOOLITTLE, James H 239
DORON, 110
DORSEY, Mr 279-280
DOSTER, 35
DOUGAL, John M 87
DOUGHMAN, Richard 51
DOUGLAS, 368 Frederick 341 Frederick B 153 Mr 153 367 Stephen 369 Stephen A 366-368
DOWNEY, Eli 50
DOWNING, Benny 53 Opal 52
DRAKE, Daniel 22 225 Frank 65 Harry 170 Isaac 65 John 355 Joshua 15 Lewis 305 Louise 50 Peter 15 305

DUBOIS, Benjamin 113-115 Daniel 113-114 Jacob 116 Norman 116 Tunis 116 Tunis V 117
DUDLEY, Silas 80
DUKE, Frank H 104 Richard 104 William 104
DUMFORD, Harold 53 Harry 53 Lydia 53
DUNCANSON, Helen 311
DUNHAM, 64 Clarence 345 P B 25
DUNLAP, 2 John 1
DUNLAVY, John 316 Rev 316
DUNLEVY, 340 A H 23 177 243 303 329 331 333 340 375 Francis 9 303-305 310 333-334 336 339 John C 177 Judge 333-334
DUNN, Willie 43
DUNSMORE, Gen 199
DURAND, 74
DURIG, Charles 170
DURRAN, Brice 75
DURRELL, Abram 131
DYCHE, Dr 107
DYE, Mr 117
DYER, Mrs Edward 108
E, M 99
EARL, James H 355
EARLY, Everett 107
EARNHART, Charles L 237 239 Eileen 52 Lt 237-239 Mrs 238-239 Sarah Guttery 237-238 Victor 52 Walter 237-238
EASLEY, Jane 52
EATON, 199 202 Jonah 198 200-201
EBERLY, D 39
EBRIGHT, 39
EBY, Henry 116-117 Mort 192 Mr 116
EDGINTON, Lawrence 51
EDWARDS, Alfred 27 Elizabeth 226
EGBERT, David 76
EISENHOWER, Dwight 12
ELBERT, Josephine 224 Samuel T 224
ELLIOT, Charles 350 John 150
ELLIOTT, 110

ELLIS, Samuel 110
ELY, Martin T 87 Phoebe 254
EMLEY, 114
ENGLERT, Jacob 139 Theresa 139
ERTEL, Drew 313 John 313 Sarah 313
ESPY, Mr 215 Nancy 215 Thomas 127 215
EVANS, Benjamin 220 David 220-221 Dr 221-223 Elizabeth Browning 206 Hannah 223-224 Hannah Smith 220 John 206 220-221 223-224 Joseph 7 Josephine 224 Margaret 224 Owen 99 246 Rachel Burnet 220-221 Sarah 206
EVERHART, 110 Emanuel 111 John 108-109 111 Nathan 111
FAIRBANKS, Mr 154
FAIRHOLM, I V 39
FALLIS, Isaiah 27 John 27 Thomas 27
FARLEY, Cardinal 236
FARMER, Mrs 132
FARR, Angelina 7
FAULKNER, David 352
FERGUSON, William 76 354 William Ii 37
FILLMORE, Pres 194
FINDLAY, James 194 231 William 213
FISCHER, Hershel I 62
FLEMING, Dora 115 J C 116
FOGLESONG, George 256
FOLEY, Harriet 113
FORAKER, Joseph B 341
FORD, Henry 389 Rose 125
FORDYCE, Thomas M 380
FORSHA, Thomas 2
FOSS, Dudley E 49
FOSTER, Daniel 76 Henry 78 James H 78 135 Jane W B 208 Miss 52 William S 139
FOUCHE, George B 139
FOWKE, Gerald 293
FOX, 110 David 225
FRANCIS, 114 Dickey 114
FRANKLIN, Benjamin 358

FRASER, Will 48
FRAZEE, John 88
FRAZER, Levi 110
FRAZIER, 110
FREEMAN, Hannah Whitehill 206
FREMONT, 228 Gen 186 196 John C 399
FRICKE, Ford C 271
FRY, Speed S 182
FRYBURGER, Frank C 83
FRYE, Albert 51
FUGATE, Thomas 129
FYFFE, W H 311
GABBARD, Verna 51
GAINES, Edmund P 79
GALBREATH, Phyllis 51
GALLAGHER, James 310
GALLAHER, Carvel 330-331 Mrs 331 Samuel 330-332 Sarah 330
GALLOWAY, James Jr 68 William A 399
GANO, John S 77 142 John Stites 141-142 225 Judge 225 Stephen 302
GARD, Stephen 305
GARRARD, Sarah Belle 228
GASKILL, Edson C 83
GATEWOOD, Theresa 83
GAUNT, 87 Nebo 86-87 93 Samuel 87 Zebulin 87 Zimri 87
GENN, Jethro 79
GEST, Erasmus 170
GILCHRIST, R Wilds 48 345
GILES, C G 358 William B 213
GIRTY, Simon 296-297
GITHENS, John 110-111
GODDARD, John 43
GOES, Wm 193
GOFORTH, William 302 Wm 211
GOODE, Burwell 206 Elizabeth 206 James S 205-206
GOODELL, Thomas 104
GORDON, Daniel K 139
GOSE, Edith 54 Rema 53 Velma 51
GOUGH, John B 358
GRAHAM, D 119 Thomas 150
GRANT, 110
GRAY, Margaret 224

GREELEY, 364
GREELY, A W 212 Seth 137
GREEN, Mr 117 Sam 100
GREGG, Hillary 44
GRETSINGER, 112
GRIFFIN, 70 Francis 303
GRIFFITHS, Catherine F 217
GRIMES, Ed 364
GROSS, James 117 James Jr 117 Mr 117 Owen 117
GROVE, L 119
GROWN, Gurtrude 49
GUERRANT, Margaret 203
GUSTIN, 233 Bethany 234 Elizabeth 234 Jeremiah 234 John 233-234 M E 345 W O 74
GUTTERY, Sarah 237-238
HACKNEY, 255
HADLEY, John 24
HAGEMAN, Henry 79 Mrs R S 346 R S 79 346
HAINES, 10 Aden 111 Noah 10
HALL, Charles 105 John T 20 Peter B 139 Rev 116
HALLAM, Bernice 138
HALSEY, Ichabod 205 James S 205
HAM, Rhoden 93
HAMILTON, Ann 274 Capt 274-275 Elizabeth 275 Frank 107 Gov 295 John 275 Maggie 275 Mary 275 Robert 273-274 Susannah 274 William 274-275 William H 87 273
HAMMEL, Enoch 74
HAMMIEL, Louise 51
HANEY, Dortha 53
HANKINSON, John 117
HANLY, Joel 129
HANNAH, Jane Osborn 341 361 Madame 361
HARBAUGH, Mrs 123
HARDIN, Col 397
HARDING, John 389 Pres 341 Warren G 161 242
HARLAN, R B 167 Thomas H 185 William 27
HARMAR, 2 Gen 126 165 382 396-398 Josiah 126 165 296 396 Lt

HARMAR (continued) Col 396
HARMON, 218 Catherine 218 Catherine F 217 Clifford 217 Clifford Burke 217 Mary Wood 217 Mr 216-219 William 216-217 William E 216 218 William Elmer 216 220 William R 216-217
HARNESBERGER, George 354
HARRELL, Nathaniel 78
HARRIS, 24 88 James 335 Samuel 24 87
HARRISON, William 72 William Henry 194
HARROD, James 394
HART, 249 Roberta 48
HARTSHORN, Patterson 150
HARTSOCK, 110 112 Byron 170 Edward 109 Jesse 111 Levi 39
HARVEY, Dr 54-55 100 Elizabeth Burgess 54 Jesse 54 100 Mr 56 Mrs 54 William 93
HATHAWAY, Andy 190 B A 119 Ephriam 75 79 323 Mr 191 Navine 193 Perry 193 W A 190
HAUSER, Charles 49
HAY, Biddle 104
HAYES, Jimmie 324 Rutherford B 102 359
HAYS, Ann 274
HAYSLIP, Alexander 109 Mr 110
HEATON, 108 Mr 109 Mrs John 108
HEIGHWAY, Samuel 44 69
HEIST, Marlin 19
HENDERSON, George W 79 87-88
HENDRICKSON, William 116
HENLEY, Wm 100
HENRI, Robert 84-86
HERALD, Elsie 51
HERRON, Joe 47
HICKS, Elias 246
HIDE, George 193
HILL, 110 David 315 Frank 156 Jacob W 378 Joseph 111 Mr 30 Samuel 111 Silas 30 William 378
HIZAR, Romona 52

HOFER, Ruth 52
HOLBROOK, Alfred 358 Prof 8
HOLCOMB, 110
HOLCRAFT, Sarah 330
HOLDCOMB, Benton 132
HOLDEN, John 31 301 Senator 301
HOLLE, Mary 5
HOLLINGSWORTH, Bert 92
   Joseph 272-273 Moses 273
   Rhoda 272-273 Rhoda Whitacre
   271 Ruthanna 273
HOLLOWAY, Cephas 261-263
   David 74 Hannah Cory 262
   Jacob 262
HOOD, 183
HOOKER, Gen 187
HOOPER, 64
HOOVER, 112
HOPKINS, 249 Thomas 7
HOPPE, Augustus 137 Edward
   Augustus 137-138 Ernst 139
   Louise 139 Mr 138
HORN, Jacob 88
HORTON, William 99-100
HOSBROOK, Archibald 130
HOUGH, Josiah 107
HOUSTON, Matthew 316 Rev 316
HOWARD, Gen 187 George 127-
   128 James Q 339 Oliver O 187
   Susan 127-128
HUGHES, Capt 242 Wm R 241
HUNT, John 322 Mr 322 Nathan
   273 Ralph W 79 150 Ruthanna
   273
HURIN, 350 Catherine 360 Silas 79
   310 323 360
HURST, Joseph 72 Mrs 72 R E 34
HUSTON, Robert 109
HUTCHINSON, Old Man 132
HUTCHINSON, O A 48
IGLEHART, John S 355
INDIAN, Black Fish 393-394 Black
   Hoof 382 Chief Blackfish 297
   Cornplanter 200 Gray Eagle 44
   Little Turtle 382 398 Red Bird 44
   Red Hawk 199 Red Jacket 200
   Tahre 382 Tecumseh 295-297

IRONS, John 61
IRWIN, Glenn 138 Mrs Charles 43
   Vivian 138
IVINS, Howard W 156-157 R 119
JACKSON, Andrew 215 227 255
   340 Col 255 Elizabeth 104 Virgil
   50
JARED, William 133
JEAN, 233 Augustin 233 Edmond
   233-234 Esther 233-234
JEFFERSON, 370
JENNINGS, David 303 James 74
   John 246
JEWETT, Thomas L 170
JOHN, Augustin 233 Augustine 234
JOHNS, Charles E 105
JOHNSON, Andrew 197 223 Jim
   364 Lyndon 12 Michael H 15
JOHNSTON, Joseph E 276
JOLLIF, John 102
JONES, 112 C E 105 Noah 110
JUTERBOCK, Richard 54
K, F 98
KAHOE, E 156
KEAN, Susannah 274
KEENE, 74
KEEVER, Al 50 Elmer 105 Elmer E
   105 George W 185 Martin 142
   Moses 119 Peter 142 Thomas
   48
KELL, Capt 179 Elizabeth 47 John
   178-179
KELLEY, Nathan 20
KELSEY, J A 105 John A 105
   Thomas 304
KEMPER, James 307-309 313 Paul
   242 Rev 308
KENAN, Joseph 80
KENDRICKS, Ada 52
KENNEDY, Herbert 156
KENRICK, Edward L 103 Walter
   103 153 Walter B 105
KENTON, Simon 296 397
KERSEY, Dr 90 Samuel C 49
   Thomas C 88
KESLING, George 340
KIBBEY, Ephriam 20

KILBURN, James 329
KING, Elder 317-318 George C 31
    Joseph 317 Mr 324 Solomon 317
KINGAN, Sharon 46
KINNEY, Coates 112 Giles 112
    John 110 Mira Cornell 112
KINSEY, David 88
KINTZEL, Alma 120
KIRBY, S 119
KIRKWOOD, William 130 William
    N 130
KITCHEL, Ellis 132 Moses 67 127
KLICK, Bob 161-162
KLING, L 119 Lewis 118
KLINGLING, John 360 Mary Ann
    345-346 360 Miss 360
KNABENSHUE, Roy 259
KNOWLTON, Samuel 311
KNOX, Henry 396
KOBLER, John 142 Rev 142
KOCH, Felix J 381
KOHR, Charles 160
KREKER, John 142
LADO, Corrine 217
LAFAYETTE, 215
LAMB, Jacob 106
LAMPERTI, 361
LAMPRECHT, William H 380
LANDER, Gen 196
LANE, Hendrick 113
LANG, Charles 72
LANGHAM, Elias 211
LARRICK, Louise 12 Louise Stetson
    11
LAWRENCE, Caroline B 208 T E
    27
LEDER, Adolph 54
LEE, Ann 313 Gen 58 Richard
    Henry 84 Robert E 276
LEITCH, William 132
LEONARD, Thomas 2
LERNER, Ike 47
LEWIS, 153 A J 184 Alexander 119
    Henry 153 155 Lillian Lee 313
    Mabelle 313 Norma 398
LINCOLN, 195 367-369 Abe 367
    Abraham 135 194 223 366 369
    371 Mary Todd 370 Mr 194 223

LINCOLN (continued)
    367 371 Mrs 367 370 Pres 176-
    177 223 371 President-elect
    369-370
LINDLEY, 15 Isaac 14 142
LINTON, Mr 168 S M 75
LITTELL, 2
LOGAN, Charlie 15-16 19 Jane 16
LONG, Charles L H 184 Charles
    L'Hommdeieu 182 Lt Col 182
LONGSTREET, 183
LONGSTRETH, Jacob 88
LONGWORTH, Nicholas 341
LOWE, Jacob D 127-128 352 Jacob
    Derrick 128
LOWRY, David 165 William 256
    354
LUCAS, Ray 43 Thomas 305
LUDLOW, Israel 228 230
LUKENS, Bill 45 Elizabeth Cleaver
    45 Levi 45 Miriam 45 120 Mrs 45
    122
LYNN, Jane 128 John 128
LYTLE, Benjamin 70 Gen 70
    William 354 William Jr 130 Wm
    68
MAAG, Earl 137 139 Eugene 53
    Frank 32 John 139
MACLEAN, J P 282
MACON, Nathaniel 213
MADDEN, Anna 35 Charles 34-35
MADISON, 370
MADJESTKA, Madame 360
MAHAN, Sight 132
MANN, Horace 358 John 48
MANNING, Samuel 79 323
MANSFIELD, E D 341 Edward D
    276
MAPLE, Frank 47 W C 345
MARCH, George R 252 John P 252
    John W 252 Mr 252
MARCONI, 268
MARKHAM, Ralph 74
MARLATT, Ellen 109 111 Ellen Mrs
    109 J W 111 Milton 52 William
    356
MARSH, E 119
MARTIN, Elizabeth 50 Samuel 74

MASON, 88 Cynthia 128 Elizabeth 128 James 126 John 126-127 Mary 126 Samuel 126 Sarah 128 William 81 126-130 William Jr 128
MASSIE, Nathaniel 68 70
MASTERS, Samuel 72 William 83
MASTIO, Ruth 53
MATHER, 39 Richard 88 150
MATTHEWS, Joseph T 139 Michael 119
MAYER, George 111
MCARTHUR, Duncan 68
MCCABE, Obidiah 356 Okey 356
MCCARREN, Frank 35 Lucy 55 Mrs Walter 94 William 35
MCCLELLAN, Gen 187
MCCLELLAND, Maria 126 Mary 126 Samuel 126
MCCLURE, Marjorie 52 Maurice 52 William 377
MCCOMAS, T B 39
MCCORMICK, Francis 142
MCCOWEN, James 129
MCCREARY, Earl 241
MCDONALD, 34 Sabin 35
MCGALLIARD, Francis 72
MCINTOSH, Elsie 51
MCKAY, A H 40 J P 40 Patience 271
MCKEEVER, Robert 52
MCKINLEY, 90 Pres 341
MCKINNEY, Abe 63
MCLAIN, Daniel 168 Judge 168
MCLEAN, 186-187 227 376 Col 186 Elizabeth 226 Fergus 224-226 304 Gen 187 J P 286 John 185-186 224-226 228 304 375 Judge 276 Mr 304 N 74 Nathaniel 226 Nathaniel Collins 185 Postmaster 227
MCMILLAN, William 210 Wm 211
MCNEMAR, 5 Rev 315-316 Richard 4 308-310 313 316
MCPHAIL, Larry 271
MEACHAM, David 318 John 313 316
MEEKS, John 127

MEIGHAN, Ephriam 131
MERRILL, M E 344 Oswald 344
MERRITT, A E 39-40 J 119
METZ, C L 299 Dr 300
MIDDLETON, Ann 315
MILLER, Catherine 252 Charlotte 252 Edwin 51 Ellen 51 Isaac 4 Joseph 252 Matilda D 252 Matthias 252 Moses 252-254 308 Moses S 252 Mr 252 Uncle Moses 253
MILLHOUSE, Robert 70
MILLIGAN, H C 35
MILLS, M 80 Mahlon 104 Mr 292 Owen 104 W C 291
MILROY, Gen 186 196
MINTLE, Aaron 111
MIRANDA, Clyde 170 Erle 52
MISEL, Harry 123-124
MITCHEL, Gen 275 277-278 O 275 O M 181 Ormsby 275-276 Ormsby McKnight 275 349 Prof 276
MIX, Tom 10
MONFORT, J G 266 John 128 Mary 128 Mr 114
MONGER, Mrs Howard 118
MONROE, 93 Charles 92 Pres 227
MORAN, Charles 170
MORDUE, H C 156
MORFORD, Cornelius 104 John 110
MORGAN, 162 Berneda 50
MORRIS, Gil 15-16 19 Isaac 307-308 Nancy 19
MORROW, 73 Gov 213-214 Jeremiah 20 69 127 137 150 171 209-213 226 250 John 213-215 Josiah 13 302 335 343 Maj 215 Mary Parkhill 213 Mr 209-210 Mrs 215 Nancy 215 Nancy Espy 215 R 40
MORTON, Joseph 72 Rhoda 72
MOSTELLER, Harry 49
MOTE, Marcus 65
MOUNT, Charles 116-117 Sarah 254
MOUNTS, William 2 14-15 68

MULFORD, Jehu 118 Marion 344
  Phebe 5
MULLIN, Isaac 7 Job 7
MULLINS, Job 7
MULLINUX, Mrs Frank Jr 238
MURDOCH, James E 263-264 341
  Mr 264-266
MURLY, John 119
MURPHY, J G 132 Sarah 128
  Stephen 131
MURRAY, 98
MYERS, John 92
NASH, Daisy 55
NEGRO, Frederick 7 Jesse Wilson 8
NELSON, Dora 107 Thomas C 78
NEWPORT, William Henry 344
NICHOLSON, Jane 7 208 Jane F
  Wales 94 Jane Wales 9
  Valentine 7 208
NICOLAY, John 370 Mr 370
NIXON, 256 Charles 88
NOBLES, Dolly Woolwine 341 360
  Milton 361
NOE, Curt 43
NULL, 18 Charles 18 Christian 15
  17-19 Emma Jane 19 Henry 17
  Jacob 17 Kathryn 18
NUNNER, Mr 124
O'BANNON, John 68
O'BRIEN, Thos 99
O'KELLY, James 204
O'NEAL, Abijah 150
O'NEALL, Abijah 10 70 Geore T
  198 J Kelly 205 Martha 206
  William 206
OBERGEFEL, M 76
OBERGEFELL, M 137
OLDFIELD, Barney 260
OSBORN, Ebenezer 304 John 68 305
OVERTON, John 70
PALMER, Ralph 33
PARCELL, 256
PARKER, Alberta 52
PARKHILL, John 127 Mary 213
PARMETER, Abram 130

PARSHALL, Oliver H 182 184
PARSONS, Samuel 200
PATTER, Mr 110
PATTERSON, John H 33
PATTON, Andy 119 William 76
PAULDING, Joseph 131
PAULIN, Martz 115
PAXTON, William 165
PAYNE, Chris 16
PEARSON, 84 Jacob 80 107-108
  110-111 Rebecca 111
PENCE, 389 Charles N 389 Harry
  389-391 Harry E 389 John
  Wesley 389 Mr 110 W 119
PERKINS, Jane 16
PERRY, 401 Walter 54
PFANZER, Fire Chief 344
PHILLIPS, 59-60 365 Arthur 52
  Hazel Spencer 89 J W 119
  Steve 58 Wendell 358
PICKET, John 60
PIERCE, Abraham 64
PITSTICK, Carl 107
PLACE, Morris 99
POISETT, G A 119
POMEROY, Mr 385
POPE, Gen 186 196
PORNO, Albino 361
PORTER, Elizabeth 205-206 John
  205 Sarah Watkins 205
POSEY, Thomas 70
POTTER, John W 13 William 64
POTTORF, Carl 33
POTTS, Edward 7 John 7 Samuel 7
POWELL, Rachel 267
PRINTZ, E R 40 H W 40
PROBASCO, Harry 381 John 251
PUGH, Achilles 7 9
PUTNAM, Aurelia 258 F W 279
  Prof 299
QUARRY, Rev 312
RAINEY, Arabella 51 June 51
RAMSEY, William 163
RANDOLPH, John 212-213 227
RANKIN, John 316 Rev 316
RANNEY, Rufus P 366
RAY, Alexander 103 Debra 103

READ, Clement 67
REEDER, Aaron 72 Annie 307
   Daniel 307-308 Daniel F 354
   David 216 308 Jacob 307 352
   Joseph 307-308 Mr 216
REES, Lewis 88
REEVES, John 256
REID, Henry 360
RENSHAW, William 83
REYNOLDS, Burt 12 Glen 54
   William 319
RHODES, Mildred 53-54 Vivian 53
RICHARDS, Don 44
RIGDON, Dr 244
RILEY, Robert 186
RIVE, Madame 361
ROACH, James 81 Mahlon 81
ROBERTSON, Daniel 87
ROBIN, Elizabeth 50
ROBLITZER, A C 35
ROGERS, Elizabeth 230 L 119 Will
   10 William 40
ROHLING, 32 Ben 31
ROOSA, Ruth 311
ROOSEVELT, Franklin Delano 271
   Theodore 202
ROSECRANS, 251 277 Gen 182
   196
ROSS, Benjamin 127 Don 19
   George 27 John 276 Ned 344
   Phineas 8 256 354 Samuel 72
   Thomas 256 Thomas R 354
ROSSBURG, 74
ROSSIGNON, Esther 233
ROTHMAN, Leslie 52
ROWLAND, Edra 51
RUCH, Mary 49
RUE, Benjamin 76
RUMMEL, G Albert 268
RUSSELL, Virgil 43
RYE, William 109
SABIN, James 185
SAGE, George R 177 375
ST CLAIR, Arthur 13 20 296 Arthur
   Jr 225 Gen 382 Gov 15
SALE, Magdalen 206 Robert 206
SANNING, Nicholas 83

SATTERTHWAITE, G W 39 John
   10 74 109 150
SAVILL, Mr 281
SCAMYHORN, Richard 398
SCHAEFER, Bob 19
SCHENCK, 113 195 Elizabeth 230
   Garrett 231 Gen 186 195-197
   229 231-232 John N C 165 John
   Noble Cumming 231 Mr 194
   Peter 231 R C 194 Rev 229-230
   Robert 194 Robert C 186 194
   243 367 Robert Cumming 194
   231 William 229-232 William C
   20 78 194 230 232 William
   Cortenus 229
SCHEURER, John 73
SCHILLING, J A 345
SCHRACK, Elizabeth 275
SCHUCHTER, Mr 301
SCHWARTZ, Harry C 343 Herb
   343-344 Ray 156 W E 92
SCHWARTZEL, Perry 160
SCOFIELD, Joseph 127 Mr 132
SCOTT, Allison L 250 Charles 400
   Dred 228 Elizabeth H 250 James
   375 Thomas 400
SCOVILLE, Blanche 361 Dr 298-
   299 S S 298
SEAMAN, Jonas 75
SEAMON, Jonas 332
SEARS, Harold 52
SEIBERT, Wilbur 6
SEIDL, Anton 361
SEIKER, Lew 342
SELLERS, Isaac 105
SERING, Samuel 307-309 Sarah
   307
SEVER, Lewis 74
SEWARD, John 127 Mason 130-
   131
SHARP, Nathan 317
SHAW, John 309 330 336
SHAWHAN, George 170
SHERMAN, 187 251 277
SHERWOOD, 88 90 Francis 87
   Frank 79 87 John 32 Jonathan
   87 93 Mabel 90

SHIPMAN, Mr 62
SIBBETT, Richard 129
SIDDON, Mrs Scott 358
SIGEL, Gen 196
SILVERS, Morris 106 Mrs 106
SIMMONS, Mrs Henry 108
SIMONTON, John 106 Lon 106
SIMPSON, Dewey 55 Philip R 186
SIMS, George 111 John 111
SKINNER, Catherine Hurin 360
SLAVE, Alfred 54 John 54 Lewis 101 Rody 54 Sam Green 100
SLUSHER, Della 51 Farrie 51 Homer 51
SMALLEY, 328 401 William 6 70 400
SMART, 35 Carroll 33-35 Mayor 34
SMITH, 112 189 Abner 309-310 Caroline 258 Catherine 252 Cynthia 206 David 184 E Kirby 188 Elizabeth 205 Elizabeth Porter 206 French 162 Gen 190 George 203 377 George James 206 George R 203 George Rapin 203 George S 203 George Stovall 203 Glen 51 Hannah 220 Hannah Whitehill Freeman 206 Harlan I 300 James 202-207 250 James M 177 205 John 69 306 340 356 John Quincy 205 John W 206 Judith 206 Junior 51 Magdalen 206 Margaret 203 Martha 206 250 Mary 206 Moses 311 Nancy 250 Philip 206 Rev 203-205 Sarah 206 Thomas 203-204 206 William 356
SNELL, Daniel 82 J W 35 Louis 34
SNIDER, Geneva 43
SNOOK, Mr 242 R D 242 Ralph 241-242 Ralph P 239-240 359 Sgt 240-242
SNYDER, Marion 161 170 370 Mr 161-162
SOLSBERRY, 128
SOTELDO, Caroline Watson 258
SOUTHERN, Frank 84-85
SPENCE, John W 82

SPENCER, 90 93 Charles A 89 Col 303 Hazel 89 John K 92 O M 302-303 Oliver M 372 Thomas R 89 Tom 89-90
SPINDLER, Rev 121
SPRINGMAN, Mrs 128-129 Rose Marie 125 130
SPROAT, Tom 19
STACK, Ruth Emma 52
STACY, J M 107
STALEY, Perry 112
STANLEY, Howard 10
STANSEL, Jeremiah 72
STANTON, Secretary 189 Secretary of War 190
STARK, Frank T 59
STARRY, William 27
STEARNE, 97
STEINER, Elizabeth 258
STEPHENSON, Thomas 246
STERNBERGER, M I 156
STETSON, John 12 John B 12-13 John Batterson 11 Louise 11-12 Stephen 11
STEVENS, Eliphalet 313 Eliphelat 311 Helen 51 Mary 313
STEVENSON, Mr 116
STITES, 15 141 Benjamin 68 140-141 Benjamin Jr 14 77 141 Benjamin Sr 77 Hezekiah 305 Major 141
STOKES, Amanda 362 Benjamin A 118-120 G W 350 Jarvis F 362
STORER, Belamy 177
STOTLER, Lillian 311
STRICKLER, Thomas G 185
STUBBS, Albert 93 Isaac 93 150 Robert 225
SUBLETT, John 392
SURFACE, Eileen 52 Mary 52 Virginia 52
SUTTON, David 14 76 143 Gen 144 James 304 Mr 364
SUYDAM, Simon 177
SWEENEY, Patrick 116
SWENY, Edwin 107
SWINK, William 160

SYMMES, 3 67 69 John Cleves 1 40 66 103 126 141 230 328-329 Judge 69 216
TAPSCOTT, Jacob M 117 Mulford 116
TAYLOR, 18 110 330-332 Baylord 358 Henry 330 332 340 William 340
TERWILLEGER, George 140
TESTERMAN, Elmo 53-54
TETRICK, Flora 130 George 134 Peter 127
THARP, John 68
THATCHER, Ann B 208
THOMAS, 251 Elijah 74 Gen 181 183 Jonas D 7
THOMPKINS, Billy 132 John 132
THOMPSON, 34-35 A C 151 B 52 Charles 33-34 Daniel 3 Darrell 51 Elder 305-306 George W 139 John 314 John A 49 John W 364 L P 184 Mr 151-152 Will S 156 Wilson 305-306
THORNBURG, Isaac 99
TICHENOR, Aaron 310 Catherine 310 Daniel 310 David 307 310 Hannah 310 Jonathan 307-310 Susannah 310
TIFFIN, Edward 210 400
TIGAR, Charles N 83 Theodore A 83
TINGLE, Jedediah 216 218 Mr 216
TIZZARD, Judge 377 Samuel 377
TOBY, H 119
TOD, Gov 188-190
TODD, Robert 2
TRABUE, Margaret 203
TRAHERN, Asa 40
TRAVISANO, Paul 16
TRIMBLE, Mr 122
TRUMAN, Harry 12
TUFTS, Belle 312 Benjamin 311 313 Benjamin Jr 311 Frank 312 Jane 312-313 Julia 312 Moses 311 313 Permelia 313 Sarah 311 Seth 311 Seth G 80
TURNER, Jabez 179 James 326 Richard 388

TYLER, Gen 195
UMPHRY, L 40
VALLANDIGHAM, Clement L 197
VAN, Ausdale Cornelius 377 Fleet A 376
VAN CAMP, 402
VANCE, Elijah 88 Elisha 88
VAN DERVEER, 114
VANDERVEER, Arthur 113 Col 182 184 192 Ethel 117 Ferdinand 182
VANDYKE, Hannah 128 John 128 Squire 132
VAN HORN, James 88
VANLANDIGHAM, Clement L 367
VAN RIPER, Victor 161
VAN RIPPER, Hans 27-29
VAN SCHOYCK, David 88
VAN TUYL, 114-115
VARNER, Martin 2
VARNUM, Joseph B 213
VENABLE, William H 178
VETTER, 112
VOORHIS, Peter 131
WAGGONER, Mrs 365
WALDSMITH, 330
WALES, Isaac 94 Jane 9 208 Jane F 94 Mrs Isaac 94 Nancy 9 208 Thomas 9 Thomas M 27
WALKER, William 131
WALL, Mr 54 56 Stephen 54
WALLACE, Elbert 105 J D 177-178 John H 62 Lew 189
WALSH, Patrick 184 Peter 132
WARD, Dora Nelson 107 Durbin 177-178 180 250 Foster 111 George 246 James W 107 Joshua 75 Maria 246 Maria Ohio 246
WASHINGTON, 58 295 370 383 396 George 209 382 401
WATKINS, Sarah 205
WATSON, 110 Mrs Culbert 108 Thomas 2
WATTS, Ira 324
WAY, Mr 98 Robert 74 98-99
WAYNE, 1 263 308 Anthony 145 274 382-383 401 Gen 382-383

WAYNE (continued)
 John 10
WEAVER, Dennis 12 Rev 116
WEBSTER, 263
WEIS, Christine 121
WELCH, Amos 27 Judith 98 S G 96 Samuel G 27 Webster 99
WELLBROOK, Ray 19
WELLER, 110
WELLS, Delma 51 Freegift 318
WESLEY, John 389
WEST, Miss 123
WHARTON, 162 Silas 103 Thomas 104
WHITACRE, Andrew 271 Aquilla 271 Jane 271-272 John 271 Loretta 53 Moses 271 Patience 272 Patience Mckay 271 Priscilla 271-272 Rhoda 271-273 Robert 271-272
WHITE, William 132
WHITEHILL, Hannah 206 Mary 206
WHITLEY, Will 160
WHITSEL, Mamie 53
WHITTLESEY, Charles 300
WICKERSHAM, 372 John 80
WIKLE, George 27
WIKOFF, Catherine 128 Peter 128 133 Peter W 73
WILCOX, 62
WILKERSON, John 24
WILLARD, H S 156
WILLIAM, J Milton 244
WILLIAMS, Capt 178-179 Enos 243 340 J Milton 242-244 Josie 49 Maj 243 Rigdon 178 251
WILLIAMSON, David 127 George 128 Hannah 128 Mary 128 Peter 128 Samuel L 105
WILLIS, Frank B 341
WILLS, Jack 33
WILSON, Americus 252 Andy 192 Bob 19 David 111 Elizabeth H 250 Frank 75 Fred 7 Grace Margaret 362 James 235 James S 251 Jeremiah M 250

WILSON (continued)
 Jesse 7-8 John 121 John Lafayette 235 363 Margaret 121 Marshall L 251 Martha 250-251 Mary Brooks 235 Mary Proctor 362 Melva 236 Melva Beatrice 235 237 363 Miss 235-236 Providence M 251 Rev Mr 329 Robert 249 251 317 329 Robert Bruce 251 Robert II 249-250 William W 251
WINTERS, Mrs 115
WITHAM, Robert 127
WITT, 124-125 Byron 123-124 Christine 121 Constance 120-123 125 Geneva 123 George Edwin 120 Mr 121 123 125 Mrs 121 124-125
WOOD, 218 Asenath 216 Charles E 217 Helen 123 Mahlon 123 Mary 217 Mr 216 William 20 120 216 331
WOODMANSEE, L D 64
WOODRUFF, Israel 75 Mrs 40
WOODWARD, Isaac 54
WOOLWINE, Laura 361
WORLEY, Joseph 317 Joshua 317-318 Malcolm 309 315 317 Rebecca 317
WORRELL, John 74 76
WRIGHT, 40 246 A G 350 Byron 156 E B 350 Jonathan 7 Jonathon 70 William 119
WYKOFF, 114
YAUGER, Peter 305
YEHRING, Mr 116
YOEMANS, E P 40
YOUNG, William C 257
YOUNGS, Benjamin S 313 316
ZEISBERGER, David 289
ZELL, George M 40
ZENTMEYER, Vess 170
ZENTMIRE, George 88
ZENTMYER, 191
ZIMMER, Mr 386

www.ingramcontent.com/pod-product-compliance
Lightning Source LLC
Chambersburg PA
CBHW050830230426
43667CB00012B/1950